State Apologies to Indigenous Peoples

This book considers the ethics and politics of state apologies made to Indigenous peoples.

The prevalent tendency to treat an apology as a speech act has maintained the focus on the state leader making the apology and not on the victims' claims. This book demonstrates the inherent shortcomings of this approach through an examination of apologies delivered to Indigenous peoples in Australia and Canada. Contrasting the texts of these apologies with Indigenous peoples' responses, the book reveals how by framing the wrongdoing according to state norms, the apologies sidelined Indigenous peoples' claims. In response, the book develops an understanding of apology as a relational process. This involves engaging Indigenous peoples in dialogue, the aim of which would be to address past injustices by fulfilling the apology's transformative promise of 'never again' to Indigenous peoples' satisfaction. The book concludes by examining more recent developments in Australia and Canada that highlight the continuing need for government accountability to fulfil this promise and ensure Indigenous peoples' rights and interests are upheld.

This book will be of considerable interest to scholars and students in the fields of law and politics, Indigenous studies; apology and forgiveness studies; transitional justice and reconciliation; settler colonialism and decolonisation.

Francesca Dominello is Senior Lecturer in the Macquarie Law School, Macquarie University Wallumattagal Campus, Sydney, Australia. She currently researches and teaches in the areas of Indigenous peoples and the law and family law from a social justice perspective.

Part of the
INDIGENOUS PEOPLES AND THE LAW
series

series editors

for information about the series and details of previous and forthcoming titles, see https://www.routledge.com/law/series/INDPPL

A GlassHouse book

State Apologies to Indigenous Peoples

Law, Politics, Ethics

Francesca Dominello

Routledge
Taylor & Francis Group
LONDON AND NEW YORK

First published 2025
by Routledge
4 Park Square, Milton Park, Abingdon, Oxon OX14 4RN

and by Routledge
605 Third Avenue, New York, NY 10158

Routledge is an imprint of the Taylor & Francis Group, an informa business

a GlassHouse book

British Library Cataloguing-in-Publication Data
A catalogue record for this book is available from the British Library

ISBN: 978-0-367-46031-0 (hbk)
ISBN: 978-1-032-79209-5 (pbk)
ISBN: 978-1-003-49101-9 (ebk)

DOI: 10.4324/9781003491019

Typeset in Sabon
by SPi Technologies India Pvt Ltd (Straive)

For Lachlan John Cozzi (21/06/2000-26/08/2022)

Contents

Preface x

1 **Introduction** 1

The focus on the Rudd and Harper apologies 1
Structure of the book 6
Overview of the book 7
How do apologies function? 8
How do the Rudd and Harper apologies function? 10
How could the Rudd and Harper apologies function more effectively? 16
Conclusion 22
Notes 23
Reference list 24

2 **Making apologies: what do they do?** 31

Introduction 31
The interpersonal apology: what is it and what does it do? 34
What makes an interpersonal apology effective? 37
The interpersonal aspects of political apologies 41
The political aspects of political apologies 43
What makes a political apology effective? 49
Conclusion 55
Notes 56
Reference list 56

3 **Sorry for what? Examining the Rudd and Harper apologies in their historical contexts** 62

Introduction 62
Why were the Rudd and Harper apologies made? 63
Protection and assimilation 63
Background of the Rudd apology 67
Background of the Harper apology 75
The significance of the Rudd and Harper apologies in advancing Indigenous peoples' claims 79
Accounts of the truth about history in the Rudd and Harper apologies 89
Conclusion 92
Notes 93
Reference list 94

4 **The Rudd and Harper apologies critically examined** 101

Introduction 101
The Rudd and Harper apologies: advancing justice and reconciliation for Indigenous peoples 103
What is wrong with this picture? Indigenous peoples' critiques of the Rudd and Harper apologies 109
The limited interpretation of history and the harms suffered in the Rudd and Harper apologies 110
The interpretation of history in the Rudd and Harper apologies translated into measures of redress 115
Settler colonialism and the Rudd and Harper apologies 121
Conclusion 130
Notes 131
Reference list 131

5 **Apology making as a relational process: re-focusing the Rudd and Harper apologies on Indigenous peoples** 136

Introduction 136
Indigenous peoples and their responses to the Rudd and Harper apologies 140
The way forward: re-conceptualising the Rudd and Harper apologies as a relational process 145
Conclusion 157
Note 158
Reference list 158

6 **Australia post-apology** 163

Introduction 163
Reparations and Stolen Generations Survivors 163
Reparations and the Bringing Them Home report 164
Compensation 167
State and territory-based redress schemes 169
Closing the gap 175
Closing the gap: Indigenous children in out-of-home care 179
The Uluru Statement from the Heart *185*
Conclusion 192
Notes 192
Reference list 193

7 **Canada post-apology** 198

Introduction 198
Reparations and Residential School Survivors 199
The monetary payments 200
Truth-telling, healing, and reconciliation 203
The TRC Calls to Action 208
Missing and Murdered Indigenous women and girls 211
Implementation of UNDRIP 215
Indigenous child welfare 221
Concluding comments 226
Reference list 227

Index 233

Preface

I began research on state apologies to Indigenous peoples after the Rudd apology was delivered in Australia in 2008. Up until that time I had been sceptical about an apology and whether it would make a difference. It was only after it was delivered, and many Indigenous peoples responded positively, that I began to take the apology more seriously. These responses changed my understanding of the apology. They illuminated what should happen after an apology is made and that it should lead to change oriented by Indigenous peoples' claims. This was ultimately the message that was conveyed by Indigenous peoples in their responses to the Rudd and Harper apologies (both made in 2008). Unfortunately, this change has not happened and much of that is due to the prevalence of settler colonialism in continuing to thwart Indigenous peoples' calls for a just resolution of their claims. In many respects, this lack of government action post-apology vindicates those Indigenous peoples who were critical of the apologies. As a strategy to counter the status quo, this book develops a relational understanding of apology making that places Indigenous peoples' claims at the centre of the process. Inherent in the making of an apology is the promise, 'never again'. The fact that apologies to Indigenous peoples, such as the Rudd and Harper apologies, are yet to fulfil this promise to Indigenous peoples' satisfaction signals the continuing need to hold governments to account post-apology. This book does this in the context of Australia and Canada by examining some recent developments in law and policy that highlight that much more work is needed to live up to the apology's promise. The developments canvassed are as of November 2023.

Chapters 1–5 of this book evolved from my PhD thesis, *Settler colonialism and apologies to Indigenous peoples: a critical analysis of the Rudd and Harper apologies* (2018), DOI:10.26190/unsworks/20375.

Chapters 2–4 also build on previous published research on the nature of apology making and critiques of the Rudd and Harper apologies that can be found here:

Dominello, F., 2014, 'Protecting the right to be a "bigot" in the wake of the "Apology to Australia's Indigenous Peoples"', *Macquarie Law Journal*, vol. 14, pp. 47–71, http://classic.austlii.edu.au/au/journals/MqLawJl/2014/15.html;

Dominello, F., 2015, 'Political apologies and their challenges in achieving justice for Indigenous peoples in Australia and Canada", *Oñati Socio-Legal Series*, vol. 7, no. 2, pp. 277–303, https://opo.iisj.net/index.php/osls/article/view/730; and

Dominello, F., 2018, 'The "Apology to Australia's Indigenous Peoples" in its historical context', in B. Bevernage and N. Wouters (eds), *The Palgrave handbook on state-sponsored history after 1945*, Palgrave Macmillan, London, pp. 817–830.

I acknowledge the lands of the Guringai people on which I live and the lands of the Wallumattagal Clan of the Dharug Nation on which I work. I pay my respects to Elders past, present, and emerging. I am also conscious that the book discusses issues that are sensitive to Indigenous peoples and that some of the Indigenous peoples who are quoted in the book have passed. The Indigenous peoples' responses discussed in the book are publicly available. Any author royalties received will be donated equally to the Aboriginal and Torres Strait Islander Healing Foundation in Australia and the National Centre for Truth and Reconciliation in Canada.

I wish to particularly thank Professor Emerita Gabrielle Meagher for encouraging me to submit a book proposal to Routledge, and staff at Routledge, especially Dr Colin Perrin and Associate Professor Mark Harris for supporting my proposal, and Ms Naomi Round Cahalin for guiding me through the publication process. I am grateful for the comments of two anonymous reviewers, the assistance and support from my research assistants, Ms Edita Grinbergs and Dr Sheikh Salauddin, the assistance from Mr Paul Taylor, and from Ms Susan Fripp and Mr Brian Ballsun-Stanton at Macquarie University. I am also grateful to Mr Paul Teerman, solicitor and Aboriginal man from the Dharug Nation for his support. Very warm and special thanks to my family, Edie, Michael, and Orlando, and my parents, Cesarina and Vincenzo, who will always be in my heart.

Chapter 1

Introduction

The focus on the Rudd and Harper apologies

The focus of this book is on two apologies which have been made to Indigenous peoples:[1] the 'Apology to Australia's Indigenous Peoples' ('the Rudd apology') made by former Australian Prime Minister Kevin Rudd on 13 February 2008 (House of Representatives, Australia, 2008); and the 'Apology to Former Students of Indian Residential Schools' ('the Harper apology') made by former Canadian Prime Minister Stephen Harper on 11 June 2008 (House of Commons, Canada, 2008, pp. 6849–6852). Both apologies relate to particular periods in the history of each nation where state laws and policies authorised the forcible removal of Indigenous children from their families, creating what is commonly referred to as the Stolen Generations in Australia and the residential school system in Canada.

Over the last few decades there have been several apologies made to Indigenous peoples in different parts of the world.[2] There have also been several of them made to Indigenous peoples in Australia and Canada.[3] Of these apologies, the Rudd and Harper apologies exemplify how such apologies can be cause for celebration, and also a source of controversy. For many years Indigenous peoples had been seeking an apology from the head of state of these nations, but even after achieving this outcome, each apology attracted mixed responses. While each of them was heralded by some as a watershed moment in advancing reconciliation, others were sceptical about whether they would lead to meaningful change. Notwithstanding these different viewpoints, this book examines how each respective apology could be used to advance Indigenous peoples' claims. In this respect, the focus of the book may be on the Rudd and Harper apologies, but the conclusions that are reached could be extended to other apologies made to Indigenous peoples in settler-colonised contexts and to apologies made in other contexts for structural forms of violence.

The main argument advanced in the book is that an apology could contribute to advancing Indigenous peoples' claims if it was treated less like a 'speech act' (which tends to focus on what the state leader says in the

DOI: 10.4324/9781003491019-1

apology) and more like a relational process (which would engage the parties in dialogue) with a view to resolving Indigenous peoples' claims. In this way, the fulfilment of the promise of 'never again', inherent in the making of an apology, would be open to negotiation between the parties. As the apology's acceptance would depend on Indigenous peoples' satisfaction, these negotiations would be guided by Indigenous perspectives on how to address past violations and prevent future ones. Only then may the pathway be set for the promise of 'never again' to be fulfilled.

To illustrate the need to shift the understanding of an apology from a speech act to a relational process, the book examines the responses of Indigenous peoples that were expressed around the time each apology was made and compares them with what each state leader said in their respective apologies. It is notable that of the two apologies, only with respect to Harper's apology were Indigenous representatives permitted to respond formally in Parliament (House of Commons, Canada, 2008, pp. 6854–6857). Phil Fontaine (Chief of the Sagkeeng First Nation and then National Chief of the Assembly of First Nations), Patrick Brazeau (member of the Algonquin community of Kitigan Zibi and then National Chief of the Congress of Aboriginal Peoples), Mary Simon (Inuk and then Inuit Tapiriit Kanatami President), Clement Chartier (then President of Métis National Council), and Beverley Jacobs (Kanienkehaka (Mohawk) community representative, Six Nations of the Grand River Territory, Bear Clan and then President of the National Aboriginal Women's Association of Canada) all responded to the apology on the floor of the House of Commons. Fontaine, Brazeau, Simon, and Chartier also addressed the Canadian Senate the following day (Senate of Canada, 2008, pp. 1503–1507). Jacobs was notably missing from the Senate. In Australia, by contrast, Tom Calma (Aboriginal Elder, Kungarakan tribal group, member of the Iwaidja tribal group, and then Aboriginal and Torres Strait Islander Social Justice Commissioner) delivered his response in the Member's Hall in Parliament House, while Patrick Dodson (Yawuru Elder and former Chairman of the Council for Aboriginal Reconciliation) addressed the National Press Club in Canberra (Calma, 2008; Dodson, 2008).[4] More generally, in each nation, the reactions of Indigenous peoples received extensive media coverage (see, for example, Fiddler, 2008; Fitzpatrick and Nguyen, 2008; Kemp, 2008; Korff, 2021; Pearson, 2008).

These responses exemplify differences in attitudes among Indigenous peoples to each respective apology. One way of understanding these differences is to consider the broader politico-legal contexts in which each apology was made. When examined in context, it is evident that each apology represented a triumph for those who had agitated for them and succeeded in overcoming the staunch opposition of the conservative forces against them. Each apology's acknowledgement that the forced removal of Indigenous children from their families was wrong makes them significant in this respect. However, it is also apparent that there were Indigenous peoples who wanted more from them. Indeed, for some Indigenous peoples, each apology represented a step closer towards forging a 'new' relationship with government that would bring the existing settler–colonised relationship to an end (Dodson, 2008; House of Commons, Canada, 2008, pp. 5856–5857 (Jacobs); Senate of Canada, 2008, p. 1505 (Simon)). Yet, when these understandings are contrasted with those conveyed in each apology, it is evident that the dismantling of the settler–colonised relationship was not on the political agenda for either Rudd or Harper.

According to settler colonial theory, colonisation is based on the logic of invasion and elimination of the Indigenous 'other' for the main purpose of gaining access to Indigenous lands (Wolfe, 2006, p. 388). This process was legitimised by the laws of the invaders, which applied to replace Indigenous peoples' authority and norms and, in many cases, severed Indigenous peoples' connections to their homelands, communities, and cultures, and compromised their overall survival and wellbeing. It was through this process that Indigenous ways of being in the world were undermined and dependencies on the state were created (Alfred, 2009, pp. 43, 52). This process of colonisation, which has more aptly been described as genocide (Barta, 1987; Chrisjohn and Young, 1997), was made possible by the promulgation of racist constructions of Indigenous peoples that functioned to deny their political authority and condoned the violation of their rights. To break down the settler–colonised relationship that was forged by these violations would require extensive changes. In terms of law and politics, it would require each respective state to accept the political authority of Indigenous peoples and their normative frameworks. Guaranteeing Indigenous rights protections would be an important part of this process. This, however, was not how either the Rudd or Harper apology saw the way forward. These apologies, made within the politico-legal order of each state, only recognised the harms suffered by Indigenous peoples according to what may be accepted as wrong according to certain state norms, not Indigenous norms and rights. Thus, rather than moving on from the nations' respective histories of colonisation, the apologies reasserted state sovereignty through the re-legitimisation of its norms. Realisations such as these explicate some of the more critical Indigenous reactions to the apologies that claimed they did not go far enough to identify and address the wrongs that have been committed against Indigenous peoples (Chrisjohn, et al., 2008; Krebs, 2008; McKinnon, 2008).

Indigenous peoples' responses provide rich insights into the significance of the Rudd and Harper apologies as well as their shortcomings. Also of significance is the way these responses provide insights into the scope of the injustices experienced by Indigenous peoples in Australia and Canada and their aspirations for the future now that the apologies have been made. However, of most significance in terms of the overall argument of the book is the way these responses provide different perspectives on the injustices perpetrated against Indigenous peoples and how to address them when compared to what was said by each state leader in their apologies. These differences highlight the importance of the understanding of apology making as relational insofar as this understanding could promote Indigenous peoples' claims. Of course, this is not the only strategy that could do this, and in this respect this approach could support a broader strategy in re-centring Indigenous perspectives in law and policy. In focusing on Indigenous peoples' responses, apology making can be reconceived as more than the state leader delivering the apology as a type of speech act, but as engaging the parties to the conflict in dialogue to advance outcomes that are responsive to Indigenous peoples' claims.

As a 'speech act' an apology can do certain things in the world. Having the authoritative voice of the head of state convey the messages of an apology to the nation is a significant aspect of a political apology (Thompson, 2008, p. 36). Indeed, an apology that is not delivered meaningfully from the point of view of its recipients can impact on its effectiveness (Capriccioso, 2010; King, 2011). And yet an apology, understood as a 'speech act', can also result in a tendency to focus on what the state actor says and what they think should be the way forward in future, which can detract from what the recipients might want. This seems to contradict how an apology should function in practice.

It is generally accepted that an apology is a means by which wrongdoers can say they are 'sorry' so they may restore or reconcile relations with the individuals or groups they have harmed. To achieve this, the recipients would need to be satisfied with the apology and accept it (Govier, 2006, p. 70). It is also true that often, to be accepted, an apology requires more than a sincere 'I'm sorry'. This may be especially so for more systemic harms, which are often the subject of a political apology. Such cases would also require reparations for the harms that have been suffered and assurances for the non-repetition of harm in future (Govier and Verwoerd, 2002, p. 72). To be sure, it may be that no matter what reparations are offered, an apology may never be accepted. Indeed, with respect to political apologies, which are often offered to many and for longstanding grievances, the responses can also be multifarious, as the responses to the Rudd and Harper apologies demonstrate. However, this does not mean that nation states can abandon the promise of 'never again' that an apology represents. Fulfilling this promise would require both sides engaging in dialogue about what 'never again' may look like in practice. This approach could subvert the tendency of state reconciliation processes being imposed on Indigenous peoples (as happened, for example, in Australia ('Editorial', 1993)). Instead, it aligns with the peacemaking model of conflict resolution that is informed by Indigenous perspectives on reconciliation and restitution (Lightfoot, 2015, pp. 23–25). Although by no means universal across Indigenous communities (Ross, 2010), this model could serve to bring all parties together to talk to one another and 'get to the bottom of a problem' and 'restore harmony and balance' in the relationship (Lightfoot, 2015, p. 24, quoting Mirsky, 2004, p. 1). In settler-colonised nations, this would involve a 'a correct rebalancing of relations between equals' through 'indication/evidence of authentic justice being restored to their status' (Graham, 2014, p, 21). To achieve this equilibrium would, no doubt, require extensive resources and reforms across a variety of areas. In this respect and considering the range of wrongdoing, 'justice' may not be confined to one concept but could span the spectrum (e.g., restorative, distributive, corrective, procedural, and retributive forms of justice). At a minimum it would require protection of the rights of Indigenous peoples as enshrined, for example, in the *United Nations Declaration of the Rights of Indigenous Peoples* ('*UNDRIP*'), which is internationally recognised as setting 'the minimum standards for the survival, dignity and well-being of the indigenous peoples of the world' (United Nations, 2007, art. 43).

Following this approach, an apology can be understood as functioning like a relational process – a dialogue which opens the lines of communication between both sides of the conflict and, most significantly, exposes the apologising side to the responses of those they have harmed. This could be crucial to decolonising settler–colonised relations considering the privileging of coloniser perspectives and consequential marginalisation of Indigenous perspectives in the colonisation process. Illuminating this issue demonstrates the importance of Indigenous perspectives in apology making and of the need for greater attention to be paid to what Indigenous peoples say during this process and into the future. In developing this understanding, the book seeks to support the ongoing attempts made by Indigenous peoples to engage in dialogue with government and bring about effective changes to the laws and policies affecting them (Graham, 2014, p. 20). The valorisation of their perspectives in the apology-making process may itself serve as a measure of reparation and contribute to the broader quest of decolonising the historical marginalisation of their perspectives and practices (Smith, 2012).

The final chapters of the book develop this approach as a strategy to support more recent attempts by Indigenous peoples to advance their respective claims in the post-apology eras in Australia and Canada. In examining some pertinent post-apology developments, the discussion highlights the ongoing importance of treating the apologies as providing a basis for change and not merely treating them as events – as speech acts – that enable a 'business as usual' approach to continue. This is particularly pertinent in the case of Australia, where several proposals have been formulated by Indigenous peoples but have been largely unmet by government. Of these, specific attention is given to the areas of reparations for the Stolen Generations, the Closing the Gap policy with a particular focus on the disproportionate numbers of Indigenous children in out-of-home care, and constitutional recognition of Aboriginal and Torres Strait Islander peoples. These areas have been chosen as they are areas of concern for many Indigenous peoples and can also be linked to the promises made in the Rudd apology. At the same time, lack of progress in these areas exemplifies how injustices are ongoing in post-apology Australia.

Similarly, with respect to Canada, there is discussion of recent developments beginning with the *Indian Residential Schools Settlement Agreement* ('*Settlement Agreement*') (2006). The *Settlement Agreement*, which came into force in 2007, was a significant outcome for the Indigenous parties and was also the only measure Harper referred to in his apology. It included provisions for monetary payments to be made to Residential School Survivors, healing and commemorative measures, and the establishment of the Truth and Reconciliation Commission of Canada ('TRC'). These provisions appear more extensive than what has been offered to the Stolen Generations in Australia, and since Prime Minister Trudeau was elected to office in 2015, his government appears to have been more responsive than Harper's (and, for that matter, any government in Australia) to Indigenous peoples' claims. For instance, the Trudeau government accepted the 94 Calls to Action as recommended by the TRC (TRC, 2015). This has led to further inquiries, such as the National Inquiry into Missing and Murdered Indigenous Women and Girls ('National Inquiry'), which concluded that the treatment of Indigenous peoples in Canada should be accepted as genocide (National Inquiry, 2019). There have also been steps made towards implementing *UNDRIP* in Canadian law with the enactment of the *Declaration on the Rights of Indigenous Peoples Act* (2021).

Differences in the developments in Australia and Canada may be linked to differences in their broader politico-legal contexts, especially to the fact that Canada is a treaty nation and Australia is not. Nevertheless, while the Trudeau government appears committed to reset the nation-to-nation relationship, the Canadian example demonstrates that meaningful long-term change requires significant action on an ongoing basis. Whether the Trudeau government is fully committed to this is debatable when its record on upholding Indigenous rights is considered. The litigation over jurisdiction for the funding of child welfare services that followed the adoption of Jordan's Principle is a case in point that is discussed along with other examples related to, for instance, Residential School Survivors' experiences of the *Settlement Agreement*, and the lack of progress in fulfilling the recommendations of the TRC, particularly with respect to missing and murdered Indigenous women and girls and implementation of *UNDRIP*. Thus, with respect to Canada it is important to remain mindful of the history of broken promises which, in terms of the focus of this book, demonstrates the continued relevance of apology making to ensure that state actors 'stay apologized' in the future (Beales, 2008).

Structure of the book

The book is divided into seven chapters. In this chapter the argument, structure, and aims of the book are outlined. In Chapter 2 various theoretical perspectives on the interpersonal and political apologies are examined to distil their similarities and differences in terms of their functions and what makes them effective. Three main claims are made: first, an apology, understood as a speech act, does not fully capture its functions in the real world; second, if an apology is to advance a process of reconciliation it must satisfy Survivors to be effective; and third, to more fully understand how apologies function and what makes them effective, apologies need to be examined in the broader contexts in which they are made. In terms of interpersonal and political apologies, the differences in understandings of their functions and effectiveness reflect their broader contexts: the social context with respect to the former; the political context with respect to the latter.

Chapter 3 builds on these arguments and examines the Rudd and Harper apologies in their broader politico-legal contexts to explicate why they were made, and in turn, why Indigenous peoples may have responded to them as they did. In terms of their more immediate politico-legal contexts, each apology was celebrated as a triumph for those who had been agitating for such an outcome. In terms of their broader politico-legal contexts, each apology, viewed as a turning point in settler–colonised relations, appeared to be finally addressing the history of settler colonialism in each nation.

Chapter 4 critically analyses the more positive interpretations of the apologies in Chapter 3 by contrasting the Indigenous responses with the texts of each apology. This analysis reveals significant shortcomings in both apologies. Most notable is the way they perpetuated the conditions of settler colonialism in each nation by upholding state norms while the rights of Indigenous peoples continued to be sidelined.

Ultimately, the analysis in Chapter 4 reveals the differences in perspectives that exist between the state leaders making the apologies and the Indigenous responses to them. In view of the way that apology making, understood as a speech act, may obfuscate these differences, Chapter 5 develops the understanding of apology making as a relational process to support Indigenous peoples in their quest for justice through the promotion of meaningful dialogue against a history of the marginalisation of their perspectives and ways of doing things. The chapter concludes, however, that transformation through dialogue will remain limited while the conditions of settler colonialism continue and are supported by state norms that authorise Indigenous rights violations. This conclusion highlights the need for reforms that will address and prevent these violations.

Chapters 6 and 7 canvass developments in Australia and Canada post-apology. The premise of these chapters is that now apologies have been made, these nations should be held to account and fulfil the promise of 'never again' by ensuring that measurable changes occur in the lives of Indigenous peoples. Recent developments are examined through this lens.

Overview of the book

In the chapters that follow, three interconnected questions are addressed: How do apologies function? How do the Rudd and Harper apologies function? How can the Rudd and Harper apologies function more effectively?

Through an examination of these questions the central claims of the book are substantiated: that an apology should promote just outcomes for Survivors; that in the context of apologies made in settler-colonised nations, the enduring legacy of settler colonialism stands in the way of justice for Indigenous peoples; and that reconceptualising apology making as relational could serve as a discursive strategy to promote Indigenous peoples' claims.

How do apologies function?

The understanding of an apology as a type of speech act stems from Austin's speech act theory, which found that utterances can perform actions in the world (Austin, 1962). An apology, according to speech act theory, acts as an expression of regret for a wrong (Austin, 1962; Searle, 1976). But as the research on apology making has developed it has become apparent that an apology can be likened more to a remedial process (Goffman, 1971, p. 109; Leech, 1983, pp. 124–125; Taft, 2000, pp. 1137–1138; Tavuchis, 1991, p. 35). This book builds on this understanding because of its potential to promote Survivor interests. Maintaining the understanding of an apology as a speech act may result in too much focus being placed on what the wrongdoer has to say, which, when translated into the political context, could function to re-legitimise state authority and do little to change the status quo for Survivors (Winter, 2014). This is arguably at odds with what an apology should do. It has been claimed that an apology involves a shift in power. The 'one who had power to harm is now opening himself or herself to the other', leaving them 'vulnerable to the responses of the other' (Govier, 2006, p. 70).

Thus, the position in the book is to treat an apology not as a speech act per se, but more like a process. In fact, an apology might be better understood as forming part of a process, most evident in how it can contribute to reconciling relationships marred by wrongdoing (Barkan and Karn, 2006, p. 7; Taft, 2000; Tavuchis, 1991). In the political context an apology often forms part of a broader process of national reconciliation. As part of this process, an apology can do more than express sorrow; it can help the nation come to terms with the truth about the past treatment of Survivors (Minow, 1998, p. 116). In this respect, an apology functions to put things on the public record (Tavuchis, 1991, p. 117).

Nonetheless, it is also evident that a political apology should do more than correct the historical record if it is to assist in promoting reconciliation between parties marred by conflict. This is especially true in cases where Survivors are still alive, or their communities are continuing to suffer from the intergenerational effects of the harms, or the harms are ongoing, as is the case in many Indigenous communities. In such cases, it may be more accurate to view an apology as a form of reparation. In this sense an apology is linked to achieving justice for the Survivors. The potential for justice rests on the messages the apology conveys – to the Survivors that they did not deserve to be treated unjustly, and to the nation that it was wrong to treat the Survivors unjustly (Celermajer, 2006, p. 155; Muldoon, 2009, p. 3; Thompson, 2008, pp. 34–37). Through this process the identities of the Survivors and the nation could be transformed – the Survivors becoming the subject of 'ethical respect' (Mihai, 2013, p. 206); the nation, through its state leader, recognising its mistakes, and committing to redress and to never repeat the injustices again. In these respects, a political apology may be understood as a transformative process for all involved as they enter a new relationship committed to justice and leave the old one marred by injustice behind them (Thompson, 2008). The effect would be to change what Nobles' theory on political apologies has described as the political membership of the nation, so that it is now inclusive of the Survivors and their claims for justice (Nobles, 2008, pp. 29, 33).

In this approach the advancement of reconciliation is inextricably linked to achieving just outcomes for Survivors (Alfred, 2005, p. 152; Corntassel and Holder, 2008; Short, 2005, pp. 268–270). An apology fits within this process by vindicating the Survivors' sense of justice through its acknowledgement that their treatment was wrong. Furthermore, a meaningful apology would do more than 'say sorry'. It would also make promises of repair and forbearance. Maintaining these promises through concrete measures of redress would be necessary to satisfy the Survivors' fuller sense of justice. Without these measures the meaningfulness of an apology may be brought into serious question (Govier and Verwoerd, 2002, p. 72), and so too may the state's claims of legitimacy.

However, these aspects of making an apology raise pertinent questions about the wrongs to be acknowledged in an apology and the measures of redress to be offered to the Survivors. The position adopted in the book is that if an apology is to lead to just outcomes, the understandings of Survivors should inform such questions. This approach is supported by the transactional view of apology making, whereby the effectiveness of an apology depends on its meaningfulness for the recipients (Lightfoot, 2015, p. 17). At a deeper level, this approach recognises the damaging effects of state-centred approaches in causing harm, and the need for Survivor-centred approaches to address, and prevent further harm.

Thus, for an apology to serve the interests of justice, the acknowledgement of wrongdoing would accord with the Survivors' understandings of their experiences of injustice. This requires a moral reassessment of history through the demonstration of other-oriented regret to Survivors. This would be followed by an offer of additional reparations, which would also be 'other-oriented' in reflecting the Survivors' understandings of the norms that have been infringed and what would be a just resolution to their claims for justice in future. In approaching the making of political apologies in this way, it becomes evident that apologies have a norm-setting function. The acknowledgement of harms suffered, translated into the norms they infringed, provides the basis for reform in the future (Smith, 2008, pp. 221, 224).

In applying this approach, the book departs from a tendency among some scholars to use abstract criteria such as whether the apology names the wrongs, accepts responsibility for them, expresses regret, and promises reform and forbearance in the future in determining the effectiveness of an apology (as exemplified by Govier (2006, pp. 68–69) and James (2008, p. 138)). It does this by emphasising the importance of Survivor perspectives in determining an apology's effectiveness and by demonstrating that its effectiveness may turn on whether the historical account of the injustices in the apology accords with their understandings. Thus, instead of applying abstract criteria, a contextual approach is adopted to discern an apology's effectiveness.

By developing this understanding, the aim is to raise greater awareness of the importance of the historical account of the wrongdoing in an apology to achieve just outcomes. An apology made in the political context should function to correct the historical record in ways that advance justice for Survivors. The contention is that the account of the harms included in the apology would inform the measures of reparation to be offered to Survivors. This is because it is logical to assume that the harms acknowledged in the apology will be the ones for which reparations will be offered.

This, in turn, raises the question: Which historical account? In answer to this question, it is claimed that an apology does not function in a vacuum but is shaped by its own politico-legal context. In other words, an apology cannot be understood as separate from the surrounding circumstances from which it emerged. Thus, to gauge the meaning and significance of an apology requires examination of the broader politico-legal context in which it was made. Such an approach would help to explicate its meaning, why it was made at the time, and why in relation to certain wrongs and not others. However, in another respect, the question 'which historical account?' is also a normative one. If it is accepted that an apology is to promote justice for Survivors, then the account of the history of injustices in an apology should accord with their understandings of the injustices. This would require examination of the broader politico-legal history of the injustices against which the account of the injustices provided in the apology can be assessed.

This is the approach adopted in the examination of the Rudd and Harper apologies: first, to demonstrate how they functioned in their immediate historical contexts; and second, to examine how they functioned in responding to Indigenous peoples' claims. Consistent with the approach in the book, the responses of Indigenous peoples are drawn on to provide insights into the claims of Indigenous peoples as the framework for analysing each apology.

How do the Rudd and Harper apologies function?

To some extent the answer to this question has been pre-determined by the politico-legal contexts in which the apologies were made. Both the Rudd and Harper apologies emerged from grassroots movements for an apology in each respective nation. When considered in the contexts of these movements, it becomes evident why they were both focused on the Stolen Generations and Residential School Survivors respectively. In fact, the history of each apology was not without controversy. Most notably, former conservative Australian Prime Minister John Howard had refused to apologise to the Stolen Generations throughout his term in office. In Canada, the Harper apology followed a largely failed attempt at an apology to Residential School Survivors in 1998 by the then Minister of Indian Affairs, Jane Stewart (Stewart, 1998). A motion in support of an apology finally passed in the House of Commons in 2007. Initially, Harper resisted the pressure for an apology, but eventually agreed after some political manoeuvring (Jung, 2010, pp. 234–235). Indeed, the fact that both apologies were made, notwithstanding their controversial backgrounds, makes them appear to be great victories for those who had been agitating for them over the years. This achievement brought hope to some that relations between Indigenous peoples and government would become an equal partnership (Calma, 2008, pp. 3–4). This seemed possible considering the struggles of Indigenous peoples in both nations for an apology, which were viewed as a testament to Indigenous peoples' survival (Dodson, 2008, pp. 22–23), and a direct challenge to the legitimacy of the state (House of Commons, Canada, 2008, p. 6854 (Fontaine)).

In terms of the content of both apologies there also appears to be much to commend them for the way they address Stolen Generations and Residential School Survivors with respect, accept that it was wrong to forcibly take Indigenous children away from their families, empathise and express regret for their suffering, and offer measures to redress their losses (cf., Celermajer, 2009, pp. 210–212). In these respects, they appear to be oriented towards achieving justice for Indigenous peoples and reconciliation on this basis. Indeed, a significant aspect of both apologies was their respective acknowledgements that the removal of Indigenous children reflected negative perceptions of Indigenous peoples and sought their elimination through the assimilation of Indigenous children into the respective mainstream societies of Australia and Canada (House of Commons, Canada, 2008, p. 6850; House of Representatives, Australia, 2008, p. 169). Furthermore, both apologies appear cognisant of the devastating consequences that the forced removal of Indigenous children has had on the individuals removed as children, their families, and broader communities (House of Commons, Canada, 2008, p. 6850; House of Representatives, Australia, 2008, p. 167).

From the point of view of the Indigenous representatives who responded in an official capacity, each respective apology had opened the path to overcoming various forms of injustice, and they used their responses as an opportunity to advance these claims. Their responses reveal that this would require a range of measures. These can be summarily listed as including the outstanding claims of those affected by the practice of forcibly removing Indigenous children. In Australia, these claims related to establishing initiatives such as a national compensation fund for Stolen Generations Survivors (Dodson, 2008, p. 22), while in Canada they included claims for redress for Residential School Survivors who had been excluded from the *Settlement Agreement* (Senate of Canada, 2008, pp. 1505–1506 (Simon; Chartier)). But it is also apparent from the Indigenous representatives' responses that more extensive measures were needed for all Indigenous peoples. In this regard, it is notable that despite the differences in the way that colonisation was legitimised in Australia (through the complete denial of Indigenous sovereignty and law) and Canada (through treaty breaches in violation of Indigenous sovereignty and law), the effects have been similar. This is evident in the responses of the Indigenous representatives who, despite their focus being on Australia or Canada, made similar claims. These related to extending basic human rights protections to Indigenous peoples aimed at overcoming the conditions of poverty in their communities evidenced by such things as poor housing and education, disproportionate numbers of Indigenous peoples in prison and children in out-of-home care, and high rates of suicide (Dodson, 2008, pp. 21–22; Senate of Canada, 2008, p. 1504 (Fontaine)). They also related to upholding culturally specific rights to help restore community relationships by addressing the unequal gendered impacts of colonisation on Indigenous women (House of Commons, Canada, 2008, p. 6856 (Jacobs)), and restoring Indigenous autonomy more broadly with a view to bringing the settler–colonised relationship to an end (Dodson, 2008, pp. 22–23). Included in these claims were calls for the active participation of Indigenous peoples in their own affairs for the realisation of their broader claims for sovereignty and self-determination (House of Commons, Canada, 2008, p. 6856 (Jacobs); Fiddler, 2008). Indigenous peoples' active involvement in their own affairs, supported by the broader non-Indigenous community, would help to create pathways to restoring Indigenous communities and would lay the foundation for a lasting settlement between Indigenous and non-Indigenous peoples (Dodson, 2008, p. 23).

Arguably, however, if the apologies were concerned with decolonising the settler–colonised relationship and supporting the exercise of greater Indigenous political authority in the future, this would have required them to come to terms with the history of colonisation in each nation and its effects on Indigenous sovereignty and law. This may have been possible if the apologies, in acknowledging the intention to eliminate Indigenous peoples through the pursuit of removing children from their families, also acknowledged that this practice formed part of the broader process of colonisation.

It was racist perceptions of Indigenous peoples' inferiority that informed the doctrines of discovery and terra nullius that applied to legitimise colonisation and the dispossession of their lands (Miller, et al., 2010). These perceptions served to erase Indigenous political autonomy and subordinate Indigenous peoples to the sovereignty of each state. The contrasting stance of superiority maintained by each state with respect to Indigenous peoples is clearly exemplified in the context of Indigenous child removals whereby these states, in asserting jurisdiction over Indigenous children and claiming to know what was best for them, effectively negated the authority of Indigenous peoples to determine their children's futures according to their laws and customs. If these connections were made in the apologies, then it may have been possible for them to acknowledge how negative perceptions of Indigenous peoples not only legitimised the practice of forcibly removing Indigenous children from their families but have underpinned the entire process of colonisation and the settler–colonised relationship it created. The consequences of the quest to assimilate Indigenous children by taking them from their families have been so devastating that they have been considered to constitute specific acts of genocide in both nations (Human Rights and Equal Opportunity Commission, 1997, pp. 270–275; Chrisjohn and Young, 1997, chap. 4).

However, an analysis of the texts of both apologies reveals that neither apology encapsulated the breadth of these claims. This may have been an inevitable outcome considering that both apologies were made within the broader context of settler colonialism. The limitations of each apology can be traced to the way they framed the harms suffered. In both apologies, the harms were largely confined to their personal and social effects on those affected by the forced child removal policies and did not extend to their legal and political effects on Indigenous peoples to support their claims for politico-legal change. In Australia, Rudd did not envisage a relationship of political equality between Indigenous peoples and government, but a relationship of social equality between Indigenous peoples and non-Indigenous peoples through the introduction of the Closing the Gap policy. While Harper went further than Rudd in acknowledging the negative cultural effects of the child removal policy, like Rudd, he did not foreshadow the creation of a new relationship in which Indigenous peoples would have increased autonomy in their affairs. Instead, he envisaged a relationship where the cultures of Indigenous peoples would be respected as any other within broader (multicultural) Canada.

One could argue that all the apologies were supposed to do was to accept that the past practice of forcibly removing Indigenous children from their families was wrong and nothing more. While some Indigenous peoples confined their claims in this way (Calma, 2008), it is evident that others did not and believed the apologies could (or should) have done more.

Most notable were the claims that the apologies marked a turning point in settler–colonised relations in each nation (e.g., Dodson, 2008; Senate of Canada, 2008, p. 1505 (Simon)). The fact that the apologies did not share this understanding ultimately helped to maintain the legitimacy of the sovereignty of each nation, enabling each state to continue to determine what is best for Indigenous peoples according to their respective laws and practices. Far from creating the conditions necessary for the establishment of a new relationship, the settler–colonised relationship was left unchanged. The result was that both apologies reiterated state sovereignty to perpetuate longstanding historical injustices against Indigenous peoples.

Arguably, it was the implicit understanding in both apologies that the authorisation of the removal of Indigenous children was a legitimate exercise of state power that effectively undercut the claims of the Indigenous representatives that the apologies would lead to broader political changes. The fact was that the legitimacy of the practice was supported by state law. In Australia, for example, the High Court of Australia in *Kruger v. Commonwealth* (1997) upheld the validity of the law authorising the forced child removal practice as had been applied by the Commonwealth in the Northern Territory. The Court rejected all the grounds raised by the Stolen Generations Survivors who sought to challenge the legality of this practice, including the claim that it amounted to genocide. Further, in *Cubillo v. Commonwealth* (2001), the Federal Court of Australia rejected the claims of Stolen Generations Survivors for compensation against the Commonwealth. The lawfulness of the practice of removing Indigenous children from their families was subsequently restated by Rudd in his apology (House of Representatives, Australia, 2008, p. 169). In turn, this finding inadvertently supported the Rudd government's refusal to establish a national compensation fund for Stolen Generations Survivors for the range of harms they have suffered.

Consequently, Rudd framed the forced removal of Indigenous children not as a legal wrong, but as a moral wrong, that is, as a violation of a core 'Aussie' value of the 'fair go' (House of Representatives, Australia, 2008, p. 169). Moreover, he conflated this wrongdoing with all the wrongs that have been committed against Indigenous peoples. As an apology addressed to 'Australia's Indigenous Peoples', the implication he seemed to make was that all Indigenous peoples should be given a fair go as other Australians in the future. In this respect, he presented the Closing the Gap policy as a key measure to address Indigenous disadvantage and the way forward to achieve reconciliation for all Australians.

In the case of Canada, Harper confined the harms suffered by the Residential School Survivors to those covered by the *Settlement Agreement*, which had been court-approved in 2007. This *Agreement* provided more extensive measures to Residential School Survivors than what Rudd had been prepared to offer Stolen Generations Survivors. This difference may be attributed to the greater acceptance of Residential School Survivors' claims for compensation in the courts. Nevertheless, the *Settlement Agreement* did not challenge the legality of the residential schools, nor resolve the question of genocide that the treatment of former residents raised. The *Settlement Agreement* was the largest class action settlement in Canada, but it did not include acceptance of legal liability by any of the defendants (*Settlement Agreement*, 2006, p. 7). Moreover, the *Agreement* did not extend to all the communities affected by the residential school system such as in Labrador and Newfoundland. However, Harper presented this *Agreement* as all that was needed to repair the harms suffered by Residential School Survivors. Furthermore, he noted the establishment of the TRC as the final phase of the *Settlement Agreement*, but confined its role 'to educate all Canadians on the Indian residential schools system' (House of Commons, Canada, 2008, p. 6850), and not to provide any additional avenues of redress to Indigenous peoples. In this respect, Harper confined the wrongdoing to the residential school system as the only injustice inflicted on Indigenous peoples that required redress.

Contrasting the texts of both apologies with the claims of Indigenous peoples reveals that the way they framed the injustices, the norms they infringed, and the reparations to make good the harms suffered were too narrow to make meaningful differences in the lives of Indigenous peoples. Ultimately, the harms acknowledged in each apology were those that could be accepted as wrong according to select state norms and values that framed the Closing the Gap policy in Australia and the *Settlement Agreement* in Canada. Implicit in the tone and logic of both apologies was that existing laws and practices of each state can produce just outcomes for Indigenous peoples. However, when the more extensive claims of Indigenous peoples are considered, the gap that continues to exist between state norms and justice for Indigenous peoples is evident. The situation for Indigenous peoples after the apologies remained one where justice was yet to come (cf., Derrida, 1992, pp. 16, 23, 24).

In this regard, the apologies appear inherently paradoxical. It can be inferred from the acceptance in both apologies that the forcible removal of Indigenous children from their families was wrong that there are limits to what states can do in exercising their powers (Reilly, 2008, p. 13). This seems to be the understanding of those Indigenous representatives who thought the apologies could (or should) eventually lead to the development of political arrangements in which Indigenous peoples would exercise greater authority and control over their own affairs. When the practice of the forcible removal of Indigenous children is viewed as forming part of the broader process of colonisation, the just response would have been to make reparations for the range of harms caused, institutionalise Indigenous rights protections, and at the very least devolve jurisdiction to Indigenous peoples with respect to child welfare. The result could have been the creation of a 'new' relationship which eventually could have led to replacing the top-down approach with a bottom-up approach in Indigenous affairs. However, at no time did either Rudd or Harper acknowledge that the exercise of state power should be placed in check. They may have accepted that the practice of removing Indigenous children was not in their best interests, but it was still lawful according to state laws. In this logic there is no room for acknowledgement of the Indigenous norms that had been violated by the removal of Indigenous children from their families. Herein the conditions of settler colonialism were perpetuated as the apologies functioned to reiterate a unitary conception of state sovereignty to the exclusion of Indigenous peoples' sovereignty and law. And in reiterating state sovereignty they reiterated the understanding that the state, through its norms and practices, knows what is best. Both Rudd and Harper may have thought they were addressing Indigenous peoples with respect. However, in maintaining the sovereign status of their respective nation state, traces of the negative perceptions of Indigenous peoples that had legitimised the acquisition of state sovereignty remained.

How could the Rudd and Harper apologies function more effectively?

As the discussion of the Rudd and Harper apologies demonstrates, while they appeared to adequately fulfil the main criteria of what makes an effective apology (naming the wrongs, accepting responsibility for them, expressing regret, and promising reform and forbearance in the future), it is evident that they did so in accordance with state norms. In contrast, the Indigenous responses demonstrated that there are alternative ways of conveying the messages of an apology to show respect, make amends for the harms suffered, and to never repeat them again in ways that could advance Indigenous claims for justice. On both sides there was an agreed understanding that the forced removal of Indigenous children was wrong, but while this acknowledgement in the apologies functioned to re-legitimise state sovereignty, in some of the Indigenous responses this acknowledgement was construed as a direct challenge to state legitimacy.

These shortcomings raise the question whether each apology should have been rejected outright as was the response of some Indigenous critics (Chrisjohn, et al., 2008; Krebs 2008; McKinnon 2008; cf., Churchill, 2008). This is an understandable reaction considering the ongoing colonial domination that the apologies exemplify. But it is also true that not all Indigenous peoples were inclined to reject them. In fact, some did find closure (Korff, 2021), while others were willing to forgive (Fitzpatrick and Nguyen, 2008). It is important to acknowledge these differences to avoid generalisations about what Indigenous peoples say and do. In terms of the argument advanced in this book, these reactions, when considered together, also reveal the various ways in which Indigenous peoples became engaged in political action in the apology process. This was evident throughout the process, and especially in the struggles of Indigenous peoples to secure an apology from each respective head of state. In speaking out about their experiences of injustice and calling on government to account for them in an apology, Indigenous peoples promoted their claims. The final chapters of the book explore how the Rudd and Harper apologies could (and have) also been used in this way in the post-apology era. The approach adopted in the book is to develop the understanding of an apology as a relational process. The aim of doing this is three-fold: first, to strengthen the understanding of an apology as a transformative process; second, to emphasise the significant role Survivors play in this process; and third, to promote Indigenous peoples' claims for justice.

A relational understanding of apology making does not deny the role that state actors play in making an apology. An apology offered by the head of state may have beneficial consequences. An apology that is officially offered by the head of state, announced in public and at the right pitch and tenor, could help to overcome conflict by changing how those on both sides see themselves and each other (Barkan and Karn, 2006, p. 7; King, 2011). Even if the apology does not work to achieve these things, an apology delivered officially by the head of state serves to acknowledge past wrongdoing, which could be effective in vindicating Survivors' experiences and raising greater public awareness of the injustices Survivors have suffered. Indeed, an apology may not only contribute to correcting the historical record; it also becomes part of the nation's history as the day the nation said 'sorry'.

Nevertheless, certain issues can arise from primarily focusing on the role of the head of state in making an apology. This approach may redeem the nation prematurely as though what happened in the past is now settled so 'we' can move on 'with the warm inner glow that will come with having said sorry' (Pearson, 2008, p. 2). Even if it is accepted that an apology requires more than a sincere 'I'm sorry', focusing only on what is said in the apology may lead to inaccurate assumptions that there is an agreed understanding of the wrongdoing, the norms they infringed, and the measures now needed to overcome the harms suffered. This issue is evident in relation to the Rudd and Harper apologies. The contrast between them and the Indigenous responses reveals the contestation that exists in the understanding of Indigenous peoples' experiences of injustice and the ways of overcoming the harms they have suffered. In turn, this analysis reveals the danger of accepting what the state leader says about these things is 'the truth', and the effect this can have in obscuring the inequality in power that exists between the parties, which can (and does) operate at the time the apology is being made. In this regard, a sincere expression of 'I'm sorry' may only eclipse the politics involved in apology making and continue to silence those to whom the apology is addressed.

Critical theoretical perspectives on the structures of power in society have been vital in revealing the interplay between discourse and power in the construction of knowledge (Foucault, 1978, 1980, chap. 5). In exposing this 'truth', critical theorists have been able to demonstrate how through the valorisation of certain ideas, and not others, the hierarchical structures of power that exist in society can be legitimised. This issue can arise in the apology-making context, for so long as state actors have control over the process, the perspective of the dominant politico-legal order will prevail in determining the content of the apology; namely, the injustices deserving of an apology and how they are to be overcome.

However, it is also important to realise these hierarchies can be challenged through the valorisation of alternative perspectives – especially the perspectives of historically marginalised groups (Parashar and Dominello, 2017, pp. 28–29). This is theoretical basis of the book and reflects this author's experience in researching and writing about the Rudd and Harper apologies and the way my understanding of apology making was influenced and shaped by the Indigenous responses to these apologies. Through this process, it became evident that apology making required reconceptualisation to ensure that Indigenous claims were not closed off by the state saying 'sorry'. An apology is after all about making things right with the people who have been wronged. This is a perspective that the collectives on either side of the apology should agree on.

As part of the process of setting things right, an apology understood as relational would involve the parties engaging in dialogue with a view to resolving the outstanding issues facing Survivors as they understand them. Based on the lessons that may be learned from the Rudd and Harper apologies, the starting point would be for Indigenous peoples to be engaged in the apology-making process from its inception in informing the apology's content and ceremony through to its delivery in responding to the apology and beyond. With respect to Indigenous peoples, acknowledging the importance of their role in the apology-making process could have deeper political consequences in helping to overcome the historical marginalisation of their perspectives. One aspect of the colonisation process has been the way that western knowledge systems have excluded Indigenous knowledges and posited western perspectives as the only source of knowledge. Critical scholars such as Aileen Moreton-Robinson (Goenpul tribe, Quandamooka nation) have responded by exposing how the western scientific paradigm, which is based on notions of neutrality and objectivity, masks the partisan nature – the whiteness – of western research (Moreton-Robinson, 2004, p. 81). Others, like Linda Tuhiwai Smith (Ngati A wa and Ngati Porou), have called for the decolonisation of academic research by decentring western perspectives and prioritising Indigenous knowledges and ways of being (Smith, 2012; cf., Ray, 2012). Similar arguments could extend to the marginalisation of Indigenous perspectives in law and politics. As Glen Coulthard (Yellowknives Dene First Nation) has argued, this marginalisation continues in the political sphere through the politics of recognition. Rather than re-centring Indigenous perspectives, the politics of recognition reinscribes settler–colonised relations by containing Indigenous peoples' claims, limiting redress for past wrongs, and maintaining state legitimacy through denial of ongoing colonial domination (Coulthard, 2014, pp. 25–49). These critiques are pertinent to apologies made in settler-colonised contexts that claim to recognise the harms suffered by Indigenous peoples, but in ways that contain the extent of the harm and the cost of redress on the state by funnelling Indigenous claims through state norms and practices.

It is contended that an apology that functions relationally may help to transform the status quo by opening the lines of communication between state actors and Indigenous peoples. However, it is also contended that little will change so long as the state's normative frameworks continue to close off Indigenous political authority. It is to be remembered that the apologies were delivered in the context of continuing settler colonialism, which the historical and contemporary removal of Indigenous children in both Australia and Canada is but one example. Bringing the settler–coloniser relationship to an end, as some Indigenous peoples thought an apology would lead to, requires extensive institutional changes. It is not possible in this book to canvass all these changes, but considering that central to the wrongs committed against Indigenous peoples are rights violations, an important aspect of any reform agenda post-apology would be to implement an Indigenous rights framework to temper the grossly unequal power dynamics of settler–colonised relations. Notably, at the time Rudd and Harper delivered their apologies, neither Australia nor Canada had endorsed *UNDRIP*, but this changed in 2009 and 2010, respectively.

Upholding the Indigenous rights in *UNDRIP* relating (among others) to self-determination and the requirement for 'free, prior and informed consent' with respect to the adoption and implementation of legislative or administrative measures affecting Indigenous peoples (United Nations, 2007, arts 3, 4, and 19) could serve as a shield against the marginalisation of Indigenous perspectives in law and policy. Incorporation of *UNDRIP* could also serve as a sword to protect Indigenous interests when their rights are violated. In making reparations for past and present rights violations, governments could also revert to international legal principles, especially the *Basic Principles and Guidelines on the Right to a Remedy and Reparation for Survivors of Gross Violations of Human Rights Law and Serious Violations of International Humanitarian Law* (United Nations, 2005), which includes measures of restitution, compensation, rehabilitation, satisfaction, and guarantees of non-repetition. Reparations made according to these principles are required to be proportionate to the gravity of the breach and the harm suffered, and be accepted as 'adequate' and 'effective' by those persons, groups, or communities entitled to them (Lenzerini, 2008, pp. 9–10, 14–15). However, considering the stronghold of settler colonialism, which even *UNDRIP* is complicit in maintaining through art. 46(1) that protects 'the territorial integrity' and 'political unity of sovereign and independent States', a rights-based approach may be limited. The state's commitment to change would be tested by what mechanisms are put in place to avoid the pitfalls of the 'politics of recognition', as identified by Coulthard, and prevent state actors from distorting Indigenous peoples' rights and continuing to infringe them.

The understanding of an apology as relational serves as a discursive strategy to focus attention on the issues facing Indigenous peoples as they understand them. This approach reveals that different perspectives can (and do) exist on the harms suffered and ways to address them and highlights the importance of Indigenous peoples' perspectives on these things as they, ultimately, are to be satisfied with the apology. Moreover, this approach also reveals how more structural changes are needed to support Indigenous perspectives if the promise of never again is to be fulfilled. The relational understanding in centring Indigenous perspectives contributes to counter the historical marginalisation of Indigenous perspectives. Through their valorisation, greater impetus for the need for changes to the dominant structures of power and knowledge may become more apparent.

The Indigenous representatives who responded to the Rudd and Harper apologies approached them as relational. Each response in its own way conveyed the understanding that the apologies required future government action and this, in turn, required further engagement with Indigenous peoples to advance their claims for justice. Of significance was their attempt to carve out a significant role for Indigenous peoples to play in the post-apology era. Negotiations between government and Indigenous peoples would mean that state actors would no longer be the ones entitled to speak. Indigenous peoples would also be entitled to speak and be listened to. In this way Indigenous peoples would steer government to fulfil the promises for reform and forbearance that the apologies represent. Instead of their perspectives being relegated to the margins, the legitimacy of their claims would be unquestionable. As Simon declared in her response to the Harper apology: '[w]e must be in the room working together with government ... Gone are the days when policy or legislative initiatives were invoked for us' (Senate of Canada, 2008, p. 1505).

A relational approach to apology making that is focused on validating Indigenous voices aligns with the Indigenous right of self-determination and starkly contrasts with the apparent state re-legitimisation approaches in both the Rudd and Harper apologies. As Indigenous peoples in Australia and Canada continue to face obstacles in the way of the realisation of their claims, a relational understanding of apology making, in emphasising the central role of Survivors to the apology-making process, could serve to hold governments accountable in ensuring that Indigenous perspectives are at the centre of future reforms. More recent developments in Australia and Canada are critically examined in this spirit.

In the case of Australia, it is evident that in the intervening period since the Rudd apology little has changed. Indeed, the socio-economic position of Indigenous peoples appears to have worsened. The Closing the Gap policy, which was the key policy commitment of the Rudd apology to address disparities in Indigenous health, education, and employment, has failed to meet its targets. Specifically, in relation to members of the Stolen Generations, they and their descendants are faring worse than other Indigenous people, but recommendations for more comprehensive reparations continue to be evaded by government (Aboriginal and Torres Strait Islander Healing Foundation, 2021). Moreover, since the Rudd apology was delivered the number of Indigenous children in out-of-home care has more than doubled, which raises concerns about the creation of a second Stolen Generation. Indeed, the entire future of reconciliation in Australia has been put into doubt by the failed referendum in 2023. The referendum, introduced by the recently elected Albanese government, sought to constitutionally enshrine an Aboriginal and Torres Strait Islander Voice to Parliament. A First Nations Voice enshrined in the Constitution was a key recommendation of the *Uluru Statement from the Heart* ('*Uluru Statement*') (2017), which also called for a treaty and truth-telling process through a Makarrata Commission. The proposed Voice to Parliament aimed to provide a forum for dialogue between Indigenous peoples and parliaments and governments at all jurisdictional levels in areas of concern for Indigenous peoples. Whether having a Voice would have led to meaningful change was uncertain, as it was intended to be advisory only. In any event, its rejection has revealed the deep divisions and racism that exists in Australia and has been devastating for its Indigenous supporters. At a time when there is much work needed to promote the rights and interests of Indigenous peoples, as the *Uluru Statement* seeks to do, the Rudd apology serves as a reminder of promises made to do better. This is following the lead of others who have appealed to the Rudd apology, and the promises of reform and forbearance it represents to them, in critiquing the status quo (Pearson, 2018; Wahlquist, 2018). These responses are a testament to the continued relevance of the apology to combat prevailing ignorance of the pressing issues facing Indigenous peoples in Australia. The relational understanding of apology making supports this understanding and the need for government accountability and leadership by attending to Indigenous peoples' claims in post-apology Australia.

In comparison to Australia, Canada has been more receptive to Indigenous peoples' claims. This can be largely attributed to the work of the TRC, which was established in 2008 as the final phase of the *Settlement Agreement*. Also of significance was the election of Prime Minister Justin Trudeau in 2015 and his commitment to fulfil the TRC's 94 Calls to Action. These 'calls' reflect the TRC's conviction to move from the 'apology to action' (TRC, 2015, p. 209) – a move that had stagnated during Harper's time in office (James, 2018, pp. 835–836).

In canvassing the developments in the post-apology era in Canada, the book's focus is on issues directly related to the strengths and weaknesses of the *Settlement Agreement* for Residential School Survivors. The government's record in implementing the TRC's Calls to Action is also canvassed. Many of the government's responses are still in their formative stages and illustrate the challenges that Indigenous peoples continue to face in the post-apology era.

A key aim of the TRC's recommendations is to reset the nation-to-nation relationship between Aboriginal peoples and the Crown. The basis of this relationship lies in the history of treaty making between Indigenous peoples and the Crown, most notably the Royal Proclamation of 1763, the provisions of which were ratified by Indigenous peoples in the Treaty of Niagara in 1764. The understanding of Indigenous peoples is that the treaties preserved their status as free and sovereign peoples (Lindberg, 2010). However, the treaties came to be understood very differently by the colonial officials who, by the 1850s, began to pursue a policy of assimilation of Indigenous peoples through legislation. The result, in sum, was that Indigenous peoples became subject to Canadian sovereignty and law. The TRC's recommendations seek to address this historical legacy through, for example, the repudiation of the doctrines of discovery and terra nullius, which were used to justify the assertion of sovereignty over Indigenous peoples and lands and the implementation of the *UNDRIP* as the framework for reconciliation (TRC, 2015, p. 199). However, the progress made in implementing the TRC recommendations has been uneven, and in some areas has been stagnant. The government has committed to aligning Canadian laws with *UNDRIP* and has, following the National Inquiry, accepted that genocide has been committed (at least against Indigenous women, girls, and 2SLGBTQQIA people) ('Trudeau accepts inquiry finding of genocide, but says focus must be on response', 2019). Nevertheless, the government's full commitment to Indigenous rights has been brought into question by notable breaches of these rights. The child welfare context is one area that is explored. In view of Canada's history of broken promises and ongoing challenges in implementing the TRC reform agenda, the understanding of apology making as relational supports the need for greater government accountability in its treatment of Indigenous peoples and infringement of their rights.

Conclusion

An apology may do many things in the world. The approach in this book is to consider how an apology made to Indigenous peoples could function to advance their claims for justice. In demonstrating that there are different perspectives on the harms suffered and ways to address them, an apology, understood as relational as opposed to a speech act, may be more equipped to focus attention on what Indigenous peoples say when apologies are made to them and what they think should be the way forward in the future. To be sure, there is not one universal Indigenous perspective, and as between Indigenous peoples in nations such as Australia and Canada their experiences of colonisation, although similar, had very different origins and require their own response. Notwithstanding these differences, both nations share a history of settler colonialism. Considering the continuing manifestations of settler colonialism as the source of Indigenous peoples' experiences of injustice, and the Indigenous responses that looked to the apologies as marking a turning point in settler–colonised relations, this book through its development of the understanding of an apology as relational, seeks to reconceptualise apology making as a process that engenders government commitment to changes in policy and law that are aligned to Indigenous peoples' claims.

Notes

1 There are differences in terminology used in Australia and Canada. For consistency, the term Indigenous peoples is used except when referring to specific individuals or communities. When citing specific sources, the book uses the terminology in those sources. It is acknowledged that at times the terminology is culturally inappropriate and insensitive, and this is not the view of the author. The terminology of 'Survivor' is also used in the book when specifically referring to Indigenous peoples' experiences of colonisation. The book uses 'victim' terminology when it is used in the literature to refer to experiences of injustice more broadly.

2 In the United States of America, there have been three apologies at the national level. The first was offered by the United States Congress in 1993 for the illegal overthrow of the Kingdom of Hawaii one hundred years earlier in 1893 ('Congress Resolution 19'). In 2000, an apology was made by Kevin Gover on behalf of the Bureau of Indian Affairs for the injustices it had inflicted on Native Americans since its inception in 1824 (Bureau of Indian Affairs, 2000). This was followed by the 'Apology to Native Peoples of the United States' (2009) in the House of Representatives, which was for 'the many instances of violence, maltreatment, and neglect inflicted on Native Peoples by citizens of the United States'.

In Norway, King Harald V publicly apologised to the Sami people in 1997 'for the injustice the Norwegian state once imposed on the Sami people through policies of Norweganization' ('King apologizes for minority repression', 1997).

In Sweden, Agriculture Minister Annika Ahnberg apologised in 1998 on behalf of the government to the Sami people for the injustices they have suffered under Swedish rule and acknowledged that 'colonisation of northern Sweden had forced the indigenous Sami off their land, and led to the Sami language being suppressed' ('Sweden apologies to Sami people', 1998).

In New Zealand, there have been many apologies and settlements offered by the Crown to individual *iwi* (Māori communities) in speeches and in legislation since 1975 when the Waitangi Tribunal was founded. In 2002, former New Zealand Prime Minister Helen Clark also apologised to Samoa for the inept and incompetent early administration of Samoa by New Zealand (Clark, 2002).

In Chile, President Michelle Bachelet issued an apology in 2010 to the descendants of five Kawesqar Indians whose remains had been shipped to Europe in the late nineteenth century and exhibited. She also acknowledged 'the mistreatment of the indigenous people was due to racist attitudes towards "our indigenous forefathers, whose human dignity was trampled upon"' ('Chile apologises over treatment of Indigenous people', 2010). She issued a further apology in 2017 to the Mapuche people (the original inhabitants of the land now known as Chile and Argentina) where she stated: 'I want, solemnly and with humility, to ask forgiveness from the Mapuche people for the errors and horrors committed or tolerated by the state in our relation with them and their communities' ('President Bachelet apologizes for "horrors" done to Indigenous Mapuche', 2017).

In El Salvador on the 518th anniversary of the landing of Christopher Columbus in the Americas in 2010, President Mauricio Funes issued an apology to the nation's Indigenous peoples 'for all the harm they have suffered over the past five centuries' ('El Salvador's President apologizes to Indigenous peoples', 2010).

In Taiwan, President Tsai Ing-wen (蔡英文) issued a formal apology in 2016 on behalf of the government to Taiwan's Indigenous people for the discrimination and neglect they suffered over the past 400 years (Office of the President Republic of China (Taiwan), 2016).

3 The Harper apology was the first apology to Indigenous peoples to be issued by a head of state in Canada. It followed two earlier apologies that had been made in 1991 and 1998 in relation to the residential school system, the first by William Van Iterson, Assistant Deputy Minister of Indian Affairs (Todd, 1991); the second by Jane Stewart, Minister of Indian Affairs and Northern Development Canada (Stewart, 1998). More recently, in 2017, Prime Minister Justin Trudeau apologised to Residential School Survivors in Newfoundland and Labrador as they had not been included in Harper's 2008 apology (Trudeau, 2017). In 2018, he also apologised (twice) to members of the Tsilhqot'in community for the hangings of six chiefs during the so-called Chilcotin War more than 150 years ago (Flynn, 2018; YouTube., n.d.). In 2018, Indigenous-Crown Relations Minister Carolyn Bennett officially apologised for the impacts of the 1923 Williams Treaties (Bennett, 2018), and in 2019 she apologised to the Ahiarmiut, a group of inland Inuit, for being forcibly removed from their homelands at Ennadai Lake in the 1940s and 1950s (Bennett, 2019). Also in 2019, Trudeau apologised for the past mistreatment by the government of Inuit with tuberculosis (Trudeau, 2019). Trudeau apologised again to Residential School Survivors in 2021 after hundreds of unmarked graves were found at residential school sites in Kamloops and Saskatchewan ('"Incredibly harmful": Trudeau apologizes for history of residential schools following discovery of unmarked graves', 2021).

In Australia, most of the apologies to the Stolen Generations were made by state and territory premiers in 1997. The premier of the Northern Territory apologised in 2001 (Australian Human Rights Commission, 2008).

4 Tom Calma was asked to speak on behalf of the two national bodies representing the Stolen Generations and their families, the National Sorry Day Committee and the Stolen Generations Alliance. In his speech he defined his role as being 'to respond to the Parliament's Apology and to talk briefly about the importance of today's events' (Calma, 2008, p. 1). Patrick Dodson was invited to speak by the National Press Club. Notably, these responses have not been treated as 'official' because they were not made in the House of Representatives. For these reasons, the 'response' made by Leader of the Opposition Brendan Nelson in the House of Representatives has been treated as the only 'official' response to the Rudd apology (McAuley, 2011, p. 21; Reilly, 2008, p. 15).

Reference list

Aboriginal and Torres Strait Islander Healing Foundation, 2021, *Make healing happen: it's time to act*, https://healingfoundation.org.au/app/uploads/2021/05/Make-Healing-Happen-Report-FINAL-May-2021.pdf

Alfred, T., 2005, *Wasáse: Indigenous pathways of action and freedom*, Broadview Press, Ontario.

Alfred, T., 2009, 'Colonialism and state dependency', *Journal of Aboriginal Health*, vol. 5, pp. 42–60.

'Apology to Native Peoples of the United States', 2009, in *Department of Defense Appropriations Act, 2010*, 19 December, http://www.copyright.gov/legislation/pl111-118.pdf

Austin, J.L., 1962, *How to do things with words*, Oxford University Press, London.

Australian Human Rights Commission, 2008, *Bringing them home: apologies by state and territory parliaments (2008)*, https://humanrights.gov.au/our-work/bringing-them-home-apologies-state-and-territory-parliaments-2008

Barkan, E. and Karn, A., 2006, 'Group apology as an ethical imperative', in E. Barkan and A. Karn (eds), *Taking wrongs seriously: apologies and reconciliation*, Stanford University Press, Stanford, pp. 3–32.
Barta, T., 1987, 'Relations of genocide: land and lives in the colonization of Australia', in I. Wallimann and M.N. Dobkowski (eds), *Genocide and the modern age: etiology and case studies of mass death*, Greenwood Press, New York.
Beales, R., 2008, 'Federal government must "stay apologized" say Aboriginal leaders', *Brantford Expositer*, 15 December.
Bennett, C., 2018, *Statement of apology for the impacts of the 1923 Williams treaties*, 17 November, https://www.rcaanc-cirnac.gc.ca/eng/1542393580430/1542393607484
Bennett, C., 2019, *Statement of apology for the relocation of the AHIARMIUT*, 22 January, https://www.rcaanc-cirnac.gc.ca/eng/1548170252259/1548170273272
Bureau of Indian Affairs, 2000, *Keynote remarks of Kevin Gover Assistant Secretary – Indian Affairs*, 8 September, https://www.bia.gov/sites/default/files/dup/assets/as-ia/opa/pdf/idc1-032248.pdf
Calma, T., 2008, *Let the healing begin: response to government to the national apology to the Stolen Generations*, 13 February, https://humanrights.gov.au/sites/default/files/content/pdf/social_justice/speech/let_the_healing_begin.pdf
Capriccioso, R., 2010, 'A sorry saga: Obama signs Native American apology resolution; fails to draw attention to it', *Indian Country Today*, 13 January, http://www.danielnpaul.com/AmericanApologyToAmericanIndians.html
Celermajer, D., 2006, 'The apology in Australia: re-covenanting the national imagery', in E. Barkan and A. Karn (eds), *Taking wrongs seriously: apologies and reconciliation*, Stanford University Press, Stanford, pp. 153–184.
Celermajer, D., 2009, *The sins of the nation and the ritual of apologies*, Cambridge University Press, Melbourne.
'Chile apologises over treatment of Indigenous people', 2010, *BBC News*, 12 January, http://news.bbc.co.uk/2/hi/americas/8455638.stm
Chrisjohn, R., Bear Nicholas, A., Stote, K., Craven (Omahkohkiaayo I'poyi), J., Wasacase, T., Loiselle, P. and Smith, A.O., 2008, 'An historic non-apology, completely and utterly not accepted', https://web.archive.org/web/20081012122924/http://www.marxmail.org/ApologyNotAccepted.htm
Chrisjohn, R. and Young, S., 1997, *The circle game: shadow and substance in the residential school experience in Canada*, Theytus Books, Penticton, http://citeseerx.ist.psu.edu/viewdoc/download;jsessionid=50335080FD3DEB0CFBF420F95FCD85DF?doi=10.1.1.110.9288&rep=rep1&type=pdf
Churchill, W., 2008, 'Healing begins when the wounding stops: Indian residential schools and the prospects for "truth and reconciliation" in Canada', *Briarpatch Magazine*, 9 June, https://briarpatchmagazine.com/articles/view/healing-begins-when-the-wounding-stops/
Clark, H., 2002, 'Helen Clark's apology to Samoa', *NZ Herald*, 4 June, https://www.nzherald.co.nz/nz/full-text-helen-clarks-apology-to-samoa/65TV2LDV6S7HHIYRDCFSC5YOZI/
'Congress Resolution 19', 1993, *United States Public Law 130–150*, 23 November, http://www.hawaii-nation.org/publawall.html
Corntassel, J. and Holder, C., 2008, 'Who's sorry now? Government apologies, truth commissions, and Indigenous self-determination in Australia, Canada, Guatemala, and Peru', *Human Rights Review*, vol. 9, no. 4, pp. 465–489, DOI:10.1007/s12142-008-0065-3

Coulthard, G., 2014, *Red skin, white masks: rejecting the colonial politics of recognition*, University of Minnesota Press, Minneapolis.

Cubillo v. Commonwealth (2001) 174 ALR 97.

Declaration on the Rights of Indigenous Peoples Act, SC, 2021, c. 14.

Derrida, J., 1992, 'Force of law: the mythical foundation of authority', in D. Cornell, M. Rosenfeld and D.G. Carlson (eds), *Deconstruction and the possibility of justice*, Routledge, New York, pp. 3–67.

Dodson, P., 2008, 'After the apology', *Arena Magazine*, April–May, vol. *94*, pp. 20–23.

'Editorial', 1993, *Aboriginal Law Bulletin*, vol. 3, no. *61*, p. 3.

'El Salvador's president apologizes to Indigenous peoples', 2010, *The Tico Times*, 13 October, http://www.ticotimes.net/2010/10/13/el-salvador-s-president-apologizes-to-indigenous-peoples

Fiddler, C., 2008, 'Gov't of Canada apologize for 100 years of atrocities', *Windspeaker*, vol. *26*, no. *4*, http://www.ammsa.com/publications/windspeaker/govt-canada-apologize-100-years-atrocities

Fitzpatrick, M. and Nguyen, L., 2008, 'Aboriginal leaders hail historic apology', *Windsor Star*, 11 June, http://www.bishop-accountability.org/news2008/05_06/2008_06_11_Fitzpatrick_AboriginalLeaders.htm

Flynn, M., 2018, 'Justin Trudeau apologizes for the brutal hanging of tribal chiefs 150 years ago', *The Washington Post*, 27 March, https://www.washingtonpost.com/news/morning-mix/wp/2018/03/27/justin-trudeau-apologizes-for-the-brutal-hanging-of-tribal-chiefs-150-years-ago/

Foucault, M., 1978, *The history of sexuality*, R. Hurley (trans.), Pantheon Books, New York.

Foucault, M., 1980, 'Two lectures', in C. Gorden (ed.), C. Gorden, L. Marshall, J. Mepham and K. Soper (trans.), *Power/knowledge*, Pantheon Books, New York.

Goffman, E., 1971, *Relations in public: microstudies of the public order*, Basic Books, New York.

Govier, T., 2006, *Taking wrongs seriously: acknowledgement, reconciliation, and the politics of sustainable peace*, Humanity Books, New York.

Govier, T. and Verwoerd, W., 2002, 'The promise and pitfalls of apology', *Journal of Social Philosophy*, vol. *33*, no. *1*, pp. 67–82, DOI:10.1111/1467-9833.00124

Graham, M., 2014, 'Aboriginal notions of relationality and positionalism: a reply to Weber', *Global Discourse: An Interdisciplinary Journal of Current Affairs and Applied Contemporary Thought*, vol. *4*, no. *1*, pp. 17–22, DOI:10.1080/23269995.2014.895931

House of Commons, Canada, 2008, *House of Commons Debates (Hansard)*, 39th Parl., 2nd Sess., vol. *142*, no. *110*, 11 June, https://www.ourcommons.ca/Content/House/392/Debates/110/HAN110-E.PDF

House of Representatives, Australia, 2008, 'Apology to Australia's Indigenous Peoples', *Parliamentary Debates*, 13 February, https://parlinfo.aph.gov.au/parlInfo/genpdf/chamber/hansardr/2008-02-13/0003/hansard_frag.pdf;fileType=application/pdf

Human Rights and Equal Opportunity Commission, 1997, *Bringing them home: report of the National Inquiry into the Separation of Aboriginal and Torres Strait Islander Children from Their Homes*, Sterling Press, Sydney.

'"Incredibly harmful": Trudeau apologizes for history of residential schools following discovery of unmarked graves', 2021, *Global News*, 26 June, https://globalnews.ca/video/7980988/incredibly-harmful-trudeau-apologizes-for-history-of-residential-schools-following-discovery-of-unmarked-graves

Indian Residential Schools Settlement Agreement, 2006, 8 May, https://residentialschoolsettlement.ca/IRS%20Settlement%20Agreement-%20ENGLISH.pdf

James, M., 2008, 'Wrestling with the past: apologies, quasi-apologies, and non-apologies in Canada', in M. Gibney, R.E. Howard-Hassmann, J. Coicaud and N. Steiner (eds), *The age of apology: facing up to the past*, University of Pennsylvania Press, Philadelphia, pp. 137–153.

James, M., 2018, 'Narrative, robustness, post-apology conduct, and Canada's 1998 and 2008 residential schools apologies', in B. Bevernage and N. Wouters (eds), *The Palgrave handbook of state-sponsored history after 1945*, pp. 831–847, Palgrave Macmillan, London, DOI:10.1057/978-1-349-95306-6_45

Jung, C., 2010, 'Canada and the legacy of the Indian residential schools: transitional justice for Indigenous people in a nontransitional society', in P. Arthur (ed.), *Identities in transition: challenges for transitional justice in divided societies*, Cambridge University Press, New York, pp. 217–250, DOI:10.1017/CBO9780511976858.008

Kemp, B., 2008, 'Putting the pain behind them', *CBC News*, 11 June, http://www.cbc.ca/news/canada/putting-the-pain-behind-them-1.710407

'King apologizes for minority repression', 1997, *Chicago Tribune*, 8 October, https://www.chicagotribune.com/news/ct-xpm-1997-10-08-9710080098-story.html

King, L.B., 2011, 'A tree fell in the forest: the US apologized to Native Americans and no one heard a sound', *Indian Country Today*, 3 December, https://tlpi.wordpress.com/2011/12/03/a-tree-fell-in-the-forest/

Korff, J., 2021, '"Sorry" apology to Stolen Generations', *Creative Spirits*, 14 January, https://www.creativespirits.info/aboriginalculture/politics/stolen-generations/sorry-apology-to-stolen-generations

Krebs, M., 2008, 'The Harper "apology" – saying "sorry" with a forked tongue', *Socialist Voice*, 29 June, http://web.archive.org/web/20110126114442/http://www.socialistvoice.ca/?p=304

Kruger v. Commonwealth (1997) 190 CLR 1.

Leech, G.N., 1983, *Principles of pragmatics*, Longman, London.

Lenzerini, F., 2008, 'Reparations for Indigenous peoples in international and comparative law: an introduction', in F. Lenzerini (ed.), *Reparations for Indigenous peoples: international and comparative perspectives*, pp. 3–26, DOI:10.1093/acprof:oso/9780199235605.003.0001

Lightfoot, S., 2015, 'Settler-state apologies to Indigenous peoples: a normative framework and comparative assessment', *Native American and Indigenous Studies*, vol. 2, no. *1*, pp. 15–39, DOI:10.5749/natiindistudj.2.1.0015

Lindberg, T., 2010, 'The doctrine of discovery in Canada', in R.J. Miller, J. Ruru, L. Behrendt and T. Lindberg (eds), *Discovering Indigenous lands: the doctrine of discovery in the English colonies*, pp. 89–125, Oxford University Press, Oxford, DOI:10.1093/acprof:oso/9780199579815.003.0004

McAuley, G., 2011, 'The national apology three years later', *Australian Studies*, vol. *3*, pp. 1–25.

McKinnon, C., 2008, 'Duplicity and deceit: Gary Foley's take on Rudd's apology to the Stolen Generations', *Melbourne Historical Journal*, vol. *36*, pp. 1–4.

Mihai, M., 2013, 'When the state says "sorry": state apologies as exemplary political judgments', *Journal of Political Philosophy*, vol. *2*, no. *1*, pp. 200–220, DOI:10.1111/j.1467-9760.2012.00418.x

Miller, R.J., Ruru, J., Behrendt, L. and Lindberg, T. (eds), 2010, *Discovering Indigenous lands: the doctrine of discovery in the English colonies*, Oxford University Press, Oxford, DOI:10.1093/acprof:oso/9780199579815.001.0001

Minow, M., 1998, *Between vengeance and forgiveness: facing history after genocide and mass violence*, Beacon Press, Boston.

Mirsky, L., 2004, 'Restorative justice practices of Native American, First Nation, and other Indigenous people of North America: part one', *Restorative Practices E-Forum*, 27 April, https://www.iirp.edu/images/pdf/natjust1.pdf

Moreton-Robinson, A., 2004, 'The possessive logic of patriarchal white sovereignty: the High Court and the Yorta Yorta decision', *Borderlands e-Journal*, vol. *3*, no. *2*, pp. 1–9, https://eprints.qut.edu.au/7690/1/7690.pdf

Muldoon, P., 2009, 'Past injustices and future protections: on the politics of promising', *Australian Indigenous Law Review*, vol. *13*, no. *2*, pp. 2–16.

National Inquiry into Missing and Murdered Indigenous Women and Girls, 2019, *Reclaiming power and place. The final report of the National Inquiry into Missing and Murdered Indigenous Women and Girls, volume 1a*, https://www.mmiwg-ffada.ca/wp-content/uploads/2019/06/Final_Report_Vol_1a-1.pdf

Nobles, M., 2008, *The politics of official apologies*, Cambridge University Press, New York, DOI:10.1017/CBO9780511756252

Office of the President Republic of China (Taiwan), 2016, 'President Tsai apologizes to Indigenous peoples on behalf of government', 1 August, https://english.president.gov.tw/NEWS/4950

Parashar, A. and Dominello, F., 2017, *The family in law*, Cambridge University Press, Melbourne.

Pearson, L., 2018, 'What good was the apology to Stolen Generations with limited reparations, more kids taken?', *ABC News*, 13 February, https://www.abc.net.au/news/2018-02-13/stolen-generations-apology-10-years-on-what-good-was-it/9422718

Pearson, N., 2008, 'When words aren't enough', *The Australian*, 12 February.

'President Bachelet apologizes for "horrors" done to Indigenous Mapuche', 2017, *The Santiago Times*, 24 June, https://santiagotimes.cl/2017/06/24/chile-president-bachelet-apologizes-for-horrors-done-to-indigenous-mapuche/

Ray, L., 2012, 'Deciphering the "Indigenous" in Indigenous methodologies', *AlterNative: An International Journal of Indigenous Peoples*, vol. *8*, no. *1*, pp. 85–98.

Reilly, A., 2008, 'The inherent limits of the apology to the Stolen Generation', *University of Adelaide Law Research Paper No. 2009–002*, DOI:10.2139/ssrn.1294101

Ross, H., 2010, "Aboriginal Australians' cultural norms for negotiating natural resources', *Cultural Survival*, 19 March, https://www.culturalsurvival.org/publications/cultural-survival-quarterly/aboriginal-australians-cultural-norms-negotiating-natural

Searle, J.R., 1976, 'A classification of illocutionary acts', *Language and Society*, vol. *5*, no. *1*, pp. 1–23.

Senate of Canada, 2008, *Debates of the Senate (Hansard)*, 39th Parl., 2nd Sess., vol. *144*, no. *69*, 12 June, https://sencanada.ca/Content/SEN/Chamber/392/Debates/pdf/069db_2008-06-12-e.pdf

Short, D., 2005, 'Reconciliation and the problem of internal colonialism', *Journal of Intercultural Studies*, vol. *26*, no. *3*, pp. 267–282, DOI:10.1080/07256860500153534

Smith, L.T., 2012, *Decolonizing methodologies research and Indigenous peoples*, 2nd edn, Zed Books, New York.

Smith, N., 2008, *I was wrong: the meanings of apologies*, Cambridge University Press, New York, DOI:10.1017/CBO9780511499258

Stewart, J., 1998, *Address by the Honourable Jane Stewart Minister of Indian Affairs and Northern Development on the occasion of the unveiling of Gathering Strength – Canada's Aboriginal Action Plan*, 7 January, https://www.rcaanc-cirnac.gc.ca/eng/1100100015725/1571590271585

'Sweden apologies to Sami people', 1998, *BBC News*, 9 August, http://news.bbc.co.uk/2/hi/europe/148164.stm

Taft, L., 2000, 'Apology subverted: the commodification of apology', *The Yale Law Journal*, vol. *109*, pp. 1135–1160, DOI:10.2307/797485

Tavuchis, N., 1991, *Mea culpa: a sociology of apology and reconciliation*, Stanford University Press, Stanford.

Thompson, J., 2008, 'Apology, justice, and respect: a critical defense of political apology', in M. Gibney, R.E. Howard-Hassmann, J. Coicaud and N. Steiner (eds), *The age of apology: facing up to the past*, University of Pennsylvania Press, Philadelphia, pp. 31–44.

Todd, D., 1991, 'Churches, feds apologize to Natives', *The Vancouver Sun*, 22 June.

'Trudeau accepts inquiry finding of genocide, but says focus must be on response', 2019, *The Canadian Press*, 4 June, https://www.youtube.com/watch?v=k81aqStX-vg

Trudeau, J., 2017, *Statement of apology on behalf of the Government of Canada to former students of the Newfoundland and Labrador residential schools*, 24 November, https://www.pm.gc.ca/en/news/backgrounders/2017/11/24/statement-apology-behalf-government-canada-former-students#:~:text=Today%2C%20I%20stand%20humbly%20before,of%20Canada%20and%20all%20Canadians

Trudeau, J., 2019, *Statement of apology on behalf of the Government of Canada to Inuit for the management of the tuberculosis epidemic from the 1940s–1960s*, 8 March, https://www.pm.gc.ca/en/news/speeches/2019/03/08/statement-apology-behalf-government-canada-inuit-management-tuberculosis#:~:text=Lives%20were%20shattered%20beyond%20repair,the%2040s%20to%20the%2060s

Truth and Reconciliation Commission of Canada, 2015, *Honouring the truth, reconciling for the future: summary of the final report of the Truth and Reconciliation Commission of Canada*, https://ehprnh2mwo3.exactdn.com/wp-content/uploads/2021/01/Executive_Summary_English_Web.pdf

Uluru Statement from the Heart, 2017, https://www.referendumcouncil.org.au/sites/default/files/2017-05/Uluru_Statement_From_The_Heart_0.PDF

United Nations, 2005, *Basic Principles and Guidelines on the Right to a Remedy and Reparation for Victims of Gross Violations of International Human Rights Law and Serious Violations of International Humanitarian Law*, General Assembly Resolution 60/147.

United Nations, 2007, *United Nations Declaration on the Rights of Indigenous Peoples*, General Assembly Resolution 61/295.

Wahlquist, C., 2018, 'Rudd's apology, 10 years on: the elusive hope of a "breakthrough moment"', *The Guardian*, 12 February, https://www.theguardian.com/australia-news/2018/feb/12/looking-back-at-rudds-apology-the-shining-hope-of-a-breakthrough-moment

Winter, S., 2014, 'Theorising the political apology', *The Journal of Political Philosophy*, vol. *23*, no. *3*, pp. 261–281, DOI:10.1111/jopp.12047

Wolfe, P., 2006, 'Settler colonialism and the elimination of the Native', *Journal of Genocide Research*, vol. *8*, no. *4*, pp. 387–409, DOI:10.1080/14623520601056240

YouTube, n.d., 'Prime Minister Justin Trudeau apologizes to the Tsilhqot'in Nation', *APTN News*, https://www.youtube.com/watch?v=_3hQYV1XEvM

Chapter 2

Making apologies

What do they do?

Introduction

The making of apologies is something people do daily. However, saying 'sorry' can mean different things depending on the context in which it is expressed. In Ancient Greece, Socrates made his famous apology to defend himself against allegations that he was guilty of corrupting the youths of Athens and did not believe in the gods (Cooper, 2002). Today, defending one's position in the form of a Socratic *apologia* may not seem to be an apology at all. Nevertheless, even today an apology may be accompanied by an excuse or explanation for one's actions (for example, 'Sorry I was late, but my bus was delayed'). Moreover, while it is usual for 'sorry' to be expressed in response to wrongs and often in response to trivial mishaps (such as bumping trolleys in the supermarket), it is not unusual to find 'sorry' expressed in contexts where no social wrong has occurred (such as to express sympathy for another when they are sick or have experienced a death in the family). Clearly these examples reveal differences in the meaning of the expressions 'I apologise' and 'I am sorry' where the former expression conveys more directly the acceptance of responsibility for a wrong and the latter does not (Gill, 2000, p. 13).

As interesting as the range of contexts may be where an 'apology' is made or the words 'I'm sorry' are expressed, this chapter examines apologies made in situations involving more serious wrongs where harm has been suffered due to the actions of another/others. These apologies are usually made in the form of 'I'm sorry. I promise I'll fix it' (Rojo, 2005, p. 64), and include additional elements such as a commitment to overcome the harm caused. In the literature these are referred to as 'moral' apologies (Govier, 2006, pp. 68–69; cf., Govier and Verwoerd, 2002, pp. 67, 72).

The reason for focusing on these types of apologies is because of their relevance to the Rudd and Harper apologies that were respectively made in Australia and Canada in 2008 (House of Commons, Canada, 2008, pp. 6849–6852; House of Representatives, Australia, 2008). In accepting responsibility for the harms caused by the forced Indigenous child removal policies,

DOI: 10.4324/9781003491019-2

both apologies included more than the expression of 'I'm sorry'. In both apologies, commitments were made for additional measures of redress. But saying these things raises a pertinent question. Does this mean that these apologies were effective?

There is no settled approach in determining the effectiveness of an apology. If it is accepted that an apology is aimed at making amends to victims, then the effectiveness of an apology would be measured according to whether it meets their interests (Brown and Levinson, 1987, p. 68). However, other perspectives suggest that an apology serves the interests of wrongdoers by restoring their social standing so they may be trusted again in the future. An apology, according to this understanding, 'saves face' of the wrongdoer (Scher and Darley, 1997, p, 128) and its effectiveness would be measured according to whether it has improved perceptions of them (Scher and Darley, 1997, p. 137).

It is important to consider these different standpoints because they can lead to very different outcomes. In the political context, an apology, treated as a 'saving face' exercise for nation states, could merely serve to redeem the state's position of power (Somani, 2011, p. 4; Sundar Rajan, 2000) and continue to silence victims and their claims (Jung, 2010, p. 234). In contrast, an apology that is focused on making things right with victims could curtail the exercise of state power. In coming to terms with the negative impact their actions have had on victims, nation states may realise they can no longer behave in that way (Reilly, 2008, p. 13). An apology's promise, 'never again', supports this position. Of course, an apology could potentially be beneficial on both sides – an apology could help the nation gain legitimacy, which had been undermined by past wrongdoing, by satisfying victims and meeting their claims.

The position adopted in this chapter is that the victims must ultimately be satisfied with the apology as only they are in the position to accept (or reject) it. This stance moves beyond treating an apology as a speech act and is based on the understanding of an apology as transactional – as involving an offer and acceptance to promote a reconciled relationship between the parties. However, the discussion extends this understanding beyond what may be described as the 'apology–forgiveness' paradigm which, in focusing on forgiveness, may have the tendency to close off the apology and the need for ongoing reform. Instead, the approach is to treat an apology as a process – a dialogue based on the state's commitment to reform – and how this could promote victims' claims as part of broader process of reconciliation. Accordingly, the effectiveness of the apology would be measured by the extent to which victims' claims are treated as central to this process.

In stating this position, it is acknowledged there are difficulties involved in achieving reconciliation on these terms, especially in circumstances where inequalities in power and resources caused by the perpetration of injustice are continuing to impact on victims during the apology process (James, 2008,

p. 137; cf., de Grieff, 2008, p. 130). These inequalities are important to keep in view with respect to apologies made to Indigenous peoples within the oppressive context of settler colonialism. However, it is important not to treat power differentials as static as this may lead to an uncritical acceptance that apologies may only serve the state and, by implication, cannot be construed differently to support victims in their quest for justice. Keeping the effects of power in view is important, but equally, countering these effects is vital to support victims and their claims. In terms of apology making, this would entail endorsing conceptualisations of apology making that promote victims' claims. This is the approach adopted in this chapter.

In particular, the focus of this chapter is on two interrelated lines of inquiry that will help to elucidate how apologies can work to meet victims' claims. On the one hand, there is the question of why apologies are made, which relates to their aims and functions and why they may be considered valuable from the point of view of victims. On the other hand, there is the question of what makes apologies meaningful or effective, which relates to what people should say when they apologise, and what they should do to promote the interests of victims. Notably, in the discussion it is evident that the meaning of apologies (i.e., how they function) and their meaningfulness for victims (i.e., whether they are effective or not), depends on the context in which they are made.

In illustrating this point, this chapter explores interpersonal (one-to-one) apologies made in the social context, before turning to consider collective (many-to-many) apologies made in the political context. It is evident that while similarities exist between interpersonal and political apologies (e.g., both types of apologies are thought to improve relationships marred by conflict), there are notable differences between them. Indeed, in both contexts the desired outcome of an apology is to promote reconciled relations. However, in this chapter it is argued that reconciliation, in the social context, is usually linked to the granting of forgiveness, while in the political context it would depend on the state providing effective measures to address past violations of victim rights and ensuring the future protection of these rights. This difference exemplifies how the functions of apologies and what makes them effective can vary depending on the context in which they are made: the social context on the one hand, and the political context on the other.

In illuminating the importance that context plays in determining the meaning and meaningfulness of an apology, the chapter argues that any assessment of an apology made in the real world requires understanding of the injustices for which it was offered, including insight into the more immediate context in which the apology was made. In this way the chapter also seeks to broaden 'the context' that researchers should consider when evaluating the functions and effectiveness of an apology. This would also include being attuned to victims' claims for justice as a basis against which to measure an apology's effectiveness. This approach of considering an apology's broader context as a framework for understanding its functions and effectiveness is developed further in Chapters 3 and 4 in examining the Rudd and Harper apologies.

The interpersonal apology: what is it and what does it do?

The conceptual foundation of apology making in western thinking was laid in speech act theory. Speech act theory, beginning with Austin's *How to Do Things with Words* (1962) and followed by Searle's *Speech Acts: An Essay in the Philosophy of Language* (1969), is based on the idea that language is a form of behaviour that is governed by rules. According to this theory there is a link between language (speech) and behaviour (act) which provides the basis for understanding how language functions. In linguistic terms utterances – speech – can perform actions in the world.

Austin's linguistic framework distinguishes between locutionary acts (the bare fact of an act of communication taking place), illocutionary acts (the act that is performed in speaking the utterance), and perlocutionary acts (the effect of the utterance on the listener) (Austin, 1962, pp. 108–109). In linguistic terms 'apologising' has been categorised as an illocutionary act, otherwise known as a performative utterance. As a performative utterance, an apology has been further categorised as *behabitive*, which is a kind of performative 'designed to exhibit attitudes and feelings' (Austin, 1962, pp. 83, 159). Similarly, for Searle, apologies are expressive illocutionary acts: the point of an apology is to express the feeling of regret (Searle, 1976, pp. 4, 12). Thus, at the most basic level, an apology acts to express sorrow for a wrong (Edmonson and House, 1981, p. 45; Tavuchis, 1991, pp. 22, 36, 109). So understood, the success of an apology would depend on the sincerity of the speaker in expressing sorrow. However, it is for this very reason that Austin himself described speech acts of the 'behabitive' kind (such as apologies) as troublesome because they have 'special scope for insincerity' (Austin, 1962, pp. 159). Thus, whether the success of making an apology can ever be accurately measured – what Austin described as the difference between a 'happy' or 'unhappy' utterance – remains an open question (Austin, 1962, p. 14).

If the speech act categories as defined by Austin are uncritically accepted, then there is the potential for the expression of a sincere 'I'm sorry' to mean that the act of apologising has been completed as soon as it is uttered and that is the end of the matter. Notably, however, Austin did not definitively specify the conditions for making a 'happy' performative utterance (such as an apology). Moreover, as the research on apologies has developed since Austin first wrote *How to Do Things with Words*, so too have the ways of understanding the concept of an apology and how it functions in society. What makes a speech act 'happy' or 'unhappy' has become a matter of debate (Derrida, 1982), and a similar observation can be made about apologies as well.

However, if an apology's effectiveness depends on its acceptance, then it becomes apparent that the person to whom the apology is addressed ultimately decides whether an apology is a 'happy' or an 'unhappy' one. This position finds support in the literature which approaches the making of an apology as transactional. For instance, in the influential book *Mea Culpa: A Sociology of Apology and Reconciliation* (1991), sociologist Tavuchis, in line with Austin's 'speech act' theory, found that the sincere expression of sorrow is essential for making a genuine interpersonal apology. He further claimed that an apology as a 'speech act' involves the speaker expressing sorrow and regret for moral wrongdoing and seeking forgiveness from the wronged party (Tavuchis, 1991, p. 22). Significantly, this approach extends the meaning of the utterance of the words 'I apologise' as an expression of remorse for the commission of a wrong, to include the desire of the wrongdoer to maintain relations with the person they have wronged. This approach has been generally understood to mean that the overall effect of a sincere apology is to restore the relationship between the parties affected by the wrongful actions. Evidently, the understanding of an apology as an utterance spoken to demonstrate sorrow for a wrong has expanded – the making of an apology has become a process that can make (or break) relationships.

Thus, in the social sciences it has been found that apologies perform 'remedial exchanges' aimed to 'set things right' and restore the relationship between the apologiser and the addressee (Goffman, 1971, p. 109; Eslami-Rasekh and Mardani, 2010, p. 96, 98; Rojo, 2005, p. 64). Notably, however, there is no agreement on who stands to benefit most from this process – whether it is the speaker, the hearer, or both. As noted above, some view an apology's function is to 'save face' of the speaker by restoring their social standing. Others consider that its function is to 'save face' of the hearer and could come at some expense to the speaker (Brown and Levinson, 1987, p. 68), while others recognise the benefits that both parties can reap from an apology. The words cannot undo the harm suffered by the hearer but, when spoken at the right tenor, they can soften negative angry emotions and, in that way, contribute to the resolution of interpersonal conflict (Frantz and Bennigson, 2005, pp. 201, 202). Similar conclusions have been drawn in emphasising the importance of forgiveness to overcome conflict. According to Tavuchis, a striking feature of an apology is its power to inspire forgiveness on the part of the person wronged: 'the helpless offender, *in consideration for nothing more than a speech*, asks for nothing less than the conversion of righteous indignation and betrayal into unconditional forgiveness and reunion' (Tavuchis, 1991, p. 35, emphasis in original).

Nevertheless, it has been in the humanities, especially in moral philosophy, that the significance of the victim in the apology process has become most apparent. Ultimately, in offering an apology the aim would be to appease the victim and restore their relationship with the wrongdoer. According to Govier and Verwoerd, making *moral amends* to victims by 'expressing *other-oriented moral regret* and appealing for forgiveness' (Govier and Verwoerd, 2002, p. 68, emphasis in original) could evoke 'an emotional shift from resentment to acceptance on the part of the victim' and create the conditions for the resumption of the relationship based on 'moral equality' (Govier and Verwoerd, 2002, p. 69). In their view, a sincere 'I'm sorry' to victims signals acknowledgement: first, the offender is acknowledging that the act was wrong and they are responsible for it; second, the offender is acknowledging '*the moral status of the victim(s), the primary person(s) to whom he* [sic] *apologizes*', namely, that the victim did not deserve to be ill-treated by the offender; and third, the offender is acknowledging the legitimacy of the victim's feelings of resentment and anger (Govier and Verwoerd, 2002, p. 69, emphasis in original). Effectively, in this process of saying '"I am sorry" or "I apologize"', the offender is acknowledging 'the *human dignity and moral worth of victims* as well as *respect for their feeling of resentment*' (Govier and Verwoerd, 2002, p. 69, emphasis in original). The significance of this for the victim would be how the offender, in 'saying sorry', is unsaying the original message of insult that the victim had 'no moral worth and [merited] no moral consideration. As Govier and Verwoerd claim: 'For one who has been humiliated or treated as worthless, such acknowledgment of dignity and human worth is profoundly significant' (Govier and Verwoerd 2002, p. 70).

Moreover, in this exchange it is important to note how power can shift between the parties in the apology process (Govier, 2006, p. 70). The power the offender once had to humiliate is now vested in the victim who has the power to forgive or not. As Lazare has claimed: 'This exchange of humiliation and power between the offender and the offended may be the clearest way of explaining how some apologies heal by restoring dignity and self-respect' (Lazare, 2005, p. 52). However, while feelings of guilt and shame may be essential to motivate the offender to accept responsibility for their actions (Coicaud and Jönsson, 2008, pp. 78–79), it is also evident that these feelings need to be tempered by empathy for the person harmed. Indeed, one may wonder if offenders would ever freely offer an apology if the experience primarily resulted in them feeling humiliated and denigrated as some have claimed (Lazare, 1995, p. 40: Olshtain and Cohen, 1990, pp. 46–47). If an apology is to realise its potential and restore relations between the parties, the offender must not only have humility to appreciate what they did was wrong, but also an understanding of the wrongs as the victim understands them. The apology would need to be motivated by the offender's empathy with the person wronged and seeing the wrongful actions in the same way. In this way, the 'apology presupposes moral agreement' between the parties that the offender's actions were wrong. As an empathetic response to the wrongdoing, the offender looks at the wrongdoing through the eyes of the victim and 'joins the victim in condemning it and others of its kind' (Govier and Verwoerd, 2002, p. 70).

Thus, a combination of complex emotions – guilt and shame, humility and empathy – are necessary for the wrongdoer to express 'other-oriented regret' and convey the message that they were wrong. In exchange, the victim may recover their sense of self-worth and self-respect and become open to forgiving the wrongdoer, improving, if not restoring, relations between them (Gill, 2000, p. 17). Indeed, although there is no obligation for the victims to forgive, they may in fact develop a sense of moral duty to respond positively to the apology and accept it (Funk-Unrau, 2004, p. 3).

By engaging in this process, it is also evident that both parties can benefit from an apology. For the offender, an apology enables them to express their feelings of guilt and remorse and re-establish their moral capacity and integrity (Gill, 2000, p. 17), while for the victim, an apology can help to alleviate any negative feelings of anger, guilt, and self-blame and restore their self-worth (Coicaud, 2009, pp. 107–108). The effect, as Taft has observed, is to restore moral balance between the parties by providing the potential for healing where the source of healing for the offender is through the expression of repentance, and for the offended through the opportunity to forgive (Taft, 2000, pp. 1137–1138). As Coicaud has further observed, an apology can open dialogue between the parties by providing an 'explanatory scheme' to promote mutual understanding and trust (Coicaud, 2009, p. 106) and create the potential for both parties to envisage a new beginning, 'cleansed from the darkest aspect of the past' (Coicaud, 2009, p. 108). Indeed, it has been found that the 'wider social web' in which the parties are enmeshed can also benefit from an apology (Coicaud, 2009, pp. 108–109; Tavuchis, 1991, p. 13) through its potential to restore social harmony more broadly (Rojo, 2005, p. 65).

In emphasising the moral dimensions of an apology, the philosophical take on apologising has brought the important role of the victim more clearly into view. In making moral amends through an apology, the wrongdoer is seeking the victim's forgiveness. The potential for forgiveness is made possible by the apologiser's demonstration of remorse for what they have done. Through the wrongdoer's expression of other-oriented regret, the victim becomes the primary consideration (cf., Kepnes, 2003, p. 103), opening the possibility for both parties to be free of past wrongdoing (cf., Celermajer 2006a, pp. 5–6). But does this mean that the effectiveness of an apology is to be measured by whether the victim forgives? The next section will explore the philosophical arguments on the question of what makes an apology effective.

What makes an interpersonal apology effective?

It is evident that the understanding of an apology as requiring a sincere expression of sorrow for a wrong in speech act theory generally informs understandings of what an apology is in the literature (Coicaud, 2009; Govier and Verwoerd, 2002; Tavuchis, 1991; cf., Smith, 2008, p. 27). However, as the understanding of apologies has developed, they appear to function more like a process than a 'speech act'. As is evident in Govier and Verwoerd's claims, a sincere apology may serve as acknowledgement of the victim and their moral worth, creating the potential for forgiveness and a restored relationship.

It is also evident in these discussions that the way the concept of an apology is understood to function coincides with the understanding of what makes an apology effective. For example, if an apology is thought to be the sincere expression of sorrow for a wrong, then the sincerity with which it was offered becomes the measure of its effectiveness (Olshtain and Cohen, 1990, p. 47). However, over time researchers have been more prescriptive in listing the elements for making an effective apology, as it has become evident that an apology may require more than sincerity to be effective (e.g., Gill, 2000, p. 14; Govier, 2006, pp. 68–69: cf., Olshtain and Cohen 1990, p. 46; Rojo, 2005, p. 64; Scher and Darley, 1997, p. 128; Schlenker and Darby, 1981, p. 272). Indeed, as philosophers have become more aware of the variables at play in the making and receiving of apologies, the elements of an apology have become more elaborate.

Of these, Smith, in his study of the social meanings of apologies in his book *I Was Wrong* (2008), has provided one of the most elaborate overviews of the range of elements that can feature in the making of an apology. In his study, Smith has developed the 'categorical apology' which he presents as reflecting the range of meanings (or values) of an interpersonal apology. Nevertheless, if one accepts that the 'meanings' of an apology also underlie its effectiveness, the twelve 'meanings' he has ascribed to the categorical apology (Smith, 2008, pp. 140–142) may also be read as general requirements for the making of an 'effective' apology. Indeed, Smith himself admits that the categorical apology sets a 'kind of benchmark for apologetic meaning', although he acknowledges that there is an inevitable variability in the apologies that are made (understandably considering the differences that exist in relationships and the wrongs that may be committed) and so therefore not all apologies may need to meet these requirements (Smith, 2008, p. 142). Smith's standards may be summarised as follows:

1 Corroborated factual record (reaching agreement and a shared understanding about what happened);
2 Acceptance of blame (the offender accepts responsibility and blame for the harm at issue (distinguishable from expressions of sympathy));
3 Possession of appropriate standing (only the offender can accept responsibility for the harm and offer an apology);
4 Identification of each harm (the offender will identify and apologise for each harm at issue and avoid apologising for the 'wrong wrong');
5 Identification of the moral principles underlying each harm (the offender will identify the moral principles underlying the harms and make explicit the values at stake in having committed the harms);

6 Shared commitment to the moral principles underlying each harm (the offender will commit to the moral principles underlying each harm, vindicating the value of the violated principles, and justifying the victim's offence caused by the breach of these values);
7 Recognition of victim as a moral interlocutor (in the apology process the offender comes to recognise and treat the victim as 'a moral agent'. No longer can the offender disregard the victim's dignity, humanity, or worth in pursuit of their own objectives);
8 Categorical regret (the offender acknowledges they have committed a wrong (as opposed to expressing sympathy that may be perceived to be justifying the consequences of their actions));
9 Performance of the apology (the offender expresses the apology to the victim and not to a third party. The victim may exercise their discretion as to whether the apology should also be presented to a broader audience or whether it should be in writing);
10 Reform and redress (the offender pledges never to repeat the same wrongs ever again, accepts sanctions for the wrongs, and provides appropriate forms of remedies and redress for the harms suffered);
11 Intentions for apologising (the intention of an apology is not to promote the self-serving objectives of the offender, but to advance the victim's well-being and affirm the values that were breached); and
12 Emotions (the offender will continue to feel guilt and sorrow about the wrongdoing, and empathy and sympathy for the victim as may be culturally appropriate in the circumstances)

(Smith, 2008, pp. 140–142).

As the requirements for apologising have become more elaborate, the question arises whether the essential message of an apology – the expression of remorse in response to a wrong – will be lost (Taft, 2000, p. 1140; Tavuchis, 1991, p. 3). However, a more pertinent question may be whether conforming to these standards will guarantee an apology's effectiveness.

There is a tendency to equate the granting of forgiveness with the apology's effectiveness. Indeed, according to Smith, philosophers from both the Analytic and Continental traditions have argued that forgiveness may only be justifiable after an offender has apologised and repented (Smith, 2008, p. 137). To reiterate the point made previously, apology and forgiveness have been viewed as acting together to complete a mutually beneficial transaction between the parties: the apology in vindicating the self-worth of the victim and forgiveness in redeeming the moral standing of the offender.

However, this argument seems to assume that forgiveness is a real possibility. There are mixed views on this. According to Arendt, forgiveness is essential if those who have committed wrongs are to ever be released from what they have done: 'Without being forgiven ... our capacity to act would ... be confined to one single deed from which we could never recover; we would remain victims of its consequences forever ... condemned' (Arendt, 1998, p. 237). Others, however, have claimed that true forgiveness is an impossible ideal to achieve (Derrida, 2001; Thompson, 2010, p. 259). This has been interpreted to mean that some wrongs are so heinous to the point that they are unforgivable. In these circumstances, an apology offered by a person who has committed such crimes would seem absurd, if not obscene. Victims might be right to condemn such a person from re-entering the moral community by refusing to accept their apology and forgive them (Coicaud, 2009, p. 102). Other analyses challenge whether such binary approaches to apology and forgiveness are helpful to understanding how they function in the practical world (Smith, 2008, p. 132). As Smith has claimed, apologies, especially for more serious harms, cannot be judged at the time they are made. An apology may only be judged over the duration of the offender's lifetime. This may depend on whether the offender has maintained their commitment to reform and forbearance, and 'any regression can diminish an apology's significance' (Smith, 2008, p. 81).

A similar observation can be made about forgiveness. Forgiveness, even when it has been granted, may not prevent the victim from later relapsing into a state of resentment and disdain; nor for that matter does a refusal to forgive preclude the victim from later forgiving the wrongdoer (Smith, 2008, pp. 132–133; cf., Thompson, 2010, pp. 268–269).

In fact, even though Smith has devised the categorical apology, in his detailed discussion of each of its aspects he shows that any number of things can go wrong that can undermine its meaningfulness. For instance, there appears to be general agreement across disciplines that in cases of serious wrongdoing an offer of repair is a necessary component of an apology (Govier and Verwoerd, 2002, p. 72; Scher and Darley, 1997; cf., Taft, 2000, p. 1140). As Govier and Verwoerd have claimed, any attempt at making moral amends must be supported by 'practical amends' if the perpetrator of the wrong is to really *mean* they are sorry. An apology that is not backed by concrete measures of reparation would, at best, seem hollow and insincere and, at worst, would likely add further insult to the original wrongdoing (Govier and Verwoerd, 2002, p. 72).

However, even when an apology is offered in conjunction with other forms of redress, the effects of the injury can continue (as cases of personal injury clearly show). As Smith has succinctly put it: 'Nothing can unscramble those eggs' (Smith, 2008, p. 83). The realisation that wrongs committed in the past may never be undone is important and reveals the challenge in determining what would constitute appropriate forms of redress, including the right balance between symbolic and practical forms.

However, the fact that this balance may never be struck – and indeed, the fact that nothing that is said or done can undo the harm that has been done, has raised issues about the possibility of forgiveness and whether an apology can in fact inspire victims to forgive. While forgiveness may, for some, be the ideal 'effect' of an apology, the reality may be that an apology is not accepted (Coicaud, 2009, pp. 100–101). This does not necessarily mean that apologies and other forms of redress are meaningless. It would appear there is general agreement across disciplines that attempts at making amends through an apology are better than no apology at all. But that does not mean that an apology, even the sincerest 'I'm sorry', will be accepted. And even when it is accepted, that does not necessarily mean that it is the end of the matter. Nevertheless, whether it is accepted or not, an apology may still be meaningful. An apology cannot change the past and replace what was lost – words are not so powerful – but it can serve as an acknowledgement of the value of what was lost and deepen awareness of, and commitment to, the relationships that are important to maintain now, and in the future (Tavuchis, 1991, p. 8). As Govier has explained, an apology 'looks *backward* to what has been done and *forward* to commitment to reform, practical amends, and a better relationship' (Govier, 2006, p. 69, emphasis in original).

Certainly, in apologising, the wrongdoer should approach the making of the apology in ways that will inspire forgiveness, but also with the knowledge that neither words nor other measures of redress may be enough to appease the victim. The offer of an apology requires the wrongdoer to be 'other-oriented' with a view to making things right with the victim. Their commitment to reform and forbearance is a commitment made to the victim that should continue to orient their behaviour in the future. In these circumstances, an apology may be understood as initiating a process of transformation for both parties with each of them taking away different messages from the apology: the victim that they did not deserve the wrongful treatment; the wrongdoer that they should refrain from committing such wrongs ever again.

The interpersonal aspects of political apologies

Turning now to consider official apologies made by governments for past injustices, it is not uncommon to find analyses of interpersonal apologies preceding discussions of official apologies (Coicaud, 2009; Coicaud and Jönsson, 2008; de Grieff, 2008; Gill, 2000; Govier, 2006, chap. 4; Govier and Verwoerd, 2002; Smith, 2008; Tavuchis, 1991; cf., Celermajer, 2009, chap. 2; Thompson, 2008). A striking example of the overlap in discourses on apologies is evident in the way that Govier and Verwoerd (2002) have seamlessly applied their understanding of the 'moral' apology in examining the collective apology phenomenon.[1] References have also been made to the literature on official apologies in discussions of interpersonal apologies. Thus, for instance, if an apology is said to empower victims in granting or withholding forgiveness (Govier, 2006, p. 70), support for this idea can be attributed to Minow who made this claim when discussing official apologies for the Holocaust (Minow, 1998, p. 115). In this respect, victims in the political context have a central role to play as they do in the interpersonal context. As Minow surmised, an apology:

> grants power to the victims, power to accept, refuse or ignore the apology. The victims may in addition seek punishment, offer forgiveness, or conclude that the act falls outside domains eligible for forgiveness. In any of these instances, the survivors secure a position of strength, respect, and specialness.
>
> (Minow, 1998, p. 115)

Evidently, victims may respond in any way they consider is appropriate. Notably, however, despite this uncertainty, it is generally recognised that, like interpersonal apologies, reconciliation of relationships is a worthwhile endeavour to pursue through the making of political apologies.

For instance, in their discussion of group apologies, Barkan and Karn hark back to Tavuchis' seminal work to illuminate how political apologies could repair damaged relationships and 'allow the parties to past injustices to go on with their lives'. In their view, an apology may help bridge the gap 'between the victim's need for acknowledgment and the perpetrator's desire to reclaim his humanity' (Barkan and Karn, 2006, p. 5; see also Coicaud and Jönsson, 2008). Furthermore, they claim that the sincere expression of 'I'm sorry' in an official apology may be 'a first step toward dampening ... discord' in cases where conflict, distrust, and misunderstanding arising from the 'legacies of historical conflict' can continue to impede the development and maintenance of co-operative partnerships (Barkan and Karn, 2006, p. 7).

In their view, the effects could be far-reaching: 'In the best cases, the negotiation of apology works to promote dialogue, tolerance, and cooperation between groups knitted together uncomfortably (or ripped asunder) by some past injustice' (Barkan and Karn, 2006, p. 7).

It is evident that in Barkan and Karn's view a sincere expression of remorse in an official apology can engender mutual healing between groups, with the potential to inspire forgiveness amongst victims and reconciliation of the relationships between victims and wrongdoers. Support for these claims can be found in the responses of Indigenous people to the Rudd apology. Murray Harrison, a Stolen Generations Survivor, remarked: 'It's been absolute closure. I was taken when I was 10 ... This apology was something I really needed to hear' (Korff, 2021). Similar sentiments were expressed in Canada in response to the Harper apology. For instance, Willie Blackwater, a prominent Residential School Survivor, wept through much of the ten-minute speech made by Harper: '"If I am able to forgive my perpetrator, I can forgive Canada", Blackwater said after the apology he felt was sincere and very moving' (Fitzpatrick and Nguyen, 2008).[2]

And, like interpersonal apologies, the effects of official apologies may extend beyond the individuals involved and be felt throughout the broader community. An official apology delivered at the right pitch may soften the broader public's attitudes towards victim groups, and vice versa. Indeed, the potential of official apologies to assist in promoting reconciliation is of significance in settler-colonised nations as far as race relations between Indigenous and non-Indigenous peoples are concerned. As King (2011) observed in response to the enactment of the 'Apology to Native Peoples of the United States' (2009), an apology 'could provide a much-needed shift in public attitudes toward tribes in the country, as well as attitudes of Native people toward the federal government'.

However, despite the overlap in how interpersonal and official apologies can function, many factors have been identified that can make them distinct from one another, leading some to question the extent to which analyses of interpersonal apologies can effectively enhance our understanding of state apologies (Celermajer, 2009; Smith, 2008; Thompson, 2008). As will become clear, their differences are explicable in terms of the functions they serve: the *moral* functions of an interpersonal apology, on the one hand, and the *political* functions of a state apology, on the other. In this sense, the value of official apologies rests on the functions they serve to enhance the political life of the nations in which they are made. Their differences are specific to the contexts in which they are made – whether the social context in the case of interpersonal apologies, or the political context in the case of official apologies. Thus, although political apologies can serve the same moral functions as interpersonal apologies, they also have their own political functions in advancing victims' claims for justice. Of course, in both contexts it could be said that an apology, particularly in relation to more egregious harms, serves to promote justice in the sense of vindicating the moral worth of victims, as well as providing an impetus for wrongdoers to provide concrete measures of redress. Nevertheless, in the political context the emphasis is less on forgiveness, as seems to be the endpoint of an interpersonal apology, and more on ensuring that the rights of victims are upheld. In the context of making apologies to Indigenous peoples, this would include a range of claims to uphold and protect their rights. Achieving such an outcome to their satisfaction may ultimately determine an apology effectiveness and whether it does, in fact, advance national reconciliation.

The political aspects of political apologies

In examining the political aspects of official apologies, it is first important to recognise that they are made in the political context where both the 'apologiser' and 'apologisee' are collective subjects. The apology itself is responding to a public wrong or wrongs committed against specific members of a group in the past (Celermajer, 2009, pp. 14–15). As a public act, the political nature of the apology has implications for the entire nation. In this respect, the potential scope of a state apology could extend further than that of an interpersonal apology: not only relationships but the histories of entire nations are at stake. As Gill has noted, these apologies have 'a role to play in the struggle to create history, to establish a certain version of events as the "official story"' (Gill, 2000, p. 22). Others have gone so far to claim that now is 'a time that seeks to establish political truth ... [and] apology has become the West's own version of a truth commission' (Howard-Hassmann and Gibney, 2008, p. 1).

Thus, if one of the functions of a state apology is to promote reconciliation, that may be as much about improving relationships marred by conflict as it is about reconciling the perpetration of past injustices in the present history of the nation (Weyeneth, 2001). An apology for past injustices is a mechanism through which acknowledgement of these injustices can take place. In this respect, the role of emotion may not be as central to a political apology as it may be in relation to an interpersonal apology. As Tavuchis remarked, the 'principal function of [a collective apology] has little, if anything, to do with sorrow or sincerity but rather with putting things on a public record' (Tavuchis, 1991, p. 117).

He is not alone in questioning the role emotion plays in the making of official apologies (Griswold, 2007, pp. 140–142; cf., Thompson, 2008, p. 36). This is because a political apology, unlike an interpersonal apology, is made on behalf of a collective whose capacity to demonstrate genuine remorse – as a collective – has been brought into serious question (Tavuchis, 1991, p. 97). Indeed, an emotional display by the state leader may detract from other more important functions of the apology.

In this regard, the official acknowledgement of historic injustices in a state apology may be better understood as contributing to the reconciliation of the past in the present and correcting the historical record of a nation (Minow, 1998, p. 116). This could help raise awareness in the general population of the facts of history as those who have suffered harm have experienced them, and thus engender a shared understanding of the history of the injustices among victim and perpetrator groups alike. Present generations of the victims of historic injustices may also feel vindicated when their understanding of historical events – their truth about history – is officially acknowledged in an apology (Bashir, 2008, pp. 55–56; Celermajer, 2006b, pp. 174–175; Govier, 2006, pp. 70–71; Minow, 1998, p. 114; Nobles, 2008, pp. 36–37; Waldron, 1992, p. 6). This is because the acknowledgement of injustices possesses symbolic significance as it stands in direct contrast to the past denial of these injustices (Govier, 2006, chap. 3). In the case of Indigenous peoples in settler-colonised nations such as Australia and Canada, this could prove to be a profoundly symbolic move when it is considered that their denigration as backward and uncivilised – as outside history – provided the discursive rationale for legitimising the acquisition of Crown sovereignty over their lands and corresponding denial of their sovereignty and law (Attwood, 1996, pp. xii–xiii).

Evidently, a political apology that does justice to the victims' accounts of history would be a significant achievement. However, it has been generally accepted that an official apology should not merely function to correct the historical record. Indeed, if all that an apology did was raise awareness of the events in a nation's history that up until that time had been repressed within the nation's collective memory, then an apology may not be entirely appropriate. Public statements of acknowledgement of these events would adequately fulfil this function (Thompson, 2008, p. 33). Given the severity of the wrongdoing that these apologies are usually acknowledging, there can (and should be) more to an official apology than 'putting things on the public record'.

In this respect, it is important to recall that a significant feature of an apology (whether in the interpersonal or political context) is the acceptance of responsibility for the harm done. As Minow put it: 'Full acceptance of responsibility by the wrongdoer is the hallmark of an apology' (Minow, 1998, p. 115). However, this may prove to be the most challenging feature of an apology. In the case of an official apology for historic injustices, the acceptance of responsibility would entail nothing less than the acceptance of transgenerational responsibility for past wrongs, which may not be immediately forthcoming as the history of the apology movement in Australia shows (Celermajer, 2006b; Thompson, 2008). Moreover, the acceptance of responsibility for past wrongdoing implies acceptance of a duty to make amends for the harms caused, giving governments even more reason to resist the calls for an apology. But when these obstacles are overcome the true value of official apologies in contributing to the just resolution of past wrongs may be finally realised (Coicaud, 2009). According to this understanding, it is the potential of a political apology to promote justice that may advance national reconciliation – not the sincere expression of remorse as may be the case of interpersonal apologies (Thompson, 2008 pp. 34–37; cf., Digeser, 2001, pp. 4–6).

So understood, an official apology can do more than put things on the public record. The acceptance of responsibility for past injustices entails the acknowledgement that the past treatment of victims was wrong. This would involve a moral reassessment of history which would convey other-oriented moral regret towards victims for the injustices they have suffered. This approach is not unlike the one described in the previous section with respect to interpersonal apologies. State leaders, in making these apologies on behalf of their nations, would accept responsibility for the injustices as victims understand them, and in naming the wrongs would convey the view that they 'have come to see their actions in the same way as their victims (i.e., as a wrongdoing) and that they firmly renounce the disrespect that those actions implied' (Muldoon, 2009, p. 3; cf., Bashir, 2008, pp. 55–59).

However, the expression of other-oriented regret through the moral reassessment of history in a political apology would have distinct political consequences. In this context, the apology can be viewed as providing a measure of reparative justice to victims. This approach is consistent with the international norms relating to the making of reparations for gross violations of human rights abuses (van Boven, 2010). In the *Basic Principles and Guidelines on the Right to a Remedy and Reparation for Victims of Gross Violations of Human Rights Law and Serious Violations of International Humanitarian Law* (United Nation, 2005), Principle 22 lists apologies among those measures of reparation aimed at satisfaction. The way these measures have been separated from the other measures of reparation, such as restitution, compensation, rehabilitation, and guarantees against repetition suggests that each measure fulfils different aims and expectations. As Thompson has claimed, drawing on Govier and Verwoerd's analysis of the 'moral apology': 'apology as part of reparative justice answers to the harm that injustice causes to the dignity of the victims' (Thompson, 2008, p. 34).

Celermajer has offered an even broader understanding of the role of apology as a measure of reparative justice that is tailored more specifically to the political context in which these apologies are made. In her view, the reparative justice that an apology performs is connected 'to address the damage to the identity of the victim and more broadly the social and political messages about history, identity and right' (Celermajer, 2006b, p. 175). As she has explained, the inclusion of 'apology' in the list of measures aimed at satisfaction suggests these measures 'operate within the *symbolic* or *discursive* dimension of harm' (Celermajer, 2006b, pp. 174–175, emphasis in original). Thus, for instance, providing an official forum for the revision of national history and acceptance of the victims' version of historical facts, which had been previously denied and silenced in the nation's history, could be understood as one of the *symbolic* or *discursive* effects of making an apology. Indeed, in the political context – where often harms are the result of violations of human rights standards – an apology provides a forum for acknowledging the history of rights violations experienced by victims. The indignity caused to the victims by the injustices would be understood in these terms: as the violation of their rights (cf., Bashir, 2008, p. 55).

The significance of Celemajer's observations lies in the way they provide the basis for developing an understanding of a political apology as functioning as a discursive strategy that can help to reconceptualise the identities of the victims, the group or institution making the apology, and the relationship that exists between them. The perpetration of injustices against the victims suggests that they were perceived as deserving of this treatment. Specifically, with respect to western nation states and their treatment of cultural minority groups, wrongdoing against these groups was often legitimised based on notions of western superiority and the corresponding inferiority – as the other – of the non-western cultural groups (Kymlicka, 1995, pp. 5–6). This issue is particularly pronounced in relation to Indigenous peoples whose perceived racial inferiority, reflected in the doctrines of discovery and terra nullius, has legitimised colonisation of their lands and denial of their sovereign rights to their lands, resources, and so on. By contrast, the making of an apology would signal that the superiority–inferiority dichotomy underpinning past wrongdoing is no longer tenable at any level of society.

Thus, the violation of the rights of victims in the past can be understood as reflecting the perception that they deserved oppressive and discriminatory treatment. An official apology, in contrast, understood as a strategy for identity transformation in the sphere of politics, makes clear that:

> past treatment of the group never was morally justified. In an official apology, the highest political authorities acknowledge that the culture of the victim group is not now, and never was, morally inferior to that of the offender group. The very identity of the victim group may be reshaped in this process.
>
> (Gill, 2000, p. 23)

So understood, an apology enacts respect and recognition (Celermajer, 2006b, p. 175). The acknowledgement of the victims in an apology is an act of respect which may make up for the disrespect shown to the victims at the time of the wrong (Thompson, 2008, p. 34). This recognition may to some extent satisfy their need for justice by addressing the indignity that had been caused by the harm. Thus, like an interpersonal apology, the demonstration of other-oriented regret could vindicate victims' moral worth. However, an apology made in the politico-legal context would go further to ensure better protection of victims' rights in the future. As Coicaud has importantly observed, for an apology to

> respect the victim ... it has to consider the individual who has been victimized [as] worthy of respect. It has to avoid paternalism or a barely veiled disdain for the person who has been made a victim. ... Short of the victim being seen 100% human, not only will his/her rights and consequently his/her status as a victim not be recognized, but ... the individual who has been wronged becomes the captive of the victim status.
>
> (Coicaud, 2009, p. 114)

In this process, the unjust treatment of victims, which had previously been shrouded by denial and rationalised by derogatory characterisations, would no longer be countenanced. Although this would, on so many levels, be challenging for nations to accept and act upon, for those nations where the wrongdoing is seen in political terms – as wrongdoing in violation of victims' rights – the offer of an apology to victims could benefit these nations also. At the political level, the apology signals the state's acceptance that it had been wrong to treat victim groups disrespectfully and without due regard and protection of their rights. In making the apology – in showing respect to those who were once denigrated and excluded by their inferior treatment – the state's image could be transformed into one committed to protecting victims' rights. In turn, this could improve public confidence in the state's leaders and institutions that had been undermined by revelations of past wrongdoing. In the case of state actors, an apology could provide a mechanism for re-invigorating public confidence in them, which in turn provides a basis for trust necessary for them to function (Gill, 2000, p. 20; Nobles, 2008, p. 32; cf., Coicaud, 2009, p. 112). Furthermore, in demonstrating a commitment to improving relations with victim groups through rights protection, a political apology may not only enhance relations between the state and its citizens but could also help to reinforce the state's commitment to human rights within the community of nations (Gibney and Roxstrom, 2001; cf., Bilder, 2008). In these respects, a political apology, like an interpersonal apology, would result in a shift in power. However, in the political context this would involve change to the way state power is exercised. When it was once the case that these nations relied on negative perceptions of victims to assert their legitimacy (Celermajer, 2006b, pp. 159, 161), now their legitimacy would depend on how effective they were in upholding victims' rights.

In these respects, the apology functions as a symbol of political inclusion – of belonging – for those to whom it is being addressed, with the potential, as Nobles has claimed, of redefining the political membership of the nation in ways that are responsive to the claims of victims for justice (Nobles, 2008, p. 19). This would include future rights protections (and Indigenous rights in the case of Indigenous peoples) as well as making reparations for past rights violations. Central to this process would be the state's commitment to adhere to the norms infringed by the wrongdoing.

It is generally accepted in apology discourses that the acceptance of responsibility for harm caused is interconnected with the identification and affirmation of the social norms breached (Eslami-Rasekh and Mardani, 2010, p. 96; Olshtain and Cohen, 1983, p. 20; Scher and Darley, 1997, p. 128; Tavuchis, 1991, p. 13). In accepting responsibility, the wrongdoer acknowledges and affirms the norms that were breached in causing the harm. In the political context it has been claimed that an apology would go further to 'help reinforce acceptance of the violated standards' by the collective and 'raise the moral threshold' of society more broadly (Brooks, 1999a, p. 3; Celermajer, 2009, p. 247; Gill, 2000, p. 20; Minow, 1998, p. 116;). However, in both contexts there is a tendency to assume there is a shared understanding of the norms that were infringed, but it is doubtful this is always the case especially in cases where there are cultural (and other intersectional) differences (Vines, 2007, pp. 13–14). This issue is particularly pertinent in relation to apologies to Indigenous peoples where there are differences in perspectives on the injustices and the norms they infringed. This is evident in Indigenous peoples' understandings of the injustices, which include violations of their rights to land, sovereignty, and culture, and which are not necessarily in the contemplation of the governments making the apologies (see Chapter 4). Presumably (although there is disagreement on this (Celermajer, 2009, pp. 206–210; de Grieff, 2008, p. 131)), if an apology is an expression of 'other-oriented moral regret', the identification of the norms that were infringed in causing harm would accord with the victims' understandings (Funk-Unrau, 2004, p. 3) and the making of reparations would be underpinned by these norms (cf., Smith, 2008, p. 224). In this regard, an apology has the potential to transform the identities of the victims and the nation, but the long-term realisation of this may depend on whether the existing normative framework of the nation can support the claims of victims for justice. If not, reforms would need to be introduced to ensure their interests are protected. Indeed, an apology may more likely fail to satisfy victims if such reforms are not forthcoming.

In this brief outline it is evident that the potential political effects of state apologies could be significantly different than interpersonal apologies when understood in terms of the contributions they can make to advance the victims' demands for justice and the implications this would have for the nations where they are made. In both contexts the acceptance of responsibility for past wrongs in an apology may serve to vindicate victims: that they did not deserve to be treated unjustly. But the potential effects of a political apology are obviously more far-reaching. In a political apology, other-oriented regret expressed in relation to past wrongs would accord with the victims' understandings of history. Following on from this, the reparations made to the victims would ensure that the harms suffered are redressed and victims' rights, previously infringed, are upheld in future. Only then may the apology signal a break from the past and the beginning of new relationship between victims and the state.

What makes a political apology effective?

Viewed in this way, the effectiveness of a political apology seems to depend less on the demonstration of remorse in seeking forgiveness (as is apparent with respect to the interpersonal apology) and more on whether the apology is followed with other forms of redress (if they have not already been offered) for past harms and to guarantee against future harms.[3]

In fact, although forgiveness is often sought in official apologies (Celermajer, 2009, p. 51), the possibility of forgiveness may be even more impossible to achieve in the political context than the interpersonal context (see also Chapter 5). Some take the position that forgiveness can only be granted by the individuals who have suffered harm (Derrida, 2001, p. 45; cf., Govier, 2002, pp. 92–95). Considering the time lapse between the wrongdoing and the apology that may exist in some circumstances this may prove difficult as many of the victims may be dead (Thompson, 2010, p. 266). But even for the remaining Survivors, issues remain. While some have argued that a collective apology in inspiring hope for a better future may also inspire forgiveness (Wenzel, et al., 2017), others have been more sceptical about whether collective apologies can engender sufficient trust or motivation among Survivors to inspire forgiveness (Hornsey, Ja Wohl and Philpot, 2015, pp. 107–108). For some Survivors an apology may seem to be 'too little, too late'. They may also doubt that the apologising collective and their representatives are truly sorry, especially if the wrongs are not being addressed and may still be ongoing as experienced by Indigenous peoples in settler-colonised states (Philpot, et al., 2013, p. 42). This is not to say that Survivors may never forgive. There have been remarkable instances where Survivors as individuals and as collectives have made statements of forgiveness. Two notable examples of collective forgiveness granted by Indigenous peoples have occurred in New Zealand (where the Wellington-based Taranaki Whanui ki Te Upoko o Te Ika responded to the 2009 Crown apology for breaches of the Treaty of Waitangi with a formal Statement of Forgiveness (Key, 2009)) and in Canada (where a 'charter of forgiveness' was signed by Elders, Residential School Survivors, and young people in response to the 2008 Harper apology ('Native residential school forgiveness granted', 2010)). However, understandably there are debates about the granting of forgiveness. While some have stressed the importance of forgiveness as a source of empowerment and healing for victims (Dillon, 2008), others have raised concerns that forgiveness can close off the past and the claims of victims for justice (Changfoot, 2009). On balance, however, forgiveness is less common in the context of political apologies than interpersonal apologies, and even if forgiveness is granted this may be separate to, and not necessarily because, an apology is made (Hornsey, Ja Wohl and Philpot, 2015, p. 108).

Nevertheless, how an apology is delivered and what is said when the apology is made may make a difference to the way it is received. Arguably, a political apology would have the greatest impact if it were delivered by an official spokesperson (for example, the head of state) during a public ceremony, and on behalf of the collective. Responsibility for wrongdoing in an official apology is not necessarily being accepted by the individual offering the apology; rather, the individual is accepting responsibility on behalf of the collective. The public aspects of the apology are necessary to engage the broader community in whose name the apology is being made; to give the apology dignity and seriousness of purpose; and to ensure that the outputs of the apology are consistent with, and do not vitiate, the apology's norm-building potential (James, 2008, pp. 138–139; cf., Thompson, 2008). In this respect, it has been argued that the authenticity of a state apology does not depend on:

> the *individual agency* of the spokesperson and his or her *personal and tearfully expressed remorse*. Rather ... the apology requires a valid representational role based on consensus within the collective and the implementation by that collective of the commitments implied in the apology.
>
> (Govier, 2006, p. 73, emphasis in original)

Thus, the emphasis is on the need for an appropriate official – an authoritative voice – who 'acknowledges and takes responsibility for an injustice committed (or allowed) by officers of the state and commits governments to avoid such injustices in the future' (Thompson, 2008, p. 36). As it has been suggested elsewhere, the significance of these apologies lies in the power of the authoritative voice delivering the apology to commit the nation to action and change (Celermajer, 2006b, p. 176).

With respect to political apologies, it is usual for the head of state to be the preferred person to deliver the moral messages of the apology (to accept responsibility for past wrongdoing and express regret to victims). The head of state is thought to be the person who best represents those individuals or collectives who have accepted that past wrongs were committed and are now resolute to address those wrongs and ensure against their repetition (Govier, 2006, p. 73). For this reason there have been times when official apologies have been criticised for being offered by the wrong person: whether because the person did not have the required standing in government to convey the moral messages of the apology forcefully enough (as in the case of the Statement of Reconciliation presented by Jane Stewart in her capacity as the Canadian Minister of Indian Affairs and Northern Affairs in 1998 (Celermajer, 2009, p. 30)); or because the person offering the apology was not perceived to be a true representative of the original wrongdoers and was not in a position to offer reparations for past wrongs (as in the case of Kevin Gover's apology to Native Americans in the US in 2000 (Buck, 2006, p. 100; Tsosie, 2006, p. 186)). The significance of an authoritative voice in making an apology is most evident in the case of the 'Apology to Native Peoples of the United States' (2009), which was heavily criticised for the failure of former President Barack Obama to read it out loud when he signed it into law in December 2009. This failure, in combination with several others, has raised concerns about whether the apology was in fact a true apology (Capriccioso, 2010; King, 2011).[4]

However, in other circumstances Indigenous peoples have been critical of the spokesperson if the delivery of the apology does not accord with their cultural standards (as happened in relation to the Rudd apology (Philpot et al., 2013, p. 42)), or the spokesperson appears to have overstepped their position in delivering an apology (as happened in Taiwan in relation to the 2016 apology to Indigenous peoples by President Tsai Ing-wen who was criticised for adopting a priest/clergyperson image when delivering the apology (Chu and Huang, 2020)).

The significance of the spokesperson's role, and the commitments they make when offering an official apology, has led some to reconsider the classification of these apologies in terms of Austin's speech act theory. In this regard, state apologies have been found to fit, not within Austin's categories of performatives as 'behabitives' (the expression of emotion), but have been classed as *commissives*, which include promises, contracts, and oaths (Austin, 1962, pp. 156–157;

Celermajer, 2006b, p. 176; cf., Schmidt, 2010, p. 61). Thus, unlike interpersonal apologies, where the emphasis is placed more on the expression of remorse and the granting of forgiveness as essential for the reconciliation of relationships, political apologies are thought to promote harmonious relationships through the official acknowledgement of responsibility for past wrongs, and the making of commitments to avoid such injustices in the future (Thompson, 2008, pp. 38–40). Political apologies provide opportunities for nations, through their spokesperson representatives, to reinvigorate their commitment to obligations that are considered essential to their national identities now that they have acknowledged that the past treatment of victims was wrong. So understood, a political apology may lead to 're-covenanting' the nation. According to Celermajer: 'the apology is ... an acknowledgment of a collective failure to live up to an ideal ethical principle and [acts as] ... a performative declaration of a new commitment, a new covenant for *now* and into the future' (Celermajer, 2009, p. 247, emphasis in original).

But making these commitments in the present imposes obligations on future generations to maintain them. Once this is accepted, then the effectiveness of an apology would ultimately depend on how the promises made in the apology are maintained in the present and future (Thompson, 2008, p. 43). Thus, like an interpersonal apology that may be judged over the lifetime of the offender, a political apology may also be judged by present and future generations to come. However, the difference with a political apology is that it will be judged according to whether the state no longer deploys its power to oppress victim groups, and whether attitudes within the broader community have changed so that unjust treatment of victims is no longer tolerated at any level in society:

> an apology achieves its goal if the perpetrator group transforms its self-understanding by living up to its ideal normative identity and by redefining the status of victims as objects of ethical respect. In this way, the apology pushes the polity towards a political and cultural context in which the wrongful actions could no longer proceed with a people's stamp of legitimacy.
>
> (Mihai, 2013, p. 206)

In these respects, the effectiveness of the apology would be measured according to whether the promises made in the apology work to address past and prevent further rights violations.

Nonetheless, there are potential problems that can arise with respect to making these commitments and maintaining them in the future. As previously noted in relation to interpersonal apologies, an apology cannot undo the harm done. Whatever measures of redress are offered with the apology, these would only serve as a substitute for what has been lost. This again raises the issue of what would be appropriate measures of redress.

In the context of political apologies, the answer to this question is usually one that is formulated by the state offering the apology. Thus, care must be taken to avoid the potential for hypocrisy in the state's offer of an apology. This means that not only are commitments for reform required in the apology, but these commitments are required to be consistently maintained in the future in ways that make a meaningful difference to the lives of victims (Gibney and Roxstrom, 2001, p. 932). In these respects, they would need to be appropriate considering the wrongs that have been committed, and adequate and effective to redress past harms and prevent future harms. Thus, the effectiveness of an apology would not depend on the victims' forgiveness, but on meeting the justice needs of victims.

However, discussions of apologies tend not to delve deeply into examining the account of the injustices for which an apology has been offered and whether the promises of reform and forbearance that are made accord with the understanding of victims. Instead, there has been a tendency to devise criteria for measuring the effectiveness of an apology, as is the approach in relation to interpersonal apologies. In some ways, as James (2008) has surmised in his coverage of the literature on political apologies, the criteria overlap with the requirements for an interpersonal apology. To begin with, he listed the five initial requirements of 'an authentic political apology', which include:

1 Naming clearly the wrong or wrongs in question;
2 Taking responsibility for the wrong;
3 Expressing regret;
4 Promising nonrepetition; and
5 Refraining from demanding forgiveness

(James, 2008, p. 138).

But in further investigating the literature and noting how a political apology serves to 'put things on the public record', requires additional measures of reparations, and publicity, ceremony, and consistency to be a genuine attempt at an apology, James modified this list and concluded that an 'authentic political apology':

1 Is recorded officially in writing;
2 Names the wrongs in question;
3 Accepts responsibility;
4 States regret;
5 Promises nonrepetition;
6 Does not demand forgiveness;
7 Is not hypocritical or arbitrary; and
8 Undertakes – through measure of publicity, ceremony, and concrete reparation – both to engage morally those in whose name apology is made and to assure the wronged group that the apology is sincere

(James, 2008, p. 139).

Criteria such as these may provide a useful checklist for identifying what should be included in an apology. At this point of the discussion, however, there is a question whether using these criteria to measure the effectiveness of an apology will in fact serve the interests of victims. Arguably, this approach may assume too readily that a shared understanding of the wrongs and how to address them is in place at the time an apology is made. This approach does not allow for differences in perspective in determining whether an apology meets these criteria. In more recent scholarship, Indigenous perspectives have been included as another criterion for determining the effectiveness of an apology (Lightfoot, 2015). Throughout this chapter the position has been that the victims' perspectives should inform the content of an apology. Any evaluation of the effectiveness of an apology requires consideration of whether the account of injustices, the norms they infringed, and the proposed reforms included in the apology reflect their perspectives on these issues. This position builds on the understanding of an apology as transactional in its reliance on victims for acceptance, but more pertinently is grounded in the understanding of an apology as transformative in seeking to include the historically excluded through the adoption of Survivor-centred responses to counter the state-centred approaches that caused them harm in the first place.

It follows from this analysis that the evaluation of an apology requires more than the application of abstract criteria against which to measure its effectiveness. It requires engagement with the history of the injustices for which an apology is offered to assess whether the interpretation of history in the apology accords with the victims' understandings. Furthermore, if it is accepted that an apology is to serve the interests of victims, then the assessment of an apology would also require engaging with the victims' perspectives on how the apology might advance their claims for justice. Accordingly, Chapter 3 explores the Rudd and Harper apologies in terms of their more immediate politico-legal contexts to explicate why some Indigenous peoples may have responded to them positively, while Chapter 4 examines the apologies from more critical Indigenous perspectives to expose their shortcomings as a response to the broader historical context of settler colonialism.

The adoption of this approach also highlights how the application of abstract criteria to assess an apology does not help to explain why a specific apology is made, and why it might be made for certain wrongs and not others. In this chapter it became evident that despite their similarities, there are striking differences in the way that interpersonal and political apologies function. In drawing out these differences one can begin to appreciate the role that context plays in shaping the understanding of how apologies function and what makes them effective. This is explored in the following chapter where the details of the respective movements in Australia and Canada for an apology are outlined. The contention is that the meaning of an apology cannot be separated from the broader politico-legal context in which the injustices took place, nor can it be separated from the more immediate context in which it was made.

Conclusion

It is evident that interpersonal and political apologies share common features and functions, but they are distinct in many respects as well. In focusing on the ethical dimensions of apology making, it is obvious that apologies can have what James describes as 'a moral core' (James, 2008, p. 137–138). An ethical approach to apology making involves the demonstration of other-oriented moral regret to appease the victim, and thereby realise the potential for reconciliation between the parties. However, due to differences in their contexts, emphasis has been placed on different aspects of interpersonal and political apologies to realise their potential to fulfil these functions.

With respect to political apologies, the emphasis is not so much on the demonstration of sincere remorse, as may be the approach in measuring the effectiveness of interpersonal apologies. Instead, the importance of putting things on the public record has been identified as a key function of a collective apology (Tavuchis, 1991, p. 117). Even so, it cannot be ignored that with any apology, the central feature is the acceptance of responsibility for past wrongs (Minow, 1998, p. 115). In relation to political apologies, this would involve morally reassessing the nation's history. The acknowledgement in an apology of injustices perpetrated against victims signals a shift in the mindset of the nation coming to terms with the truth about its past: in accepting the truth, the nation accepts that the past treatment of victims was wrong.

Whether in relation to interpersonal or political apologies, the acceptance of responsibility for past wrongs represents a show of respect to victims, conveying messages that their past treatment was wrong and that they never deserved to be treated unjustly (Govier and Verwoerd, 2002; Thompson, 2008). Moreover, with respect to both types of apologies, additional measures of redress would likely be required for harms suffered. However, while the endpoint of an interpersonal apology seems to be forgiveness, the endpoint of a political apology is justice. Setting on this path requires the state to reappraise its obligations towards those to whom an apology is addressed. As a demonstration of other-oriented moral regret, it would be necessary for the perspectives of victims to be reflected in the apology and in any future reform agenda. The inference that can be drawn from this approach is that the head of state, in offering the apology, would also be affirming the normative order of the victims in naming the wrongs in accordance with their understanding of history, and making amends to them in ways that meet their claims for justice. In this way, the potential for official apologies to advance reconciliation *and* promote justice becomes evident; the realisation of victims' claims, and ultimately providing the basis for the state's claims to legitimacy in the future.

Notes

1 Not everyone has managed to do this. For instance, Smith, in his study of collective apologies, applied each of the elements of the categorical apology only to find them wanting in each respect (Smith, 2008, chap. 10). More specifically, de Grieff has questioned whether the exchange of 'humiliation and power' in an interpersonal apology (Lazare, 2005, p. 52) can realistically occur in a state apology (de Grieff, 2008, p. 130).

2 Willie Blackwater is well known for speaking out with other Residential School Survivors about the rape and beatings he suffered as a child at the Port Alberni Residential School on Vancouver Island in British Columbia. These revelations led to the criminal conviction of his former dormitory supervisor, Arthur Plint, who was sentenced to 11 years' imprisonment: *R. v. Plint* (1995). Civil proceedings in the Supreme Court of Canada were subsequently brought by several former students of the Alberni Residential School. Although Plint was named as a defendant, the main issue turned on whether damages for sexual assault should be apportioned between the United Church and the federal government. The Court ultimately found they could: *Blackwater v. Plint* (2005).

3 In this regard an apology, in the context of making reparations to victims, tends to be treated as one of many of the measures of reparations required to address past wrongs. See generally the essays in Brooks (1999b) and Lenzerini (2008). However, by no means is it universally accepted that public apologies should be offered in conjunction with additional forms of reparations. For example, Cunningham, in emphasising the importance of sincerity and acceptance of the apology for improving relations between the parties, has argued that reparation, in money or goods, may follow, but can occur independently from apology (Cunningham, 1999, p. 291). In contrast, Alter (1999) has claimed that some concrete form of reparation is one of the essential elements of the apology process. Celermajer has adopted a different perspective altogether, arguing that an apology is less about sentiment and compensation and is more a means by which a nation can transform its identify and reconsider the norms underpinning its political culture that supported the conditions for the wrongs to occur in the first place (Celermajer, 2006b, p. 155).

4 On 16 December 2010, approximately one year after he signed the 'Apology to Native Peoples of the United States' (2009), President Obama acknowledged the importance of the apology and his support for it: '[L]last year, I signed a resolution, passed by both parties in Congress, finally recognizing the sad and painful chapters in our shared history—a history too often marred by broken promises and grave injustices against the First Americans. ... It's a resolution I fully supported—recognizing that no statement can undo the damage that was done; what it can do is help reaffirm the principles that should guide our future. It's only by heeding the lessons of our history that we can move forward' (Great Plains Tribal Chairman's Association, 2010). Notably, he still did not read the apology out loud.

Reference list

Alter, S., 1999, *Apologising for serious wrongdoing: social, psychological and legal considerations: final report for the Law Commission of Canada*, http://dalspace.library.dal.ca/bitstream/handle/10222/10273/Alter%20Research%20Apology%20EN.pdf

'Apology to Native Peoples of the United States', 2009, in *Department of Defense Appropriations Act, 2010*, 19 December, http://www.copyright.gov/legislation/pl111-118.pdf

Arendt, H., 1998, *The human condition*, 2nd edn, University of Chicago Press, London.
Attwood, B., 1996, 'Introduction', in B. Attwood (ed.), *In the age of Mabo*, Allen & Unwin, Sydney, pp. vii–xxxviii.
Austin, J.L., 1962, *How to do things with words*, Oxford University Press, London.
Barkan, E. and Karn, A., 2006, 'Group apology as an ethical imperative', in E. Barkan and A. Karn (eds), *Taking wrongs seriously: apologies and reconciliation*, Stanford University Press, Stanford, pp. 3–32.
Bashir, B., 2008, 'Accommodating historically oppressed social groups: deliberative democracy and the politics of reconciliation', in B. Bashir and W. Kymlicka (eds), *The politics of reconciliation in multicultural societies*, Oxford University Press, Oxford, pp. 48–69.
Bilder, R.B., 2008, 'The role of apology in international law', in M. Gibney, R.E. Howard-Hassmann, J. Coicaud and N. Steiner (eds), *The age of apology: facing up to the past*, University of Pennsylvania Press, Philadelphia, pp. 13–30.
Blackwater v. Plint, [2005] 3 SCR 3.
Brooks, R.L., 1999a, 'The age of apology', in R.L. Brooks (ed.), *When sorry isn't enough: the controversy over apologies and reparations for human injustice*, New York University Press, New York, pp. 3–12.
Brooks, R.L. (ed.), 1999b, *When sorry isn't enough: the controversy over apologies and reparations for human injustice*, New York University Press, New York.
Brown, P. and Levinson, S.C., 1987, *Politeness: some universals in language usage*, Cambridge University Press, Cambridge.
Buck, C., 2006, '"Never again": Kevin Gover's apology for the Bureau of Indian Affairs', *Wicazo Sa Review*, vol. *21*, no. *1*, pp. 97–126, DOI:10.1353/wic.2006.0002
Capriccioso, R., 2010, 'A sorry saga: Obama signs Native American apology resolution; fails to draw attention to it', *Indian Country Today*, 13 January, http://www.danielnpaul.com/AmericanApologyToAmericanIndians.html
Celermajer, D., 2006a, 'From the Levinasian apology to the political apology: reflections on ethical politics', *Australasian Political Studies Association Conference*, 25–27 September, University of Newcastle, Newcastle.
Celermajer, D., 2006b, 'The apology in Australia: re-covenanting the national imagery', in E. Barkan and A. Karn (eds), *Taking wrongs seriously: apologies and reconciliation*, Stanford University Press, Stanford, pp. 153–184.
Celermajer, D., 2009, *The sins of the nation and the ritual of apologies*, Cambridge University Press, Melbourne.
Changfoot, N., 2009, 'Canada's Truth and Reconciliation Commission for Indian residential schools: Whose truth? Whose reconciliation?', *Annual Meeting of the Canadian Political Science Association*, https://www.cpsa-acsp.ca/papers-2009/Changfoot.pdf
Chu, R.X. and Huang, C.T., 2020, 'The day after the apology: a critical discourse analysis of President Tsai's national apology to Taiwan's Indigenous peoples', *Discourse Studies*, vol. *23*, no. *1*, pp. 84–101, DOI:10.1177/1461445620942875
Coicaud, J., 2009, 'Apology: a small yet important part of justice', *Japanese Journal of Political Science*, vol. *10*, no. *1*, pp. 93–124, DOI:10.1017/S1468109908003393
Coicaud, J. and Jönsson, J., 2008, 'Elements of a road map for a politics of apology', in M. Gibney, R.E. Howard-Hassmann, J. Coicaud and N. Steiner (eds), *The age of apology: facing up to the past*, University of Pennsylvania Press, Philadelphia, pp. 77–91.

Cooper, J.M. (rev), 2002, *Plato. Five dialogues: Euthyphro, Apology, Crito, Meno, Phaedo*, G.M.A. Grube (trans.), 2nd edn, Hackett, Indianapolis.

Cunningham, M., 1999, 'Saying sorry: the politics of apology', *Political Quarterly*, vol. *70*, no. *3*, pp. 285–293, DOI:10.1111/1467–923X.00231

De Grieff, P., 2008, 'Apologies in national reconciliation processes', in M. Gibney, R.E. Howard-Hassmann, J. Coicaud and N. Steiner (eds), *The age of apology: facing up to the past*, University of Pennsylvania Press, Philadelphia, pp. 120–136.

Derrida, J., 1982, 'Signature event context', in A. Bass (trans.), *Margins of philosophy*, Harvester Press, Sussex, pp. 309–330.

Derrida, J., 2001, *On cosmopolitanism and forgiveness*, M. Hughes (trans.), Routledge, New York.

Digeser, P.E., 2001, *Political forgiveness*, Cornell University Press, New York.

Dillon, A., 2008, 'Does the apology bring about healing', *Aboriginal and Islander Health Worker Journal*, vol. *32*, no. *4*, p. 6.

Edmonson, W.J. and House, J., 1981, *Let's talk and talk about it: a pedagogic interactional grammar of English*, Urban & Schwarzenberg, München.

Eslami-Rasekh, A. and Mardani, M., 2010, 'Investigating the effects of teaching apology speech act, with a focus on intensifying strategies, on pragmatic development of EFL learners: the Iranian context', *Journal of Language Society and Culture*, vol. *30*, pp. 96–103.

Fitzpatrick, M. and Nguyen, L., 2008, 'Aboriginal leaders hail historic apology', *Windsor Star*, 11 June, http://www.bishop-accountability.org/news2008/05_06/2008_06_11_Fitzpatrick_AboriginalLeaders.htm

Frantz, C.M. and Bennigson, C., 2005, 'Better late than early: the influence of timing on apology effectiveness', *Journal of Experimental Social Psychology*, vol. *41*, no. *2*, pp. 201–207, DOI:10.1016/j.jesp.2004.07.007

Funk-Unrau, N., 2004, 'Potentials and problems of public apologies to Canadian Aboriginal peoples', *9th Biennial National Conference of Conflict Resolution Network Canada, Academic Institute of Interaction*, 2–4 June, Kitchener.

Gibney, M. and Roxstrom, E., 2001, 'The status of state apologies', *Human Rights Quarterly*, vol. *23*, no. *4*, pp. 911–939, DOI:10.1353/hrq.2001.0051

Gill, K., 2000, 'The moral functions of an apology', *The Philosophical Forum*, vol. *31*, no. *1*, pp. 11–27, DOI:10.1111/0031–806X.00025

Goffman, E., 1971, *Relations in public: microstudies of the public order*, Basic Books, New York.

Govier, T., 2002, *Forgiveness and revenge*, Routledge, London, DOI:10.4324/9780203870136

Govier, T., 2006, *Taking wrongs seriously: acknowledgement, reconciliation, and the politics of sustainable peace*, Humanity Books, New York.

Govier, T. and Verwoerd, W., 2002, 'The promise and pitfalls of apology', *Journal of Social Philosophy*, vol. *33*, no. *1*, pp. 67–82, DOI:10.1111/1467–9833.00124

Great Plains Tribal Chairman's Association, 2010, 'President Obama acknowledges need for Native American apology', *Business Wire*, 20 December.

Griswold, C.L., 2007, *Forgiveness: a philosophical exploration*, Cambridge University Press, New York, DOI:10.1017/CBO9780511619168

Hornsey, M.J., Ja Wohl, M. and Philpot, C.R., 2015, 'Collective apologies and their effects on forgiveness: pessimistic evidence but constructive implications', *Australian Psychologist*, vol. *50*, no. 2, pp. 106–114, DOI:10.1111/ap.12087

House of Commons, Canada, 2008, *House of Commons Debates (Hansard)*, 39th Parl., 2nd Sess., vol. *142*, no. *110*, 11 June, https://www.ourcommons.ca/Content/House/392/Debates/110/HAN110-E.PDF

House of Representatives, Australia, 2008, 'Apology to Australia's Indigenous Peoples', *Parliamentary Debates*, 13 February, https://parlinfo.aph.gov.au/parlInfo/genpdf/chamber/hansardr/2008-02-13/0003/hansard_frag.pdf;fileType=application/pdf

Howard-Hassmann, R.E. and Gibney, M., 2008, 'Introduction: apologies and the West', in M. Gibney, R.E. Howard-Hassmann, J. Coicaud and N. Steiner (eds), *The age of apology: facing up to the past*, University of Pennsylvania Press, Philadelphia, pp. 1–9.

James, M., 2008, 'Wrestling with the past: apologies, quasi-apologies, and non-apologies in Canada', in M. Gibney, R.E. Howard-Hassmann, J. Coicaud and N. Steiner (eds), *The age of apology: facing up to the past*, University of Pennsylvania Press, Philadelphia, pp. 137–153.

Jung, C., 2010, 'Canada and the legacy of the Indian residential schools: transitional justice for Indigenous people in a nontransitional society', in P. Arthur (ed.), *Identities in transition: challenges for transitional justice in divided societies*, Cambridge University Press, New York, pp. 217–250, DOI:10.1017/CBO9780511976858.008

Kepnes, S., 2003, 'Ethics after Levinas: Robert Gibbs why ethics? Signs of responsibilities', *Modern Theology*, vol. *19*, no. *1*. pp. 103–115, DOI:10.1111/1468-0025.t01-1-00211

Key, J., 2009, 'PM welcomes acceptance of Crown apology', *Beehive.gov.nz*, 30 July, http://beehive.govt.nz/release/pm-welcomes-acceptance-crown-apology

King, L.B., 2011, 'A tree fell in the forest: the US apologized to Native Americans and no one heard a sound', *Indian Country Today*, 3 December, https://tlpi.wordpress.com/2011/12/03/a-tree-fell-in-the-forest/

Korff, J., 2021, '"Sorry" apology to Stolen Generations', *Creative Spirits*, 14 January, https://www.creativespirits.info/aboriginalculture/politics/stolen-generations/sorry-apology-to-stolen-generations

Kymlicka, W., 1995, *The rights of minority cultures*, Oxford University Press, New York.

Lazare, A., 1995, 'Go ahead, say you're sorry', *Psychology Today*, vol. *28*, no. *1*, pp. 40–43.

Lazare, A., 2005, *On apology*, Oxford University Press, New York.

Lenzerini, F. (ed.), 2008, *Reparations for Indigenous peoples: international and comparative perspectives*, Oxford University Press, New York.

Lightfoot, S., 2015, 'Settler-state apologies to Indigenous peoples: a normative framework and comparative assessment', *Native American and Indigenous Studies*, vol. 2, no. *1*, pp. 15–39, DOI:10.5749/natiindistudj.2.1.0015

Mihai, M., 2013, 'When the state says "sorry": state apologies as exemplary political judgments', *Journal of Political Philosophy*, vol. 2, no. *1*, pp. 200–220, DOI:10.1111/j.1467-9760.2012.00418.x

Minow, M., 1998, *Between vengeance and forgiveness: facing history after genocide and mass violence*, Beacon Press, Boston.

Muldoon, P., 2009, 'Past injustices and future protections: on the politics of promising', *Australian Indigenous Law Review*, vol. *13*, no. 2, pp. 2–16.

'Native residential school forgiveness granted', 2010, *CBC News*, 12 June, https://www.cbc.ca/news/canada/native-residential-school-forgiveness-granted-1.956939

Nobles, M., 2008, *The politics of official apologies*, Cambridge University Press, New York, DOI:10.1017/CBO9780511756252

Olshtain, E. and Cohen, A., 1983. 'Apology: a speech act set', in N. Wolfson and E. Judd (eds), *Sociolinguistics and language acquisition*, Newbury House, Rowley, pp. 18–36.

Olshtain, E. and Cohen, A., 1990, 'The learning of complex speech act behaviour', *TESL Canada Journal/Revue TESL Du Canada*, vol. *7*, no. *2*, pp. 45–65.

Philpot, C., Balvin, N., Mellor, D. and Bretherton, D., 2013, 'Making meaning from collective apologies: Australia's apology to its Indigenous peoples', *Peace and Conflict: Journal of Peace Psychology*, vol. *19*, no. *1*, pp. 34–50, DOI:10.1037/a0031267

R. v. Plint, [1995] BCJ No. 3060.

Reilly, A., 2008, 'The inherent limits of the apology to the Stolen Generation', *University of Adelaide Law Research Paper No. 2009–002*, DOI:10.2139/ssrn.1294101

Rojo, L., 2005, '"Te quería comentar un problemilla ..." The speech act of apologies in Peninsular Spanish: a pilot study', *Hipertexto*, vol. *1*, pp. 63–80, https://www.utrgv.edu/hipertexto/_files/documents/articles/hipertexto-01/laura-rojo.pdf

Scher, S.J. and Darley, J.M., 1997, 'How effective are the things people say to apologize? Effects of the realization of the apology speech act', *Journal of Psycholinguistic Research*, vol. *26*, pp. 127–140, DOI:10.1023/A:1025068306386

Schlenker, B.R. and Darby, B.W., 1981, 'The use of apologies in social predicaments', *Social Psychology Quarterly*, vol. *44*, pp. 271–278, DOI:10.2307/3033840

Schmidt, T., 2010, 'We say sorry: apology, the law and theatricality', *Law Text Culture*, vol. *14*, no. *1*, pp. 55–78.

Searle, J.R., 1969, *Speech acts: an essay in the philosophy of language*, Cambridge University Press, Cambridge.

Searle, J.R., 1976, 'A classification of illocutionary acts', *Language and Society*, vol. *5*, no. *1*, pp. 1–23.

Smith, N., 2008, *I was wrong: the meanings of apologies*, Cambridge University Press, New York, DOI:10.1017/CBO9780511499258

Somani, A., 2011, 'The apology and its aftermath: national atonement or the management of minorities?', *Postcolonial Text*, vol. *6*, no. *1*, pp. 1–18.

Sundar Rajan, R., 2000, 'Righting wrongs, rewriting history', *Interventions*, vol. *2*, no. *2*, pp. 159–170, DOI:10.1080/136980100427289

Taft, L., 2000, 'Apology subverted: the commodification of apology', *The Yale Law Journal*, vol. *109*, pp. 1135–1160, DOI:10.2307/797485

Tavuchis, N., 1991, *Mea culpa: a sociology of apology and reconciliation*, Stanford University Press, Stanford.

Thompson, J., 2008, 'Apology, justice, and respect: a critical defense of political apology', in M. Gibney, R.E. Howard-Hassmann, J. Coicaud and N. Steiner (eds), *The age of apology: facing up to the past*, University of Pennsylvania Press, Philadelphia, pp. 31–44.

Thompson, J., 2010, 'Is apology a sorry affair? Derrida and the moral force of the impossible', *Philosophical Forum*, vol. *41*, no. *3*, pp. 259–274, DOI:10.1111/j.1467-9191.2010.00362.x

Tsosie, R., 2006, 'The BIA's apology to Native Americans: an essay on collective memory and collective conscience', in E. Barkan and A. Karn (eds), *Taking wrongs seriously: apologies and reconciliation*, Stanford University Press, Stanford, pp. 185–212.

United Nations, 2005, *Basic Principles and Guidelines on the Right to a Remedy and Reparation for Victims of Gross Violations of International Human Rights Law and Serious Violations of International Humanitarian Law*, General Assembly Resolution 60/147.

Van Boven, T., 2010, 'The United Nations Basic Principles and Guidelines on the Right to a Remedy and Reparation for Victims of Gross Violations of International Human Rights Law and Serious Violations of International Humanitarian Law', *United Nations Audiovisual Library of International Law*, http://legal.un.org/avl/pdf/ha/ga_60-147/ga_60-147_e.pdf

Vines, P., 2007, 'The power of apology: mercy, forgiveness or corrective justice in the civil liability arena', *Public Space: The Journal of Law and Social Justice*, vol. *1*, no. *1*, pp. 1–51.

Waldron, J., 1992, 'Superseding historic injustice', *Ethics*, vol. *103*, no. *1*, pp. 4–28.

Wenzel, M., Anvari, F., de Vel-Palumbo, M. and Bury, S.M., 2017, 'Collective apology, hope, and forgiveness', *Journal of Experimental Social Psychology*, vol. *72*, pp. 75–87, DOI:10.1016/j.jesp.2017.05.003

Weyeneth, R.R., 2001, 'The power of apology and the process of historical reconciliation', *The Public Historian*, vol. *23*, no. *1*, pp. 9–38, DOI:10.1525/tph.2001.23.3.9

Chapter 3

Sorry for what? Examining the Rudd and Harper apologies in their historical contexts

Introduction

It is evident that at least in theory interpersonal and political apologies share common features. An apology understood as expressing other-oriented moral regret – as seeing the wrongdoing and the harm caused through the eyes of the victims – would demonstrate acceptance of responsibility for the wrongdoing, respect for the victims, and acknowledgement that they did not deserve to be treated wrongly. However, while the endpoint of an apology may be to advance reconciliation, in relation to a political apology it may not be appropriate to equate this in terms of forgiveness, as may be the case for an interpersonal apology. It may be that Survivors as individuals and collectives may respond with forgiveness, but considering its political context, the assessment of an apology may depend more on the state meeting its commitments to change now and in the future. Thus, the main criterion for evaluating a political apology may be whether it helps to create the necessary conditions for reconciliation by achieving just outcomes for members of the harmed group. The focus of this chapter is to identify what this would entail by drawing on a sample of Indigenous responses to the Rudd and Harper apologies.

The chapter begins by summarising the background of each apology to explain their significance in terms of their broader and more immediate historical contexts. The discussion then turns to examine some of the more positive responses of Indigenous peoples to each apology. Evident in these claims was the understanding that the apologies would result in the creation of a 'new' relationship between Indigenous peoples and each state. The final section of the chapter demonstrates how these Indigenous reactions are aligned to the understanding of critical theories on the history of settler–colonised relations, which ascribe the injustices experienced by Indigenous peoples to the ongoing process of colonisation. They reflect an understanding that the settler–colonised relationship needs to end if the claims of Indigenous peoples are to be realised. In making these claims the importance of the historical account included in an apology becomes apparent as the basis for making adequate and effective reparations to Indigenous peoples.

DOI: 10.4324/9781003491019-3

Why were the Rudd and Harper apologies made?

It is notable that the Rudd apology was addressed to 'Australia's Indigenous Peoples' and broadly acknowledged their 'past mistreatment'. More specifically, the apology was focused 'on the mistreatment of those who were Stolen Generations—this blemished chapter in our nation's history' (House of Representatives, Australia, 2008, p. 167). In contrast, Harper in his apology specifically addressed 'Former Students of Indian Residential Schools' and extended his apology 'to aboriginal peoples for Canada's role in the Indian residential schools system' (House of Commons, Canada, 2008, p. 6850).

The discussion below outlines to the broader and more immediate historical contexts of the apologies to explicate why they were made and why making them was significant.

Protection and assimilation

In their apologies, Rudd and Harper each conveyed their understanding of the injustices caused by the forcible removal of Indigenous children from their families. In Australia, this practice was first pursued as part of the policy of protection that was adopted by the various Australian jurisdictions from the 1860s to 1910s. The assimilation policy replaced the protection policy in the 1950s and remained in place until the 1970s. The establishment of residential schools in Canada also formed part of a policy of assimilation. Control over these schools was first vested in the Canadian government in the 1870s. The last school was closed in 1996.

The protection policy in Australia was informed by social Darwinism which supported the view that Indigenous peoples would eventually die out in the face of western civilisation (Markus, 1994, p. 78). This belief arose from the catastrophic effects of colonisation and reflected conceptions of Indigenous peoples as inferior beings and unable to withstand these effects (Behrendt, 2010, p. 186).

Originally the policy of protection applied to 'full blood' Aboriginal people as they were then called. Reserves were established to segregate them from the broader white population. These reserves were established, euphemistically, to help 'smooth the dying pillow' (Bolton, 1982, p. 59). In reality, the administrators of the reserves were given wide discretionary powers over Indigenous peoples in areas such as residence, employment, and marriage (Wearne, 1980, p. 15). The exercise of these powers was largely unfettered by the rule of law (Behrendt, et al., 2019, p. 25).[1]

However, it soon became clear that the Aboriginal race was not 'dying out', most evident in the birth of so-called 'half-caste' children. This raised the concern that Indigenous peoples would not die out as expected; instead, their numbers would increase and the children would inherit the negative traits of their race.[2] To deal with this 'problem', protection legislation was amended which authorised the forcible removal of Indigenous children from their families. The theory behind the policy was that 'full blood Aborigines' would die out, the 'half-caste' children would be absorbed into white society, and the Aboriginal race would 'disappear' forever (Renes, 2011, p. 33). It was not until the 1960s and 1970s that explicitly race-based legislation targeting the removal of Indigenous children was finally repealed.

Proponents of the practice of separating children from their families considered that it was in the children's best interests. However, this sentiment was administered through a policy that adversely discriminated against Indigenous peoples and was authorised through laws that reflected racist perceptions of Indigenous peoples as a 'child race' in need of protection. The intention was never to protect the rights of Indigenous peoples, but the rights of the colonisers. As Cecil Cook, Chief Protector of the Northern Territory from 1927 to 1939, surmised: 'the native actually has become an intruder in a white man's country. Politically the Northern Territory must always be governed as a white man's country, by the white man for the white man' (quoted by Markus, 1990, p. 90). Apparently securing the land for 'the settlers' was vital, regardless of what the consequences were for Indigenous peoples. This was presented as a perfectly legitimate use of state power because it was considered as something positive for the entire nation. As A.O. Neville, Chief Protector of Western Australia, remarked in 1937:

> the native population is increasing. What is to be the limit? Are we going to have a population of 1,000,000 blacks in the Commonwealth, or are we going to merge them into our white community and eventually forget that there ever were any Aborigines in Australia?
>
> (Commonwealth of Australia, 1937, p.11).

Although evidently discriminatory in the way the practice singled out Indigenous peoples for adverse treatment, the practice also had genocidal intentions in the way it sought the complete eradication of Indigenous peoples as distinct peoples through the removal of Indigenous children from their families. This had been the conclusion of the former Human Rights and Equal Opportunity Commission ('HREOC') in its report, *Bringing Them Home* ('*BTH*') where it found that the forced removal of Indigenous children was genocide as it entailed the forcible transfer of children from one group to another group pursuant to Article 2(e) of the *Convention on the Prevention and Punishment of the Crime of Genocide* ('*Genocide Convention*') (United Nations, 1948, discussed in HREOC, 1997, pp. 270–275). As it was further put in *BTH*: 'Culture, language, land and identity were to be stripped from the children in the hope that the traditional law and culture would die by losing their claim on them and their sustenance of them' (HREOC, 1997, p. 202). Evidently, the destruction of culture would spell the end of the connections of Indigenous peoples to their lands, customs, and laws, the effects of which resulted in 'the loss of language, family dispersion and the cessation of cultural practices' (Dudgeon, et al., 2010, p. 30).

The policy of protection in Australia was eventually abandoned in the mid-twentieth century in favour of a policy of assimilation. The shift in policy was originally rationalised in the late 1930s to achieve full absorption of the Aboriginal race to advance the interests of white Australia (Commonwealth of Australia, 1937). Implementation of the policy was delayed by World War II. When finally introduced in the 1950s, the policy sought to create a culturally homogenous Australia (Broome, 1994, pp. 171–173). The policy was defined at the 1961 Native Welfare Conference of Federal and State Ministers in these terms:

> The policy of assimilation means ... that all aborigines and part-aborigines are expected ... to attain the same manner of living as other Australians and to live as members of a single Australian community enjoying the same rights and privileges, accepting the same responsibilities, observing the same customs and influenced by the same beliefs, hopes and loyalties as other Australians.
>
> (Hasluck, 1961, p. 1)

Ostensibly, the aim of assimilation was to achieve equal rights and privileges. Underpinning this approach was the principle of formal equality which adopts a colour-blind stance to promote the equal treatment of everyone in society (discussed further below). However, the representation of the concept of equality as neutral and value-free obscures the way it can be used to condone discriminatory practices and privilege dominant normative systems. In practice, the application of the principle does not preclude the unequal (and discriminatory) treatment of those who are not the same. In the context of colonisation, assimilation meant that Indigenous laws and customs could continue to be denigrated (and ignored), and white Australian norms and practices would continue to set the standard against which Indigenous peoples were measured (and could be found lacking). Thus, Indigenous peoples' purported deficiencies could still legitimise adverse treatment as they had done under the protection policy. In the area of child welfare, the non-conformity of Indigenous families with white Australian nuclear family values resulted in more Indigenous children being removed from their families.[3] There was little regard given to Indigenous child-rearing practices and little reflection on the impacts of colonisation that caused the socio-economic inequalities between Indigenous and non-Indigenous families that could result in children being taken away.

In Canada, the government had similar intentions in administering the residential school system, but it was implemented through different measures. The residential school system, which had been first established by the Christian churches in the early 1800s, came under the control of the federal government in the 1870s. The schools were the cornerstone of the policy of assimilation that the Canadian government was rigorously pursuing at the time in the exercise of its power under s. 91(24) of the *Constitution Act* (1867) with respect to 'Indians, and Lands reserved for the Indians'.[4] Like in Australia, the aim of assimilation was 'to terminate the cultural, social, economic, and political distinctiveness of Aboriginal peoples by absorbing them into mainstream Canadian life and values' (Hanson, 2009a).

The policy of assimilation had been gradually adopted over the course of the 1800s.[5] As in Australia, its adoption was based on the understanding that it would benefit Indigenous peoples. However, it was an approach infused with notions belittling of Indigenous peoples as they were assigned the status of 'wards or children of the state', while the colonisers, in their 'wisdom and duty', assigned themselves the task of aiding 'the Red man in lifting himself out of his condition of tutelage and dependence' (Harry, 2009, p. 11, quoting Canada's Department of the Interior, 1876). While this attitude reflected a concern for Indigenous peoples to achieve full citizenship, in practice, it reinforced a relationship of dependency between Indigenous peoples and the Crown and was aligned with conceptions of Indigenous racial inferiority and of white superiority. Not only was assimilation an affront to Indigenous peoples' humanity, but it undermined their political, cultural, and economic autonomy as it was a direct breach of the treaties they had signed with the intent of protecting their ongoing relationships to their lands (Truth and Reconciliation Commission of Canada, 2012, pp. 7–11).

The policy was given legal authority through the enactment of the *Indian Act* (1876) (still in force), which consolidated all prior federal legislation affecting Indigenous peoples. Its effect was to impose a regime of control over Indigenous peoples. More broadly, the *Indian Act* has been described as:

> highly invasive and paternalistic, as it authorizes the Canadian federal government to regulate and administer in the affairs and day-to-day lives of registered Indians and reserve communities. This authority has ranged from overarching political control, such as imposing governing structures on Aboriginal communities in the form of band councils, to control over the rights of Indians to practice their culture and traditions. The Indian Act has also enabled the government to determine the land base of these groups in the form of reserves, and even to define who qualifies as Indian in the form of Indian status.
>
> (Hanson, 2009a)

As an instrument of assimilation, the *Act* also contained provisions for the compulsory enfranchisement of Indigenous peoples (that had particularly dire consequences for women married to non-Indian men and their children)[6] and the imposition of the residential school system on their families and communities.

It is not difficult to see where the policy of assimilation was headed: to eliminate, whether by enfranchisement or education, those Indigenous peoples who could lay claim to Indian Status, and thereby secure Indigenous lands for settlement. In 1920, Duncan Campbell Scott, the first Superintendent of the Residential Schools, explicitly acknowledged this intention when he claimed: 'I want to get rid of the Indian problem ... Our object is to continue until there is not a single Indian in Canada that has not been absorbed into the body politic, and there is no Indian question, and no Indian department' (quoted in Treaty 6 Education, n.d.).

Indeed, in all the history of the *Indian Act*, the establishment of the residential school system stands out as the gravest attack on Indigenous peoples' humanity and autonomy. Guided by the edict 'Kill the Indian in the child' (a phrase which had been coined by Scott), the establishment of these schools set out to destroy the seeds of Indian culture by civilising the children in Europeans ways so that they could be absorbed into the broader Canadian society.

Initially, it was believed that the introduction of a schooling system would provide Indigenous children with a western education without compromising traditional educational practices (Truth and Reconciliation Commission of Canada, 2012, p. 49). Provision was made for the establishment of 'schools on reserves' in a number of treaties that were signed in the 1870s (Miller, 2013). Ultimately, and in breach of these treaties, many of the schools that were established involved the custodial institutionalisation of children far from their communities.

In fact, whether the intention was really to provide the children with a western education – or to save any children for that matter – was highly questionable. For instance, Scott knew that the children in the schools were at a much greater risk of disease and death than in their tribal communities. But he chose to ignore this evidence, claiming that it 'does not justify a change in the policy of this department which is geared toward a final solution of our Indian problem' (Farber, 2013).

It is evident from this (albeit) brief overview of the state-sanctioned removal of Indigenous children from their families that there is much that the governments of Australia and Canada should be sorry for. However, while the pursuit of this practice was devastating for many, it is also evident that the removal of children was only one of many injustices inflicted on Indigenous peoples. Therefore, to understand why the specific focus of the apologies was on the Stolen Generations and the residential schools respectively, it is necessary to consider their own historical backgrounds.

Background of the Rudd apology

In Australia, the momentum for an apology to the Stolen Generations grew after the recommendation for an apology was made in *BTH*, which was tabled in the Australia Parliament in 1997 (HREOC, 1997). The HREOC inquiry was established by the former Labor Keating government in response to calls by Indigenous agencies, individuals, and communities for greater awareness and support for people who had been forcibly removed as children (Buti, 2002; Short, 2008, pp. 92–93).

At the time of its release, *BTH* attracted mixed reactions – and some vehement attacks (Wootten, 1998). Political conservatives were especially critical of the report and throughout this period they remained steadfast in their view that the whole idea of 'Stolen Generations' was a myth (Manne, 2001, p. 82). The finding of genocide in *BTH* was the most controversial for these critics who cast doubt on how many children were removed, and claimed for any children who had been removed that it was in their best interests (Manne, 2001, p. 75). The recommendations relating to reparations calling for a national apology (HREOC, 1997, p. 287) and the payment of monetary compensation to the Stolen Generations (HREOC, 1997, p. 282) were also met with criticism. Notably, the Labor Keating government, which could have been more receptive to the HREOC findings, was no longer in power. Earlier in 1992, Prime Minister Paul Keating delivered the 'Redfern Speech' in which he recognised some of the fundamental injustices inflicted by non-Aboriginal Australians on Indigenous peoples, including how '[w]e took the children from their mothers' (Department of the Prime Minister and Cabinet, 1992, p. 2). In 1996, leader of the Liberal–Coalition party, John Howard, was elected Prime Minister. His government proved unable to accept any wrongdoing had been committed against Indigenous peoples.

With respect to *BTH*, the Howard government's objections were interrelated. It rejected the finding of genocide, claiming that the past treatment of Indigenous peoples was in the best interests of the children concerned. This interpretation of history was also supported by decisions of the Australian federal courts, which rejected the claims of Stolen Generations Survivors that the practice amounted to genocide (*Kruger v. Commonwealth* (1997)) and their claims for compensation for the effects of this practice (*Cubillo v. Commonwealth* (2001)). These decisions also supported the government's refusal to make an apology and set up a compensation scheme as the government maintained it was not legally obliged to offer either of them. In maintaining this stance, the government strictly adhered to the liberal understanding of responsibility for wrongful actions. It maintained that an apology to Indigenous peoples would imply that present generations of Australians were responsible for the actions of earlier generations. This would create an injustice for ordinary Australians in the present time, particularly because it was not so clearly apparent that the past treatment of Indigenous peoples was wrong (Govier, 2006, pp. 217–218).

The government did acknowledge that the past treatment of Indigenous peoples was regrettable by today's standards. However, the way forward was not to dwell on the past through symbolic gestures such as an apology, but to introduce practical measures that would address Indigenous socio-economic disadvantage. Thus, the government's response to *BTH* was to offer AU$63 million in rehabilitative measures to address some of the consequences of family separation (Herron, 2000, p. ii).

However, these measures did not reflect the spirit of the *BTH* recommendations. *BTH* contained the testimonies of hundreds of Indigenous peoples affected by the forced child removal practice. These testimonies revealed the devastating consequences of the practice, not only for the individuals who had been removed, but also for their families and communities, with continuing intergenerational effects on Indigenous communities across Australia. In the report it was estimated that between 1910 and 1970 at least one in three to one in ten children had been removed (HREOC, 1997, p. 37); they were often not told the truth about the circumstances of their removal; denied knowledge of their Indigenous identity; forbidden to practice their traditions and speak their languages, and would be punished if they did so; and were often subjected to racism, neglect, and physical and sexual abuse. The long-term cultural effects included loss of cultural knowledge, loss of language, and loss of cultural identity. The flow-on effects included further land dispossession, as evidenced by the difficulties now facing Stolen Generations Survivors seeking native title rights to land. The practice of removal also affected personal attachments and parenting skills, which has led to a cycle of children being removed from one generation to the next (HEROC, 1997, chap. 11).

In light of this evidence, the report found that the practice of forcibly removing Indigenous children from their families was in violation of a number of international human rights laws, most notably the *Genocide Convention* (United Nations, 1948) and the *International Convention on the Elimination of All Forms of Racial Discrimination* (United Nations, 1965), and had breached common law rights by depriving children of their liberty, their parents of their parental rights, and involved abuses of power and breaches of guardianship duties (HEROC, 1997, chap. 13). In response to these violations the report set out several recommendations aimed at making reparations. Using the van Boven principles as a framework,[7] these included acknowledgement and apology, guarantees against repetition, restitution, rehabilitation, and monetary compensation (HREOC, 1997, p. 651). In total, *BTH* made 54 recommendations, which also extended to child welfare and juvenile justice regimes in line with international human rights principles, and specifically the right of self-determination. In framing the future response to Indigenous affairs according to these principles, the aim was to prevent repetition of past practices, address the present over-representation of Indigenous children in the child welfare and juvenile justice systems, and thereby ensure their wellbeing in the future (HREOC, 1997, chap. 26).

Most of the *BTH* recommendations remain unimplemented, and the attempt to implement some (such as child welfare reforms according to the principle of self-determination) has not been as they were intended (see

Chapter 6). This is further evidenced by the rehabilitative measures introduced by the Howard government. These were not framed in terms of meeting Australia's human rights obligations as set out in *BTH*. They formed part of the government's broader political strategy whereby it abandoned the existing policies of self-determination and reconciliation and replaced them with its own policy of 'practical reconciliation'. These changes in policy reflected the government's ideological stance that it was:

> committed to common rights for all Australians. … The Government supports additional measures to ensure equality of opportunity … necessary to overcome specific disadvantages experienced by Indigenous people. Neither the Government nor the general community, however, is prepared to support any action which would entrench additional, special or different rights for one part of the community.
>
> (Commonwealth of Australia, 2002, pp. 1, 17)

In this respect, for example, the government's refusal to set up a compensation fund was consistent with its refusal to accord Stolen Generations Survivors special rights when the ordinary course for other Australians was to claim compensation in court (see generally, Herron, 2000, pp. 38–51).

To appreciate the significance of this shift in policy, some account of earlier developments is needed. The policy of self-determination had been first introduced by former Labor Prime Minister Gough Whitlam. Its introduction followed the 1967 referendum which amended the *Commonwealth of Australia Constitution Act* (1900) to give the Commonwealth Parliament power to make laws with respect to Aboriginal and Torres Strait Islander peoples. At the time, Indigenous peoples and their supporters thought that Commonwealth oversight of Indigenous affairs could address their appalling and discriminatory treatment by the state governments. However, this change did not bring the discrimination to an end. The introduction of a national policy of self-determination for Indigenous peoples did, nonetheless, result in the introduction of a range of measures. Most notably, during this period most Australian states and territories enacted land rights schemes, and a Commonwealth statutory body named the Aboriginal and Torres Strait Islander Commission ('ATSIC') was established in 1989. It was through ATSIC that Indigenous peoples became formally involved in the processes of government.

However, the scope of the policy of self-determination was limited. It was administered through government and did not extend to recognise Indigenous political autonomy or laws. In the 1980s, many Indigenous representatives sought a treaty with the Commonwealth government to give effect (among other things) to their aspiration for complete control over their own affairs and recognition of their sovereignty and rights, including the establishment of a national land rights scheme (Northern and Central Land Councils,

1988). A treaty never eventuated owing to the failure of former Labor Prime Minister Bob Hawke to attract bipartisan support. An inquiry in 1986 into the recognition of Aboriginal customary law, with a view to shielding Indigenous peoples from the discriminatory effects of Australian law, also proved largely ineffective (Aboriginal and Torres Strait Islander Social Justice Commissioner of the Human Rights and Equal Opportunity Commission, 2003).

It was also in the 1980s that interest in the history of forced child removals began to generate among non-Indigenous academics. The term 'Stolen Generations' was first used by historian Peter Read in writing on the history of the removal of Indigenous children in New South Wales (Read, 1982). In fact, since the 1960s historians had shown an increasing interest in the history of settler–colonised relations. Their work has been vital in exposing the violence of dispossession in the initial stages of colonisation (Reynolds, 1982); and in identifying the racism that underpinned the policies of protection and assimilation that created the Stolen Generations (Markus, 1987). The work of these 'new historians' has been particularly significant, not only in breaking the silence in mainstream Australia that had shrouded the history of colonisation in Australia since the late nineteenth century, but also in bringing into question particular understandings of settler–colonised relations – especially the idea that came to pervade mainstream accounts that settlement was mostly peaceful and benevolent towards Indigenous peoples (Attwood, 1996, pp. 101–102).

Indigenous academics and activists have been vital to this research in writing about their cultures and the nature of their laws and customs and in seeking justice for violations of their cultural rights (Langford, 1983). A notable example is the role that Murray Islanders, Eddie Mabo, David Passi, and James Rice played in bringing proceedings in the High Court of Australia where they sought a declaration on behalf of the Meriam people for recognition of their rights to the Murray Islands in the Torres Strait. The result was the landmark *Mabo v. Queensland (No. 2)* ('*Mabo*') (1992) decision. In *Mabo*, the High Court found that the Australian common law recognised the concept of native title, which was grounded in the laws and customs of Indigenous peoples. In reaching this decision, the Court also overturned the colonisers' refusal (supposedly justified by the terra nullius doctrine) to recognise Indigenous peoples as the original owners of their lands. The logical implication of this finding was that the sovereignty of Indigenous peoples had also survived. However, the Court refused to question the acquisition of British sovereignty over the Australian territories. This gave rise to the need for a just settlement of Indigenous peoples' claims to sovereignty, but this was not the course of action adopted at the time. Instead, the Keating government introduced the *Native Title Act* (1993) ('*NTA*'), but this has proven to provide even less protection to native title than the common law (Bartlett, 2014).

In some ways, developments such as the 1967 referendum, the adoption of the policy of self-determination, and the High Court decision in *Mabo* reflected a changed attitude among white Australians towards Indigenous peoples. Yet, it is also evident that full support for Indigenous peoples' claims was lacking, and they were entertained only to the extent that they did not disturb the balance of power in the hands of the colonisers. Indeed, once Howard became Prime Minister it became increasingly apparent that his intention was to wind back the meagre gains Indigenous peoples had made. Among the many examples to support this claim, the 1998 amendments to the *NTA* stand out, along with the 2007 imposition of the Northern Territory Emergency Response ('the Intervention'), which was implemented under the *Northern Territory National Emergency Response Act* (2007). With respect to the former, the Howard government's amendments to the *NTA* have been found to be in violation of Australia's obligations to eliminate racial discrimination as they have provided greater protection to non-Indigenous property interests and have further undermined the protection of native title in Australian law (Hoffman, 2000). The Intervention was also found to have been imposed on Indigenous peoples in violation of their rights to self-determination and freedom from racial discrimination (Amnesty International, n.d., p. 10). Introduced in response to allegations of rampant family violence and child sexual abuse in remote communities of the Northern Territory, the government (with Labor Party support) used the Intervention to impose punitive controls on designated communities (such as the 'management' of welfare payments through strict mutual obligation requirements) (Proudfoot and Habibis, 2015). Reminiscent of the protection era and set to achieve the same outcome of stamping out cultural differences (by attacking Aboriginal land rights and customary law), the Intervention exacerbated community hardships (evidenced by increase in children in out-of-home care and criminal detention of children and adults, increase in family violence, suicide, and self-harm, increase in unemployment, and overcrowded housing) (Gibson, 2017). Nevertheless, despite its failings, aspects of this model (which was renamed Stronger Futures by the Labor Gillard government in 2012) were extended to other communities across the country (Behrendt and McCausland, 2008). By 2022, some of these measures had been repealed or had lapsed, but some, such as the paternalistic policy of income management, have remained in the Northern Territory (Australian Government, 2023).

These developments demonstrate the ease with which Indigenous peoples' rights can be infringed in Australian law and attest to the fragile status of Indigenous peoples in Australian law and policy. With respect to the Howard government, they were consistent with its stance on reconciliation and self-determination.

In 1991, the Royal Commission into Aboriginal Deaths in Custody ('RCIADIC') presented its findings on the causes of the high number of Aboriginal deaths in police custody. The RCIADIC had been appointed by the Hawke Labor government in 1987. Its report was significant in providing the most comprehensive overview of the injustices experienced by Indigenous peoples in Australia up to that time. One of its more notable findings was that 43 people of the 99 deaths in custody examined had been separated from their families (Royal Commission into Aboriginal Deaths in Custody, 1991, vol. 1. para. 2.2.9). The report also came at a time when the Labor government was seeking to find a solution to its failure to secure support for a treaty from the opposing conservative parties. The result was the adoption of a national policy of reconciliation which seemingly endorsed the RCIADIC's recommendation that:

> all political leaders and their parties recognise that reconciliation between the Aboriginal and non-Aboriginal communities in Australia must be achieved if community division, discord and injustice to Aboriginal people are to be avoided.
>
> (Royal Commission into Aboriginal Deaths in Custody, 1991, vol. 5. para. 38.32)

The reactions of some Indigenous people were cautious and sceptical. They had not been properly consulted and were wary that issues such as sovereignty, a treaty, and a national land rights scheme were not included on the reconciliation agenda ('Editorial', 1993, p. 3). The introduction of this process, however, was supported by all political parties and all levels of government were urged to:

> address progressively Aboriginal disadvantage and aspirations in relation to land, housing, law and justice, cultural heritage, education, employment, health, infrastructure, economic development and any other relevant matters.
>
> (*Council for Aboriginal Reconciliation Act* (1991), (e))

The Council for Aboriginal Reconciliation ('CAR') was the national statutory body established to lead the process of reconciliation. Most notably, recommendations 5 and 6 in CAR's final report went further than originally envisaged in calling for a treaty aimed at achieving the protection of 'the political, legal, cultural and economic position of Aborigines and Torres Strait Islanders' and legislation 'which would unite all Australians by way of agreement, and which would enable outstanding issues of reconciliation to be resolved' (CAR, 2000a, chap. 10).

However, the Howard government rejected these recommendations on the basis that they 'would be divisive, would undermine the concept of a single Australian nation, would create legal uncertainty and future disputation' (Commonwealth of Australia, 2002, p. 23). Earlier in 2000, the Howard government had also published a revised version of *The Australian*

Declaration Towards Reconciliation, which had been previously published by CAR (2000b) where the references in CAR's version to Aboriginal customary law, an apology for past injustices, and self-determination were deleted. The Howard government claimed that it could not endorse customary law because it 'believes all Australians are equally subject to a common set of laws', and it could not endorse the term 'self-determination' because it 'implies the possibility of a separate Indigenous state or states' (Commonwealth of Australia, 2002, p. 10). Following this, and as part of the Intervention in 2007, the Howard government enacted provisions prohibiting consideration of customary law in bail and sentencing in the Northern Territory (*Crimes Act* (1914), s. 16AA). Furthermore, in the intervening time, the government dismantled ATSIC in 2005 based on claims that it had mismanaged government funds and lacked support and accountability (Behrendt, 2005, pp. 4–5). For the Howard government, ATSIC was a 'failed experiment', but in abolishing ATSIC, the government effectively silenced 'a vocal critic' of the government's position on native title and its violation of Indigenous rights both domestically and internationally (Behrendt, 2005, pp. 4, 6). The demise of ATSIC effectively spelled the end of the self-determination policy and led to the return of Indigenous service delivery to the bureaucratic mainstream (Behrendt, 2005, pp. 6–7).

The government's approach may be explicable in terms of its commitment to the principle of formal equality, according to which all Australians should be accorded equal treatment and provided with the same opportunities. However, the government's espousal of formal equality obscured how Indigenous policy during Howard's term was underpinned by neoliberal concerns to promote economic efficiency, self-sufficiency, and accountability, especially in remote communities where many residents were (and are) dependent on welfare. The aim was for Indigenous peoples to become responsible and productive members of society (Howard-Wagner and Kelly, 2011, p. 106). The recognition of specific Indigenous cultural rights would be counterproductive as this would contradict the neoliberal logic that informs the deregulated market economy (Altman and Fogarty, 2010). Thus, instead of a rights-based approach that could be used by Indigenous peoples to hold government to account, the government adopted a welfare-based approach (such as the Intervention) that it used to maintain control over Indigenous peoples' lives.

This approach was also supported by the government's ideological concerns about the effect that Indigenous peoples' claims could have on the image and identity of the nation. Ultimately, these concerns were expressed through the history wars that escalated during this period between the 'new historians' and the 'New Right historians', the latter of whom sought to reinvigorate an idealised version of Australian history as one of progress and peaceful settlement and reject what they described as the 'black armband history' of the new historians (Blainey, 1993). In the case of the Stolen

Generations, the New Right's portrayal of their removal as being for their own good contrasted with the suggestion that it was racially motivated genocide as had been claimed in *BTH*. Howard also explicitly rejected the 'black armband' view of history, which in his opinion:

> reflects a belief that most Australian history since 1788 has been little more than a disgraceful story of imperialism, exploitation, racism, sexism and other forms of discrimination. I take a very different view. I believe that the balance sheet of our history is one of heroic achievement and that we have achieved much more as a nation of which we can be proud than of which we should be ashamed.
>
> (Howard, 1996, p. 9)

In aligning himself with the Right in this way, Howard demonstrated the conservative cultural bias of his politics, which he justified by relying on the principle of formal equality to reject claims for specific rights for Indigenous peoples.

Nevertheless, Howard's government did not have universal support from the Australian public. This was most evident with respect to the issue of an apology, especially in the public support shown for the commemoration of a National Sorry Day on 26 May 1998 as part of National Reconciliation Week; the millions who signed sorry books at the time; and the People's Walk for Reconciliation on 28 May 2000 which saw hundreds of thousands of Australians walk across the Harbour Bridge in support of an apology and reconciliation. Howard's refusal to apologise, in particular, was seen as unjust by many non-Indigenous peoples, not only because it was a refusal to acknowledge that the past treatment of Indigenous peoples was wrong, but more pertinently, his refusal brought shame on the entire nation and '*deprived white Australia of its ability to declare its pride in itself to others*' (Ahmed, 2004, p. 112, emphasis in original). Evidently, the supporters who maintained this sentiment had their own political agenda in seeking to re-legitimise the nation and their place in it by offering an apology to Indigenous peoples. Rudd harnessed this sentiment during the 2007 election campaign, promising to make an apology the first item on the agenda of his government if elected.

Background of the Harper apology

As in Australia, the apology movement in Canada had also grown from the grassroots, but unlike in Australia where the movement had large-scale involvement for the broader non-Indigenous population, in Canada it mostly involved Survivors of the residential school system who began to speak out about their experiences in the 1980s and 1990s. Phil Fontaine (then Grand Chief of the Assembly of Manitoba Chiefs) was one of a number of Survivors who spoke out about the abuse he suffered while attending a Roman Catholic residential school in Fort Alexander, Manitoba, and used his experience to call for recognition of the abuse, for compensation, and an apology for the inherent racism involved (Assembly of First Nations, 2015). Disclosures of abuse soon led to commencement of court proceedings by former residents.

Another significant development was the establishment in 1991 of the Royal Commission on Aboriginal Peoples ('RCAP') in response to disputes involving Indigenous peoples concerning their land rights, self-government, and political autonomy more generally. The RCAP completed its report in 1996 and made extensive recommendations in response to the constitutional, political, economic, social, and cultural concerns of Indigenous peoples (Nobles, 2008, p. 74). The report is also noted for its role in raising awareness about the effects of the residential schools. The RCAP recommended, as HREOC had done in Australia, that apologies be made 'by those responsible' (RCAP, 1996b, vol. 1, p. 367).

There is extensive literature on the effects (and intergenerational effects) of the residential school system on its former residents, estimated to have been 150,000 in number (see generally, Calgary, 2007). Many parallels can be drawn between the experiences in Australia and Canada of Indigenous children removed from their families: their exposure to physical, sexual and emotional abuse, and neglect; how they were denied their cultures, languages, and belief systems, and made to feel inferior; how many lost their lives; how their suffering of trauma has been intergenerational and continues to undermine their life chances; and their shared understanding that what was done to them was genocide (Treaty 6 Education, n.d.).

However, Canada's approach appears to have been more responsive than Australia's. In 1998, the then Minister of Indian Affairs, Jane Stewart, introduced *Gathering Strength: Canada's Aboriginal Action Plan* ('*Gathering Strength*') in response to the RCAP recommendations (Stewart, 1998). C$350 million was allocated for the establishment of the Aboriginal Healing Foundation ('AHF') designed to address the intergenerational effects of the residential school system on Survivors. Another notable difference from the Australian experience was the relative success of claims for compensation, although litigation was not without its drawbacks. Apart from the extensive delays and cost of going to court (Hennessy, 2008, pp. 6–7), the law was only equipped to provide individualised justice, and not community-based supports, and even then, only individual harms related to sexual and physical abuses were accepted, while claims of loss of language and culture were not. The inadequacies of the law resulted in trials of alternative approaches. These culminated in the establishment of an Alternative Dispute Resolution Process in 2003, but it soon became obvious that this process was also flawed (Assembly of First Nations, 2004). The sheer number and success of claims by Survivors, including class action claims such as the Cloud class action that had been successfully initiated in court, led the government to seek an alternative solution. Negotiations for a resolution of outstanding legal claims began in 2005; agreement was reached between all parties in 2006; and in 2007 the *Indian Residential Schools Settlement Agreement* ('*Settlement Agreement*') (2006) came into effect after it had been approved in courts across the country. This *Agreement* allocated C$1.9 billion for Common Experience Payments and C$960 million for an Independent Assessment Process as compensation to Residential School Survivors. It also provided C$60 million for the establishment of a Truth and Reconciliation Commission; C$20 million for the establishment of a Commemoration Fund; and another C$125 million to extend the life of the AHF until September 2014.

Of notable contrast to Canada was that even after Rudd made his apology, his government, like its predecessor, refused to set up a compensation fund. In Canada, under the *Settlement Agreement*, individual Residential School Survivors were eligible to apply for a Common Experience Payment, to be paid in recognition of the negative impacts of the residential school system. The amount was based on the time spent in the system (an initial C$10,000 plus C$3,000 for each year in a school). Survivors seeking additional compensation (for sexual and/or physical abuse, other forms of abuse, and loss of income) applied through an Independent Assessment Process. The maximum amount payable was C$275,000 (for abuse) and an additional C$250,000 (for loss of income).

Notwithstanding the extent of these measures, they have not been without their critics. For example, when the AHF was first introduced as part of *Gathering Strength*, it was criticised by different Indigenous groups for being 'too little, too late' (Nobles, 2008, p. 76). This criticism is understandable considering that *Gathering Strength* was presented as the government's response to the RCAP, but ultimately fell short of satisfying its main recommendations. These included providing greater recognition of Aboriginal peoples in Canada as 'nations' with 'a right to govern themselves and, in general, a strong desire to do so in partnership with Canada' and pursuing a decolonisation agenda to renew nation-to-nation relations based on the principles of recognition, respect, sharing, and responsibility (RCAP, 1996a, pp. 3, 13–15).

Furthermore, when Stewart launched *Gathering Strength* in 1998, she also issued a 'Statement of Reconciliation', in which she acknowledged the role of the federal government in establishing and administering the residential schools and expressed regret for the sexual and physical abuse suffered by students in the schools (Stewart, 1998). However, this statement did not satisfy all Indigenous groups. Its main failings were that it was not a clear statement of apology; it had not been offered by Jean Chrétien, the Prime Minister at the time; it was never put on the official record; and its focus on physical and sexual abuse ignored the more extensive social and cultural harms suffered by Indigenous peoples (Funk-Unrau, 2014, p. 142).

It was not until Stephen Harper's apology in 2008 that the calls of Residential School Survivors for an apology seemed to be finally answered. However, the making of this apology was not without controversy. In 2007, a motion for a formal apology introduced by former First Nations member of Parliament Gary Merasty had passed unanimously in the House of Commons. However, the Conservative party was in power, not the Liberal party, and an apology was not immediately forthcoming. The idea was initially rejected by Harper's Conservative government, which claimed that the residential schools had been established with the benign intent of educating Indigenous children, and that the need for an apology would be determined only after the Truth and Reconciliation Commission issued its final report. It was only after some political wrangling that Harper finally announced he would offer an apology (Jung, 2010, pp. 234–235).

Nevertheless, there was general mistrust of Harper among Indigenous peoples in Canada and concerns about whether he could deliver an apology they would find appropriate. The conservatism with which he had been approaching Indigenous issues impacted negatively on his credibility (Fiddler, 2008; Jung, 2010, pp. 234–235), and raised serious questions about whether he could deliver a meaningful apology. The doubts were further exacerbated by his refusal to accept the demands of Indigenous representatives for a meaningful consultation process to settle the wording of the apology. Unlike Harper, the Rudd government had engaged in consultation, albeit that the Stolen Generations representatives had to concede on certain points, and Rudd repeatedly refused to consider compensation and would have the final say on the apology's wording (Macklin, 2018). But in Canada, Harper's refusal to consult triggered harsh reactions and threats to reject the apology before it had even been delivered (Horelt, 2011, p. 362). Even on the day of the apology, there was controversy over whether Harper would allow prominent Indigenous leaders to respond in the House of Commons. Moreover, only hours before the apology was scheduled, Pierre Poilievre, the Member for Nepean-Carlton, criticised the apology and the *Settlement Agreement* in a radio interview, claiming: 'My view is that we need to engender the values of hard work and independence and self-reliance. That's the solution in the long run – more money will not solve it' (MacCharles, 2008). He apologised for his comments in the House of Commons the following day. Calls for his resignation were rejected by Harper.

Nevertheless, when Harper did finally deliver the apology, it was evident that it brought relief for many. Most notably, Fontaine (then National Chief of the Assembly of First Nations) declared: 'Finally, we heard Canada say it is sorry' (House of Common, Canada, 2008, p. 6854). And, as with the reactions of some Indigenous peoples to the Rudd apology, the feeling in Canada was that it marked a turning point in the settler–colonised relationship and a step towards the just resolution of the issues facing Residential School Survivors, and indeed all Indigenous peoples.

The significance of the Rudd and Harper apologies in advancing Indigenous peoples' claims

There were many aspects of the Rudd and Harper apologies that made them appear to be important gestures at the time they were delivered. In this section some of these aspects will be reviewed.

To begin with there were their public aspects. Both apologies were delivered by the head of state, 'within *the space of government*: namely, the national parliament of each country' (MacLachlan, 2013, p. 184). Not only did this mean that the apologies were put on the 'official record', but they were *read out loud* in Parliament. What made this even more significant was that the delivery of each apology was televised live outside Parliament and across the nation. The significance of this was captured by Shawn Atleo (a hereditary chief of the Ahousaht First Nation and then British Columbia Assembly of First Nations Regional Chief) who said in an interview:

> An apology is a very high level political recognition ... We're grabbing onto some hope that it will be a moment that will lead to a better tomorrow, that the general populace is finally going to be made aware of those severely disruptive policies over generations. ...
>
> This is the permanent record. ... This is what will be told 100 years from now
>
> (Fitzpatrick and Nguyen, 2008)

Also, of significance was the strong and visible presence of Indigenous peoples both inside and outside each parliament. The apologies in both nations received standing ovations and as each apology was televised live there were visible signs of emotion from the many thousands of Indigenous people in the various audiences (Campion-Smith, 2008; Hopper, 2008; Kemp, 2008). In Australia, the fact that there were politicians on both sides of politics who supported the apology and that Indigenous and non-Indigenous peoples came together in celebration was viewed as a significant step for reconciliation (Philpot, et al., 2013, p. 42).

Notably, in both nations Indigenous representatives were present on the floor of Parliament but only in Canada did they respond to the apologies in Parliament and these responses were subsequently reproduced in the official record (House of Commons, Canada, 2008, pp. 6855–6857 (Brazeau; Chartier; Fontaine; Jacobs; Simon); cf., Calma, 2008; Dodson, 2008). The delivering of the speeches in the House of Commons in Canada was particularly significant considering Harper's earlier opposition and the inference of nation status that their presence implied.

The apologies themselves were considered by some Indigenous peoples to represent a watershed moment in each nation's history. Accordingly, they were welcomed as positive gestures of reconciliation (Fitzpatrick and Nguyen,

2008; Gartrell, 2008). As Dodson (former Chairman of the Council for Aboriginal Reconciliation) remarked in his response to the Rudd apology:

> It [the apology] is a page that future generations of Australians might read with pride, recognising the moment when hope re-emerged; the moment we confronted our past and embarked on a journey of social revival characterised by vision, wisdom, courage and nation building. It is a watershed renaissance moment.
>
> (Dodson, 2008, p. 21)

In a similar vein, Calma (then Aboriginal and Torres Strait Islander Social Justice Commissioner) recognised:

> Today is an historic day.
>
> It's the day our leaders – across the political spectrum – have chosen dignity, hope and respect as the guiding principles for the relationship with our first nations' peoples. …
>
> For today is not just about the Stolen Generations – it is about every Australian.
>
> Today's actions enable every single one of us to move forward *together* – with joint aspirations and a national story that contains a shared past and future.
>
> (Calma, 2008, pp. 1–2)

There were similar reactions in Canada. Brazeau (then National Chief of the Congress of Aboriginal Peoples) claimed: 'Not only is it a historic day, but it is a positive step forward in the history of this great country of ours' (House of Commons, Canada, 2008, p. 6855).

Chartier (then President of Métis National Council) also welcomed the apology, despite his mixed emotions over the exclusion of most of the Métis people not only from the *Settlement Agreement* and the apology, but from most other government policies and programs available to Indigenous peoples (Senate of Canada, 2008, pp. 1506–1507):

> I said that the Métis Nation would be here to share this day with those people who have waited for so long. We want to celebrate, and we do celebrate, with them, with you, with all Canadians, because this is a day for all Canadians. It is a day for us to move forward.
>
> (House of Commons, Canada, 2008, p. 6856)

But even as a gesture of reconciliation, the apologies were not seen as restoring relations between Indigenous and non-Indigenous peoples. For many Indigenous peoples, the relationship had never been harmonious to start with. Instead, the apologies were viewed as a break from the past, and the start of a new relationship. As Fontaine declared:

> What happened today signifies a new dawn in the relationship between us and the rest of Canada. ...
>
> [the apology signifies] ... a respectful and, therefore, liberating relationship between us and the rest of Canada.
>
> (House of Commons, Canada, 2008, pp. 6854–6855)

Similarly, Simon (then Inuit Tapiriit Kanatami President) announced: 'a new day has dawned, a new day heralded by a commitment to reconciliation and building a new relationship with Inuit, Métis and first nations' (House of Commons, Canada, 2008, p. 6855).

Evidently, these reactions highlight the significance of each apology not only as an act of reconciliation, but also as a great achievement in overcoming the obstacles in the way of them being made – Stephen Harper's reluctance, and John Howard's refusal to apologise.

Thus Harper, in acknowledging that 'the Government of Canada *now* recognizes that it was wrong to forcibly remove children from their homes' (House of Commons, Canada, 2008, p. 5680, emphasis added), appeared to reflect his government's changed attitude to this issue. More pertinently, given that successive governments in the past had failed to recognise that this was wrong, Harper's apology was a welcome gesture and was, as Fontaine put it, 'nothing less than the achievement of the impossible' (House of Commons, Canada, 2008, pp. 6854–6855).

In Australia, the long-awaited 'sorry' delivered by Rudd in Australia seemed particularly satisfying in view of Howard's racist stance on Indigenous politics ('Tiga Bayles – response to the 2008 apology', 2018). Unlike Howard, Rudd had accepted that an apology was the right thing to do without question, qualifications, or excuses. Rudd directly responded to the various arguments Howard and other opponents had made against an apology. For example, Rudd acknowledged that '[s]ome people have asked, "Why apologise?"' (House of Representatives, Australia, 2008, p. 168). Rudd responded to this question, first by dispelling any suggestion that the history of the Stolen Generations was a myth by pointing to the testimonies in *BTH* and other personal records as evidence that what had been done was wrong. He further rejected the view, maintained by the conservative Right, that 'the policy of generic forced separation was somehow well motivated, justified by its historical context' (House of Representatives, Australia, 2008, p. 169). Rudd then turned to consider another objection centred on 'the argument of intergenerational responsibility' (House of Representatives, Australia, 2008, p. 169). Rudd dealt with this issue by reminding his audience that 'the forced removal of Aboriginal children was happening as late as the early 1970s.

The 1970s is not exactly a point in remote antiquity' (House of Representatives, Australia, 2008, p. 169). In this way, he implicated present members of Parliament who had been previously serving and had supported the enactment of the laws that authorised the forced removal of Indigenous children.

Finally, Rudd acknowledged there was a further reason for an apology and that was because:

> reconciliation is in fact an expression of a core value of our nation—and that value is a fair go for all. There is a deep and abiding belief in the Australian community that, for the stolen generations, there was no fair go at all. There is a pretty basic Aussie belief that says it is time to put right this most outrageous of wrongs.
>
> (House of Representatives, Australia, 2008, p. 169)

> In taking this course Rudd was explicit in distinguishing his approach from the former Howard government: from the nation's parliament there has been a stony and stubborn and deafening silence for more than a decade; a view that somehow we, the parliament, should suspend our most basic instincts of what is right and what is wrong; a view that, instead, we should look for any pretext to push this great wrong to one side, to leave it languishing with the historians, the academics and the cultural warriors, as if the stolen generations are little more than an interesting sociological phenomenon. But the stolen generations are not intellectual curiosities. They are human beings; human beings who have been damaged deeply by the decisions of parliaments and governments. But, as of today, the time for denial, the time for delay, has at last come to an end.
>
> (House of Representatives, Australia, 2008, p. 168)

He continued, claiming:

> This is not, as some would argue, a black-armband view of history; it is just the truth: the cold, confronting, uncomfortable truth—facing it, dealing with it, moving on from it. Until we fully confront that truth, there will always be a shadow hanging over us and our future as a fully united and fully reconciled people. It is time to reconcile. It is time to recognise the injustices of the past. It is time to say sorry. It is time to move forward together.
>
> (House of Representatives, Australia, 2008, p. 169)

This sentiment was also reflected by Calma who, in his response, commended leaders across the political spectrum for giving the apology their support:

> Through one direct act, Parliament has acknowledged the existence and the impacts of past policies and practices of forcibly removing Indigenous children from their families.

> And by so doing, has paid respect to the Stolen Generations. For their suffering and their loss. For their resilience. And ultimately, for their dignity. ...
>
> This is not about black armbands and guilt. It never was.
>
> It is about belonging. ...
>
> By acknowledging and paying respect, Parliament has now laid the foundations for healing to take place and for a reconciled Australia in which everyone belongs.
>
> (Calma, 2008, pp. 1–2).

Dodson made a similar point, quoting the author Richard Flanagan in his response: 'What Black Australia offers to the nation is not guilt about our history but an invitation to our future' (Dodson, 2008, p. 20). This sentiment was echoed by other Indigenous people: 'It was never about guilt. It's history. The truth is the truth' (Neil Barney, Melbourne, quoted by Korff, 2021).

Also of significance was the way that the role of Indigenous peoples in the apology process was understood as representing a change in the dynamics of the settler–colonised relationship and providing the impetus for changes to their political, social, and economic status.

Most notably, Fontaine acknowledged how the Harper apology had been forged from the struggles of Indigenous peoples in their attempts to raise awareness of the truth and make demands for justice:

> We heard the Government of Canada take full responsibility for this dreadful chapter in our shared history. We heard the Prime Minister declare that this will never happen again. ...
>
> Brave survivors, through the telling of their painful stories, have stripped white supremacy of its authority and legitimacy. The irresistibility of speaking truth to power is real.
>
> Today is not the result of a political game. Instead, it is something that shows the righteousness and importance of our struggle.
>
> (House of Commons, Canada, 2008, p. 6854)

So understood, the apology was to be collectively celebrated as 'we ... stand on the dignity of who we are and celebrate our survival' (Grand Chief Edward John of the First Nations Summit, quoted by Kemp, 2008). In this respect, the apology was interpreted as a testament to the Survivors: 'The outstanding reality behind the apology is the extent and complexity of the resistance of our people to the assimilation project that was the purpose of the Indian residential schools experience' (Senate of Canada, 2008, p. 1503 (Fontaine)).

According to Fontaine, at the heart of that project was an understanding of Indigenous culture as inferior – an understanding which many internalised and suffered greatly. However, through a history of suffering and struggles for survival and more recent struggles for justice – compensation, commemoration, healing, a truth commission, and now an apology – the Survivors had restored their dignity and pride: 'We have fought the denial of our existence, and our people today are working hard to take the future into our own hands' (Senate of Canada, 2008, p. 1504 (Fontaine)).

Simon conveyed a similar sentiment by speaking in her Inuit language in her response to Harper's apology 'because I wanted to illustrate to you that our language and culture are still strong' (House of Commons, Canada, 2008, p. 6855). In her speech at an Inuit gathering the previous day, she summed up the significance of the suffering of the Residential School Survivors and their struggles for an apology, noting ultimately that 'the Inuit and other aboriginal peoples of Canada, whatever the struggles and oppressions and injustices of history, are here today ... and we will be here tomorrow' (Simon, 2008).

However, it was also evident in these responses that Harper's apology was viewed as creating the impetus for action on the outstanding issues facing Residential School Survivors, as well as those facing Indigenous peoples more broadly.

With respect to the former, both Simon and Chartier called for specific protection of the rights of those Inuit and Métis Residential School Survivors who had been excluded from the *Settlement Agreement* (Senate of Canada, 2008, pp. 1505–1506). There were different reasons for their exclusion, varying from region to region. In an interview, Simon explained (for example) that the Inuit who attended schools in Labrador were excluded from the *Agreement* because they were run by the provincial government and not by the federal government. 'There's no record of them being at that school, even though they were', she explained; yet these students suffered the same abuses and effects as other Residential School Survivors and their children (Fiddler, 2008). This sense of exclusion extended to the apology. For instance, the three Inuit representatives who flew from Labrador to Ottawa to hear the apology interpreted their exclusion from the *Settlement Agreement* and the fact they had not been formally invited to Ottawa as meaning that the apology was not 'intended for us' (Kemp, 2008).

Métis Survivors who attended church-run, government-sanctioned schools, and thousands more who attended day schools run by religious orders, had also been excluded from the *Settlement Agreement.* Their exclusion, as Chartier explained in the Senate: 'is part of a general pattern of exclusion starting with the refusal of the federal government to accept constitutional responsibility to deal with the Métis nation under section 91.24 of the Constitution Act, 1867' (Senate of Canada, 2008, p. 1506).

As a result, Chartier further explained, Métis peoples have been excluded from a range of policies and programmes which automatically apply to other Indigenous peoples because they do not come under federal jurisdiction. His basic claim, therefore, was for Métis peoples to stop being the 'exception': 'We want to stop being the "except-able" people; we want to be the "accepted" people. We want to get there soon because our people are suffering' (Senate of Canada, 2008, p. 1507).

With respect to the issues facing Indigenous peoples more broadly, Fontaine drew on the struggles and triumphs of Residential School Survivors to insist that '[w]e know we have many difficult issues to handle. There are many fights still to be fought' (House of Commons, Canada, 2008, p. 6854). In the Senate, he elaborated on the need for basic human rights protections:

> We want to rid ourselves of the terrible conditions that impede too many of our communities. We want to eradicate First Nations' poverty. We want to become real contributors to Canada's prosperity. We want our children to go to school in an environment that is conducive to learning. We want our communities to have safe drinking water. We want to be able to address the severe housing crisis that too many of our communities face.
>
> We want our children, the approximately 27,000 First Nation children who are in state care, to be returned to their families and their communities. We want the many young men and women who are incarcerated to be set free. We want to be able to provide our young men and women with the hope that their lives will be better, that they will be respected and that there will be opportunities for them to create for themselves a lives worthy of living, so that we do not experience some of the highest suicide rates in the world. We do not want to see our children end up in gangs.
>
> We want what the rest of the country has. We want what every Canadian expects from their governments, and that expectation is to be treated fairly and justly.
>
> We want what Canadians expect in their own lives. We do not want any more than other Canadians have. We are certainly not interested in depriving anyone, but we expect to be treated fairly and justly.
>
> (Senate of Canada, 2008, p. 1504)

Jacobs (then President of the National Aboriginal Women's Association of Canada) further recognised that the wrongs committed against Indigenous peoples amounted to nothing less than 'major human rights violations' which needed to be addressed: 'What is it that this government is going to do in the future to help our people?' she asked the members of the House of Commons (House of Commons, Canada, 2008, p. 6857). In acknowledging the impacts of genocidal policies such as the residential schools on Indigenous communities, and specifically the impacts on women and the matriarchal system that holds communities together, Jacobs identified the need to rebuild relationships and revitalise language, culture, and spirituality for all men and women to make sure 'we have strong nations again' (House of Commons, Canada, 2008, p. 6856). She elaborated on what was needed in an article published in the same year where she called on government for a process:

> to ensure that the financial resources are in place to deal with all of the impacts we are dealing with today. When our languages are fully revitalized, then we will know that change has occurred. When Aboriginal

> women are no longer targets of violence, then we know that change has occurred. When our Nations our flourishing and no longer living in poverty, then we know that change has occurred. I look forward to the day when we are no longer fighting for equality because we have reclaimed our way of being.
>
> (Jacobs, 2008, p. 225)

Respect would be central to the implementation of this process. In an interview after the apology, Jacobs explained that those in government 'need to start respecting us as a people in those original relationships and [accepting] that we can make decisions on our own and we know what needs to be done in our communities' (Fiddler, 2008). She was not alone. Simon in both the Senate and the House of Commons also claimed that the apology offered an opportunity to both the Inuit and the government to transform their relationship from one based on unfulfilled promises into one based on 'respect for who we are, our traditions, history, language and culture' (Senate of Canada, 2008, p. 1505):

> Let us now join forces with the common goal of working together to ensure that this apology opens the door to a new chapter in our lives as aboriginal peoples and in our place in Canada. …
>
> This can be achieved only when dignity, confidence and respect for traditional values and human rights once again become part of our daily lives and are mirrored in our relationships with governments and other Canadians.
>
> (House of Common, Canada, 2008, p. 6856)

Simon also made it clear that the success of the new relationship would depend on government action *and* the involvement of Aboriginal peoples:

> We must be in the room working together with government to build this new relationship.
>
> Gone are the days when policy or legislative initiatives were invoked for us.
>
> (Senate of Canada, 2008, p. 1505)

Similar sentiments were expressed in Australia with respect to the Rudd apology. For instance, both Calma and Dodson drew on the moral force of an apology in reconciling relationships to support the development of a 'new' relationship based on a consultative and participatory model, with Indigenous peoples taking an active role in the development and administration of future Indigenous policies. Calma drew on the way the apology had come about in Australia as providing the model for future dealings between Indigenous peoples and the state. The discussions with representatives of the Stolen

Generations prior to Rudd making the apology were seen by him as the first steps in a new partnership for implementation of the reforms proposed in *BTH* (Calma, 2008, pp. 3–4). Accordingly, he called on governments across Australia to implement all the remaining recommendations in *BTH* and on the federal government for leadership to make this happen. He also called for a whole-of-government approach to create a partnership with Stolen Generations groups, Link Ups, and other service providers for specific assistance to those affected by the forced child removal practice, tailored to their specific circumstances, and with their ongoing consultation and participation (Calma, 2008, pp. 3–4).

Dodson's suggestions were based on a similar model but envisaged more extensive reforms. His understanding of the apology 'as an epic gesture on the part of the Australian settler state to find accommodation with the dispossessed and colonised' was translated into the need to develop:

> practical public policy that recognises the fact that Indigenous society – which draws on thousands of years of cultural and religious connection to Australian lands – has survived. We are capable of creating a relationship where the imperatives of Indigenous life are understood and respected by governments and institutionalised as part of good governance. ...
>
> What greater achievement could we bequeath our children than a nation united, where its Indigenous people and their cultures, laws and languages are central to the foundations of the nation-state?
>
> (Dodson, 2008, pp. 22, 23)

In these respects, he drew on the survival of Indigenous cultural traditions, evidence of broader national support for the recognition of Indigenous peoples, and the impact of the apology itself, as supporting a more far-reaching reform agenda. Indeed, he referred to the opening of Parliament by a historic Welcome to Country ceremony the previous day as evidence of how Australia's institutions, steeped in the Westminster tradition, could change:[8] 'I look forward to the Usher of the Black Rod one day carrying a woman's digging stick, a powerful symbol of sustenance and strength' (Dodson, 2008, pp. 21–22).

Of particular significance was how Dodson drew on Rudd's metaphor for the apology as 'a new page in Australia's history' (House of Representatives, Australia, 2008, p. 167) as a way of re-imagining Australia 'as a different place' (Dodson, 2008, p. 21). The new Australia he imagined would be:

> A place where Aboriginal citizens no longer live in third world conditions. A place where our kids are safe. A place where community rights – of choice, consultation, participation and responsibility – matter more than administrative procedures and public sector management guidelines.
>
> (Dodson, 2008, p. 21)

To make this imagined world a reality, Dodson called for the adoption of a more holistic approach to the unfinished business in Australia that would ensure protection for the rights of Indigenous peoples. In summary, these included:

1 Constitutional recognition;
2 Supporting Aboriginal regional governance structures for the better delivery of services and for the development of strategies to address the key issues facing Aboriginal communities;
3 Addressing the overrepresentation of Aboriginal people in Australian prison systems;
4 Addressing Aboriginal health and the significant gap in life expectancy which exists between Indigenous and non-Indigenous peoples;
5 Addressing suicide, drug taking and general despair that exists in so many Aboriginal communities;
6 Delivering citizenship services to Aboriginal communities which most other Australians take for granted;
7 Providing educational facilities and curricula that would enable Indigenous youth to compete in the mainstream economy and develop regional and culturally relevant industries in Aboriginal communities;
8 Addressing urgent housing needs for shelter and security;
9 Sustaining Aboriginal languages and cultural practices;
10 Reforming native title laws;
11 Compensating members of the Stolen Generations;
12 Redirecting Indigenous policy away from the neoliberalism that currently informs it – most notably in the form of the Intervention; and
13 Joining the global consensus on the *United Nations Declaration on the Rights of Indigenous Peoples* by ratifying and adopting it into national legislation, policy, and practice

(Dodson, 2008, pp. 21–23).

Although he acknowledged that a great deal of work would be needed to make the necessary changes a reality, he took the government's talk of building bridges of engagement and building a national consensus as opening the opportunity for dialogue between government and Indigenous peoples. Through such dialogue, the terms of their evolving relationship could be negotiated so that the 'appalling relationship which is at the heart of the apology' would, in time, be replaced by one based on trust, transparency, and integrity (Dodson, 2008, p. 23). In these respects, he recognised the need for Indigenous peoples to work in partnership with government, and with the support of non-Indigenous Australians, 'to address the legacy of our shared history, create pathways to reconstruct Indigenous communities and build a consensus for a lasting settlement between Indigenous people and the Australian nation-state' (Dodson, 2008, p. 23).

These calls for reform in Australia and Canada were not new. What was distinctive about them in this context was the belief that each apology had the potential to transform settler–colonised relations and forge a 'new' relationship in which Indigenous peoples' rights would be protected and they would have control of their affairs. It was the role that Indigenous peoples had played in the movements for an apology – whether through the consultation process in Australia, or in the struggle for an apology in Canada – which was now seen as legitimising their future involvement in the development and administration of Indigenous policies.

However, also evident in these responses was acceptance that change would not happen overnight. Each apology was a step – and not the end – of the process of reconciliation and would need further action to be accepted as a genuine attempt at reconciliation. Any changes would require support from non-Indigenous peoples (Dodson, 2008, p. 23; House of Commons, Canada, 2008, p. 6855 (Fontaine; Simon)) and their successful implementation would require government action – especially resources – for without them the apology 'won't mean a thing at all in the long run' (Peter Ballentyne, Cree Nation band member from Saskatchewan, quoted by Fiddler, 2008).

Accounts of the truth about history in the Rudd and Harper apologies

The acknowledgement in each apology of the truth of the history of Indigenous peoples' wrongful treatment was significant on a personal level, as evidenced by individual responses in Australia that highlighted the Rudd apology's significance for being 'the first time someone in government say that they feel sorry for us and for all that has happened to us'; for vindicating the stories of so many 'that we weren't lying about our own history, or what we went through'; and for seeing those affected 'for what's happened to them ... [which] lifted some of the shame and the pain off their shoulders' (Philpot, et al., 2013, pp. 41–42).

The acknowledgement of the truth was also seen as central to creating the conditions for a new partnership. In Australia, this understanding was made explicit by both Calma and Dodson who viewed the Rudd apology as a new beginning based on the 'truth' of the stories told by the Aboriginal and Torres Strait Islander peoples interviewed in *BTH*. As Dodson remarked: 'We know these stories are as true as they are sad. Parliament has now accepted the complicity of Australian governments in a misguided attempt to destroy our people' (Dodson, 2008, p. 20).

Equally evident in Dodson's response in Australia, and Simon's and Jacobs' responses in Canada, was the understanding that the apologies had created the potential to bring the settler–colonised relationship to an end. Indeed, the impression given by Fontaine was that Indigenous peoples, in exposing the truth about the residential schools, had completely 'stripped white supremacy of its authority and legitimacy ... [which] shows the righteousness and importance of our struggle' (House of Commons, Canada, 2008, p. 6854).

Statements such as these appear to link the respective histories of the Stolen Generations and the residential schools to the broader history of colonisation and the colonisers' drive to eliminate Indigenous peoples. If the Rudd and Harper apologies gave the impression that they were addressing the history of colonisation, it might be because they seemed cognisant of that history and its genocidal intentions. In Australia, Rudd acknowledged how in some quarters 'the forced extractions of children of so-called "mixed lineage" were seen as part of a broader policy of dealing with "the problem of the Aboriginal population"'. He further noted how their removal was treated by some as the solution to this problem because it would result in 'the complete disappearance of the black race, and the swift submergence of their progeny in the white' (House of Representatives, Australia, 2008, p. 169, quoting the Northern Territory Protector of Natives, Cecil Cook). In apologising to the Stolen Generations, he acknowledged 'the pain, suffering and hurt of these Stolen Generations, their descendants and for their families left behind'; 'the breaking up of families and communities'; '[a]nd for the indignity and degradation thus inflicted on a proud people and a proud culture' (House of Representatives, Australia, 2008, p. 167).

Similarly in Canada, Harper acknowledged how the:

> [t]wo primary objectives of the residential school system were to remove and isolate children from the influence of their homes, families, traditions and cultures, and to assimilate them into the dominant culture. These objectives assumed that aboriginal cultures and spiritual beliefs were inferior and unequal. Indeed, some sought, as was infamously said, 'to kill the Indian in the child'.
>
> (House of Commons, Canada, 2008, p. 6850)

In his apology he acknowledged the consequences of the schools' 'lasting and damaging impact on aboriginal culture, heritage and language'; 'the emotional, physical and sexual abuse and neglect of helpless children, and their separation from powerless families and communities' that took place in the schools; and the 'social problems that continue to exist in many communities today' (House of Commons, Canada, 2008, p. 6850).

One could construe such admissions as accepting that the attempt to eliminate Indigenous peoples through the forced removal of their children had been wrong and had caused a range of harms which both leaders were now willing to redress. Pertinently, the inference to an intent to eliminate Indigenous peoples raises the issue of genocide made possible by the denial of Indigenous political autonomy and infringement of their rights. Conceding that the removal of Indigenous children was a direct attack on Indigenous peoples' culture alludes to an attack on their political autonomy, which is intrinsic to Indigenous culture. This is evident in the inherent rights Indigenous peoples claim to have over their lands (Behrendt, 2010, pp. 173–174; Lindberg, 2010, pp. 89–91) and children (Butler, 1993; Harris-Short, 2012, p. 150).

In this regard, it is important to acknowledge that while colonisation was institutionalised through the (albeit implicit) application of the doctrines of discovery and terra nullius over the lands of Indigenous peoples in nations such as Australia and Canada (Ritter, 1996; Sanders, 1990), it has been a process that infused every facet of Indigenous peoples' lives through the subjugation of Indigenous peoples to the laws and policies of the colonisers. As was noted in Chapter 1, settler colonialism is structured by invasion and governed by the logic of elimination. It 'destroys in order to replace' and is primarily motivated by access to, and control of, territory (Wolfe, 2006, p. 388). It has been further claimed that the key mode of elimination is the persistent denial of Indigenous peoples' political autonomy (Macoun and Strakosch, 2013, p. 429) by insistence on their purported cultural deficiencies and corresponding valorisation of attributes of the colonisers as progressive and enlightened (see generally, Rose, 1996).

Another significant claim made by settler-colonial theorists and reflected in Indigenous critical perspectives (Corntassel, 2012, Watson, 2016) is that the process of colonisation is an ongoing one (Wolfe, 2006, p. 388), which has assumed a variety of forms over time. In this respect, the references in the Rudd apology to the removal of Indigenous children as a means of achieving the 'complete disappearance' of 'the problem of the Aboriginal population', and in the Harper apology to the edict to 'kill the Indian in the child' that underpinned the residential schools, reflect the attitudes of prominent administrators of the practice in each nation respectively (e.g., Cecil Cook in Australia; Duncan Campbell Scott in Canada) who explicitly sought to rid Indigenous peoples of their lands for good. These attitudes attest to the drive to eliminate Indigenous peoples that the practice of forcibly removing Indigenous children from their families formed an integral part.

The consequences of colonisation have been devastating for Indigenous peoples' connections to their lands and families and capacity to exercise political autonomy and self-determination. Indeed, it has been claimed that the only options colonisation has made available to Indigenous peoples have been those of destruction, dependency, or assimilation (Alfred, 2009, p. 53; see also Steering Committee for the Review of Government Service Provision, 2009). Decades of 'colonial exploitation and a prolonged systematic attempt to destroy Indigenous people and culture' have been identified as the main causes of Indigenous impoverishment and disadvantage today (Dudgeon, et al., 2010, p. 35; Kirmayer, Simpson and Cargo, 2003, p. 15).

This discussion can also explain why some Indigenous peoples reacted as they did to the Rudd and Harper apologies. If some Indigenous peoples interpreted each apology as a step towards bringing the settler–colonised relationship to an end, it is because colonisation itself is ultimately the source of the injustices experienced by Indigenous peoples. If these apologies for the forcible removal of children could be seen as a step in this direction, it is because the physical separation of Indigenous children from their families was part of the colonial project in its quest to undermine their political autonomy and eliminate them from their lands. In the words of Aboriginal Elder and Stolen Generations campaigner Brian Butler:

> Colonisation did not just take away our land, not just forbid us to practice our religion and custom, speak our language or observe our laws. In doing all these things it also challenged and tried to destroy our rights to our children. We have always maintained our sovereignty in these matters ...
>
> Our children are no less important than our land ... without one there will be no guarantee of the other.
>
> (Butler, 1993, p. 12)

Furthermore, if some Indigenous peoples looked to the Rudd and Harper apologies as the beginning of a new relationship in which Indigenous peoples would have a degree of political autonomy, it is because they challenge the legitimacy of state sovereignty and assert their own inherent right to sovereignty as inherited from their ancestors (Lindberg, 2010, pp. 89–90). These claims are further strengthened by the fact that despite the claims of past governments that they have sought to protect Indigenous peoples and promote their best interests, the devastating consequences of Indigenous peoples' subordination to state laws and policies have repeatedly demonstrated the converse is in fact true. According to Indigenous peoples, as evidenced in some of their responses to the Rudd and Harper apologies, their continuing survival and wellbeing depend on the creation of jurisdictional space so that they can have, as Jacobs put it, 'strong nations again' (House of Commons, Canada, 2008, p. 6856).

Saying 'sorry' for the forced removal of Indigenous children could have resulted in the creation of jurisdictional space, since the making of an apology, as previously discussed in Chapter 2, requires the wrongdoer to see the injustices as the victims see them, and redress them accordingly. Whether Rudd and Harper shared this understanding will be explored in the next chapter.

Conclusion

In light of this discussion, it is apparent that some Indigenous peoples looked to the Rudd and Harper apologies as a step in overcoming the legacies of colonisation, notwithstanding that each apology was focused on the forced removal of Indigenous children. This is understandable considering that the practice of removal was symptomatic of the broader project of colonisation and not separate from it. The inference to be drawn from the Rudd and Harper apologies was that their acceptance that the forced removal of Indigenous children was wrong might extend to an acceptance that it had involved an illegitimate use of state power in perpetuating the denial of the legitimacy of Indigenous political autonomy and law. The effects of this include the range of social, economic, and political areas of Indigenous peoples' lives upon which colonisation has had negative impacts. To address these effects would require transforming the existing settler–colonised relationship through the creation of a partnership between Indigenous and non-Indigenous peoples. Through this partnership, the legacies of those who did and did not survive the attempts made to eliminate them, and of those who struggled for the truth of this history to be accepted in an apology, would live on through the realisation of Indigenous peoples' claims for justice. Indeed, the realisation of such claims would further testify to Indigenous peoples' survival of the processes of colonisation, as made manifest in their struggles for an apology.

Notes

1 Two examples that demonstrate some of the more oppressive aspects of this era were in the areas of employment and child welfare, creating what is commonly referred to respectively as 'Stolen Wages' (Senate Standing Committee on Legal and Constitutional Affairs, 2006) and the 'Stolen Generations'. The issues of stolen lands, stolen wages, and stolen children are interrelated. Under the policy of protection, the removal of Indigenous peoples from the land would make more land available for the colonisers, while the removal of the children from what was perceived to be the negative influences of tribal life would produce an exploitable source of labour.

2 In Australia, legal constructions of Aboriginality based according to bloodlines also applied to erase the existence of Indigenous kinship ties and ties to land. As the number of 'half-caste' children increased, legislators modified the definition of 'an Aborigine' to include more and categories of people that they could assert control over and regulate their sexual relations and marriage choices (Markus, 1987, pp. 49–53).

3 A similar approach to child welfare was adopted in Canada in the latter half of the twentieth century, creating what is now referred to as the 'Sixties Scoop', which relates to the removal of thousands of children from their families into the care of non-Indigenous families. Like the Australian experience, it was believed that because the children were not being cared for according to middle-class Euro-Canadian values, they were not being adequately cared for at all (Hanson, 2009b).

4 Note that at the time of confederation the Canadian Parliament did not assume jurisdiction over the Inuit or Métis peoples. However, the policy of assimilation applied to them as is evident in the history of the residential school system during which time all children from distinct Indigenous communities were 'completely vulnerable to forced removal and institutionalisation to expedite the goal of assimilation' (Morse, 2008, p. 43).

5 In 1850, the Province of Canada (then a British Colony) began to pass legislation which gave it authority to determine who possessed Indian Status. Between 1857 and 1874 more legislation was enacted which created (among others) a process of

enfranchisement that was designed to strip Indigenous peoples of their Indian Status so they may become full British subjects; gave the federal government exclusive jurisdiction over Indigenous peoples and their lands; introduced the concepts of Status and non-Status Indians; and placed severe restrictions on Indigenous land ownership (Harry, 2009, pp. 9–10).

6 Colonial patriarchy was infused in the *Indian Act* in ways that undermined traditional family ties and connections to land. In particular, the *Indian Act* imposed an artificial patriarchal structure on Aboriginal communities by placing a stronger emphasis on male lineage in its definition of Indian Status. The effect was to exclude Indian women married to non-Indian or non-Status Indian men and their descendants from residing on the reservation and from sharing in the benefits available to their communities (Harry, 2009, pp. 18–19). Moreover, the *Indian Act* explicitly denied Indian Status to the Métis and Inuit peoples (Makarenko, 2008). Amendments to the *Indian Act* have proven to be ineffective in overcoming all its sexist aspects (Lovelace Nicholas and Francis, 2022).

7 These principles have since been adopted in the *Basic Principles and Guidelines on the Right to a Remedy and Reparation for Victims of Gross Violations of International Human Rights Law and Serious Violations of International Humanitarian Law* (United Nations, 2005).

8 Matilda House Williams, Ngamberi-Ngunnawal Elder and a traditional custodian of the land on which the Australian Parliament House stands, addressed members of both Houses of Parliament in the Member's Hall in Parliament House as part of the Welcome to Country ceremony to mark the opening of the 42nd sitting of Parliament. She was accompanied by her son and grandchildren. The grandchildren handed a message stick to the Prime Minister and House delivered her speech to the members of both Houses of Parliament. The ceremony was accompanied by Aboriginal and Torres Strait Islander dancers and singers from around the country who were there to celebrate the occasion with the Ngamberi-Ngunnawal traditional owners. Notably, House's interpretation of the Welcome to Country ceremony on this occasion was consistent with Calma's and Dodson's understandings of the apology as bringing Indigenous and non-Indigenous peoples together on mutual terms:

> 'Prime Minister, my grandchildren have handed you a gift, a message stick, a tangible symbol of today's ceremony.
>
> 'The message stick is a means of communication used by our peoples for thousands of years. They tell the story of our coming together. With this renewed hope, our pride and our strength is refreshed'
>
> (quoted in McAuley, 2011, p. 9).

Reference list

Aboriginal and Torres Strait Islander Social Justice Commissioner of the Human Rights and Equal Opportunity Commission, 2003, *Submission to the Northern Territory Law Reform Committee Inquiry into Aboriginal Customary Law in the Northern Territory*, https://humanrights.gov.au/our-work/legal/sju-submission-inquiry-aboriginal-customary-law-nt

Ahmed, S., 2004, *The cultural politics of emotion*, Edinburgh University Press, Edinburgh.

Alfred, T., 2009, 'Colonialism and state dependency', *Journal of Aboriginal Health*, vol. 5, pp. 42–60.

Altman, J. and Fogarty, B., 2010, 'Indigenous Australians as "no gaps" subjects: education and development in remote Australia', in I. Snyder and J. Nieuwenhuysen (eds), *Closing the gap in education: improving outcomes in southern world societies*, Monash University Publishing, Victoria, pp. 109–128, http://hdl.handle.net/1885/9738

Amnesty International, n.d., *The NT intervention and human rights*, https://www.amnesty.org/en/wp-content/uploads/2021/05/SEC010032010ENGLISH.pdf

Assembly of First Nations, 2004, *Report on Canada's dispute resolution plan to compensate for abuses in Indian residential schools*, https://collections.irshdc.ubc.ca/index.php/Detail/objects/8639

Assembly of First Nations, 2015, *Residential schools – a chronology*, https://www.rememberingthechildren.ca/history/index.htm

Attwood, B., 1996, 'Introduction', in B. Attwood (ed.), *In the age of Mabo*, Allen & Unwin, Sydney, pp. vii–xxxviii.

Australian Government, 2023, *Enhanced income management – Northern Territory*, https://www.dss.gov.au/families-and-children-programs-services-welfare-reform-enhanced-income-management/enhanced-income-management-northern-territory

Bartlett, R., 2014, 'Indigenous rights in and control of resource development: the contrast between the Australian and Canadian law of native title', *Australian Resources and Energy Law Journal*, vol. *33*, no. *3*, pp. 311–324.

Behrendt, L., 2005, *The abolition of ATSIC – implications for democracy*, Democratic Audit of Australia – November 2005, https://library.bsl.org.au/jspui/bitstream/1/679/1/200511_behrendt_atsic.pdf

Behrendt, L., 2010. 'The doctrine of discovery in Australia', in R.J. Miller, J. Ruru, L. Behrendt and T. Lindberg (eds), *Discovering Indigenous lands: the doctrine of discovery in the English colonies*, Oxford University Press, Oxford, pp. 171–186.

Behrendt, L., Cunneen, C., Libesman, T. and Watson, N., 2019, *Aboriginal and Torres Strait Islander legal relations*, 2nd edn, Oxford University Press, Australia.

Behrendt, L. and McCausland, R., 2008, *Welfare payments and school attendance: an analysis of experimental policy in Indigenous education*, https://web.archive.org/web/20150322174005/http:/www.aeufederal.org.au/Publications/2008/LBehrendtpaper.pdf

Blainey, G., 1993. 'Drawing up a balance sheet of our history', *Quadrant*, vol. *38*, no. *7–8*, pp. 10–15.

Bolton, G.C., 1982, 'Aborigines in social history: an overview', in R.M. Berndt (ed.), *Aboriginal sites, rights and resource development*, University of Western Australia Press, Perth, pp. 59–68.

Broome, R., 1994, *Aboriginal Australians*, 2nd edn, Allen & Unwin, Sydney.

Butler, B., 1993, 'Aboriginal children: back to origins', *Family Matters*, no. *35*, pp. 7–12.

Buti, A., 2002, 'The removal of Aboriginal children: Canada and Australia compared', *University of Western Sydney Law Review*, vol. *6*, no. *1*, pp. 26–37.

Calgary, S.G., 2007, 'Aboriginal healing methods for residential school abuse and intergenerational effects: a review of the literature', *Journal of Native Social Work*, vol. *6*, pp. 11–32.

Calma, T., 2008, *Let the healing begin: response to government to the national apology to the Stolen Generations*, 13 February, https://humanrights.gov.au/sites/default/files/content/pdf/social_justice/speech/let_the_healing_begin.pdf

Campion-Smith, B., 2008, *Harper officially apologizes for Native residential schools*, https://www.thestar.com/news/canada/2008/06/11/harper_officially_apologizes_for_native_residential_schools.html

Commonwealth of Australia, 1937, *Aboriginal welfare: initial conference of Commonwealth and state Aboriginal authorities*, 21–23 April, https://aiatsis.gov.au/sites/default/files/catalogue_resources/20663.pdf

Commonwealth of Australia, 2002, *Commonwealth government response to the Council for Aboriginal Reconciliation final report – Reconciliation: Australia's challenge*, Department of Immigration and Multicultural and Indigenous Affairs, Canberra.

Commonwealth of Australia Constitution Act, 1900, 63 & 64 Vict., c. 12, s. 9 (Imp.).

Constitution Act, 1867, 30 & 31 Vict., c. 3 (UK).

Corntassel, J., 2012, 'Re-envisioning resurgence: Indigenous pathways to decolonization and sustainable self-determination', *Decolonization: Indigeneity, Education & Society*, vol. *1*, no. *1*, pp. 86–101.

Council for Aboriginal Reconciliation, 2000a, *Reconciliation: Australia's challenge*, http://www5.austlii.edu.au/au/orgs/car/finalreport/contents.htm

Council for Aboriginal Reconciliation, 2000b, *The Australian declaration towards reconciliation*, http://www5.austlii.edu.au/au/orgs/car/finalreport/appendices01.htm

Council for Aboriginal Reconciliation Act, 1991 (Cth).

Crimes Act, 1914 (Cth).

Cubillo v. Commonwealth (2001) 174 ALR 97.

Department of the Prime Minister and Cabinet, 1992, *Speech by the Hon Prime Minister, P.J. Keating MP*, 10 December, https://pmtranscripts.pmc.gov.au/sites/default/files/original/00008765.pdf

Dodson, P., 2008, 'After the apology', *Arena Magazine*, April–May, vol. *94*, pp. 20–23.

Dudgeon, P., Wright, M., Paradies, Y., Garvey, D. and Walker, I., 2010, 'The social, cultural and historical context of Aboriginal and Torres Strait Islander Australians,' in N. Purdie, P. Dudgeon and R. Walker (eds), *Working together: Aboriginal and Torres Strait Islander mental health and wellbeing principles and practice*, Department of Health and Aging, Canberra, Department of Health and Aging, Canberra, pp. 25–42.

'Editorial', 1993, *Aboriginal Law Bulletin*, vol. *3*, no. *61*, p. 3.

Farber, B.M., 2013, 'Op-ed: the troubling legacy of Duncan Campbell Scott', *BishopAccountability.org*, 26 August, https://www.bishop-accountability.org/news2013/07_08/2013_08_26_Farber_OpedThe.htm

Fiddler, C., 2008, 'Gov't of Canada apologize for 100 years of atrocities', *Windspeaker*, vol. *26*, no. *4*, http://www.ammsa.com/publications/windspeaker/govt-canada-apologize-100-years-atrocities

Fitzpatrick, M. and Nguyen, L., 2008, 'Aboriginal leaders hail historic apology', *Windsor Star*, 11 June, http://www.bishop-accountability.org/news2008/05_06/2008_06_11_Fitzpatrick_AboriginalLeaders.htm

Funk-Unrau, N., 2014, 'The Canadian apology to Indigenous Residential School Survivors: a case study of renegotiation of social relations', in M. Mihai and M. Thaler (eds), *On the uses and abuses of political apologies*, Palgrave Macmillan, London, pp. 138–153, DOI:10.1057/9781137343727_8

Gartrell, A., 2008, '"New era" dawns after Indigenous apology', *The Sydney Morning Herald*, 13 February, https://www.smh.com.au/national/new-era-dawns-after-indigenous-apology-20080213-1rv4.html

Gibson, P., 2017, '10 impacts of the NT intervention', *NITV*, 21 June, https://www.sbs.com.au/nitv/article/10-impacts-of-the-nt-intervention/vzia753tx

Govier, T., 2006, *Taking wrongs seriously: acknowledgement, reconciliation, and the politics of sustainable peace*, Humanity Books, New York.

Hanson, E., 2009a, *The Indian Act*, First Nations and Indigenous studies, University of British Columbia, https://indigenousfoundations.arts.ubc.ca/the_indian_act/

Hanson, E., 2009b, *Sixties scoop*, First Nations and Indigenous studies, University of British Columbia, http://indigenousfoundations.arts.ubc.ca/sixties_scoop/

Harris-Short, S., 2012, *Aboriginal child welfare, self-government and the rights of Indigenous children: protecting the vulnerable under international law*, Ashgate, Farnham.

Harry, K., 2009, *The Indian Act & Aboriginal women's empowerment: what front line workers need to know*, Battered Women's Support Services, https://www.bwss.org/wp-content/uploads/theindianactaboriginalwomensempowerment.pdf

Hasluck, P., 1961, *The policy of assimilation*, *Decisions of Commonwealth and State Ministers at the Native Welfare Conference*, 26–27 January, Canberra, https://aiatsis.gov.au/sites/default/files/catalogue_resources/18801.pdf

Hennessy, P., 2008, 'Resolving claims of abuse in Native residential schools: the court's role in Canada's settlement process', *9th Biennial Conference of the International Association of Women Judges*, 25–28 March, Panama City, Panama.

Herron, J., 2000, *Federal government submission: Senate Legal and Constitutional References Committee inquiry into the Stolen Generations*, Parliament of Australia, Canberra.

Hoffman, S., 2000, 'United Nations Committee on the Elimination of Racial Discrimination: consideration of Australia under its early warning measures and urgent action procedures', *Australian Journal of Human Rights*, vol. *6*. no. *1*, pp. 13–33.

Hopper, T., 2008, 'Harper's apology paves way for Native health care reforms', *Yukon News*, 14 June, http://yukon-news.com/news/harpers-apology-paves-way-for-native-health-care-reforms

Horelt, M., 2011, 'Performing reconciliation: a performance approach to the analysis of political apologies', in N. Palmer, D. Granville and P. Clark (eds), *Critical perspectives on transitional justice*, Intersentia, Cambridge, pp. 347–370.

House of Commons, Canada, 2008, *House of Commons Debates (Hansard)*, 39th Parl., 2nd Sess., vol. *142*, no. *110*, 11 June, https://www.ourcommons.ca/Content/House/392/Debates/110/HAN110-E.PDF

House of Representatives, Australia, 2008, 'Apology to Australia's Indigenous Peoples', *Parliamentary Debates*, 13 February, https://parlinfo.aph.gov.au/parlInfo/genpdf/chamber/hansardr/2008-02-13/0003/hansard_frag.pdf;fileType=application/pdf

Howard, J., 1996, 'The liberal tradition: the beliefs and values which guide the federal government', Annual Sir Robert Menzies Lecture, Monash University, Melbourne, 18 November, https://pmtranscripts.pmc.gov.au/sites/default/files/original/00010171.pdf

Howard-Wagner, D. and Kelly, B., 2011, 'Containing Aboriginal mobility in the Northern Territory: from "protectionism" to "interventionism"', *Law Text Culture*, vol. *15*, pp. 102–134.

Human Rights and Equal Opportunity Commission, 1997, *Bringing them home: report of the National Inquiry into the Separation of Aboriginal and Torres Strait Islander Children from their Homes*, Sterling Press, Sydney.

Indian Act, 1876, Vict. 39, c. 18.

Indian Residential Schools Settlement Agreement, 2006, 8 May, https://residentialschoolsettlement.ca/IRS%20Settlement%20Agreement-%20ENGLISH.pdf

Jacobs, B., 2008, 'Response to Canada's apology to Residential School Survivors', *Canadian Woman Studies/Les Cahiers De La Femme*, vol. *26*, no. *3, 4*, pp. 223–225.

Jung, C., 2010, 'Canada and the legacy of the Indian residential schools: transitional justice for Indigenous people in a nontransitional society', in P. Arthur (ed.), *Identities in transition: challenges for transitional justice in divided societies*, Cambridge University Press, New York, pp. 217–250, DOI:10.1017/CBO9780511976858.008

Kemp, B., 2008, 'Putting the pain behind them', *CBC News*, 11 June, http://www.cbc.ca/news/canada/putting-the-pain-behind-them-1.710407

Kirmayer, L., Simpson, C. and Cargo, M., 2003, 'Healing traditions: culture, community and mental health promotion with Canadian Aboriginal peoples', *Australasian Psychiatry*, vol. *11*, no. *1*, pp. 15–23, DOI:10.1046/j.1038-5282.2003.02010.x

Korff, J., 2021, '"Sorry" apology to Stolen Generations', *Creative Spirits*, 14 January, https://www.creativespirits.info/aboriginalculture/politics/stolen-generations/sorry-apology-to-stolen-generations

Kruger v. Commonwealth (1997) 190 CLR 1.

Langford, R., 1983, 'Our heritage – your playground', *Australian Archaeology*, vol. *16*, pp. 1–6.

Lindberg, T., 2010, 'The doctrine of discovery in Canada', in R.J. Miller, J. Ruru, L. Behrendt and T. Lindberg (eds), *Discovering Indigenous lands: the doctrine of discovery in the English colonies*, pp. 89–125, Oxford University Press, Oxford, DOI:10.1093/acprof:oso/9780199579815.003.0004

Lovelace Nicholas, S.M. and Francis, B., 2022, 'First Nations women, children deserve federal action to address ongoing Indian Act discrimination', *SenCA+ Magazine*, 28 July, https://sencanada.ca/en/sencaplus/opinion/first-nations-women-children-deserve-federal-action-to-address-ongoing-indian-act-discrimination/

Mabo v. Queensland (No. 2) (1992) 175 CLR 1.

MacCharles, T., 2008, 'Conservative MP apologizes for "hurtful" remarks', *Toronto Star*, 13 June, https://www.thestar.com/news/canada/2008/06/13/conservative_mp_apologizes_for_hurtful_remarks.html

Macklin, J., 2018, 'How we said sorry: reflecting on the apology, a decade on', *Meanjin Quarterly*, https://meanjin.com.au/essays/how-we-said-sorry-reflecting-on-the-apology-a-decade-on/

MacLachlan, A., 2013, 'Government apologies to Indigenous peoples', in A. MacLachlan and A. Speight (eds), *Justice responsibility and reconciliation in the wake of conflict*, Springer, Dordrecht, pp. 183–203, DOI:10.1007/978-94-007-5201-6_11

Macoun, A. and Strakosch, E., 2013, 'The ethical demands of settler colonial theory', *Settler Colonial Studies*, vol. *3*, no. *3–4*, pp. 426–443, DOI:10.1080/2201473X.2013.810695

Makarenko, J., 2008, *The Indian Act: historical overview*, re:politics, https://repolitics.com/features/the-indian-act-historical-overview/#early

Manne, R., 2001, *In denial: the Stolen Generations and the right*, Australian Quarterly Essay, Black Inc., Melbourne.

Markus, A., 1987, 'Under the Act', in B. Gammage and P. Spearritt (eds), *Australians 1938*, Fairfax, Syme & Weldon Associates, Sydney, pp. 47–53.

Markus, A., 1990, *Governing savages*, Allen & Unwin, Sydney.

Markus, A., 1994, *Australian race relations 1788–1993*, Allen & Unwin, Sydney.

McAuley, G., 2011, 'The national apology three years later', *Australian Studies*, vol. *3*, pp. 1–25.

Miller, J.R., 2013, *Residential schools and reconciliation*, Active History, http://activehistory.ca/papers/history-papers-13

Morse, B.W., 2008, 'Government responses to the Indian residential schools settlement in Canada: implications for Australia', *Australian Indigenous Law Review*, vol. *12*, no. *1*, pp. 41–59.

Native Title Act, 1993 (Cth).

Nobles, M., 2008, *The politics of official apologies*, Cambridge University Press, New York, DOI:10.1017/CBO9780511756252

Northern and Central Land Councils, 1988, 'The Barunga Statement', *Land Rights News*, vol. *29*, p. 26.

Northern Territory National Emergency Response Act, 2007 (Cth).

Philpot, C., Balvin, N., Mellor, D. and Bretherton, D., 2013, 'Making meaning from collective apologies: Australia's apology to its Indigenous peoples', *Peace and Conflict: Journal of Peace Psychology*, vol. *19*, no. *1*, pp. 34–50, DOI:10.1037/a0031267

Proudfoot, F. and Habibis, D., 2015, 'Separate worlds: a discourse analysis of mainstream and Aboriginal populist media accounts of the Northern Territory Emergency Response in 2007', *Journal of Sociology*, vol. *51*, no. 2, pp. 170–188, DOI:10.1177/1440783313482368

Read, P., 1982, *The Stolen Generations: the removal of Aboriginal children in New South Wales 1883 to 1969*, Government Printer, Sydney.

Renes, C.M., 2011, 'The Stolen Generations, a narrative of removal, displacement and recovery', in C.M. Renes (ed.), *Lives in migration: rupture and continuity*, University of Barcelona, Spain, pp. 30–49.

Reynolds, H., 1982, *The other side of the frontier*, Penguin, Ringwood.

Ritter, D., 1996, 'The "rejection of terra nullius" in Mabo: a critical analysis', *Sydney Law Review*, vol. *18*, no. *1*, pp. 5–33.

Rose, D., 1996, 'Land rights and deep colonising: the erasure of women', *Aboriginal Law Bulletin*, vol. *3*, no. *85*, pp. 6–13.

Royal Commission into Aboriginal Deaths in Custody, 1991, *Royal Commission into Aboriginal Deaths in Custody national report*, http://www.austlii.edu.au/au/other/IndigLRes/rciadic/index.html

Royal Commission on Aboriginal Peoples, 1996a, *Highlights from the report of the Royal Commission on Aboriginal Peoples*, Minister of Supply and Services Canada, https://static1.squarespace.com/static/562e7f2ae4b018ac41a6e050/t/59d0024a9f74567b7ee58b43/1506804313123/RCAP_reading.pdf

Royal Commission on Aboriginal Peoples, 1996b, *Report of the Royal Commission on Aboriginal Peoples*, Ottawa.

Sanders, D., 1990, 'The Supreme Court of Canada and the "legal and political struggle" over Indigenous rights', *Canadian Ethnic Studies*, vol. *22*, no. *3*, pp. 122–129.

Senate of Canada, 2008, *Debates of the Senate (Hansard)*, 39th Parl., 2nd Sess., vol. *144*, no. *69*, 12 June, https://sencanada.ca/Content/SEN/Chamber/392/Debates/pdf/069db_2008-06-12-e.pdf

Senate Standing Committee on Legal and Constitutional Affairs, 2006, *Unfinished business: Indigenous stolen wages*, https://www.aph.gov.au/Parliamentary_Business/Committees/Senate/Legal_and_Constitutional_Affairs/Completed_inquiries/2004-07/stolen_wages/report/index

Short, D., 2008, *Reconciliation and colonial power: Indigenous rights in Australia*, Ashgate, Aldershot.

Simon, M., 2008, *Speeches in response to apology to Residential School Survivors, Tuesday June 10, 2008, Tungasuvvingat Inuit Gathering*, http://web.archive.org/web/20130720141250/https://www.itk.ca/media/speech/speeches-response-apology-residential-school-survivors

Steering Committee for the Review of Government Service Provision, 2009, *Overcoming Indigenous disadvantage: key indicators 2009*, https://www.pc.gov.au/ongoing/overcoming-indigenous-disadvantage/2009/key-indicators-2009.pdf

Stewart, J., 1998, *Address by the Honourable Jane Stewart Minister of Indian Affairs and Northern Development on the occasion of the unveiling of Gathering Strength – Canada's Aboriginal Action Plan*, 7 January, https://www.rcaanc-cirnac.gc.ca/eng/1100100015725/1571590271585

'Tiga Bayles – response to the 2008 apology', 2018, in JOL Admin (ed.), *Responses to the national apology to the Stolen Generations*, 12 February, State Library of Queensland, https://www.slq.qld.gov.au/blog/responses-national-apology-stolen-generations-brisbane

Treaty 6 Education, n.d., *Residential schools: the legacy continues*, https://treaty6education.lskysd.ca/residentialschools2.html

Truth and Reconciliation Commission of Canada, 2012, *Canada, Aboriginal peoples, and residential schools: they came for the children*, https://publications.gc.ca/collections/collection_2012/cvrc-trcc/IR4-4-2012-eng.pdf

United Nations, 1948, *Convention on the Prevention and Punishment of the Crime of Genocide*, General Assembly Resolution 260 A (III).

United Nations, 1965, *International Convention on the Elimination of All Forms of Racial Discrimination*, General Assembly Resolution 2106 (XX).

United Nations, 2005, *Basic Principles and Guidelines on the Right to a Remedy and Reparation for Victims of Gross Violations of International Human Rights Law and Serious Violations of International Humanitarian Law*, General Assembly Resolution 60/147.

Watson, I., 2016, 'First Nations and the colonial project', *Inter Gentes*, vol. *1* no. *1*, pp. 30–39.

Wearne, H., 1980, *A clash of cultures: Queensland Aboriginal policy (1824–1980): an analysis of the Aborigines Act 1971–79, regulations of 1972 and by-laws*, Uniting Church of Australia, Brisbane.

Wolfe, P., 2006, 'Settler colonialism and the elimination of the Native', *Journal of Genocide Research*, vol. *8*, no. *4*, pp. 387–409, DOI:10.1080/14623520601056240

Wootten, H., 1998, 'Ron Brunton & bringing them home', *Indigenous Law Bulletin*, vol. *4*, no. *12*, pp. 4–8.

Chapter 4

The Rudd and Harper apologies critically examined

Introduction

The discussion in the previous chapter provided insight into why some Indigenous peoples may have responded positively to the Rudd and Harper apologies. These reactions may be explicable in terms of their broader and more immediate histories of the apologies; specifically, the struggles of Indigenous peoples, and their ultimate success, in securing an apology in each nation. They may also reflect certain understandings of the content of each apology. The focus of the apologies on the history of the forced removal of Indigenous children from their families was understood as leading the way towards a just resolution for those affected by this practice. More broadly, some construed the apologies as taking a step closer towards ending the settler–colonised relationship and realising Indigenous peoples' broader claims for justice.

This chapter critically examines both apologies to determine whether Rudd and Harper shared the same understanding. In particular, the focus is on the account of the history of injustice in each apology and whether this account could result in outcomes that are consistent with the claims of Indigenous peoples as were outlined in Chapter 3. A historical account that accords with Indigenous peoples' perspectives not only vindicates Indigenous peoples' understandings of the wrongs committed against them but provides a framework for understanding the measures needed to overcome the harms suffered.

To begin, the chapter assesses the apologies against the main criteria for making an apology (naming the wrongs; accepting responsibility for them; expressing regret for the wrongdoing; and making commitments for forbearance and reform in the future). It is apparent that when measured against these criteria the apologies appear to be advancing justice for Indigenous peoples and reconciliation on this basis. However, a closer analysis of both apologies shows this was not entirely the case.

DOI: 10.4324/9781003491019-4

This becomes evident in the second part of the chapter when the apologies are examined from the perspectives of Indigenous peoples. This discussion highlights a point that was made in Chapter 2 regarding the dangers of assuming that when an apology is made there is a shared understanding of the wrongs and how to address them. Such a stance depends on the existence of a singular truth and does not make allowance for differences in perspective on 'the truth'. This approach may only obscure the imbalance of power that exists at the time an apology is made with the effect of reinforcing dominant viewpoints and marginalising Survivor viewpoints. Once it is accepted that different perspectives exist, it is no longer possible to accept representations of 'the truth' at face value. If it is accepted that an apology should aim to satisfy victims, then it is essential that it is evaluated from their perspectives.

As is evident in this chapter, when the content of the Rudd and Harper apologies are considered from more critical Indigenous perspectives, it is apparent that both apologies have limitations. Their shortcomings can be traced to the limited range of harms for which each leader was prepared to accept responsibility. Evidently, both apologies were attempting to respond to certain historical injustices experienced by Stolen Generations and Residential School Survivors. Yet, the harms as identified in each apology was largely limited to the effects of this practice that could fit established state norms. Similarly, the measures offered to redress these harms were ones that were consistent with these norms.

In developing this critique of the Rudd and Harper apologies, the discussion draws on Indigenous peoples' more negative assessments of the apologies. In many ways these critiques reflect similar aspirations of those who responded more positively to the apologies. Their main differences relate mostly to whether the apologies had the potential to realise Indigenous peoples' various claims. As the argument is developed in this chapter, it is apparent that neither apology fully acknowledged the extent of the harms suffered by the Stolen Generations and Residential School Survivors and related these harms to the broader process of colonisation. This critique reveals that neither apology really intended to change the power dynamics of the settler–colonised relationship. Instead, the final part of the chapter exposes the various ways the apologies perpetuated settler colonialism in continuing to deny Indigenous peoples' political autonomy and protection of their rights through the maintenance of the legitimacy of state sovereignty and laws.

Evidently, the apologies functioned in a paradoxical way. In making them, both Rudd and Harper sought to acknowledge and accept responsibility for (some) wrongs, but in a way that did not ultimately challenge the authority of the state to commit these wrongs. This analysis illuminates that each apology was a manifestation of the ongoing history of colonisation in maintaining the legitimacy of state power at the expense of Indigenous peoples' claims. Indigenous peoples would remain subordinate to the state and its norms, allowing each state to continue to assert what is best for them.

The Rudd and Harper apologies: advancing justice and reconciliation for Indigenous peoples

At first glance, the Rudd and Harper apologies seem to advance national reconciliation by seeking to redress Indigenous peoples' experiences of injustice. Each of them conveys an understanding of history that appears to accord with Indigenous understandings. Moreover, each leader seemed committed to reconciling history and relations in these settler-colonised nations by declaring that this treatment was wrong and accepting responsibility for it. These reconciliatory aspects are interlinked with achieving a measure of justice for Indigenous peoples. Through the expression of regret for the harms suffered, the apologies conveyed the message of respect to restore the dignity that had been harmed by the wrongdoing. Finally, each apology outlined a reform agenda to ensure against repetition of harm in the future. The following account provides a summary of these aspects in each apology. Evidently, each apology appears to adequately fulfil these criteria. However, as will be subsequently apparent, when the apologies are measured against more critical Indigenous perspectives, they both clearly fall short of meeting these Indigenous peoples' expectations.

If one of the requirements for achieving reconciliation is the acknowledgement of 'the truth' of the past, both apologies appear to advance reconciliation by the way they substantiate the facts of past injustices inflicted on Indigenous peoples. The declaration in each apology that events in the past were wrong is important in this respect. In the Rudd apology, the wrongfulness of past actions related generally to the 'past mistreatment' of Australia's Indigenous peoples and more specifically 'on the mistreatment of those who were Stolen Generations—this blemished chapter in our nation's history' (House of Representatives, Australia, 2008a, p. 167). In this respect, Rudd moved from acknowledging the wrongfulness of 'the laws and policies of successive Parliaments and governments that have inflicted profound grief, suffering and loss on these our fellow Australians' to acknowledging 'especially' the wrongfulness of the laws and policies that authorised 'the removal of Aboriginal and Torres Strait Islander children from their families, their communities and their country' (House of Representatives, Australia, 2008a, p. 167).

It is with respect to the wrongs inflicted on the Stolen Generations that Rudd set out details of the historical record. He first referred to the personal experience of Warumungu woman Nanna Nungala Fejo, who at the time of the apology was in her 80s and who, according to Rudd's account, had been wrongly removed from her warm and loving family at age four:

> Tears flowing, her mum tried clinging to the sides of the truck as her children were taken away to the Bungalow in Alice, all in the name of protection. ...

> [She] never saw her mum again. After she left the mission, her brother let her know that her mum had died years before, a broken woman fretting for the children that had literally been ripped away from her.
>
> (House of Representatives, Australia, 2008a, p. 168)

The veracity of her story is further evidenced by Rudd who identified it as one of the 'thousands, tens of thousands, of them: stories of forced separation of Aboriginal and Torres Strait Islander children from their mums and dads over the better part of a century' (House of Representatives, Australia, 2008a, p. 168). These stories are further substantiated by Rudd's reference to the *Bringing Them Home* report ('*BTH*') (Human Rights and Equal Opportunity Commission ('HREOC'), 1997) which contains firsthand testimonies of Stolen Generations members (House of Representatives, Australia, 2008a, p. 168).

In addition to these personal accounts, Rudd presented external criteria to measure the extent of the harm by referring to specific statistics that confirm the number of children removed between 1910 and 1970 to be in the vicinity of 'between 10 and 30 per cent', estimating the total number of children to be 50,000 (House of Representatives, Australia, 2008a, p. 169).[1] Significantly, he also acknowledged the source of the wrongdoing 'as part of a broader policy of dealing with "the problem of the Aboriginal population"' and specifically condemned the fact that those responsible for the removal of Indigenous children held the view that by removing the children, 'the problem of our half-castes ... will quickly be eliminated by the complete disappearance of the black race' (House of Representatives, Australia, 2008a, p. 169).

In similar vein, the Harper apology is addressed to Indigenous peoples who had been forcibly removed from their families and subjected to the Indian residential school system. In providing an account of the harms suffered by these children, Harper noted how:

> Many were inadequately fed, clothed and housed. All were deprived of the care and nurturing of their parents, grandparents and communities.
>
> First nations, Inuit and Métis languages and cultural practices were prohibited in these schools.
>
> Tragically, some of these children died while attending residential schools, and others never returned home.
>
> (House of Commons, Canada, 2008, p. 6850)

Like Rudd, Harper also provided an objective measure of the extent of harm: 'For more than a century, Indian residential schools separated over 150,000 aboriginal children from their families and communities' (House of Commons, Canada, 2008, p. 6849). Furthermore, Harper acknowledged the role of the Canadian government in the administration of the policy: 'The Government of Canada built an educational system in which very young children were often forcibly removed from their homes and often taken far from their communities' (House of Commons, Canada, 2008, p. 6850). Harper expanded on the government's involvement in the 'development and administration of these schools' that began in the 1870s, noting that there were '[o]ne hundred and thirty-two federally supported schools located in every province and territory except Newfoundland, New Brunswick, and Prince Edward Island' (House of Commons, Canada, 2008, pp. 6849–6850).

He further exposed that the rationale of the policy was to fulfil 'two primary objectives' to 'remove and isolate children from the influence of their homes, families, traditions and cultures, and to assimilate them into the dominant culture' (House of Commons, Canada, 2008, p. 6850). He acknowledged that these assumptions were based on the understanding that 'aboriginal cultures and spiritual beliefs were inferior and unequal' (House of Commons, Canada, 2008, p. 6850). Notably, he referred to the motivation behind the policy, which was to 'kill the Indian in the child' and condemned it outright: 'Today, we recognize that this policy of assimilation was wrong, has caused great harm, and has no place in our country' (House of Commons, Canada, 2008, p. 6850).

In setting out these details, both Rudd and Harper interlinked their acknowledgement that the state-sanctioned practice of forcibly removing Indigenous children from their families was wrong with their acceptance of responsibility for the harms caused by this practice. In the Rudd apology, this occurred immediately in the preamble where, in listing the harms suffered sentence by sentence, Rudd punctuated each with the phrases 'we apologise' or 'we say sorry' (House of Representatives, Australia, 2008a, p. 167). But it is in the body of the apology that Rudd offered an unequivocal apology to the Stolen Generations:

> To the stolen generations, I say the following: as Prime Minister of Australia, I am sorry. On behalf of the government of Australia, I am sorry. On behalf of the parliament of Australia, I am sorry. I offer you this apology without qualification. We apologise for the hurt, the pain and suffering that we, the parliament, have caused you by the laws that previous parliaments have enacted. We apologise for the indignity, the degradation and the humiliation these laws embodied. We offer this apology to the mothers, the fathers, the brothers, the sisters, the families and the communities whose lives were ripped apart by the actions of successive governments under successive parliaments. In making this apology, I would also like to speak personally to the members of the stolen generations and their families: to those here today, so many of you; to those listening across the nation—from Yuendumu, in the central west of the Northern Territory, to Yabara, in North Queensland, and to Pitjantjatjara in South Australia.
> (House of Representatives, Australia, 2008a, pp. 169–170)

Of note is that his acceptance of responsibility extended to the intergenerational responsibility of former Australian governments, which the former Howard government had refused to accept. As Rudd put it: 'The uncomfortable truth for us all is that the parliaments of the nation, individually and collectively, enacted statutes and delegated authority under those statutes that made the forced removal of children on racial grounds fully lawful' (House of Representatives, Australia, 2008a, p. 169).

Harper also extended a rather lengthy apology to the Residential School Survivors 'on behalf of the Government of Canada and all Canadians':

> I stand before you, in this chamber so central to our life as a country, to apologize to aboriginal peoples for Canada's role in the Indian residential schools system.
>
> To the approximately 80,000 living former students and all family members and communities, the Government of Canada now recognizes that it was wrong to forcibly remove children from their homes, and we apologize for having done this.
>
> We now recognize that it was wrong to separate children from rich and vibrant cultures and traditions, that it created a void in many lives and communities, and we apologize for having done this.
>
> We now recognize that in separating children from their families, we undermined the ability of many to adequately parent their own children and sowed the seeds for generations to follow, and we apologize for having done this.
>
> We now recognize that far too often these institutions gave rise to abuse or neglect and were inadequately controlled, and we apologize for failing to protect you.
>
> Not only did you suffer these abuses as children, but as you became parents, you were powerless to protect your own children from suffering the same experience, and for this we are sorry. ...
>
> We are sorry.
>
> (House of Commons, Canada, 2008, p. 6850)

Thus, in each apology the acceptance of responsibility is underlined by the repetition of the word 'sorry' for the harms suffered. The resolve of each leader is further evidenced by their commitments to forbearance in the future: Rudd declaring in the preamble that 'the injustices of the past must never, never happen again' (House of Representatives, Australia, 2008a, p. 167), and Harper announcing '[t]here is no place in Canada for the attitudes that inspired the Indian residential schools system to ever prevail again' (House of Commons, Canada, 2008, p. 6850). Notably, in this regard, Rudd and Harper's reactions appear not to be motivated by feelings of guilt or shame as one might expect (cf., Gaita, 1999, pp. 87–106), but may be better understood as an empathetic response to Indigenous peoples' suffering of harm.

The message is one of regret that Indigenous peoples were treated unjustly, and they now deserve an apology (cf., Muldoon, 2009, pp. 3–4).

For instance, after Rudd gave his account of the facts of history (such as Nanna Fejo's story and the stories contained in *BTH*), he declared:

> There is something terribly primal about these firsthand accounts. The pain is searing; it screams from the pages. The hurt, the humiliation, the degradation and the sheer brutality of the act of physically separating a mother from her children is a deep assault on our senses and on our most elemental humanity. ...
>
> These stories cry out to be heard; they cry out for an apology.
>
> (House of Representatives, Australia, 2008a, p. 168)

Similarly, Harper's acknowledgement and acceptance of responsibility for past harms was expressed in ways that could appeal to Indigenous peoples. Among these, he acknowledged that the residential school policy had a 'profoundly negative ... lasting and damaging impact on aboriginal culture, heritage and language'; that any positive experiences of the residential schools have been 'far overshadowed by tragic accounts of the emotional, physical and sexual abuse and neglect of helpless children, and their separation from powerless families and communities'; and that 'the legacy of Indian residential schools has contributed to social problems that continue to exist in many communities today' (House of Commons, Canada, 2008, p. 6850). Moreover, he appealed directly to Residential School Survivors in acknowledging how, for instance, '[t]he burden of this experience has been on your shoulders for far too long. The burden is properly ours as a government, and as a country' (House of Commons, Canada, 2008, p. 6850). Most significantly in this regard was his implicit acknowledgement of the role of Indigenous peoples to the apology's ultimate success. As noted in Chapter 2, it is common in apology discourses to measure the effectiveness of an apology according to whether victims forgive the wrongdoer or not. Harper appeared conscious of this when he stated: 'The Government of Canada sincerely apologizes and asks the forgiveness of the aboriginal peoples of this country for failing them so profoundly' (House of Commons, Canada, 2008, p. 6850).[2]

Through the respective displays of regret for these wrongdoings, each apology served as a measure of justice in conveying the message that the treatment of Indigenous peoples was undeserved, and this acknowledgement would set each nation on the path towards reconciliation. However, this did not mean that each respective apology was expected to undo the harm done. Rudd seemed clear about this when he addressed the Indigenous members in the audience and acknowledged: 'there is nothing I can say today that can take away the pain you have suffered personally. Whatever words I speak today, I cannot undo that. Words alone are not that powerful; grief is a very personal thing' (House of Representatives, Australia, 2008a, p. 170). But, in turn, he also addressed the non-Indigenous members in the audience to 'imagine if this had happened to us. Imagine the crippling effect. Imagine how hard it would be to forgive' (House of Representatives, Australia, 2008a, p. 170). In this way, Rudd adopted an empathetic stance in looking at the situation – from the point of view of the Stolen Generations, on the one hand, and non-Indigenous Australians on the other – and thereby bridged the gulf between them by forging a shared understanding that what had been done to the Stolen Generations was wrong. Thus, Rudd presented the apology as though it is the missing link that will unite all Australians. As Rudd surmised: 'My proposal is this: if the apology we extend today is accepted in the spirit of reconciliation in which it is offered, we can today resolve together that there be a new beginning for Australia. And it is to such a new beginning that I believe the nation is now calling us' (House of Representatives, Australia, 2008a, p. 170).

It is notable that in forging this new beginning for Australia, Rudd employed the metaphor of 'building a bridge between Indigenous and non-Indigenous Australians' and that by crossing that bridge together they will 'embrace a new partnership' (House of Representatives, Australia, 2008a, p. 170). It is at this moment that he outlined the practical measures of redress to be implemented, noting that 'unless the great symbolism of reconciliation is accompanied by an even greater substance, it is little more than a clanging gong' (House of Representatives, Australia, 2008a, p. 170). The one he placed most emphasis on was 'closing the gap between Indigenous and non-Indigenous Australians on life expectancy, educational achievement and employment opportunities' (House of Representatives, Australia, 2008a, p. 170). In the language in which he spoke it might seem logical that the building of a bridge between Indigenous and non-Indigenous peoples would translate into ensuring that all Australians have equal opportunities in life. This may seem appropriate considering the history of discrimination and lack of basic rights protections experienced by Indigenous peoples which many other Australians have enjoyed. This approach may also seem logical considering the way he framed the wrongdoing according to what he claimed was public opinion on the subject at the time, that is, the forced removal of Indigenous children was a violation of a core 'Aussie' value of the 'fair go'. By implication, the way to address the legacies of past wrongs was to ensure that all Indigenous peoples are guaranteed the same 'fair go' as other Australians in the future, and in that way achieve reconciliation for all Australians (House of Representatives, Australia, 2008a, p. 169).

Harper also seemed to use his apology as a way of bridging the gulf that exists between Indigenous and non-Indigenous Canadians, acknowledging that 'the absence of an apology has been an impediment to healing and reconciliation' (House of Commons, Canada, 2008, p. 6850). Like Rudd, Harper presented his apology as the beginning of something new for Canada, although in directly addressing Residential School Survivors in the audience he was cognisant of the fact that '[y]ou have been working on recovering from this experience for a long time, and in a very real sense we are now joining you on this journey' (House of Commons, Canada, 2008, p. 6850). Moreover, in likening the process to a 'journey', it is important to point out that Harper considered his apology as part of a broader process of 'healing, reconciliation and resolution' (House of Commons, Canada, 2008, p. 6850). In this respect, he also showed awareness that more than an apology would be needed to fulfil these goals. In his view, the *Indian Residential Schools Settlement Agreement* ('*Settlement Agreement*') (2006) that had been implemented in 2007 would provide the roadmap for the future. As part of that process Harper looked to the establishment of the proposed Truth and Reconciliation Commission of Canada ('TRC'). According to Harper,

> it will be a positive step in forging a new relationship between aboriginal peoples and other Canadians, a relationship based on the knowledge of our shared history, a respect for each other and a desire to move forward with a renewed understanding that strong families, strong communities and vibrant cultures and traditions will contribute to a stronger Canada for all of us.
>
> (House of Commons, Canada, 2008, p. 6851)

What is wrong with this picture? Indigenous peoples' critiques of the Rudd and Harper apologies

In Chapter 3 some of the more positive reactions of Indigenous peoples to the apologies were explored. However, neither apology received unanimous support and it is these more negative assessments that help to expose the shortcomings of both apologies.

To begin with, the responses which seemed most dismissive of the apologies reiterate a sad but true fact about apologies – they cannot undo the harm that was done. As simply expressed by one Stolen Generations Survivor: 'It's not doing anything for me, it won't give back my years' (Rhonda Maynard, East Davenport, Tasmania, quoted by Korff, 2021b).

In fact, while the apologies may have been accepted by some Indigenous peoples, they still were not enough to erase their painful memories (Kemp, 2008). Reactions like these powerfully bring home the fact that an apology is a poor form of compensation. But as was evident in the above discussion, the apologies were not intended to undo the harm that was done – how could they? They did, however, represent acceptance that forcibly removing Indigenous children was wrong. Nevertheless, not all Indigenous peoples in Australia and Canada respectively were convinced that the Rudd and Harper apologies would advance their claims.

In exploring these responses, the aim is not to discredit those who reacted positively to the apologies and may have found closure from the experience, but to understand why the apologies were not equipped to advance Indigenous peoples' broader claims as outlined in Chapter 3.

The limited interpretation of history and the harms suffered in the Rudd and Harper apologies

Considering the range of reactions to the apologies, it immediately becomes apparent that not everyone was receptive to them. Some rejected them outright. When asked: 'What do you think the [Rudd] apology means to blackfellas in general?' Gary Foley (Aboriginal activist, historian, and member of the Gumbaynggirr people) responded:

> Given the duplicitous wording of it all, it means nothing. It is completely without meaning. Some people have responded emotionally to what they perceived is the intent, but their perceptions of the intent and the actual wording of the apology are two completely different things.
>
> (McKinnon, 2008, p. 1)

As was discussed in Chapter 3, some Indigenous peoples in Australia and Canada saw the potential for the respective apologies to the Stolen Generations and Residential School Survivors as opening the way to resolving their claims and the broader issue of colonisation. However, when the text of both apologies is examined, it is apparent that this was not what Rudd and Harper intended to achieve.

If the process of colonisation is structured by the logic of elimination, there are instances in each apology that appear cognisant of this and prepared to condemn it. For instance, in the case of Rudd, he acknowledged that the state policy of forcibly removing Indigenous children was 'deliberate' and 'calculated' and was: 'taken to such extremes by some in administrative authority that the forced extractions of children of so-called "mixed lineage" were seen as part of a broader policy of dealing with "the problem of the Aboriginal population"' (House of Representatives, Australia, 2008a, p. 169).

He further alluded to the racist and genocidal intentions of government officials aimed to ensure 'all native characteristics of the Australian aborigine are eradicated'. According to one official, quoted by Rudd, '[t]he problem of our half-castes ... will quickly be eliminated by the complete disappearance of the black race, and the swift submergence of their progeny in the white' (House of Representatives, Australia, 2008a, p. 169). Moreover, in the apology Rudd also rejected the claim that 'the policy of generic forced separation was somehow well motivated, justified by its historical context' (House of Representatives, Australia, 2008a, p. 169). Rudd's apparent rejection of this claim was even more significant as it had been accepted by the former Howard government that the practice of removal was in fact in the best interests of the children when judged by the standards of the time of their removal.

This argument had been effectively applied in Australian law to reject the claims made by Stolen Generations Survivors that their treatment amounted to genocide (*Kruger v. Commonwealth* (1997)) and should be compensated (*Cubillo v. Commonwealth* (2001)).

However, despite his apparent condemnation of the practice, Rudd never directly challenged the lawfulness of removing Indigenous children from their families. Consequently, the state's authority to eliminate Indigenous peoples on racial grounds remained intact. This authority was beyond question on the circular logic that it had never been successfully challenged in Australia before. When asked why he had not used the word 'genocide', Rudd replied that genocide 'has a specific definition in international law and I don't believe [it] is either appropriate or helpful in describing the event[s] as they occurred or ... in taking the country forward' (Jones, 2008). However, his reluctance to engage with the genocide question does not necessarily reflect international developments (see Chapter 7); rather they reflect domestic developments, not only in the Australian courts, but also in the conservative response to the finding of genocide in the *BTH* report. Rudd's deflection of the issue was subsequently criticised. As John Moriarty, a Stolen Generations Survivor, claimed in response to the Rudd apology:

> It doesn't tell what the Stolen Generation really is ... I'm questioning the cultural genocide aspect. I think it's an appeasement in the sense that it's saying sorry, but it doesn't get down to the real crux of the issue, in my view, that people like me were taken away from their full-blooded mothers to breed out the culture. It doesn't come to that. It doesn't hit home with me.
>
> ('Kevin Rudd's national apology to Stolen Generations', 2008; see also Polya, 2008)

Instead, it is apparent from the text of the apology that Rudd confined the extent of the harms suffered by the Stolen Generations to the impact on their familial ties and consequential effects of these losses. In this respect, Rudd established a common understanding of the wrongdoing, which was founded on the value of the family as the fundamental social institution for all of humankind that had been violated by the practice of forcibly removing Indigenous children from their families (cf., Muldoon, 2009, p. 4). These losses were important to acknowledge. As Rudd put it, quoting Nanna Fejo in the apology:

> I asked Nanna Fejo what she would have me say today about her story. She thought for a few moments then said that what I should say today was that all mothers are important. And she added: 'Families—keeping them together is very important. It's a good thing that you are surrounded by love and that love is passed down the generations. That's what gives you happiness.'
>
> (House of Representatives, Australia, 2008a, p. 168)

However, by framing the harms in terms of 'breaking up of families' Rudd evaded mentioning any other social or economic cost of this practice, such as the malnourishment, maltreatment, emotional, sexual and physical abuse, and labour exploitation to which the children were often exposed while in institutional care, and which were well documented in *BTH* (HREOC, 1997, chap. 10).

Furthermore, in confining the losses to their personal effects, Rudd evaded expanding on the details of the cultural harms inflicted on the Stolen Generations and only made fleeting references in the preamble to the apology to the impact of the removal of Indigenous children 'from their families, their communities and their country' and to 'the indignity and degradation … [of the breaking up of families] inflicted on a proud people and a proud culture' (House of Representatives, Australia, 2008a, p. 167). There was also no mention of the ongoing individualised harms suffered by the Stolen Generations such as the higher levels of abuse, mistreatment, poverty, and dislocation from family ties than other Indigenous peoples, and corresponding higher rates of imprisonment and health problems than other Indigenous peoples. Nor was there any mention of ongoing group harms arising from community dislocation which has meant loss of culture, language, and land for many; and that the cycle of removing Indigenous children from their communities continues (HREOC, 1997, chap. 11). Rudd's limited understanding of the harms inflicted on the Stolen Generations did not do justice to their suffering, but so too in focusing so much on the Stolen Generations, Rudd ignored other historical injustices, such as the massacres, and more recent injustices, such as the Northern Territory Emergency Response ('the Intervention') (Philpot, et al., 2013, pp. 42–43).

Similar limitations were evident in Harper's apology. With respect to the residential schools, Harper seemed prepared to accept responsibility for a broader range of harms than Rudd in his apology. Harper referred not only to the personal losses caused by the separation of children from their families, but also the neglect, abuse, and cultural harms inflicted in the schools, as well as the ongoing social and intergenerational effects of the system on Survivors, their families, and communities. Nevertheless, the Harper apology shares similar limitations in not making the connections between the harms suffered by Residential School Survivors and their broader legal and political implications for Indigenous peoples in Canada. Harper acknowledged that the underlying intention of forcibly removing Indigenous children was 'to kill the Indian in the child' and 'assimilate them into the dominate culture' on the understanding that 'aboriginal cultures and spiritual beliefs were inferior and unequal' (House of Commons, Canada, 2008, p. 6850). However, these allusions to the elimination of Indigenous peoples were never connected to the broader process of colonisation, nor to the more specific claim that the residential school system amounted to genocide.

It is also notable that despite Harper's admission 'that it was wrong to separate children' (House of Commons, Canada, 2008, p. 6850), he repeatedly claimed that it is only 'now' that this had become obvious. Considering the government's reluctance to issue an apology, it may be true that it was only *now* accepting this practice was wrong. However, this position not only contradicts earlier official reports that documented the lethal conditions in the schools, which were subsequently documented in the Royal Commission on Aboriginal Peoples report in 1996 (MacLachlan, 2013, p. 194); but it also contrasts starkly with the history of Indigenous peoples' opposition to the residential school system which was adamant then as much as it is now. The logical inference that has been drawn from Indigenous resistance to the residential school system was that it was in direct violation of Indigenous peoples' sovereignty and self-determination (Henderson and Wakeham, 2009, p. 8).

The failure of the Harper apology to acknowledge that the residential school system was an act of genocide; the way the apology was made on behalf of the Canadian government instead of making those responsible for the genocide accountable for their crimes; and its failure to acknowledge the school system as having played a key role in the process of Canadian colonialism were listed as some its greatest deficiencies (Krebs, 2008). Indeed, these deficiencies led Mike Krebs (Indigenous activist of mixed Blackfoot and European descent) to question whether anything positive could come from the apology when the wrongs and the solutions to them had been framed by government and not by Canada's Indigenous peoples (Krebs, 2008; see also Churchill, 2008). In fact, some doubted the apology was actually an apology because Harper avoided admitting what truly had happened by failing to declare: ***'I'm sorry the Canadian government committed genocide against you. It was a criminal action on our part'*** (Chrisjohn, et al., 2008, emphasis in original).

Moreover, some were critical of Harper for not having fully listed the breadth of the injustices caused to Indigenous culture and law and the wide-ranging and long-term effects it has had on Indigenous communities across Canada. As Lynda Gray (member of the Tsimshian Nation and Executive Director of the Urban Native Youth Association) noted, the broader effects of the residential school system went 'beyond the overwhelming destruction of our families and individual lives':

> Some of the important things that the prime minister chose not to share with Canadians include the destruction of the cultural and spiritual traditions that would have helped our communities to recover from the residential-school experiences and the learned negative behaviours of violence, women-hating, homophobia, and elder abuse. …
>
> If the assimilationist policies of the Canadian government had not destroyed or severely compromised the systems that our ancestors had developed in the areas of negotiating, governance, caring for the land, and child-rearing, we would not be facing many of the broader community issues that we are today.
>
> (Gray, 2008)

Gray also criticised Harper for failing to acknowledge the gross inadequacy of the level of education received by the children in residential schools which has resulted in Indigenous children underachieving in mainstream schools in contemporary times:

> This is due to the learned fear of educational institutions, the social issues we face that stem from Canadian assimilation policies, and the racism that persists throughout this country as nonaboriginal people judge us for those social issues we are forced to overcome due to all of the external forces that led to them.
>
> (Gray, 2008)

Another notable aspect of the assimilation policy that went unacknowledged was the process of compulsory enfranchisement that was designed to strip Indian Status under the *Indian Act* (1876).[3] As noted in Chapter 3, enfranchisement and the residential school system violated treaty agreements that have been made between Indigenous peoples and the Crown. In an apology seeking 'healing, reconciliation and resolution' (House of Commons, Canada, 2008, p. 6850), an appropriate course would have been to acknowledge that the Crown had breached the obligations it owed to Indigenous peoples according to these treaties and commit to restoring the nation-to-nation relationship these treaties represent to Indigenous peoples (cf., Dorrell, 2009, pp. 34–35).

This was one of the aspirations expressed in Canada; namely, that in his apology Harper would acknowledge the history of treaty making in Canada and the fact that Canada has not lived up to the spirit of the treaties that were made. For instance, prior to the delivery of the Harper apology in Canada, Phil Morin, a Residential School Survivor, expressed his hope that Harper:

> will say that they will do everything they can to share the resources in this country that rightfully belong to First Nations people. We can't continue to live how we do, with one society benefiting more than the other. That was not the spirit and intent of the treaty. We were supposed to co-exist peacefully.
>
> (Fiddler, 2008)

Ultimately, however, Harper did not acknowledge the history of treaty making in Canada and the need to revisit the inequalities that were created because of broken treaties.

It may well be that it was only *now* that the Canadian government had accepted that the residential school system was wrong – the success of those Indigenous peoples who had secured the *Settlement Agreement* was vital in this regard. But in accepting these claims and not others the impression Harper gave was that the residential school system had been the only state-sanctioned initiative to impact negatively on Indigenous peoples in Canada.

Thus, in light of this discussion it seems unsurprising that there were Indigenous peoples in both nations who dismissed the apologies for not having gone far enough to acknowledge and address the wrongs that have (and continue to be) committed against them. The way that both apologies focused on the policy of forcibly separating Indigenous children, removed from its broader historical context, is at odds with the interrelationship that exists between the range of wrongs inflicted upon Indigenous peoples. It is evident from the Indigenous perspectives canvassed above that the forced separation of Indigenous children from their families is not the only wrongdoing experienced by Indigenous peoples. On the contrary, it formed part of what has been described to be 'a larger web of racist and oppressive government policies that have unjustly structured and limited the scope of indigenous life and life chances' (Jung, 2009, p. 2), and may rightly be described as genocide.

The interpretation of history in the Rudd and Harper apologies translated into measures of redress

The significance of the limited interpretation of the harms caused by the forced removal of Indigenous children becomes even more apparent when the limited measures of redress offered in each apology are examined. In both apologies, there were promises for 'reform' made and maintained post-apology.[4] In Australia, Rudd's key measure was the introduction of the policy of Closing the Gap between Indigenous and non-Indigenous peoples in the areas of health, education, and employment. In Canada, Harper promised to fulfil the final requirement of the *Settlement Agreement* and establish the TRC (see also Chapters 6 and 7). In this section, the focus is to examine how these measures correlate with the understanding of the harms as detailed in each apology. As outlined in the previous section, the understanding of the harms caused by the forced removal of Indigenous children was limited when contrasted to certain Indigenous understandings. When considered in terms of the measures of redress offered in each apology it is apparent that in confining the harms to certain losses, the cost on the state was also contained.

As this discussion reveals, the problem may not be whether states keep their promises, but in the actual promises that are made. Indeed, the problem may relate to the kinds of harms that were identified in the apologies and the way they were translated into the norms that were infringed. As Smith has observed, an apology requires 'the offender to name each specific offense, identify the moral principle breached by each offense, and endorse this underlying principle'. Ultimately, in his opinion, these elements are linked to each other. 'Depending on the principles which are identified in an apology, subsequent reform might shift accordingly' (Smith, 2008, pp. 221, 224).

Thus, in the Australian case, Rudd may have lamented the fact that the forced removal of Indigenous children was 'fully lawful', but this claim impliedly sidelined claims relating to genocide and compensation. As noted in the previous chapter, these claims could be sidelined as they had not gained mainstream political or legal acceptance. Instead, he framed the harms solely in terms of the personal effects of forcibly removing Indigenous children – the pain and suffering of separating a child from its mother. Indeed, his claim was that 'there is nothing I can say today that can take away the pain you have suffered personally' (House of Representatives, Australia, 2008a, p. 170). While there is truth in such a statement for many Stolen Generations Survivors, that does not mean that reparations should not be made. On the contrary, the significant losses suffered by Stolen Generations Survivors warrant reparations. Making reparations in line with international human rights standards and principles was central to the recommendations in *BTH* and continues to be a significant issue for many Survivors (Aboriginal and Torres Strait Islander Healing Foundation, 2021). This is exemplified by the issue of compensation (discussed in Chapter 6). However, even before delivering the apology the Rudd government announced that it would not set up a compensation package for the Stolen Generations, and by reducing the harms to their personal effects, it depoliticised any claims for compensation and made them seem offensive. Brendan Nelson, then Leader of the Opposition, in his response to the Rudd apology was particularly explicit on this point: 'There is no compensation fund for this—nor should there be. How can any sum of money replace a life deprived of knowing your family?' (House of Representatives, Australia, 2008b, p. 174). Notably, there were Indigenous people who saw through such rhetoric. As Noel Pearson (Director of the Cape York Institute for Policy and Leadership from the Guugu Yimithirr Aboriginal community) succinctly put it: 'Black fellas will get the words, the white fellas will keep the money' (Pearson, 2008, p. 4).

Logically, Rudd's acceptance on behalf of all Australian governments that the forced child removal practice was wrong should have led to the establishment of a national compensation fund for Stolen Generations Survivors. Indeed, as he had rejected the logic upon which the legality of the removal of Indigenous children had been found to depend – that is, that the policy 'was somehow well motivated, [and] justified by its historical context' (House of Representatives, Australia, 2008a, p. 169), his government's refusal to offer compensation appeared hypocritical and immoral. As Ghillar Michael Anderson (Aboriginal activist, Senior Law Man, Elder, and leader of the Euahlayi Nation) put it:

> Many people argue that the effort on the part of former PM Kevin Rudd to apologise was worth hearing and that it did serve to act as a catalyst towards improving and easing the trauma of our people, but then to say that our people are not worthy of reparation and compensation for those affected is yet another major slap in the face for the survivors and their families of the Stolen Generations.
>
> (Anderson, 2013)

Rudd, however, elided such arguments. The fact remained that Commonwealth liability had never been positively determined in court and, therefore, there was no perceived legal obligation to set up such a fund. Nor was there any apparent political motivation to do so as many Australians were opposed to compensation (Korff, 2021a).

In the absence of an explicit legal or political justification to pay compensation to Stolen Generations Survivors, Rudd framed the wrongs they experienced as a violation of 'a core value of our nation—and that value is a fair go for all' (House of Representatives, Australia, 2008a, p. 169). In his view, this is how the broader community saw the wrongs committed against the Stolen Generations: 'There is a deep and abiding belief in the Australian community that, for the stolen generations, there was no fair go at all' (House of Representatives, Australia, 2008a, p. 170). Notably, however, after framing the wrongs in this way he did not provide any comprehensive measures specifically aimed at addressing the losses suffered by Stolen Generations Survivors (save the extension of family reunification services such as Link-Up (House of Representatives, Australia, 2008a, p. 171)). Instead, he introduced the Closing the Gap policy in the areas of health, education, and employment that would extend to all Indigenous peoples. In making this announcement, Rudd gave the impression that the social and economic disadvantages experienced by Indigenous peoples across the nation would finally be addressed. Some Indigenous peoples took this to mean that the apology was finally acknowledging the consequences of white settlement on the broader Indigenous population (Patterson, 2009, p. 22). More specifically, it appeared that the government was endorsing an initiative, backed by Indigenous and non-Indigenous service providers, and endorsed by the Aboriginal and Torres Strait Islander Social Justice Commissioner (2005), to 'Close the Gap' on Indigenous health and life expectancy within twenty-five years.

However, adopting this initiative, and not any recommendations made in the numerous reports relating to Indigenous peoples in the preceding decades (including *BTH*), exposed the government's limited vision in addressing Indigenous peoples' claims, and the apology was criticised for its limited approach (Philpot, et al., 2013, pp. 42–43). Pertinently, the introduction of the Closing the Gap policy in an apology addressed to 'Australia's Indigenous Peoples' conveyed the view that this was the only measure needed to redress all the injustices inflicted on Indigenous peoples. The policy was presented as the bridge that would guide the nation to create a new partnership between Indigenous and non-Indigenous Australians (House of Representatives, Australia, 2008a, p. 171). On closer examination, however, it is apparent that as a policy aimed at Indigenous socio-economic disadvantage, Rudd had not significantly departed from the concerns of previous governments to achieve equal outcomes for Indigenous peoples measured against non-Indigenous standards. Notably, the Closing the Gap policy was informed by the same rationale (to promote equal opportunity) and policy objective (to address socio-economic disadvantage of Indigenous communities) as the former Howard government's 'practical reconciliation' policy (Howard, 2000). In effect, it was assimilation by another name. This is particularly concerning considering that Indigenous children were removed under the auspices of the assimilation policy. However, Rudd avoided this fact by not explicitly referring to the policies of protection and assimilation and instead confined his apology to the events which took place between 1910 and 1970 as part of 'a broader policy of dealing with "the problem of the Aboriginal population"' (House of Representatives, Australia, 2008a, p. 169).

Arguably, if the apology was to respond to the broader effects of colonisation in Australia, it would have identified the violation of Indigenous peoples' sovereignty and laws as central to the harms suffered, and the need to redress these effects by accepting their claims for political autonomy through treaty making and rights protection. However, in framing the violations experienced by the Stolen Generations (and Indigenous peoples more broadly) in terms of the mainstream 'Aussie fair go', the inference Rudd seemed to draw was that all Indigenous peoples should be given a fair go like other Australians and not a 'fair go' as Indigenous peoples may understand the term, which would require measures to address the broader impacts of colonisation (Rose, 1984). Thus, Rudd's declaration in the apology that the Stolen Generations had been denied 'a core value of our nation – and that value is a fair go for all' (House of Representatives, Australia, 2008a, p. 169), alluded to their inequality of treatment when compared to other Australians and nothing more. Further, he emphasised the necessity – out of respect for 'our Indigenous brothers and sisters' – to address this discrepancy and nothing else (House of Representatives, Australia, 2008a, p. 171). Notably, 'respect' in this context is informed by liberal values of equal regard and respect which Rudd applied to Indigenous people as members of the family of humankind as opposed to the way it could be applied according to theories of difference (Fraser, 1995, pp. 68–93; Young, 1990, pp. 48–63), where differences require positive affirmation through the implementation (in this case) of culturally specific rights. However, he also did not mean that closing the gap would extend citizenship rights to Indigenous peoples and thereby create an obligation on the state to uphold these rights. Instead, he listed 'respect, cooperation and mutual responsibility as the guiding principles of this new partnership on closing the gap' (House of Representatives, Australia, 2008a, p. 170). These are some of the key principles that underpin the neoliberal state where the role of government is to maximise private wealth and minimise welfare dependency by imposing mutual obligations on individuals so that they become economically responsible and self-sufficient. This approach is directly at odds with an apology in which responsibility for past wrongs was apparently and unequivocally accepted by the head of state. Rather, it aligns more broadly with social welfare policy in Australia which is based on the principle of mutual obligations. This is also concerning considering that the mutual obligations regime has disproportionately impacted on Indigenous communities, and its more stringent requirements have had more devasting effects. This has been clearly illustrated by the Intervention (see Chapter 3), which has been a direct affront to Indigenous peoples' human rights. Indeed, for Indigenous critics such as Foley, the apology could not be seen as a positive gesture while the government continued to endorse the Intervention, which in his view was another manifestation of the assimilation policy (McKinnon, 2008, p. 1).

Evidently, Indigenous peoples' broader claims for such things as a treaty and rights protection would continue to remain off the political agenda under Rudd. His focus was on redressing the socio-economic gaps informed by a neoliberal policy agenda and not the political gaps that exist between Indigenous and non-Indigenous communities. Rudd did acknowledge the need for 'a new partnership [between Indigenous and non-Indigenous Australians] for closing the gap' that required 'flexible, tailored, local approaches', appropriate for regional and remote communities 'to achieve commonly agreed national objectives' (House of Representatives, Australia, 2008a, p. 171). However, whether this was possible in the absence of an Indigenous rights framework was doubtful. In any case, the new partnership was not imagined to be an equal one, for when it came to ensuring the success of closing the gap and devising future national policies (such as the establishment of a joint policy commission and constitutional recognition) (House of Representatives, Australia, 2008a, p. 171) Rudd emphasised the need for bipartisan agreement, and not necessarily Indigenous peoples' agreement, meaning that the top-down approach to Indigenous politics would likely continue undisturbed. This was a far cry from the relationship that Indigenous representatives such as Dodson envisaged for future relations in Australia after the apology based on open dialogue and negotiation between government and Indigenous peoples (Dodson, 2008).

The fact that the Rudd apology did not create the conditions to increase Indigenous autonomy and control over their own affairs has been identified as one of its weaknesses (New South Wales, Parliament, Legislative Council, General Purpose Standing Committee No. 3, 2016, p. 67). These limitations of the apology can be directly linked to the narrow understanding of the harms and measures to address them and has raised further concerns that the apology merely glossed over the truth and dismissed it as having been dealt with (McKinnon, 2008, p.1). This seems most apparent in the way that Rudd addressed the apology to 'Australia's Indigenous Peoples', but in naming the wrongs committed against them he referred only to the forced child removal practice as though it was the only aberration in the history of settler–colonised relations in Australia and confined the measures of redress for this history of injustice to the Closing the Gap policy.

Turning to Harper's apology, as was noted above, he acknowledged a broader range of harms suffered by the Residential School Survivors than Rudd in relation to the Stolen Generations. This may be attributed to the successes of Residential School Survivors in the Canadian courts and in ultimately securing the *Settlement Agreement* from the former Martin government (which included monetary, truth-telling, healing, and commemorative provisions for Residential School Survivors). These successes eluded Indigenous peoples in Australia. Nevertheless, Harper was more concise in setting out the roadmap for the future. This may be because he, unlike Rudd, was specifically focused on apologising to Residential School Survivors, and not to all Indigenous peoples in Canada. However, like the Rudd apology that was specifically focused on the Stolen Generations (despite being addressed to 'Australia's Indigenous Peoples'), Harper's focus on the Residential School Survivors also gives the impression that what happened to them was the only aberration in the history of settler–colonised relations in Canada. This understanding is further reinforced by the way that Harper emphasised the *Settlement Agreement*, which he described as giving 'us a new beginning and an opportunity to move forward together in partnership' (House of Commons, Canada, 2008, p. 6850). As the only measure of redress that is mentioned in his apology, it would seem he was confident that it would not only overcome the harms caused by residential school system, but also would be enough to reset the relationship between Indigenous and non-Indigenous Canadians.

In this respect, it is possible to connect the harms Harper identified to those which the *Settlement Agreement* sought to address. Accordingly, for instance, it can be inferred that 'the emotional, physical and sexual abuse and neglect of helpless children' Harper identified in the apology (Harper 2008, p. 6850) would be compensated through the Independent Assessment Process, established as part of the *Settlement Agreement*; while the intergenerational effects of the schools 'on aboriginal culture, heritage and language' and the broader 'social problems that continue to exist in many communities today' (House of Commons, Canada, 2008, p. 6850) would be addressed through the work of the Aboriginal Healing Foundation, whose life had been extended under the *Settlement Agreement*. Harper further noted that 'healing, reconciliation and resolution' (House of Commons, Canada, 2008, p. 6850) would be realised through the work of the TRC, which was to be established as the final stage of the *Settlement Agreement*. Notably, in this regard, he confined the TRC's role to only one of its stated mandates 'to educate all Canadians on the Indian residential schools system' (House of Commons, Canada, 2008, p. 6850).

If this analysis is accepted, then it is evident that Harper relied on the *Settlement Agreement* to curtail the provision of any additional avenues of redress to Indigenous peoples. This was already apparent at the time Harper delivered his apology in relation to the Inuit and Métis Residential School Survivors who had been excluded from the *Settlement Agreement* (Senate of Canada, 2008, pp. 1505–1506 (Simon; Chartier)). But even with respect to the Residential School Survivors to whom the *Agreement* applied, it was criticised for several reasons (Chrisjohn, et al., 2008; Corntassel and Holder, 2008; Jung, 2009, pp. 2–3; Krebs, 2008). Specifically, these measures failed to bring the perpetrators of the genocide to justice (or lead to further investigations of students who had gone missing after leaving the schools); they failed to address the land rights issues arising from the children's removal from their traditional homelands; the economic measures of redress were grossly inadequate in addressing Indigenous socio-economic disadvantage; and these measures failed to compensate the families of those who had died before the *Agreement* came into effect or address the intergenerational effects of past child removals on Indigenous communities, particularly the continuing cycle of child removals by child welfare authorities. More broadly, these measures were criticised by Indigenous peoples for focusing on the effects of the residential school system when government responsibility extends beyond individual Survivors and includes collective and cultural harms suffered by Indigenous communities, languages, and cultures more broadly (Jung, 2009, p. 2). These criticisms demonstrate that the Harper government ultimately possessed a limited understanding of the injustices experienced by Indigenous peoples which translated into inadequate measures of redress.

Viewed holistically, this discussion reveals how measures such as the Closing the Gap policy in Australia and the *Settlement Agreement* in Canada, although they reflect certain Indigenous aspirations, conform to the accepted standards and norms of each nation state. They do not, for instance, extend beyond the accepted norms to other Indigenous aspirations relating to self-determination and other rights protections. Essentially, these developments reflect a lack of political will to change the institutional structures and norms of the state to promote these broader claims. Indeed, with respect to the apologies that were made, both were delivered in the House of Parliament and the House of Commons in Australia and Canada respectively, which means they were both protected by parliamentary privilege, and thus had no legal effect. Each apology was in effect a non-justiciable act of sovereignty. There was only a moral imperative for each nation to uphold the promises that were made in each respective apology. Ultimately, the fact that both nations kept these promises may be because their fulfilment was aligned to, and did not challenge, the politico-legal order of either state. To put it another way, if neither the Rudd nor the Harper apology constructed the wrongs as violations of Indigenous peoples' rights it is because the norms of each state had not recognised these rights. This, in turn, enabled both to remain in denial of the existence of these rights. The discussion that follows explores the various ways that both apologies in fact maintained the legitimacy of state power and in doing so perpetuated settler colonialism by continuing to deny the existence of Indigenous norms and practices.

Settler colonialism and the Rudd and Harper apologies

In Chapter 2, the making of an apology was described as a transformative process. In terms of the nation, one transformative effect of an apology would be the realisation that there are just some things that governments cannot do. The acknowledgement of wrongdoing in a political apology suggests there are limits to state power and its exercise. As Reilly has argued: 'to be genuine, the apology requires a certain *loss* of sovereignty' (Reilly, 2008, p. 13, emphasis in original). The corresponding transformative effect for victims would arise from the message of respect conveyed in the apology that they did not deserve to be treated unjustly which would be followed by the introduction of measures (if none were already in place) to ensure their rights, violated by the wrongdoing, are protected to prevent future violations. This course seems to logically follow the acceptance of responsibility for wrongs committed against victim groups and the making of promises of reform and forbearance in an apology. And yet, neither the Rudd nor the Harper apology brought into question the authority of the state to remove Indigenous children from their families as the basis for introducing reforms aimed at protecting the rights of Indigenous peoples in the future. Instead, it may be more correct to say that each apology served to consolidate state power and reassert its legitimacy in response to the exposition of past wrongdoing (Winter, 2014).

In this sense (as noted in Chapter 2), these apologies as 'speech acts' can be understood in Austin's terms not as a behabitive (the expression of emotion) or as a commissive (the making of a promise), but as an *exercitive* which relates to speech used for 'exercising of powers, rights, or influence' (Austin, 1962, pp. 150, 154–155). Indeed, both apologies may be categorised as exercitive insofar as they are performed as official acts of state: as motions passed within the respective parliaments of each nation. So understood, an exercitive would need to be made in a certain way to have validity and meaning. The procedures used in making these apologies require that certain official requirements are met for them to succeed in parliament. These procedures have been inherited from the European societies that formally engaged in the process of colonisation (Veracini, 2010, p. 105). Thus, in practice, the legal and political processes used for making these apologies (and any legal or political process for determining other measures of reparations more generally) have originated from the same institutional traditions and structures as the ones which had instituted the oppressive laws and policies that adversely affected Indigenous peoples in the first place. So understood, the making of these apologies does not function to limit sovereignty, but to reiterate it (Anker, 2014). Evidently, this reveals an inherent paradox in the making of political apologies insofar as they function, not as a limit on state authority, but to reinforce and sustain it (Reilly, 2012).

This is further exemplified by the promises of future forbearance made in each apology. For instance, Rudd in his apology resolved that 'the injustices of the past must never, never happen again' (House of Representatives, Australia, 2008a, p. 167). And yet, as Reilly has observed, at no stage did 'the apology resile from the power of the State to enact laws of removal or its power to enforce them. In fact, the apology confirms the power of the State to pass the laws' (Reilly, 2008, p. 13). As Rudd made it clear in the apology, 'the forced removal of children on racial grounds [was] fully lawful'. In making this claim, Rudd exposed a serious deficiency in Australian law: 'put simply, the laws that our parliaments enacted made the stolen generations possible. ... The problem lay with the laws themselves' (House of Representatives, Australia, 2008a, p. 169). He even appeared to lament that this was the legal position. Nevertheless, at no time in the apology did Rudd consider how the law could be redeemed, whether by offering reparations to the Stolen Generations according to the international standards as set out in *BTH*, or legally enshrining Indigenous rights such as the right to self-determination to empower Indigenous peoples and prevent similar laws from being made.

Furthermore, in finding that the forced removal of Indigenous children was lawful according to Australian law, Rudd also omitted to add that this practice was in direct conflict with Aboriginal and Torres Strait Islander customary laws relating to children and their care (HREOC, 1997, chap. 22), and thus a direct affront to their inherent right to sovereignty. Evidently, the polarity that exists between the two systems of laws remained intact. The fact that Indigenous child welfare has continued to be largely biased against Indigenous child-rearing practices further supports this claim (Cripps, 2012, p. 28).

In making promises of forbearance in an apology focused on the Stolen Generations, it would have been appropriate to acknowledge the need for law reform to prevent the removal of Indigenous children in violation of their rights. This is a pertinent issue in contemporary times as Indigenous children continue to be removed from their families and placed with non-Indigenous carers at disproportionate rates (see Chapter 6). It is important to highlight this issue because at the time Rudd delivered his apology it did not feature as something that needed attention, and only in 2020 did out-of-home care become a Closing the Gap target. However, in the absence of commitment to uphold Indigenous self-determination and cultural rights, child welfare systems continue to be repeating mistakes of the past. The effect is assimilation as Indigenous peoples continue to be subject to mainstream standards rather than treated as subjects with their own rights.

Similar observations can be made with respect to the Harper apology for the residential school system. Notwithstanding Harper's claim that 'we recognize that this policy of assimilation was wrong, has caused great harm, and has no place in our country' (House of Commons, Canada, 2008, p. 6850), this was ultimately inconsistent with the contemporary reality of the disproportionate number of Indigenous children in non-Indigenous care settings. Contemporary Indigenous child welfare laws and policies are a striking example of the continuation of the project of assimilation which the residential school system in Canada left incomplete (Jung, 2009, p. 3; Sinclair, 2016). Thus, whether Harper's apparent promise of forbearance in the apology that '[t]here is no place in Canada for the attitudes that inspired the Indian residential schools system to ever again prevail' (House of Commons, Canada, 2008, p. 6850) was a true possibility remained doubtful so long as colonial attitudes continued to prevail in Canada (Henderson and Wakeham, 2009, p. 2).

In this regard, Harper may have apologised for separating children from their homes and 'from rich and vibrant cultures and traditions, that ... created a void in many lives and communities' (House of Commons, Canada, 2008, p. 6850), but he, like Rudd, did not go so far and acknowledge that the policy infringed their rights and accordingly the corresponding need for the adoption of an Indigenous rights framework. In failing to make these connections, the apology appears to have only gone so far to accept Indigenous cultures in a social (that is, multicultural) sense which continues to be assimilationist in continuing to deny Indigenous peoples' sovereign status and maintain their subordination to the state. Harper's failure to acknowledge that the entire residential school system was itself a violation of Indigenous rights is most evident when he acknowledged that '[s]ome former students have spoken positively about their experiences at residential schools', but goes on to say that 'these stories are far overshadowed by tragic accounts of the emotional, physical and sexual abuse and neglect of helpless children, and their separation from powerless families and communities' (House of Commons, Canada, 2008, p. 6850). Thus, his apology avoided constructing the residential schools as a systemic injustice; only some of its effects were unjust.

But if both Rudd and Harper could sideline Indigenous peoples' claims for political autonomy and rights, it was because they upheld the norms and values of each state. These norms are not only structured and administered in ways to exclude these claims; they also reflect the virtues and goodness of each nation and its people. In this way, both the state's norms and its people were placed beyond reproach. Accordingly, each leader managed to ensure there was no need to change state norms to align with Indigenous peoples' rights, nor was there a need to change the outlook of the broader non-Indigenous population on this issue.

Of the two apologies, the Rudd apology most clearly demonstrated an unfailing faith in the goodness of 'this great country, Australia' (House of Representatives, Australia, 2008a, p. 167). Rudd warmly described the Australian people as 'a passionate lot. We are also a very practical lot. For us, symbolism is important but, unless the great symbolism of reconciliation is accompanied by an even greater substance, it is little more than a clanging gong' (House of Representatives, Australia, 2008a, p. 170). He further upheld values that are central to the Australian national identity – particularly the value of the 'fair go' – as the foundation of a just and reconciled future for Indigenous and non-Indigenous peoples.

In the case of Harper, he expressed a similar sentiment in an interview at the G20 Pittsburgh Summit in September 2009 (three months after his apology to Residential School Survivors) where he presented this overview of the history of Canada:

> We are one of the most stable regimes in history. There are very few countries that can say for nearly 150 years they've had the same political system without any social breakdown, political upheaval or invasion. We are unique in that regard. We also have no history of colonialism.
>
> (Wherry, 2009)

This comment attests to the virtues and goodness of the Canadian nation, which obviously no revelation of past wrongdoing has been able to disturb, despite the several number of apologies for past transgressions that have been made. Specifically, this statement also reveals that the history of colonisation of Indigenous peoples in Canada would not, most likely, have been in Harper's contemplation when he made the apology.

Far from addressing the effects of the history of colonisation that the forced child removal practice exemplifies, each leader, in naming the wrongs, identifying the harms, and offering measures of redress, did so in a manner that completely sidelined this history and thus the potential of each apology to account for it, and respond to it. Some Indigenous peoples may have thought that the apologies could set each nation on the path to forging a new relationship which would presumably bring the settler–colonised relationship to an end. As previously discussed in Chapter 3, this understanding was partly based on the acceptance of 'the truth' in each apology that the forced removal of Indigenous children was wrong but, as has become evident in this chapter, the understanding of this truth in the Rudd and Harper apologies was not the same. The involvement of Indigenous peoples in the apology-making process had also been thought by some as forming the basis of a new partnership that would lead to Indigenous peoples exercising greater control over their own affairs. However, it would seem this is not the way Rudd and Harper interpreted this history either.

In the Rudd apology, Rudd made a point of mentioning that in offering an apology to the Stolen Generations he was fulfilling an election promise to the Australian people (House of Representatives, Australia, 2008a, p. 167), and thereby he was implicitly acknowledging the support for an apology in the broader population, but there is no specific mention of the active role that Indigenous peoples played in the apology-making process. Furthermore, Rudd may have envisaged the creation of a partnership between Indigenous and non-Indigenous peoples through the implementation of the Closing the Gap policy, but it was one aimed at attaining comparable standards of living between them; policy decision making power would remain squarely in the hands of government.

Harper in his apology gave greater recognition to the role of Indigenous peoples in speaking out about the abuse they have suffered, how this is 'a testament to their resilience as individuals and to the strength of their cultures' (House of Commons, Canada, 2008, p. 6850), and how their combined efforts culminated in the *Settlement Agreement* which, in his opinion, 'gives us a new beginning and an opportunity to move forward together in partnership' (House of Commons, Canada, 2008, p. 6850). However, like Rudd, the partnership he envisaged was not one that would lead to greater Indigenous involvement in the political life of the nation. Instead, Harper thought this new partnership would strengthen the cultural life of Canadian society. In this respect, he looked to the proposed work of the TRC as:

> a positive step in forging a new relationship between Aboriginal peoples and other Canadians, a relationship based on the knowledge of our shared history, a respect for each other and a desire to move forward together with a renewed understanding that strong families, strong communities and vibrant cultures and traditions will contribute to a stronger Canada for all of us.
>
> (House of Commons, Canada, 2008, p. 6851)

Thus, despite each apology heralding the beginning of a new partnership, elements of the settler–colonised relationship remained present as each leader continued in his own way to pursue the assimilation of Indigenous peoples by continuing to deny the existence of Indigenous sovereignty and laws. The impression given by both is that Indigenous peoples would now be treated as equal citizens against a history of being treated unequally. However, in the absence of law and policies to uphold and protect the rights of Indigenous peoples, the effect was to continue to subject Indigenous peoples to state norms. Although these norms may appear committed to notions of neutrality and equality, they have in fact internalised mainstream values that may result in discriminatory treatment of Indigenous peoples. Thus, the situation remained one where mainstream non-Indigenous values would continue to set the standard against which Indigenous peoples could be measured and found lacking.

If this analysis is accepted, then it also exposes the limits of each apology as an expression of regret for past wrongdoing. In Chapter 2, the understanding of apology making as expressing other-oriented regret for victims of injustice demonstrated the potential of an apology to enact respect and recognition of victims and overcome the disrespect caused by past injustices. This show of respect serves as a measure of reparative justice at the time the apology is made but would prove to be an empty gesture in the absence of measures to redress the harms suffered and ensure past rights violations are not repeated. Showing respect to victims would be a long-term commitment and measured by the extent to which the nation upheld the rights violated by the wrongdoing. However, the discussion in this chapter has shown how each apology fell short in making promises for future reform and forbearance of this nature. In the case of Australia, Rudd appeared to be committed to change by essentially acknowledging that 'a business as usual' was not working, but the introduction of the Closing the Gap policy as 'the new beginning' for the nation was a short-sighted response in view of the range of claims advanced by Indigenous peoples. A similar conclusion can be reached in relation to Harper's focus in his apology on the *Settlement Agreement* as forging the path forward to creating a new relationship in Canada. More significantly, these limited measures of redress, framed according to accepted state norms and not in terms of Indigenous rights standards, undermined the intimations of respect made in each of them and replicated the conditions of settler colonialism.

Thus, for instance, the acknowledgement in the Rudd apology of the 'indignity and degradation ... inflicted on a proud people and a proud culture' appears to be attempting to convey to Indigenous peoples 'a real respect rather than a thinly veiled contempt' (House of Representatives, Australia, 2008a, p. 170) as had been the case in the past. However, in the absence of acknowledgement of Indigenous sovereignty and laws, this reference echoes romantic notions of the 'noble savage' – a conception which reflects the notion of terra nullius and the understanding that Indigenous peoples do not have their own laws and social organisation that the doctrine implies. Although the terra nullius doctrine was presumably overturned by the High Court in *Mabo v. Queensland (No. 2)* (1992), it continues to underpin Australian law through the non-recognition of Aboriginal sovereignty and laws. In not acknowledging these 'uncomfortable' truths in the apology, Rudd also repeated mistakes made in the past (and present) by neglecting to mention that Indigenous peoples have their own conceptions of sovereignty and laws that survived the acquisition of British sovereignty. Notable in this respect is the way he portrays the apology as the opportunity to reconcile 'the entire history of the often bloody encounter between those who emerged from the Dreamtime a thousand generations ago and those who, like me, came across the seas only yesterday' (House of Representatives, Australia, 2008a, p. 171). But in failing to acknowledge what was at stake during this violent encounter – the genocide of Indigenous peoples made possible by the denial of their sovereignty and violation of their rights to life, land, and culture – he left the historical narrative of peaceful settlement of Australia largely undisturbed. The new and unified Australia he imagined was one in which 'we' – presumably white Australia – can move on:

> It is for the nation to bring the first two centuries of our settled history to a close, as we begin a new chapter. We embrace with pride, admiration and awe these great and ancient cultures we are truly blessed to have among us – cultures that provide a unique, uninterrupted human thread linking our Australian continent to the most ancient prehistory of our

> planet. Growing from this new respect, we see our Indigenous brothers and sisters with fresh eyes, with new eyes, and we have our minds wide open as to how we might tackle, together, the great practical challenges that Indigenous Australia faces in the future.
>
> (House of Representatives, Australia, 2008a, p. 171)

Effectively, in claiming to be bringing the 'first two centuries of our *settled* history to a close', Rudd evaded the question of genocide, and many of the other effects of white 'settlement', including its effects on Indigenous sovereignty and laws. Indeed, in bringing this history to a close, it would seem these issues have been settled as far as Rudd was concerned. This is further evident in his claim that 'we are truly blessed to have [them] among us' which showed complete disregard of the history of colonisation and continuing invasion in the absence of Indigenous peoples' consent. According to Rudd, all that was left to be resolved were 'the great practical challenges that Indigenous Australia faces in the future'. In the absence of acceptance of Indigenous sovereignty and laws, these challenges are to be met by state policies and laws. Rudd may have intimated empathetically that 'we' are seeing Indigenous people with 'new eyes', and that together 'we' will tackle the practical problems facing Indigenous Australia, but at this very moment of recognition he reinscribed settler-colonial constructs by recasting Indigenous people to prehistoric times devoid of their own temporal sovereignty and laws. In this logic, history repeated itself as the colonial mindset continued to construct the 'Aboriginal problems' that need fixing, and to promote state policies and laws as providing the best (and only) solutions to these problems. In this state of play the dynamics of the settler–colonised relationship have not changed, and it will not change so long as government continues to dictate what is best for Indigenous peoples.

In contrast, the way that Harper addressed Residential School Survivors in his apology as 'survivors' and acknowledged the abuse they suffered in the residential schools appears to be a significant acknowledgement of 'their resilience as individuals and to the strengths of their cultures' (House of Commons, Canada, 2008, p. 6850). Addressing Indigenous peoples as Survivors represents a show of respect. Discursively, it signals a changed attitude towards Indigenous peoples. Whereas the assimilation of the residential schools had been justified on the understanding that Indigenous peoples' cultures and beliefs system were inferior and unequal, the reference to 'survivors' in the apology correlates with the understanding that what had been done to them was wrong. Nevertheless, Harper's use of the term did not fully grasp Indigenous peoples' understandings of the notion of 'Survivor' – as surviving the denial of their very existence as Indigenous peoples (House of Commons, Canada, 2008, p. 6854 (Fontaine)). If that had been what Harper intended, he would have expressly acknowledged the survival of Indigenous peoples as distinct peoples with their own sovereignty and laws and accepted the inherent rights that are bound up in their cultures, which should now guide future reform agendas. In failing to recognise the agency of Indigenous peoples in this way, Harper recast Indigenous peoples and the state in their roles within the settler–colonised relationship. Rather than going on to cast Indigenous peoples as agents with rights, Harper went on to describe Survivors as 'recovering from this experience' (House of Commons, Canada, 2008, p. 6850), an understanding that connotes they are sick and need to recover, and pathologises and depoliticises their experiences. As for the role of the state, Harper in recognising that the residential schools were evidence of the government 'failing to protect you' (House of Commons, Canada, 2008, p. 6850), and apologising for this, positioned the state to reclaim its role as Indigenous peoples' protector. Harper could do this now that he had redeemed the state by apologising and in the absence of recognition of Indigenous peoples' ability to take care of their own affairs.

So long as the settler–colonised relationship remains intact, the regret and ultimately the respect expressed in each apology operates as expression of colonial power. It confirms what Yellowknives Dene scholar Glen Coulthard has identified as an intrinsic problem with state recognition (Coulthard, 2014). While acts of reconciliation, such as apologies, may be sought by Survivors to gain recognition of past injustices, their scope is determined by government perceptions of the harms suffered and how to overcome them. In both the Rudd and Harper apologies there was a degree of mutual recognition as they accepted that the removal of Indigenous children from their families was wrong, but the absence of recognition of this practice as an element of settler colonialism meant that the broader effects of colonisation could continue to be ignored. As noted in Chapter 2, an apology as a show of respect to victims, signals that the disrespect inherent in their past mistreatment was wrong and perceptions of their inferiority that facilitated their denigration can no longer be countenanced. Both Rudd and Harper appeared to condemn such perceptions, but not far enough. In the context of settler-colonised nations such as Australia and Canada, perceptions of Indigenous inferiority legitimised the acquisition of Crown sovereignty and had the flow on effects of supressing Indigenous sovereignty and rights with dire consequences for Indigenous peoples. By not addressing these deeper issues, notions of inferiority and superiority that have historically underpinned the settler–colonised relationship remained undisturbed. Although both leaders appeared to discredit such notions, they did not overcome them. Each leader may have responded to the damage caused by the racist pursuit of removing Indigenous children from their families by seeking to valorise Indigenous peoples' cultures as forming part of the fabric of their respective nation. Nevertheless, in failing to provide the jurisdictional space needed to support Indigenous peoples on their healing journey, the effect was to recast their inferior status as victims – not as the victims of injustice in recognition of the violation of their rights, as the term has been used in apology discourses

(Coicaud, 2009, p. 114), but as lacking agency and ability to take care of their own affairs. Thus, by casting Indigenous peoples in the role of victim, these nations maintained their sovereignty through the denial of Indigenous conceptions of sovereignty.

Conclusion

It is apparent that both the Rudd and Harper apologies share similar shortcomings. In both, the recognition of the injustices caused by the forcible removal of Indigenous children is treated as though *now* each government has recognised the errors of its ways, and the path has *now* been set for healing and reconciliation. But in confining their apologies to the harms that could be recognised according to state norms, these nations have left many of the claims of Indigenous peoples unanswered. The effect is to evade the broader politico-legal implications that the state-sanctioned practice of forcibly removing Indigenous children has had for Aboriginal sovereignty and laws. In these ways, each nation has left the scope of their powers in making laws and policies with respect to Indigenous peoples intact. In turn, each nation has maintained the legitimacy of its own sovereign power in determining the course of action to pursue in Indigenous affairs in future. Each leader may imagine that their respective apology has created the conditions for a new partnership with Indigenous peoples, but the terms of this new relationship remained under state control. In this respect, the values underpinning each nation would continue to serve as a beacon in determining the ongoing obligations they have towards Indigenous peoples. This will continue to be the case so long as these nations pay lip service to the importance of culture for Indigenous peoples in the absence of measures that accept their sovereignty and uphold their rights.

Viewed in this way, the treatment of a state apology as a 'speech act' whereby the head of state accepts responsibility and offers measures of redress for past injustices may assume too readily that the state is conveying a common understanding of the norms that were violated in causing the harm, and of the norms now required to be upheld in introducing measures of redress and ensuring against the repetition of harm in the future. The emphasis is on the head of state to make these commitments in the apology, which enables them to decide how the injustices are to be framed and what commitments to make to redress them. For Indigenous peoples, their perspectives on their experiences of injustice and the reparations needed to overcome them remain compromised and marginalised in this process. Thus, the transformative potential of state apologies to change perceptions and approaches to Indigenous peoples and their affairs is overshadowed by state institutional understandings of these issues. All the while, these political aspects of the apologies are obscured by their emotional aspects as the expression of regret and respect in each apology, seemingly other-oriented towards

Indigenous peoples, further obfuscates Indigenous peoples' broader claims. In the case of the Rudd and Harper apologies, in claiming to know what went wrong and what is to be done about it, neither of them created space for Indigenous viewpoints on these matters. The chapter that follows considers how apologies made to Indigenous peoples in settler-colonised nations could be utilised more effectively to promote Indigenous peoples' claims for justice through the development of a relational understanding of apology making.

Notes

1 Indeed, although Rudd estimated that 50,000 children were removed in this period, others have estimated the number of children removed was 100,000 (Attwood, 2001, p. 166). Compare the lower estimate calculated by Manne (2001, pp. 25–7) and even lower estimate by Windschuttle (2009, p. 617). The destruction of records and poor recordkeeping has made it difficult to accurately assess how many children were removed.

2 However, as was also noted in Chapter 2, making an apology conditional on the granting of forgiveness is generally considered inappropriate. Harper's intention in asking for forgiveness is equivocal and such a request was notably absent in Rudd's apology.

3 Despite their experiences of oppression under the *Indian Act*, Indigenous peoples have in the past resisted past attempts to repeal it because it represents (albeit distortedly) Indigenous-Crown relations. This is evident in the vehement opposition to the attempt made in the 1960s by the Canadian government, led by former Liberal Prime Minister Pierre Trudeau, to implement the White Paper on Indian Policy (Department of Indian Affairs and Northern Development, 1969) and dismantle Indian reserves; abolish Indian Status; and transfer federal services for Indigenous peoples to the provinces. Its aim was to dismantle the collective rights of Status Indians and facilitate their integration in the Canadian mainstream. Informing this process was liberal principles of individualism and formal equality (see generally, Coates, 2008, pp. 6–12). More recently, some First Nations have raised concerns about the *Indian Act* being repealed now that the *United Nations Declaration on the Rights of Indigenous Peoples Act Action Plan* (Department of Justice Canada, 2023) has been adopted (Morrisseau, 2023).

4 Note that Rudd had intimated that he would establish a joint policy commission led by him and the Leader of the Opposition, Brendan Nelson, to oversee Indigenous policy – an initiative that Nelson did not support. He also mentioned the issue of a referendum to recognise the 'first Australians' in the Constitution (see Chapter 6).

Reference list

Aboriginal and Torres Strait Islander Healing Foundation, 2021, *Make healing happen: it's time to act*, https://healingfoundation.org.au/app/uploads/2021/05/Make-Healing-Happen-Report-FINAL-May-2021.pdf

Aboriginal and Torres Strait Islander Social Justice Commissioner, 2005, *Social Justice Report*, https://humanrights.gov.au/our-work/aboriginal-and-torres-strait-islander-social-justice/publications/social-justice-report-5

Anderson, M., 2013, *The apology is still an empty vessel*, Sovereign Union – First Nations Asserting Sovereignty, 12 February, http://nationalunitygovernment.org/content/apology-still-empty-vessel-sovereign-union

Anker, K., 2014, 'Symptoms of sovereignty? Apologies, Indigenous rights and reconciliation in Australia and Canada', in R. Buchanan and P. Zumbansen (eds), *Law in transition: human rights, development and transitional justice*, pp. 245–267, Hart Publishing, Oxford, DOI:10.5040/9781474201841.ch-014

Attwood, B., 2001, 'The Stolen Generations and genocide: Robert Manne's In denial: the Stolen Generations and the right', *Aboriginal History*, vol. *25*, pp. 163–172.

Austin, J.L., 1962, *How to do things with words*, Oxford University Press, London.

Chrisjohn, R., Bear Nicholas, A., Stote, K., Craven (Omahkohkiaayo I'poyi), J., Wasacase, T., Loiselle, P. and Smith, A.O., 2008, 'An historic non-apology, completely and utterly not accepted', https://web.archive.org/web/20081012122924/http://www.marxmail.org/ApologyNotAccepted.htm

Churchill, W., 2008, 'Healing begins when the wounding stops: Indian residential schools and the prospects for "truth and reconciliation" in Canada', *Briarpatch Magazine*, 9 June, https://briarpatchmagazine.com/articles/view/healing-begins-when-the-wounding-stops/

Coates, K., 2008, *The Indian Act and the future of Aboriginal governance in Canada*, National Centre for First Nations Governance, http://fngovernance.org/ncfng_research/coates.pdf

Coicaud, J., 2009, 'Apology: a small yet important part of justice', *Japanese Journal of Political Science*, vol. *10*, no. *1*, pp. 93–124, DOI:10.1017/S1468109908003393

Corntassel, J. and Holder, C., 2008, 'Who's sorry now? Government apologies, truth commissions, and Indigenous self-determination in Australia, Canada, Guatemala, and Peru', *Human Rights Review*, vol. *9*, no. *4*, pp. 465–489, DOI:10.1007/s12142-008-0065-3

Coulthard, G., 2014, *Red skin, white masks: rejecting the colonial politics of recognition*, University of Minnesota Press, Minneapolis.

Cripps, K., 2012, 'Indigenous children's "best interests" at the crossroads: citizenship rights, Indigenous mothers and child protection authorities', *International Journal of Critical Indigenous Studies*, vol. *5*, no. 2, pp. 25–35, DOI:10.5204/ijcis.v5i2.88

Cubillo v. Commonwealth (2001) 174 ALR 97.

Department of Indian Affairs and Northern Development, 1969, *Statement of the Government of Canada on Indian policy*, Indian and Northern Affairs Canada, Ottawa.

Department of Justice Canada, 2023, *United Nations Declaration on the Rights of Indigenous Peoples Act Action Plan 2023–2028*, 21 November, https://www.justice.gc.ca/eng/declaration/ap-pa/index.html

Dodson, P., 2008, 'After the apology', *Arena Magazine*, April–May, vol. *94*, pp. 20–23.

Dorrell, M., 2009, 'From reconciliation to reconciling: reading what "we now recognize" in the Government of Canada's 2008 residential schools apology', *ESC English Studies in Canada*, vol. *35*, pp. 27–45, DOI:10.1353/esc.0.0165

Fiddler, C., 2008, 'Gov't of Canada apologize for 100 years of atrocities', *Windspeaker*, vol. *26*, no. *4*, http://www.ammsa.com/publications/windspeaker/govt-canada-apologize-100-years-atrocities

Fraser, N., 1995, 'From redistribution to recognition? Dilemmas of justice in a "post-socialist" age', *New Left Weekly*, vol. *212*, pp. 68–93.

Gaita, R., 1999, *A common humanity: thinking about love and truth and justice*, Text Publishing, Melbourne.

Gray, L., 2008, 'Why silence greeted Stephen Harper's residential-school apology', *The Georgia Straight*, 12 June, http://www.straight.com/article-150021/unyas-lynda-gray-responds-prime-ministers-apology

Henderson, J. and Wakeham, P., 2009, 'Colonial reckoning, national reconciliation?: Aboriginal peoples and the culture of redress in Canada', *ESC English Studies in Canada*, vol. *35*, pp. 1–26, DOI:10.1353/esc.0.0168

House of Commons, Canada, 2008, *House of Commons Debates (Hansard)*, 39th Parl., 2nd Sess., vol. *142*, no. *110*, 11 June, https://www.ourcommons.ca/Content/House/392/Debates/110/HAN110-E.PDF

House of Representatives, Australia, 2008a, 'Apology to Australia's Indigenous Peoples', *Parliamentary Debates*, 13 February, https://parlinfo.aph.gov.au/parlInfo/genpdf/chamber/hansardr/2008-02-13/0003/hansard_frag.pdf;fileType=application/pdf

House of Representatives, Australia, 2008b, 'Apology to Australia's Indigenous Peoples', *Parliamentary Debates*, 13 February, http://parlinfo.aph.gov.au/parlInfo/genpdf/chamber/hansardr/2008-02-13/0004/hansard_frag.pdf;fileType=application%2Fpdf

Howard, J., 2000, 'Practical reconciliation', in M. Grattan (ed.), *Reconciliation: essays on Australian reconciliation*, Bookman Press, Melbourne, pp. 88–96.

Human Rights and Equal Opportunity Commission, 1997, *Bringing them home: report of the National Inquiry into the Separation of Aboriginal and Torres Strait Islander Children from their Homes*, Sterling Press, Sydney.

Indian Act, 1876, Vict. 39, c. 18.

Indian Residential Schools Settlement Agreement, 2006, 8 May, https://residentialschoolsettlement.ca/IRS%20Settlement%20Agreement-%20ENGLISH.pdf

Jones, T., 2008, 'Tony Jones talks to Prime Minister Kevin Rudd', *ABC Lateline*, 14 February, http://www.abc.net.au/lateline/content/2007/s2163296.htm

Jung, C., 2009, *Transitional justice for Indigenous peoples in a non-transitional society*, International Center for Transitional Justice, https://www.ictj.org/sites/default/files/ICTJ-Identities-NonTransitionalSocieties-ResearchBrief-2009-English.pdf

Kemp, B., 2008, 'Putting the pain behind them', *CBC News*, 11 June, https://www.cbc.ca/news/canada/putting-the-pain-behind-them-1.710407

'Kevin Rudd's national apology to Stolen Generations', 2008, *News Corp Australia Network*, 13 February, https://web.archive.org/web/20131115041438/http://www.news.com.au/national/pm-moves-to-heal-the-nation/story-e6frfkw9-1111115539560

Korff, J., 2021a, 'Compensation for Stolen Generation members', *Creative Spirits*, 8 August, https://www.creativespirits.info/aboriginalculture/politics/compensation-for-stolen-generation-members#toc2

Korff, J., 2021b, '"Sorry" apology to Stolen Generations', *Creative Spirits*, 14 January, https://www.creativespirits.info/aboriginalculture/politics/stolen-generations/sorry-apology-to-stolen-generations

Krebs, M., 2008, 'The Harper "apology" – saying "sorry" with a forked tongue', *Socialist Voice*, 29 June, https://web.archive.org/web/20110126114442/http://www.socialistvoice.ca/?p=304

Kruger v. Commonwealth (1997) 190 CLR 1.

Mabo v. Queensland (No. 2) (1992) 175 CLR 1.

MacLachlan, A., 2013, 'Government apologies to Indigenous peoples', in A. MacLachlan and A. Speight (eds), *Justice responsibility and reconciliation in the wake of conflict*, Springer, Dordrecht, pp. 183–203, DOI:10.1007/978-94-007-5201-6_11

Manne, R., 2001, *In denial: the Stolen Generations and the right*, Australian Quarterly Essay, Black Inc., Melbourne.

McKinnon, C., 2008, 'Duplicity and deceit: Gary Foley's take on Rudd's apology to the Stolen Generations', *Melbourne Historical Journal*, vol. *36*, pp. 1–4.

Morrisseau, M., 2023, 'Canada's UNDRIP plan draws mixed reactions from Indigenous leaders', 23 June, *ICT*, https://ictnews.org/news/canadas-undrip-plan-draws-mixed-reactions-from-indigenous-leaders

Muldoon, P., 2009, 'Past injustices and future protections: on the politics of promising', *Australian Indigenous Law Review*, vol. *13*, no. *2*, pp. 2–16.

New South Wales, Parliament, Legislative Council, General Purpose Standing Committee No. 3, 2016, *Reparations for the Stolen Generations in New South Wales: unfinished business*, https://www.parliament.nsw.gov.au/lcdocs/inquiries/1645/Final%20report%20-%20Reparations%20for%20the%20Stolen%20Generations%20in%20NSW%20-%2023%20June%202016%20-%20with%20covers.pdf

Patterson, J., 2009, 'The politics of sorry', *Australian Quarterly*, vol. *81*, no. *2*, pp. 19–25.

Pearson, N., 2008, 'When words aren't enough', *The Australian*, 12 February.

Philpot, C., Balvin, N., Mellor, D. and Bretherton, D., 2013, 'Making meaning from collective apologies: Australia's apology to its Indigenous peoples', *Peace and Conflict: Journal of Peace Psychology*, vol. *19*, no. *1*, pp. 34–50, DOI:10.1037/a0031267

Polya, G., 2008, 'Australian Aboriginal genocide. Australia's "sorry", genocide denial & hypocrisy', *MWC News*, 14 February, https://sites.google.com/site/aboriginalgenocide/australian-aboriginal-genocide

Reilly, A., 2008, 'The inherent limits of the apology to the Stolen Generation', *University of Adelaide Law Research Paper No. 2009–002*, DOI:10.2139/ssrn.1294101

Reilly, A., 2012, 'Sovereign apologies', in J. Evans, A. Genovese, A. Reilly and P. Wolfe (eds), *Sovereignty: frontiers of possibility*, University of Hawai'i Press, Honolulu, pp. 196–219.

Rose, D.B., 1984, 'The saga of Captain Cook: morality in Aboriginal and European Law', *Australian Aboriginal Studies*, vol. 2, pp. 24–39.

Senate of Canada, 2008, *Debates of the Senate (Hansard)*, 39th Parl., 2nd Sess., vol. *144*, no. *69*, 12 June, https://sencanada.ca/Content/SEN/Chamber/392/Debates/pdf/069db_2008-06-12-e.pdf

Smith, N., 2008, *I was wrong: the meanings of apologies*, Cambridge University Press, New York, DOI:10.1017/CBO9780511499258

Sinclair, R., 2016, 'The Indigenous child removal system in Canada: an examination of legal decision-making and racial bias', *First Peoples Child and Family Review*, vol. *11*, no. 2. pp. 8–18.

Veracini, L., 2010, *Settler colonialism: a theoretical overview*, Palgrave Macmillan, New York.
Wherry, A., 2009, 'What he was talking about when he was talking about colonialism', *Macleans*, 1 October, http://www.macleans.ca/politics/ottawa/what-he-was-talking-about-when-he-talked-about-colonialism
Windschuttle, K., 2009, *The fabrication of Aboriginal history volume 3: the Stolen Generations 1881–2008*, Macleay Press, Sydney.
Winter, S., 2014, 'Theorising the political apology', *The Journal of Political Philosophy*, vol. 23, no. 3, pp. 261–281, DOI:10.1111/jopp.12047
Young, I.M., 1990, *Justice and the politics of difference*, Princeton University Press, Princeton.

Chapter 5

Apology making as a relational process

Re-focusing the Rudd and Harper apologies on Indigenous peoples

Introduction

State apologies conform to the norms and practices of the nations in which they are made. This appears to be the conclusion that can be drawn from the discussion in Chapter 4. As the examination of the Rudd and Harper apologies showed, the wrongs acknowledged in each of them were aligned to accepted norms. Ultimately, it was these norms that provided the framework for overcoming the harms caused. In Australia, this was evident with the formal adoption of the Closing the Gap policy in the *National Indigenous Reform Agreement (Closing the Gap)* (Council of Australian Governments, 2009), while in Canada, the *Indian Residential Schools Settlement Agreement* ('*Settlement Agreement*') (2006) provided the framework for the resolution of Indigenous peoples' outstanding claims. While both measures were aligned to Indigenous aspirations in each respective nation, it remained the case that they were determined according to state norms. In the case of Australia, where there had never been legal acceptance of Stolen Generations' claims for compensation, Rudd in his apology appealed to the notion of the 'fair go' to promote the Closing the Gap policy. The aim was to achieve equality of outcomes for Indigenous peoples vis-à-vis non-Indigenous peoples, while Indigenous-specific claims would continue to be sidelined (see also Chapter 6). Residential School Survivors seemingly appeared to do better in Canada in securing the *Settlement Agreement*. However, while it was approved by the courts it did not include any admissions of liability and aspects of its processes and administration proved inaccessible and ineffective and placed unfair and inequitable burdens on Survivors (see Chapter 7).

Ultimately, these apologies continued to perpetuate denial of the normative systems of Indigenous peoples and to present state norms and governance structures as the only legitimate framework for resolving the issues now facing Indigenous peoples. In each apology the wrongdoing was contained and framed to fit established state norms. Consequently, Indigenous peoples would continue to remain in a subordinate position to the state,

DOI: 10.4324/9781003491019-5

contrary to those who believed that each apology marked a new era in Indigenous–state relations.

The purpose of this chapter is to examine how these effects could be countered by shifting attention in the apology-making process to what Indigenous peoples say in response to the apologies made to them. In the wider literature on apologies, this aspect of the process remains underdeveloped. It is more usual than not for the focus to be on the state leader making the apology and what they say and how they say it. This might be because of the emphasis that has been placed on the delivery of an apology. Ensuring that it is offered officially by the head of state, in public and at the right pitch and tenor, is considered essential to help change how each side of a conflict might see the other and thus overcome the conflict that might exist between them (Barkan and Karn, 2006, p. 7; King, 2011). However, whether this approach can result in appropriate reforms is doubtful when the focus is on what the state leader is saying, and it is assumed everyone will benefit equally from the apology. Ultimately, such an approach obscures the inequality in power that exists in society, and how it can (and does) operate at the time the apology is being made to exclude and marginalise victim perspectives on reform options.

Thus, it might be more the case that state leaders will use their displays of emotion in delivering the apology to offset making adequate and effective reparations to victims. This problem could arise because an apology, as a speech act, is generally understood as performing actions in the world. As an expression of sorrow for a wrong, an apology can give the appearance that what happened in the past is now settled once and for all (Jung, 2010, p. 234) so that 'we' can move on 'with the warm inner glow that will come with having said sorry' (Pearson, 2008, p. 2). However, it might be for this very reason that political apologies have been dismissed as seductive, feel-good strategies (Cowlishaw, 2009, p. 358) that function to divert attention away from the need for measurable changes to the lives of those who have suffered and who (like Indigenous peoples) continue to suffer from the effects of past (and present) wrongs (Dodson, 2000, p. 269; Thompson, 2008, p. 32). In light of these shortcomings it would appear that critics are right to dismiss apology making 'as nothing more than a cheap effort at assuaging lingering guilt concerning some misdeeds from the past', while those who make them can 'feel morally superior to those who came before them' (Cunningham, 1999, p. 288; Gibney and Roxstrom, 2001, p. 912) without having to do much more than apologise.

It is likely that state leaders would be fully aware of the political benefits they can reap from making an apology at the right pitch to their audiences. Indeed, the emotional aspects of making an apology may only obscure the politics involved. As became evident in the previous chapter, both Rudd and Harper apparently expressed other-oriented regret and appeared willing to make reparations for past wrongdoing, but in ways that reinforced state power in ascribing the harms suffered by Indigenous peoples and how to overcome them. This stance enabled each respective leader to redeem the virtue of their respective nation, while they continued to elide the breadth and depth of the impacts of colonisation on Indigenous peoples. The acknowledgement of suffering recast Indigenous peoples as needing a cure, and the proposals for a cure were based on their worthiness of respect. Nevertheless, on both understandings, Indigenous peoples' claims for specific rights, such as self-determination, were effectively precluded. The acknowledgement of their suffering sidestepped their capacity for self-determination, while the recognition of their human worth applied to place them on par with everyone else in each nation. In this way, each apology served to re-legitimise state sovereignty over Indigenous peoples as it would seemingly apply to other citizens in the polity, obscuring Indigenous-specific claims, and maintaining state authority to know what would be best for Indigenous peoples in the future.

The fact that these deeper political issues can be depoliticised by the emotional aspects of apology making raises the question whether state apologies should be done away with altogether. Ultimately, this may not be ideal as there are Survivors who continue to call for them and find them meaningful. At the same time, their shortcomings cannot be ignored. Considering these tensions, a more pertinent question may be whether they can be used more effectively to realise the transformative potential of an apology, and in the case of apologies to Indigenous peoples disrupt the settler–colonised relationship.

This chapter seeks to address this issue by refocusing attention on the role of Indigenous peoples in the apology-making process and considering how their role could be recast in political terms, as opposed to sidelining their claims as happened in the Rudd and Harper apologies. The aim is to place Indigenous peoples at the centre of the process. This shift in focus also involves reconsidering the role of emotion in the apology-making process to ensure the apology is attuned to the needs of Indigenous peoples and prevent it from being used as a means of meeting the emotional (and thereby the political) needs of those who identify with the apologising nation state. The basis for this approach is grounded in the understanding of an apology as a relational process – state actors may deliver the apology, but only victims can decide whether to accept or reject it. The fate of the apology lies in their hands. So understood, the process would be empowering for victims and would not merely serve to reiterate the power of the apologising state. If this understanding garnered stronger support, it could become less easy for governments to sideline Indigenous claims post-apology.

The chapter is divided into two parts. The first part revisits Indigenous peoples' responses to the Rudd and Harper apologies discussed previously in Chapters 3 and 4. Clearly, while some found closure, others looked to the apologies to provide the impetus for more far-reaching reforms, while others still rejected them outright. Also of significance, particularly considering the correlation made in this book between reconciliation and justice, is how the Indigenous representatives in their formal responses did not greet the apologies with forgiveness but with gratitude. In this respect, they did not treat the apologies as an endpoint, but as a step in the broader process of reconciliation. The effectiveness of the apologies – and the possibility of forgiveness – would depend on future government commitment and action to advance just outcomes for Indigenous peoples.

The second part of the chapter considers how the understanding of an apology as a relational process could further support such claims because, unlike an apology understood as a 'speech act', a relational understanding brings the recipients of the apology into focus. While this understanding derives from a transactional understanding based on the relationship between apology and forgiveness, it refrains from using notions of forgiveness and acceptance as completing an apology. Instead, it treats an apology as opening the lines of communication between the parties and is more akin to Indigenous conflict resolution processes (see Chapter 1). Moreover, in political terms, the effect of a relational approach not only treats the apologising state as engaged in political action, Indigenous peoples are similarly engaged. Viewed in this way, it becomes possible to consider how Indigenous peoples' role in determining the effectiveness of an apology may not be about forgiveness (although this may be of significance to some Survivors), but in political terms can create a site of political resistance and space to assert Indigenous claims. In this respect, in developing the understanding of apology making as relational, this chapter is also developing the understanding of apology making as transformative whereby an apology's promise of 'never again' is fulfilled by giving precedence to Indigenous understandings of what is best for them and provide counter perspectives to what state actors might think is best.

In many respects, the argument developed in this chapter is addressed to the various parties involved in the apology-making process, including those scholars who research in this field. The chapter also adopts the stance that there is an ethical responsibility to resist the quest of settler colonialism to eliminate Indigenous peoples through continued denial of their political autonomy and infringement of their rights, the consequences of which have been grimly felt by many, including those impacted by the forced Indigenous child removal policies and laws. In developing the understanding of apology making as relational, this chapter seeks to contribute to this endeavour by doing what the Rudd and Harper apologies did not do, but which the Indigenous representatives who responded sought to do, which is to focus attention on what Indigenous peoples have to say and thereby support their claims and how they may envisage the way forward. Through the constitutive power of language, which in this chapter is to shift the discourse of apology making from speech act to relational process, Indigenous peoples' perspectives are brought into view to strengthen the moral imperative of an apology to promote their claims for justice.

Nevertheless, it is equally important to be attuned to the current reality of inequality that exists in Indigenous–state relations, evidenced by continuing rights violations, and that dialogue in the absence of robust Indigenous rights protections may ultimately fail to achieve lasting change. Accordingly, the chapter concludes by calling for more far-reaching institutional changes, such as the implementation of an Indigenous rights framework, to create a more level playing field. This approach has its own set of shortcomings, but considering the rights infringed throughout the process of colonisation it seems imperative that following an apology, institutional changes are made, which at the very least provide avenues for Indigenous peoples to assert their rights.

Indigenous peoples and their responses to the Rudd and Harper apologies

The responses of Indigenous peoples to the Rudd and Harper apologies reveal a diverse range of reactions. Some responses attested to the far-reaching intergenerational impacts of the forced Indigenous child removal practice and how an apology served as recognition of these impacts. This is reflected in this statement by Archie Roach, Stolen Generations Survivor and Gunditjmara and Bundjalung Elder: '[It's] an apology not just for me, but for my mother and for my father and for my children who carry the burden and carry the weight of what happened to us stolen kids' (Archie Roach, Aboriginal singer and song-writer, reproduced in Korff, 2021).

In terms of gauging their effectiveness, some appeared to treat them as they would an interpersonal apology. Some looked for sincerity in the way they were delivered (Kemp, 2008; Wright, 2008), while others were so moved by the experience they were inspired to forgive (Fitzpatrick and Nguyen, 2008). The positive reactions revealed the personal significance of the apologies for some Survivors, while the more negative reactions reflect the apologies' shortcomings and how an apology made very little difference to their lives (Korff, 2021). In some cases, the apology's significance was felt even though the direct Survivors were no longer alive (Tillett, 2010), but equally the fact that loved ones had died long before the apology was reason to dismiss it for being too late (Philpot, et al., 2013, p. 42).

Also evident in these responses was acknowledgement of the significance of the apologies for the Survivors as well as each nation. As discussed in Chapter 3, the apologies were hailed as watershed moments in the history of each nation for their contribution to the reconciliation process. In Calma's view, for instance, the Rudd apology not only provided 'healing' for the Stolen Generations, but for the entire Australian nation. 'Let your healing, and the healing of the nation, begin', he declared as he concluded his speech on the day of the apology (Calma, 2008, p. 4). This understanding was also shared by some Stolen Generations Survivors and other Indigenous peoples as they acknowledged the significance of the apology in terms of their own personal histories, and in terms of the history of the nation and improving

Indigenous and non-Indigenous relations based on a shared truth that the forced removal of Indigenous children was wrong (Korff, 2021). It is notable, however, that while some individual Survivors may have reacted positively, this did not necessarily equate with forgiveness. If there was forgiveness it may have been separate from the apology and if there was no forgiveness it may have been because government actions did not warrant it (Philpot, et al., 2013, pp. 44–45).

None of the Indigenous representatives included pronouncements of forgiveness in their official responses to the apologies either. Indeed, in some of their responses was the understanding that forgiveness – if it was to be granted at all – could only be granted on an individual basis. This understanding was inferred by Dodson when he addressed Stolen Generations Survivors in his response:

> To the children of those who were removed, I challenge you to find the courage to forgive but never to forget what was done to your families and to take from their stories the commitment and courage to prevail as proud Aboriginal people.
>
> (Dodson, 2008, p. 21)

Others reiterated that the granting of forgiveness would be dependent on the achievement of just outcomes for Indigenous peoples. For instance, Simon in her statement in the Senate on the day following the Harper apology acknowledged that forgiveness was a matter of individual choice. At the same time, she made a point of saying: 'As leader of the organization representing the Inuit of Canada, I believe that real and lasting forgiveness must be earned. It will be forthcoming only when it is clear that government is willing to act' (Senate of Canada, 2008, p. 1505).

Notably, instead of forgiveness, each representative expressed gratitude in their responses, particularly for the leadership that both Rudd and Harper had showed in overcoming the challenges that had stood in the way of making their respective apologies. It is important to make this distinction to avoid confusing their expressions of gratitude with forgiveness. Their expressions of gratitude seemed to relate more specifically to the immediate histories of the apologies. They were grateful that the apologies had been made, and understandably so considering no other government had come forward to make an apology. In Australia, Dodson expressed his appreciation for the apology as a 'courageous and welcome step' (Dodson, 2008, p. 20), while Calma expressed his gratitude to Rudd:

> Prime Minister, can I thank you for your leadership on this issue. ...It is far more difficult to try and unite people than to divide them.
>
> Your efforts should be praised universally for attempting to create a bridge between the many diverse elements of our society.
>
> (Calma, 2008, p. 3)

Notably the sentiment was echoed by Indigenous peoples in the audience who expressed their gratitude by wearing T-shirts on the day which had the simple message 'Thanks' printed on them.

In Canada, gratitude – not forgiveness – also underlined the reactions of the representatives who responded to the Harper apology in Parliament. In this respect, Fontaine was clear when he addressed the Senate: 'We accepted the apology with gratitude' (Senate of Canada, 2008, p. 1503). Gratitude for the apology and recognition of Harper's leadership in making the apology was a sentiment that was expressed by all the other Indigenous representatives in the House of Commons in response to the apology (House of Commons, Canada, 2008, pp. 6855–6857 (Brazeau; Simon; Chartier; Jacobs)).

Thus, it is evident that the apologies were of great personal significance for some, while they were of historical and political significance for others. In fact, there are responses where the personal, historical, and political significance of these apologies were treated as inextricably linked. In a speech at a Tungasuvvingat Inuit gathering the day before the Harper apology, Simon drew these links together:

> June 11th 2008 will be a day in which we, as Inuit and as aboriginal people, can take some comfort.
>
> Comfort that the sad history and sad legacy of abuse at schools attended by Inuit and other aboriginal students will be fully and forcefully exposed to the public eye.
>
> Comfort that the various efforts in the past to deny, minimize or rationalize that abuse will be forever discredited.
>
> Comfort that the accountability of the Government of Canada will be acknowledged and that an apology will be given.
>
> (Simon, 2008)

In these terms, any comfort Indigenous peoples could derive from the apologies depended on the public acknowledgement of the truth about the past and the government's acceptance of responsibility for the injustices Indigenous peoples have suffered. Indeed, when these aspects seem absent the veracity of a state apology may seriously come into question. This was strikingly illustrated in Australia in relation to the conservative Liberal–Coalition opposition leader Brendan Nelson's apology delivered in response to the Rudd apology (House of Representatives, Australia, 2008b). His implied defence of John Howard's refusal to apologise and expressed support of recent Coalition interventionist policies imposed on Indigenous communities in the Northern Territory resulted in members of the audience turning their backs on him while he read out his speech (Gartrell, 2008). It is also important to point out with respect to the Rudd and Harper apologies that there were Indigenous peoples who rejected them outright for not owning up to the truth of the genocide and bringing the perpetrators to justice (see, e.g., Chrisjohn, et al., 2008; 'Kevin Rudd's national apology to Stolen Generations', 2008).

Moreover, even for those Indigenous representatives who responded positively to the apologies it was apparent that more than the acknowledgement of the truth was needed. Achieving just outcomes for Indigenous peoples would ultimately measure the effectiveness of each apology. The reaction of Anishinabek Nation Grand Council Chief John Beaucage reflected this attitude:

> We are so proud that many Anishinabek lived long enough to hear Canada's apology to them. But the true test of Mr. Harper's words will be his government's actions to help our children have a better future than their parents and grandparents.
>
> (Kemp, 2008).

In Chapter 3, the responses of the Indigenous representatives who responded formally to each apology were discussed in greater detail. Broadly, these responses revealed there was a need to address the effects of the forced child removal practice. There was also the need to address the broader effects of colonisation. Moreover, evident in these responses was how working on achieving these ends could advance reconciliation. On the one hand, there were calls for unity between Indigenous and non-Indigenous peoples to work towards rebuilding strong and healthy Indigenous communities (e.g., House of Commons, Canada, 2008, p. 6855 (Simon); see also Dodson, 2008, p. 23). Fontaine expressed this imperative most emphatically:

> The attempts to erase our identities hurt us deeply. But it also hurt all Canadians and impoverished the character of this nation.
>
> We must not falter in our duty now. Emboldened by this spectacle of history, it is possible to end our racial nightmare together.
>
> (House of Commons, Canada, 2008, p. 6855)

On the other hand, their perspectives revealed the need for the relationship between Indigenous and non-Indigenous peoples to, as Jacobs claimed, respect Indigenous peoples' self-determination 'as a people … and that we can make decisions on our own and we know what needs to be done in our communities' (Fiddler, 2008).

It was evident in such responses that institutionalising a new relationship in place of the settler–colonised relationship, and the potential for the apologies to contribute to this process, was being treated as a real and necessary possibility. Indigenous peoples assuming an official role in the political landscape of each nation with the aim of gaining control over their affairs was considered vital in this regard. Indeed, even those Indigenous peoples who criticised the apologies (as discussed Chapter 4) sought a similar outcome.

The main difference between the Indigenous representatives who responded positively to the apologies and those who did not appeared to turn on whether they thought the apologies could make any difference to the achievement of just outcomes. For instance, Calma used his response to the Rudd apology as an opportunity to call on government to implement the remaining recommendations of the *Bringing Them Home* report (Human Rights and Equal Opportunity Commission, 1997) which would, among other things, have included the setting up of a compensation fund for the Stolen Generations (Calma, 2008, pp. 3–4). The fact that no fund was set up led to criticisms, like the one made by Anderson, that the apology was 'an empty vessel' (Anderson, 2013). Likewise, Simon declared in her response to the Harper apology that the new relationship with government requires that '[w]e must be in the room working together with government ... Gone are the days when policy or legislative initiatives were invoked for us' (Senate of Canada, 2008, p. 1505). A similar aspiration can be inferred from Krebs' criticisms of that apology, particularly when he claimed that such an outcome cannot follow an apology where the state continues to determine outcomes for Indigenous peoples (Krebs, 2008).

These responses are only a sample and do not represent all Indigenous peoples' perspectives on the Rudd and Harper apologies and the range of harms they were seeking to have addressed. The offer of measures (such as the Closing the Gap policy and the *Settlement Agreement*) also showed that both Rudd and Harper understood that more than a sincere 'I'm sorry' would be needed to make their respective apologies meaningful. However, when measured against the more critical Indigenous perspectives in Chapter 4, it became evident that there are substantive differences in understanding regarding the effects of the injustices, the reforms required to address them, and the role of Indigenous peoples in resolving them. This discussion demonstrated the importance of the way that history is interpreted in an apology to attain just outcomes. The contestation over history (especially of colonisation) can be seen reflected in the different reform agendas put forward by government in the apologies and Indigenous peoples in their responses and is further reflected in how they each thought reconciliation could be achieved in future: the state would continue to exercise jurisdiction over Indigenous peoples; whereas Indigenous peoples sought jurisdictional space to conduct their own affairs. Yet, it was each state's perspective on history, supported by their respective normative frameworks, which prevailed in each apology. This enabled both states to maintain the legitimacy of their powers to continue to drive Indigenous policy. Simultaneously, the potential that some Indigenous peoples envisaged for power to shift in their favour was curtailed.

The next part of this chapter considers how a different outcome could be supported by changing how apology making is conceptualised. Briefly, the approach that is adopted depends on the understanding of an apology as a relational process, which is aimed to create leeway in the apology context for

Indigenous peoples to push the boundaries that have been set by government around the issues they continue to face in settler-colonised nations. This approach recognises that just as some Indigenous peoples saw themselves as engaged in political action in their struggles to secure an apology, so too in responding to these apologies they were engaged in political action. Indeed, their responses could provide effective resistance to colonial power, for while states may make the apologies, only Survivors can determine their fate. In this dynamic, the fate of an apology may ultimately depend on whether the claims of Survivors have been satisfied. Essentially, this means that after an apology the claims of Survivors can no longer be ignored. So understood, apology making conceived as relational deepens understanding of the potential of the apology process to provide room for Indigenous peoples to articulate their claims for justice and have those claims acted upon. However, as becomes evident below, implementing this understanding in practice is not without obstacles.

The way forward: re-conceptualising the Rudd and Harper apologies as a relational process

As became evident in Chapter 2, an apology may assist to overcome conflict created by injustice. At the time of the injustice, the wrongdoers were in a position of power with respect to the victims and acted as though they could treat them as they pleased. An apology is one way the wrongdoer can acknowledge that their actions were wrong and make up for them. A sincere 'I'm sorry' sends the message that victims did not deserve to be treated unjustly. In this way, an apology serves as a show of respect for the victims in the present, which has the potential to make up for the disrespect the wrongdoer had once shown to them. An apology, as implied in this understanding, functions to unite the parties based on their shared understanding that the past treatment of the victims was wrong. It is for this reason that the potential of an apology to promote reconciliation between the parties is considered one of its most vital functions.

Nevertheless, as important as the making of an apology can be to reconciling (or improving) relationships, the role that victims play in the apology process (and the reconciliation process for that matter) cannot be ignored. This is because the effectiveness of an apology depends on satisfying victims, as they determine the fate of the apology and whether to accept or reject it. Understood in these terms, an apology involves a shift in power between the wrongdoer and the person/s wronged: in apologising the wrongdoer becomes vulnerable to the responses of those they have wronged. In turn, the apology process would be empowering for victims. They may choose to grant or withhold forgiveness. They may even ignore the apology. In accepting or rejecting the apology, the fate of the apologiser, and possibly even the future relations between the parties, is placed in the victims' hands (Tavuchis, 1991, p. 35; cf. Coicaud and Jönsson, 2008, p. 79).

The point of making these observations is to demonstrate how the making of an apology gives victims scope to respond to the apology and imposes an obligation on the apologiser to listen and act accordingly:

> the apology process institutionalizes a symbolic exchange whereby the speaker provides a social legitimation of the pain of the listener and the social and moral norms held by the listener in the hope that the listener will respond in some reciprocal manner.
>
> (Funk-Unrau, 2004, p. 3)

In this exchange, the roles are reversed as the apologiser 'places her/himself at the mercy of the listener who may or may not accept the apology' (Funk-Unrau, 2004, p. 3). According to Funk-Unrau, 'a sincere apology implies vulnerability on the part of the apologiser and a willingness to accept the demands and judgment of the one who has been wronged' (Funk-Unrau, 2004, p. 10). And even when Survivors do not forgive, the withholding of forgiveness can also be empowering for them. According to Minow, the victims are the ones 'who remind the community about what can, and cannot, be forgiven. The authority to view a violation as beyond forgiveness marks one of the survivors' contributions to the community's moral sense' (Minow, 1998, p. 116).

These understandings highlight the central role of victims to the apology-making process which, in turn, is central to a relational understanding of apology making. Once this is accepted it would no longer make sense to treat an apology merely as a 'speech act' – which in the political context may translate the expression of sorrow into the re-legitimisation of state sovereignty. Instead, understood as a relational process an apology may be better viewed as making room for dialogue between the parties – where the reactions to the apologies are treated seriously (if not more so) than the apologies themselves. Importantly, the shift in power that a relational understanding may inspire could shift the frame of reference for future action to give precedence to Indigenous perspectives in directing change.

However, apology discourses have not ventured far into analysing the political implications of the participation of victims in the apology-making process and how this can form part of the broader resolution process. In some respects, apology discourses may rush too quickly toward reaching a resolution by emphasising how victims may respond to an apology by granting forgiveness (Govier and Verwoerd, 2002, p. 69). Although these discourses also recognise that victims have the power to decide whether to grant forgiveness or not (Govier, 2006, p. 70), this is not usually followed by an examination of how this could translate into future negotiations between victims and perpetrators. Moreover, this assumes that whether victims grant or withhold forgiveness, either response can be empowering. Whether this is so is a debateable issue and may depend on how 'empowerment' is understood. In the context of making apologies to Indigenous peoples, and as has been advanced in this chapter, empowerment requires victims having the means to realise their claims for justice.

In forgiveness discourses the tendency, however, has not been to connect the notion of forgiveness with the advancement of justice, but instead to frame forgiveness somewhat apolitically in terms of changing the psychological state of victims: the granting or withholding of forgiveness relates to whether victims are willing (or not) to move on and let go of feelings of resentment (Butler, 1827; Larocco, 2016, pp. 25–26). Moreover, while it is true that forgiveness may be granted (or withheld) independently of an apology, when an apology has been offered, some may view it as incomplete without forgiveness and may be dismayed when victims do not grant forgiveness in their responses to an apology. Indeed, this criticism was implicit in some of the commentary on Indigenous peoples' responses to both the Rudd and Harper apologies (Mackay, 2009; James, 2018).

Those who subscribe to this view consider forgiveness as creating the pathway to true healing for victims: without forgiveness, healing may be impossible (Dillon, 2008). So understood, the granting of forgiveness is viewed as the ideal outcome for victims because it may assist them to overcome the negative effects of being the 'victims': with forgiveness, the victim identity dissolves, and a person's true power emerges (Tolle, 2005). In this way, forgiveness may be seen as facilitating 'a freedom within the individual, a release from the pain and trauma that enables one to move on and live in the world without grudges or hatred' (Changfoot, 2009, p. 7). As Archbishop Desmond Tutu put it, forgiveness is 'the best form of self-interest' because it enables people 'to survive and emerge still human despite all efforts to dehumanize them' (Tutu, 1999, p. 52).

Others, by contrast, appear more attuned to the way the personal benefits of forgiveness may extend to other social and political benefits as well. As Minow has explained:

> Through forgiveness, we can renounce resentment, and avoid the self-destructive effects of holding on to pain, grudges, and victimhood. The act of forgiving can reconnect the offender and the survivor and establish or renew a relationship; it can heal grief; forge new, constructive alliances; and break cycles of violence.
>
> (Minow, 1998, p. 14)

Accordingly, the personal benefits of forgiveness – the cessation of resentment and bitterness – could extend to the rest of society. Victims who forgive may no longer harbour resentment and the compulsion to seek revenge which could help avert a cycle of violence from developing. In granting forgiveness victims can reconnect and recognise the common humanity of those who have wronged them, which, at the collective level, may strengthen a broader sense of the commonality of humankind and assist in promoting stability and democracy in society more broadly (Arendt, 1998).

Nevertheless, there are still those who are wary of the granting of forgiveness. Concerns have been raised about whether it can benefit victims and relieve them of negative feelings about the past (Changfoot, 2009). Forgiveness theorists may espouse the power that forgiveness gives to victims to rise above negative situations and see them in a different light (Spezzano, 1999, p. 4), but when those negative situations have not changed in reality (and settler-colonised contexts are one example of this) it becomes questionable whether forgiveness is in fact an appropriate response. There is, therefore, an understandable concern that the notion of forgiveness may have a coercive effect on victims and close off their claims for justice. The concern may be summed up by a key motif in forgiveness discourses which is 'to forgive and forget'. In other words, 'get over it and move on'. It is important to acknowledge, however, that there need not be a direct correlation between forgiving and forgetting. As was noted above, Dodson, in response to the Rudd apology, stated to Survivors: 'I challenge you to find the courage to forgive but never to forget' (Dodson, 2008, p. 21). It is notable how Dodson separated forgiving from forgetting, which is contrary to the usual correlation, 'forgive and forget'. The idea of 'forgiving without forgetting' has the potential to separate the act of forgiving from the act of seeking justice. This is possible if forgiveness is considered more in relation to the benefits it can have for the person wronged (such as overcoming hurt and anger) and not to the potential benefits it can have for wrongdoers (such as being 'let off the hook').

This is a significant distinction to make as it provides scope for victims to forgive for their own sake while they may also continue to pursue their claims for justice. However, as the experience in Australia has shown, the perception among politicians that the Rudd apology was 'accepted' largely justified their adoption of a 'business as usual' approach, as though forgiveness had in fact been granted (Brennan and Higgins, 2018).

Evidently, there are different ways forgiveness can function. For victims, granting forgiveness may promote healing; it can be withheld on condition of future action; or it may never be granted because the conditions may not allow for it. For wrongdoers, being granted forgiveness may also promote healing in terms of their relationships with those they have harmed; if withheld it sends the message that more action is needed; but if granted it may merely serve the pragmatic ends of the wrongdoers to bring the past to a close. This is the most concerning outcome. When it comes to apology making, it is the correlation that exists between apology and forgiveness that may raise the expectations of the perpetrators (and the wider population) for victims to respond to the apology with forgiveness. This highlights the ambiguous position victims can be placed when they are offered an apology as they may feel as though they have a moral obligation to forgive. This could effectively undermine their power 'to respond any way [they] desire' (Funk-Unrau, 2004,

p. 3). Thus, instead of benefiting the victims, the granting of forgiveness may exonerate the wrongdoers prematurely and thus release them from their obligations to make meaningful reparations. Indeed, forgiveness may be sought by wrongdoers merely to relieve them of responsibility for their transgressions, while victims may be left not feeling relieved of the past at all.

Ultimately, however, perpetrators' true intentions may never be known. Ostensibly, Harper (House of Commons, Canada, 2008, p. 5850) in asking for forgiveness in his apology on behalf of the Government of Canada could be construed as an acknowledgement of Indigenous peoples' power to determine Canada's fate. However, this gesture may have been mere political manoeuvring. Considering the way Harper contained the harms and measures of redress in his apology, he seemed more intent on moving the nation forward than concerned about whether Indigenous peoples granted forgiveness or not. Notably, there were Residential School Survivors and others in Canada who came together to collectively respond to the Harper apology with forgiveness. The impression they gave was that this was for their own healing and empowerment ('Native residential school forgiveness granted', 2010), but whether this was the government's understanding remains to be seen.

Nevertheless, even for perpetrators who desire forgiveness, it is not always forthcoming, and an apology may in fact be rejected outright. A notable development in forgiveness discourses has been to expose the inherent difficulties involved in the granting of forgiveness (especially in extreme cases of wrongdoing). Forgiveness may be the ideal effect of an apology, but it may be an impossible ideal to achieve especially if it requires nothing less than forgiving the unforgivable (Derrida, 2001). Thus, it is often conceded that forgiveness may not be granted. As noted in the previous section, the Indigenous responses to the Rudd and Harper apologies give the general impression that forgiveness is considered an individual matter, and not a collective one. And even then, individuals may not forgive. As Grand Chief Edward John of the First Nations Summit said in a release issued by the First Nations Leadership Council with respect to the Harper apology:

> The responses to the apology are both individual and collective. It is extremely important that we respect the many survivors who, in their own discretion and time, will consider the prime minister's apology and determine how, in their own interest, each of them will deal with it.
>
> (Kemp, 2008)

However, the problem remains that the granting of forgiveness could compromise the claims of victims for justice and close off the potential of an apology to promote these claims. One can then appreciate why Indigenous representatives such as Simon were careful to distinguish between those individuals who at a personal level may have found the strength to forgive while she, in her political capacity as President of the Inuit, held off granting forgiveness. Indeed, it may be the withholding of forgiveness that possesses the greatest political value for victims because of its potential to stave off closure and thus maintain the possibility for just outcomes on their terms. In this respect, it is important to recall a desired endpoint of a state apology is the just resolution of past wrongs – forgiveness, if it is to be granted at all, may be conditional on such an outcome. To reiterate what Simon stated in the Senate: 'The magnitude of yesterday's historic apology and request for forgiveness will be measured in the future actions of government' (Senate of Canada, 2008, p. 1505).

Reinforcing the understanding that official apologies not only have the potential to provide a measure of justice for victims, but also form part of a broader process of reform, is important especially in the case of Indigenous peoples whose calls for justice have been too often ignored. Indeed, as is evident from the responses to the apologies, there are Indigenous peoples who consider that a failure to make adequate and effective reparations for past wrongs can be detrimental to the long-term success of the apologies that are offered to them. The relational understanding of apology making serves to promote this stance in orienting attention to Indigenous peoples' claims.

This relational understanding stands in contrast to the understanding of apology making as a 'speech act', which in focusing on what the head of state says in an apology and the significance of the head of state in performing this act has tended to sideline the importance of the role of Survivors in the apology process and what they have to say in response. Indeed, even more critical appraisals of the Rudd and Harper apologies maintain this focus (e.g., Holder, 2014; cf. Reilly, 2012), which ultimately comes at the expense of victims and their perspectives.

This point is illustrated by the way Calma's and Dodson's responses to the Rudd apology were treated. Neither Calma nor Dodson responded in the House of Representatives and therefore they were not given the opportunity to 'formally accept' the apology before Parliament. In the absence of Indigenous peoples making 'official' responses in Parliament, the delivery of the apology – as an official *speech* to the nation – has been interpreted as not allowing for or not requiring their acceptance: 'Although the public gallery was full of Aboriginal people witnessing the apology, the success of its delivery and its acceptance did not depend on their presence' (Reilly, 2008, p. 15).

Considering how in the apology itself Rudd appeared oblivious of Indigenous peoples' specific involvement in the apology movement and instead claimed to be fulfilling an election promise to the Australian people by making the apology, it seems unsurprising that Indigenous peoples' role in the apology proceedings would be confined to that of spectator, there only 'to register the emotional content of the event' (Stephens, 2008). The apology was not treated as theirs because: 'the apology was not intended for them. The true recipients of the apology were those white Australians who watched and wanted to be made to feel as if they had taken part in something good' (Stephens, 2008).

Indeed, to the extent that the drive for an apology in Australia was motivated by white Australians' feelings of guilt and shame about Australia's past treatment of Indigenous peoples (cf. Celermajer, 2009, pp. 190–193; Muldoon, 2009, pp. 10–11), the apology was framed in such a way as to alleviate these negative feelings. Notable, in this regard, is the way Rudd accepted intergenerational responsibility on behalf of the present Parliaments of the nation, but not for the present generation of Australian people as though they are not in any way responsible for what has been done to Indigenous peoples. Moreover, in retelling the story of the forced removal of the Warumungu woman Nanna Nungala Fejo, and the way that she finally forgave the Aboriginal stockman who decades earlier had assisted two white welfare men to forcibly remove her from her mother (House of Representatives, Australia, 2008a, p. 168), Rudd circumscribed the need to ask for forgiveness. In this way, the apology *and* the granting of forgiveness were neatly contained within the one speech, making it easy for white Australians and their political representatives to move on in the belief that they had done something good by supporting an apology, and thus enabling them to restore pride in themselves and their nation. Indigenous peoples, in contrast, were left with the potential pangs of guilt in the event they did in fact reject the apology. According to Rudd: 'if the apology we extend today is accepted in the spirit of reconciliation in which it is offered, we can today resolve together that there be a new beginning for Australia' (House of Representatives, Australia, 2008a, p. 170). In this way, Rudd inadvertently acknowledged the importance of Indigenous peoples' acceptance of the apology for its success, but at the same time he seemed to give Indigenous peoples little choice but to respond positively to it, or else their rejection of the apology would mean the end of reconciliation for Australia.

Considering the history of political exclusion of Indigenous peoples from the workings of government, the failure to include Indigenous representatives in a formal capacity during the apology proceedings in Parliament is an obvious failing of the Rudd apology. Nevertheless, the fact remains that Indigenous peoples *did* make speeches in response to the apology, and the general lack of acknowledgement of their responses and their importance to the apology in the literature is problematic. The immediate effect of this failure is to reinforce the understanding that only what the head of state says in the apology is important, which reinforces the assumption of the absolute sovereignty of the Crown, while Indigenous peoples' role is confined to that of '"passive witnesses" to the apology's performance' (Reilly, 2008, p. 15).

Ultimately, the extensive focus on what is said, at the expense of what is said in response to an apology, could have the effect of silencing victims and trivialising the importance of their involvement in the apology process and the reconciliation process more broadly. Acknowledging these responses as forming a part of the apology process is important, particularly in the case of Indigenous peoples whose experiences of being silenced has been intrinsic to their experiences of injustice. Whether victims grant or withhold forgiveness, indeed, whatever their attitudes to an apology may be, amounts to a response. As was evident in the official responses of the Indigenous representatives to the Rudd and Harper apologies, none of them explicitly accepted or rejected them but they were thankful for them. Arguably, in expressing gratitude for the apologies they recognised that forgiveness was not yet possible; instead, they recognised the importance of keeping the lines of communication open to engender a working partnership with government which they believed could be possible now an apology had been made. At the same time, by not accepting the apologies outright, they used their role in responding to the apologies as an opportunity to express their own positions on the future direction of the process of reconciliation. Unfortunately, however, while it seems that the making of an apology has the potential to open the space for Survivor empowerment, as long as what is said in the apologies continues to attract most of the attention, there is a danger that the understanding of the wrongs and the way to address them will continue to be framed in terms of the perspective of the politico-legal order of the state and not from the perspectives of Indigenous peoples.

There has been literature since the apologies were made that has focused on the ritual aspects of the apologies and acknowledged the importance of the presence of Survivors during the apology ceremony for the apology's overall success (Horelt, 2011; MacLachlan, 2013). In the case of the Harper apology, the presence of the Aboriginal, Inuit, and Métis representatives who were seated on the floor of the House of Commons as Harper made his apology, and the acclamation with which they received the apology, were considered essential to its success (Horelt, 2011, p. 366). Moreover, in Australia, the Aboriginal and Torres Strait Islander people who filled the public gallery and the distinguished visitors' gallery in Parliament House were identified as 'the proxy recipients of the apology, standing in for the thousands watching elsewhere' (McAuley, 2011, p. 6). The images of their reactions to the apology, as they were broadcast across the country, have come to be accepted as an important part of the historical record of the apology's proceedings (McAuley, 2011, p. 6). As has become clearer from these analyses, the reactions of those to whom the apologies were addressed – the Stolen Generations in the case of Australia; the Residential School Survivors in the case of Canada – have been crucial to the overall assessment of these apologies from the point of view of the spectators in the broader mainstream audience. The media coverage of the apologies has been crucial in this regard in documenting a cross-section of responses of Indigenous peoples.

The focus on the ceremonial aspects of the apologies in these analyses could also assist in re-orienting apology discourses to better appreciate the role of Indigenous peoples in the apology process – especially in the apology ritual – while also raising the political profile of Indigenous peoples and their claims. This is particularly evident in discussions of the Harper apology.

For instance, MacLachlan has recognised the political significance of the presence of the Indigenous leaders in their capacity as representatives of '*nations*' in the House of Commons on the day of the apology in Canada (MacLachlan, 2013, p. 199). Speaking in the House of Commons was a historic first for Indigenous peoples in Canada and was profoundly significant, especially considering the 'huge debate' over whether these representatives should be allowed to respond to the apology in the Commons, which was resolved only one hour before the apology was delivered (Beales, 2008; Fitzpatrick and Nguyen, 2008).

Overall, the presence of these Indigenous representatives during the proceedings was seen by both Indigenous and non-Indigenous Canadians as the most moving aspect of the apology. In particular, the presence of Phil Fontaine, Chief of the Assembly of First Nations, '[w]earing the appurtenances of his office, standing in that chamber, in the company of other aboriginal leaders' (Murphy, 2008), was considered as having profound political significance: 'Receiving and responding to a formal apology, when understood as a gesture between political bodies and peoples, not individuals, cemented recognition in Canadian consciousness that the Assembly of First Nations *was* a political body deserving of formal address' (MacLachlan, 2013, p. 199).

Fontaine's presence 'on the floor of the House of Commons – to speak in one's own voice, in one's own right [capacity] to the country' (quoted by MacLachlan, 2013, p. 199), was evidently not only moving, but also of deep political significance: 'Way to go Phil! You are our leader!' was the reaction of one man in the gallery when Fontaine rose to speak (Fitzpatrick and Nguyen, 2008).

The incorporation of traditional rituals in the apology ceremony also added an important dimension to the overall proceedings in Canada. It was reported that the rituals had commenced at dawn when Indigenous peoples gathered on an island in the Ottawa River below Parliament Hill. They began by offering morning prayers for those who did not live to hear the apology. They burned tobacco to honour the spirits of those who had died and offered prayers to help those haunted by cultural loss, physical abuse, and sexual assaults. When it came time for Harper to make his apology, he met with 11 special guests (Indigenous representatives and a handful of Survivors) and together they walked down to the Commons where the apology was delivered. After the apology senior officials, including Prime Minister Harper and Indian Affairs Minister Chuck Strahl and their guests, participated in a smudging ceremony. During the ceremony a smouldering dish was brought before the Prime Minister, and an Elder swished the smoke toward him with a feather. Harper fanned the smoke over his head, his face, and his chest, as if washing with water, and finally rested his hand on his heart. At the conclusion of the proceedings, Harper and Strahl offered tobacco and tea to the guests and Harper presented a framed statement of the apology to the 11 special guests (Campion-Smith, 2008; Fitzpatrick and Nguyen, 2008).

The performance of this ceremony was consistent with the relational understanding in the way it was oriented towards the other. Apology, understood as a relational process awaiting 'the response of the other', also 'require[s] that the ways in which the other sees the world ... be taken into account' (Miller, 2006, p. 11). The inclusion of a smudging ceremony at the end of the session in the House of Commons seemed particularly significant as it conveyed respect for the customs of Indigenous peoples in contrast to the gross lack of respect for their cultural values in the past. The cultural appropriateness of the ceremony for Indigenous peoples also seemed to make the apology proceedings appear more authentic. The performance of the ceremony as a cross-cultural exchange involving the Prime Minister, senior government officials, and the Indigenous representatives effectively symbolised the new dawn in the relationship between Indigenous peoples and the state and thus reinforced the understanding of the apology as marking a transition in Canadian settler–colonised relations (Horelt, 2011, p. 365).

In bringing Indigenous and non-Indigenous cultures together in these ways, the apology appears to have been a profound accomplishment, and may be contrasted with the delivery of Rudd apology, which was criticised by some Indigenous people for not adhering to Indigenous cultural protocols at all (Philpot, et al., 2013, pp. 42–43). However, a more detailed examination of the ceremonial aspects involved in the delivery of the Harper apology reveals the extensive amount of work still needed to achieve an equal partnership between Indigenous peoples and the state. Notably, the smudging ceremony was not conducted in the House of Commons, but outside on Parliament Hill. Moreover, while the presence of the Indigenous leaders on the floor of the House of Commons was a historic first, and the success of their struggle to speak on that occasion should be celebrated for challenging Canada's politico-legal order that has historically oppressed Indigenous peoples, a closer look reveals how heavily that order was being guarded even while the apology was being delivered. This is apparent by the fact that before the representative leaders could deliver their responses this needed to be endorsed by a motion passed by unanimous consent of the House of Commons in accordance with its rules, practices, and traditions. Further, in a keynote address at a conference in 2012, Elijah Harper, Oji-Cree leader and Residential School Survivor, explained that when the apology was being delivered by Harper in the House of Commons, the Speaker of the House was in his rightful location (in the Speaker's chair), and the House of Commons Mace was in its rightful location (on the Clerk's table). These practices symbolise that Parliament is in official proceedings and they are always in place even when foreign dignitaries or heads of state speak in the House of Commons. However, when it was the Indigenous leaders' turn to speak, the Speaker of the House left his chair, returned to the floor, and the House of Commons Mace was moved to a non-official location, indicating that Parliament was no longer in formal session (Gehl, 2013).

The inference to be drawn from these actions was that as far as the government was concerned the Indigenous representatives were not to be treated or recognised as the official representatives of 'Nations'. In this respect, there was an obvious disjuncture between the rituals used during the apology ceremony and what Harper had said in the apology when he called for 'a new beginning and an opportunity to move forward together in partnership' (House of Commons, Canada, 2008, p. 6850). From an Indigenous perspective, the effect of the disjuncture was to reaffirm the disenfranchised status of Indigenous peoples in Canadian society and 'the fork-tongue discourse' of the colonial state.[1] Moreover, their treatment as 'guests' throughout the apology proceedings undermined any sense that they may have had a 'right' to be a part of the proceedings.

Nuanced analyses of state apologies like these add special meaning to the adage that 'actions speak louder than words'. It should therefore come as no surprise that the Indigenous representatives approached the apology on a 'let us wait and see what happens' basis by identifying a number of conditions on which future acceptance of the apology would ultimately depend. Analyses like these also illuminate the importance of Indigenous peoples' responses to the apologies. In that regard, whether Indigenous peoples were involved in an official capacity during an apology's performance is an important consideration, but it should not detract from what they say in their responses. Their responses provide alternative ways of understanding the wrongs that were committed and how to address them. In turn, they expose the dangers of taking what is said (and done) in an apology at face value – lest the apology be accepted as a genuine act of reconciliation.

Indigenous peoples' involvement, whether by engaging in discussions leading up to the apology (in the Australian case) or by demanding to be heard on the floor of the House of Commons (in the Canadian case), demonstrated that they viewed their participation in the apology process as playing a significant part in the broader process of reconciliation and the creation of a 'new' relationship between them and the nation state. The development of the understanding of an apology as a relational process in this chapter has sought to provide a framework to support these aspirations and advance Indigenous peoples' perspectives on how reconciliation can be achieved in view of their understandings of the wrongs in need of redress. And yet, the fact remains that the interpretations of history and perspectives on reconciliation that informed the content of the Rudd and Harper apologies and the measures required for the resolution of past wrongs were underpinned by state norms. The literature in the field also seems mostly focused on the significance of what is said in the apologies without much systematic analysis of what is said in response to them (e.g., Muldoon, 2009, p. 12; Dorrell, 2009, p. 40). Even when researchers have turned to consider Indigenous peoples' responses, they seem mostly motivated by what these responses say about whether forgiveness has been granted or not (e.g., Philpot, et al., 2013).

Considering the discussion in this chapter it is imperative to begin to reconsider the significance of the apologies that are made and refocus attention on what Indigenous peoples have to say in response to them. The overall impression given by the Indigenous representatives' responses was that the apologies would lead to engagement, dialogue, and change to the status quo as proposed by Indigenous peoples. This is explored in the following two chapters on post-apology Australia and Canada. In canvassing developments in post-apology Australia and Canada, these chapters serve as a reminder of the need for action after an apology and not complacency. At a minimum, action would lead to Indigenous rights protections as a response to historical and ongoing rights infringements.

Not all Indigenous peoples may agree with a rights-based approach. For example, Jeff Corntassel (Cherokee Nation) has claimed rights are 'state-centric' and in opposition to the inherent responsibilities Indigenous peoples have with respect to their relationships with their land and communities (Corntassel, 2012, p. 92). Irene Watson (Tanganekald, Meintangk, and Boandik, Aboriginal Nations) has extended the critique to the international community for failing to recognise First Nations Peoples as sovereign peoples and thereby enabling their subordination to state sovereignty (Watson, 2016, p. 35). Intrinsic to both arguments is that whether in international law or domestic law, the autonomy and laws of Indigenous peoples have been suppressed, the effect being that any Indigenous 'rights' may be thwarted by the state as it determines the scope of any rights (if any) it is willing to protect. For example, the *United Nations Declaration of the Rights of Indigenous Peoples* ('*UNDRIP*') (United Nations, 2007) may set minimum standards for 'the survival, dignity and well-being of the indigenous peoples of the world' (art. 43). However, *UNDRIP* also asserts that none of its provisions are intended to 'dismember or impair, totally or in part, the territorial integrity or political unity of sovereign and independent States' (art. 46(1)). The Australian context is replete with examples of conservatives successfully voicing concerns about preserving Australian unity to thwart the protection of Indigenous rights (e.g., in the context of native title law, entering a treaty, and recognising customary law and the right of self-determination) (McRae, et al., 2009, pp. 292–294, 685). It is important to bear all this in mind, as it demonstrates the expanse of state power in legitimising Indigenous rights violations and that the decolonisation of the settler–colonised relationship would require a range of alternative strategies and interventions. As both Corntassel and Watson claim, cultural resurgence through the exercise of Indigenous legal autonomy is vital in this regard.

Nevertheless, there are Indigenous peoples who assert their rights, which is evident in movements to implement *UNDRIP* in both Australia and Canada (discussed in Chapters 6 and 7). Ensuring that Indigenous peoples have choice and control over their futures and how they will live would be central to the full realisation of these rights (Holder and Corntassel, 2002, p. 139).

This has been the understanding adopted in this book, for instance, in framing the forced removal of Indigenous children from their families as infringing Indigenous peoples' right to autonomy to determine how they will live and acknowledging the need for more robust protection of this right to address and curb further rights violations in future.

Developments in international law reveal the potential of rights protections to shield Indigenous peoples from rights violations. There have been notable cases in which Indigenous peoples have successfully made claims in international law against both Australia and Canada for human rights violations, for example, with respect to the claim of racial discrimination arising from the Northern Territory Emergency Response in Australia (Anaya, 2010), and the claim of sex discrimination against Indigenous women under the *Indian Act* (1876) in Canada (*Sandra Lovelace v. Canada*, 1981). These examples demonstrate that human rights mechanisms can be used to vindicate claims of rights violations, but the fact that these rights violations were not adequately resolved and other rights violations have continued, despite international condemnation, is indicative of the legal gaps that exist domestically in the protection and enforcement of Indigenous rights and the need to fill these gaps as a measure of reparation. This solution has its challenges as Indigenous rights continue to be subordinate to state sovereignty. However, it is for this very reason that the relational understanding of apology making – in valorising Indigenous claims – could be useful strategy to support more rigorous approaches to realise Indigenous peoples' rights claims in ways that finally do place a check on state power. How Australia and Canada have responded post-apology is explored in the following two chapters.

Conclusion

Overall, this chapter has sought to contribute further to the understanding of the political functions of official apologies. More specifically, this chapter has sought to further examine the role of Indigenous peoples in the apology process. In developing the understanding of an apology as a relational process, the chapter has considered how an apology provides Survivors with the right to respond which places them at the centre of the process. In this way, the chapter has helped to deepen the understanding of the making of official apologies as a form of political action, not only for those who make them, but also for those to whom they are made. In placing Indigenous peoples at the centre of the process the aim has been to demonstrate how an apology can create a forum for Indigenous peoples to articulate their truths about the past and their aspirations for the future. The conclusion to be drawn from this analysis is that making an apology should be treated as a process in which Indigenous peoples have a central role. This relational understanding of apology making creates space for discussions about the way forward in the future – debates that in the post-apology era should be guided by Indigenous peoples' claims for justice. However, until there is a greater awareness of this potential and it has legal and political backing, there is a risk that the act of apologising will continue to be treated as a 'solo performance' of those who make them, while the voices of Indigenous peoples continue to be silenced and ignored (Mackay, 2009). With this in mind, the following two chapters explore developments in post-apology Australia and Canada using the relational understanding of apology making as the framework for analysis and impetus for government accountability to Indigenous peoples post-apology.

Note

1 A similar argument has been raised in relation to the way that the historic Welcome to Country ceremony (which marked the opening of Parliament the day before the Rudd apology (see Chapter 3)) was managed in Australia to ensure that it did not undermine the Westminster traditions upon which the Australian system of government has been founded. Most notable was the way that the mainstream audience (including Prime Minister Rudd and Leader of the Opposition Brendan Nelson) treated the ceremony as entertainment instead of accepting it as a mode of communication for the traditional custodians to convey their continuing connections to their homelands. In contrast, Indigenous peoples in the audience recognised the political significance of the ceremony. For instance, Bob Randall (Elder of the Yankunytjatjara people and Stolen Generations Survivor) saw the Welcome to Country ceremony as being of even greater significance than the Rudd apology: 'It changes everything ... [T]he colonisers remained colonisers until yesterday but now the Ngunnawal people have welcomed the parliament it gives us a responsibility for maintaining them as guests. ... This will bring in a new energy' (quoted by McAuley, 2011, pp. 11–12).

Reference list

Anaya, J., 2010, *Observations on the Northern Territory Emergency Response in Australia*, https://www.ncca.org.au/files/Natsiec/NTER_Observations_FINAL_by_SR_Anaya_.pdf

Anderson, M., 2013, *The apology is still an empty vessel*, Sovereign Union – First Nations Asserting Sovereignty, 12 February, https://nationalunitygovernment.org/content/apology-still-empty-vessel-sovereign-union

Arendt, H., 1998, *The human condition*, 2nd edn, University of Chicago Press, London.

Barkan, E. and Karn, A., 2006, 'Group apology as an ethical imperative', in E. Barkan and A. Karn (eds), *Taking wrongs seriously: apologies and reconciliation*, Stanford University Press, Stanford, pp. 3–32.

Beales, R., 2008, 'Federal government must "stay apologized" say Aboriginal leaders', *Brantford Expositer*, 15 December.

Brennan, B. and Higgins, I., 2018, 'Stolen Generations Survivors disappointed after Malcolm Turnbull skips 10th anniversary event', *ABC News*, 13 February, https://www.abc.net.au/news/2018-02-13/stolen-generations-survivors-disappointed-with-pm-not-at-event/9425990

Butler, J., 1827, *Fifteen sermons preached at the Rolls Chapel: sermon VIII*, Project Canterbury, https://anglicanhistory.org/butler/rolls/index.html

Calma, T., 2008, *Let the healing begin: response to government to the national apology to the Stolen Generations*, 13 February, https://humanrights.gov.au/sites/default/files/content/pdf/social_justice/speech/let_the_healing_begin.pdf

Campion-Smith, B., 2008, *Harper officially apologizes for Native residential schools*, https://www.thestar.com/news/canada/2008/06/11/harper_officially_apologizes_for_native_residential_schools.html

Celermajer, D., 2009, *The sins of the nation and the ritual of apologies*, Cambridge University Press, Melbourne.

Changfoot, N., 2009, 'Canada's Truth and Reconciliation Commission for Indian residential schools: Whose truth? Whose reconciliation?', *Annual Meeting of the Canadian Political Science Association*, https://www.cpsa-acsp.ca/papers-2009/Changfoot.pdf

Chrisjohn, R., Bear Nicholas, A., Stote, K., Craven (Omahkohkiaayo I'poyi), J., Wasacase, T., Loiselle, P. and Smith, A.O., 2008, 'An historic non-apology, completely and utterly not accepted', https://web.archive.org/web/20081012122924/http://www.marxmail.org/ApologyNotAccepted.htm

Coicaud, J and Jönsson, J., 2008, 'Elements of a road map for a politics of apology', in M. Gibney, R.E. Howard-Hassmann, J. Coicaud and N. Steiner (eds), *The age of apology: facing up to the past*, University of Pennsylvania Press, Philadelphia, pp. 77–91.

Corntassel, J., 2012, 'Re-envisioning resurgence: Indigenous pathways to decolonization and sustainable self-determination', *Decolonization: Indigeneity, Education & Society*, vol. *1*, no. *1*, pp. 86–101.

Council of Australian Governments, 2009, *National Indigenous Reform Agreement (Closing the Gap)*, https://www.voced.edu.au/content/ngv%3A49067

Cowlishaw, G., 2009, 'A multiplicity of meanings: an ethnographic reflection on Kevin Rudd's apology on behalf of the nation to Australia's Indigenous peoples in January 2008', in N. Mookherjee (ed.), 'Ethics of apology: a set of commentaries', *Critique of Anthropology*, vol. *29*, no. *3*, pp. 358–360, DOI:10.1177/0308275X09336703

Cunningham, M., 1999, 'Saying sorry: the politics of apology', *Political Quarterly*, vol. *70*, no. *3*, pp. 285–293, DOI:10.1111/1467-923X.00231

Derrida, J., 2001, *On cosmopolitanism and forgiveness*, M. Hughes (trans.), Routledge, New York.

Dillon, A., 2008, 'Does the apology bring about healing', *Aboriginal and Islander Health Worker Journal*, vol. *32*, no. *4*, p. 6.

Dodson, P., 2000, 'Lingiari: until the chains are broken', in M. Gratton (ed.), *Reconciliation: essays on Australian reconciliation*, Bookman Press, Melbourne, pp. 264–274.

Dodson, P., 2008, 'After the apology', *Arena Magazine*, April–May, vol. *94*, pp. 20–23.

Dorrell, M., 2009, 'From reconciliation to reconciling: reading what "we now recognize" in the Government of Canada's 2008 residential schools apology', *ESC English Studies in Canada*, vol. *35*, pp. 27–45, DOI:10.1353/esc.0.0165

Fiddler, C., 2008, 'Gov't of Canada apologize for 100 years of atrocities', *Windspeaker*, vol. *26*, no. *4*, https://www.ammsa.com/publications/windspeaker/govt-canada-apologize-100-years-atrocities

Fitzpatrick, M. and Nguyen, L., 2008, 'Aboriginal leaders hail historic apology', *Windsor Star*, 11 June, https://www.bishop-accountability.org/news2008/05_06/2008_06_11_Fitzpatrick_AboriginalLeaders.htm

Funk-Unrau, N., 2004, 'Potentials and problems of public apologies to Canadian Aboriginal peoples', *9th Biennial National Conference of Conflict Resolution Network Canada, Academic Institute of Interaction*, 2–4 June, Kitchener.

Gartrell, A., 2008, '"New era" dawns after Indigenous apology', *The Sydney Morning Herald*, 13 February, https://www.smh.com.au/national/new-era-dawns-after-indigenous-apology-20080213-1rv4.html

Gehl, L., 2013, 'Stephen Harper speaks in fork tongue: Elijah Harper's thoughts on the apology', *Black Face Blogging*, 3 October, https://www.lynngehl.com/2/post/2013/03/stephen-harper-speaks-in-fork-tongue-elijah-harpers-thoughts-on-the-apology.html

Gibney, M. and Roxstrom, E., 2001, 'The status of state apologies', *Human Rights Quarterly*, vol. *23*, no. *4*, pp. 911–939, DOI:10.1353/hrq.2001.0051

Govier, T., 2006, *Taking wrongs seriously: acknowledgement, reconciliation, and the politics of sustainable peace*, Humanity Books, New York.

Govier, T. and Verwoerd, W., 2002, 'The promise and pitfalls of apology', *Journal of Social Philosophy*, vol. *33*, no. *1*, pp. 67–82, DOI:10.1111/1467-9833.00124

Holder, C., 2014, 'Reasoning like a state: integration and the limits of official regret', in M. Mihai and M. Thaler (eds), *On the uses and abuses of political apologies*, Palgrave Macmillan, London, pp. 203–219, DOI:10.1057/9781137343727_12

Holder, C.L. and Corntassel, J.J., 2002, 'Indigenous peoples and multicultural citizenship: bridging collective and individual rights', *Human Rights Quarterly*, vol. *24*, no. *1*, pp. 126–151, DOI:10.1353/hrq.2002.0012

Horelt, M., 2011, 'Performing reconciliation: a performance approach to the analysis of political apologies', in N. Palmer, D. Granville and P. Clark (eds), *Critical perspectives on transitional justice*, Intersentia, Cambridge, pp. 347–370.

House of Commons, Canada, 2008, *House of Commons Debates (Hansard)*, 39th Parl., 2nd Sess., vol. *142*, no. *110*, 11 June, https://www.ourcommons.ca/Content/House/392/Debates/110/HAN110-E.PDF

House of Representatives, Australia, 2008a, 'Apology to Australia's Indigenous Peoples', *Parliamentary Debates*, 13 February, https://parlinfo.aph.gov.au/parlInfo/genpdf/chamber/hansardr/2008-02-13/0003/hansard_frag.pdf;fileType=application/pdf

House of Representatives, Australia, 2008b, 'Apology to Australia's Indigenous Peoples', *Parliamentary Debates*, 13 February, https://parlinfo.aph.gov.au/parlInfo/genpdf/chamber/hansardr/2008-02-13/0004/hansard_frag.pdf;fileType=application%2Fpdf

Human Rights and Equal Opportunity Commission, 1997, *Bringing them home: report of the National Inquiry into the Separation of Aboriginal and Torres Strait Islander Children from their Homes*, Sterling Press, Sydney.

Indian Act, 1876, Vict. 39, c. 18.

Indian Residential Schools Settlement Agreement (*'Settlement Agreement'*), 2006, 8 May, https://residentialschoolsettlement.ca/IRS%20Settlement%20Agreement-%20ENGLISH.pdf

James, M., 2018, 'Narrative, robustness, post-apology conduct, and Canada's 1998 and 2008 residential schools apologies', in B. Bevernage and N. Wouters (eds), *The Palgrave handbook of state-sponsored history after 1945*, Palgrave Macmillan, London, pp. 831–847, DOI:10.1057/978-1-349-95306-6_45

Jung, C., 2010, 'Canada and the legacy of the Indian residential schools: transitional justice for Indigenous people in a nontransitional society', in P. Arthur (ed.), *Identities in transition: challenges for transitional justice in divided societies*, Cambridge University Press, New York, pp. 217–250, DOI:10.1017/CBO9780511976858.008
Kemp, B., 2008, 'Putting the pain behind them', *CBC News*, 11 June, https://www.cbc.ca/news/canada/putting-the-pain-behind-them-1.710407
'Kevin Rudd's national apology to Stolen Generations', 2008, *News Corp Australia Network*, 13 February, https://web.archive.org/web/20131115041438/https://www.news.com.au/national/pm-moves-to-heal-the-nation/story-e6frfkw9-1111115539560
King, L.B., 2011, 'A tree fell in the forest: the US apologized to Native Americans and no one heard a sound', *Indian Country Today*, 3 December, https://tlpi.wordpress.com/2011/12/03/a-tree-fell-in-the-forest/
Korff, J., 2021, '"Sorry" apology to Stolen Generations', *Creative Spirits*, 14 January, https://www.creativespirits.info/aboriginalculture/politics/stolen-generations/sorry-apology-to-stolen-generations
Krebs, M., 2008, 'The Harper "apology" – saying "sorry" with a forked tongue', *Socialist Voice*, 29 June, https://web.archive.org/web/20110126114442/https://www.socialistvoice.ca/?p=304
Larocco, S., 2016, 'The temporality of forgiveness: memory, counter-memory, rearticulation', in F. Dominello and D.H. Pereyra (eds), *Forgiveness in perspective*, Inter-disciplinary Press, Oxford, pp. 25–40.
Mackay, H., 2009, 'It's a sorry state of affairs when forgiveness is not the main objective', *The Sydney Morning Herald*, 17 November, https://www.smh.com.au/opinion/politics/its-a-sorry-state-of-affairs-when-forgiveness-is-not-the-main-objective-20091115-igav.html
MacLachlan, A., 2013, 'Government apologies to Indigenous peoples', in A. MacLachlan and A. Speight (eds), *Justice responsibility and reconciliation in the wake of conflict*, Springer, Dordrecht, pp. 183–203, DOI:10.1007/978-94-007-5201-6_11
McAuley, G., 2011, 'The national apology three years later', *Australian Studies*, vol. *3*, pp. 1–25.
McRae, H., Nettheim, G., Anthony, T., Beacroft, L., Brennan, S., Davis, M. and Janke, T., 2009, *Indigenous legal issues: commentary and material*, 4th edn, Thomson Reuters, Sydney.
Miller, B.G., 2006, 'Bringing culture in: community responses to apology, reconciliation, and reparations', *American Indian Culture and Research Journal*, vol. *30*, no. *4*, pp. 1–27, DOI:10.17953/aicr.30.4.36h56wkm72hj85u0
Minow, M., 1998, *Between vengeance and forgiveness: facing history after genocide and mass violence*, Beacon Press, Boston.
Muldoon, P., 2009, 'Past injustices and future protections: on the politics of promising', *Australian Indigenous Law Review*, vol. *13*, no. 2, pp. 2–16.
Murphy, R., 2008, 'The day the House stood still', *The Globe and Mail*, 14 June, https://www.theglobeandmail.com/news/national/the-day-the-house-stood-still/article720368/
'Native residential school forgiveness granted', 2010, *CBC News*, 12 June, https://www.cbc.ca/news/canada/native-residential-school-forgiveness-granted-1.95693999

Pearson, N., 2008, 'When words aren't enough', *The Australian*, 12 February.
Philpot, C., Balvin, N., Mellor, D. and Bretherton, D., 2013, 'Making meaning from collective apologies: Australia's apology to its Indigenous peoples', *Peace and Conflict: Journal of Peace Psychology*, vol. *19*, no. *1*, pp. 34–50, DOI:10.1037/a0031267
Reilly, A., 2008, 'The inherent limits of the apology to the Stolen Generation', *University of Adelaide Law Research Paper No. 2009–002*, DOI:10.2139/ssrn.1294101
Reilly, A., 2012, 'Sovereign apologies', in J. Evans, A. Genovese, A. Reilly and P. Wolfe (eds), *Sovereignty: frontiers of possibility*, University of Hawai'i Press, Honolulu, pp. 196–219.
Sandra Lovelace v. Canada, 1981 Communication No. 24/1977: Canada 30/07/1981, UN Doc. CCPR/C/13/D/24/1977.
Senate of Canada, 2008, *Debates of the Senate (Hansard)*, 39th Parl., 2nd Sess., vol. *144*, no. *69*, 12 June, https://sencanada.ca/Content/SEN/Chamber/392/Debates/pdf/069db_2008-06-12-e.pdf
Simon, M., 2008, *Speeches in response to apology to Residential School Survivors, Tuesday June 10, 2008, Tungasuvvingat Inuit Gathering*, https://web.archive.org/web/20130720141250/https://www.itk.ca/media/speech/speeches-response-apology-residential-school-survivors
Spezzano, C., 1999, *If it hurts, it isn't love: secrets of successful relationships*, Hodder & Stoughton, London.
Stephens, S., 2008, 'The apology and the moral significance of guilt', *ABC News*, 2 May, https://www.abc.net.au/news/2008-02-25/the-apology-and-the-moral-significance-of-guilt/1053240
Tavuchis, N., 1991, *Mea culpa: a sociology of apology and reconciliation*, Stanford University Press, Stanford.
Thompson, J., 2008, 'Apology, justice, and respect: a critical defense of political apology', in M. Gibney, R.E. Howard-Hassmann, J. Coicaud and N. Steiner (eds), *The age of apology: facing up to the past*, University of Pennsylvania Press, Philadelphia, pp. 31–44.
Tillett, A., 2010, 'Tearful Wyatt thanks Rudd for apology', *The West Australian*, 30 September, https://thewest.com.au/news/australia/tearful-wyatt-thanks-rudd-for-apology-ng-ya-196784
Tolle, E., 2005, *A new Earth: awakening to your life's purpose*, Dutton, New York.
Tutu, D., 1999, *No future without forgiveness*, Doubleday, New York.
United Nations, 2007, *United Nations Declaration on the Rights of Indigenous Peoples*, General Assembly Resolution 61/295.
Watson, I., 2016, 'First Nations and the colonial project', *Inter Gentes*, vol. *1*, no. *1*, pp. 30–39.
Wright, T., 2008, 'Outburst of emotion echoes across the land', *The Age*, 14 February, https://www.theage.com.au/news/national/australias-new-beginning/2008/02/13/1202760398783.html

Chapter 6

Australia post-apology

Introduction

This chapter canvasses more recent developments in Australia post-apology. The premise of this chapter is that now the apology has been made, the apology's promise of 'never again' imposes an obligation on the government to ensure that measurable changes are made to the lives of Indigenous peoples in accordance with their claims. The relational understanding of apology making supports this understanding. The focus of the discussion is on providing redress to Stolen Generations Survivors; closing the gap on institutional inequalities and socio-economic disadvantage with a particular focus on contemporary Indigenous child removals; and achieving constitutional reform. These areas have been chosen as they are areas of concern for many Indigenous peoples, and they link to promises Rudd made in his apology. Despite this convergence in understanding, Indigenous peoples continue to face ongoing injustices in these and other areas. The stout resistance to changing the status quo has been most recently illustrated by the failed referendum to institutionalise dialogue between Indigenous peoples and Parliament and the Executive through a constitutionally enshrined Aboriginal and Torres Strait Islander Voice to Parliament. The proposal on its own had drawbacks; nevertheless, it had the potential to set in train more far-reaching reforms. Ultimately, it is argued that in the present political climate, where Indigenous rights protection remains off the political agenda, Indigenous peoples' claims continue to be marginalised and established state structures and norms continue to prevail. As the history of the Stolen Generations, and colonisation more broadly, has shown, for Indigenous peoples caught within these structures the negative consequences will likely continue unabated.

Reparations and Stolen Generations Survivors

As was noted in Chapter 3, an apology to the Stolen Generations was one of the 54 recommendations made by the Human Rights and Equal Opportunity Commission ('HREOC', 1997) in its report, *Bringing Them Home* ('*BTH*'),

DOI: 10.4324/9781003491019-6

which was tabled in the Australian Parliament in 1997. The report was a significant feat in cataloguing the government policies, laws, and practices across all the Australian states and territories that sanctioned the forcible removal of Indigenous children from their families and communities, and in documenting the experiences and destructive effects on those impacted by removal. The recommendations contained in *BTH*, which were in response to the hundreds of testimonies and submissions by Stolen Generations Survivors and others received during the inquiry, provide a comprehensive roadmap for change. However, despite the calls for their implementation, few have been fully implemented. This general failure to act in response to *BTH* reinforces the doubt cast on the integrity of the Rudd apology, as became evident in Chapter 4. One of the key aspects of an apology is to make amends for past wrongs. As the apology specifically focused on the Stolen Generations, a relational understanding of apology making supports the introduction of reforms that would respond to their claims. In the absence of adequate and effective reparation, a catch-22 situation has arisen where the actions (and inactions) of government continue to cause injustice as the ripple effects of the trauma caused by the original policies continue to be felt in communities. Accordingly, the need to address the injustices experienced by the Stolen Generations is central to the discussion in this section. This includes discussion of the framework for making reparations to the Stolen Generations as set out in *BTH*, the relevance of that framework today, and the deficiencies in government actions that continue to impede a satisfactory resolution of the claims of Stolen Generation Survivors.

Reparations and the Bringing Them Home report

Chapter 11 of *BTH* provides a comprehensive overview of the far-reaching effects on those impacted by the past Indigenous child removal policies. The response in *BTH* was to lay responsibility for all this suffering primarily at the feet of the governments that authorised the practice. It found the treatment of the children removed infringed basic principles of English law imported by the Australian colonies, namely: deprivation of liberty; abolition of parental rights; abuses of power; and breach of guardianship obligations (HREOC, 1997, pp. 265). The evidence also supported findings of criminal victimisation including widespread sexual and physical abuse. In addition to these findings, *BTH* found that the forcible removal of Indigenous children infringed basic human rights, specifically relating to racial discrimination (HREOC, 1997, pp. 266–267) and genocide (HREOC, 1997, pp. 270–275).

Following the identification of the wrongs as breaches of fundamental human rights, *BTH* set out a reparations scheme based on international standards under the headings of acknowledgment and apology; guarantees against repetition; measures of restitution; measures of rehabilitation; and monetary compensation (HREOC, 1997, pp. 280–283, citing van Boven, 1996). Further, in line with these standards, *BTH* recommended that reparations be made to all victims, whether as individuals, families, or communities, directly or indirectly, affected by the forcible removal practice (HREOC, 1997, p. 283).

In their entirety, these recommendations provided a starting point for achieving a just resolution of the injustices experienced by Stolen Generations Survivors. However, in the intervening period since the *BTH* report was released, the evidence suggests that the impacts of removal have worsened. According to key indicators related to economic outcomes (such as poverty, unemployment and welfare reliance); social outcomes (particularly relating to homelessness and homeownership); health outcomes (such as disability and chronic disease); and law and justice outcomes (particularly relating to violence, discrimination and incarceration), it has been found that Stolen Generations Survivors continue to be worse off than other Indigenous peoples who were not removed (Aboriginal and Torres Strait Islander Healing Foundation ('Healing Foundation'), 2021, p. 21). It has also been found that socio-economic disadvantage of Survivors is being compounded by ageing and disability, as it was estimated that by 2022 all Survivors (estimated nationally to be 33,600 in 2018–2019) will be over 50 (Healing Foundation, 2021, p. 5). The disadvantage and discrimination experienced by Survivors has had flow-on effects on their descendants (estimated to be 142,200 in 2018–2019). It has been found that material wellbeing of descendants (based on household income) is better than other Indigenous peoples (Healing Foundation, 2021, p. 58). Nevertheless, other indicators show that the effects of intergenerational trauma have made them worse off, evidenced by, for example, an increase of family and lateral violence in communities, substance abuse and other addictions, behavioural problems and mental illness, contemporary child removals, children in the juvenile justice system, and adult criminalisation (Healing Foundation, 2017, pp. 20–21). However, the services and resources required to respond to the complex and intersecting needs of Survivors and intergenerational trauma of descendants continue to be inadequate. Ultimately, this highlights how little has been done by governments since *BTH* was released to overcome the wrongs caused by past child removal policies and laws and that the momentum for this change, rather than increasing, appears to have stagnated. As stated by Florence Onus, a descendant of the Birri-Gubba and Kairi/Bidjara clans and inaugural chairperson of the Healing Foundation:

> Our people have demonstrated our resilience time and time again but more needs to be done to support the Stolen Generations and their families. We need to recognise the work yet to be done to move forward from saying sorry.
>
> (Onus, 2023)

Soon after the apology, the Healing Foundation was established in 2009. Introduced by the Council of Australian Governments ('COAG') as part of the Closing the Gap policy and developed in consultation with Aboriginal and Torres Strait Islander peoples, the Healing Foundation funds and supports projects that focus on addressing the legacy of colonisation, and in particular the history of forced child removals. The Healing Foundation has supported numerous initiatives to support Stolen Generations Survivors, services, and organisations to lead and develop their own healing programs (Healing Foundation, 2022). These measures demonstrate the practical importance of self-determination to the healing process. Nevertheless, there is still a felt need for governments, especially the Commonwealth, to take responsibility and make reparations. The Healing Foundation's report in 2017, marking the 20th anniversary of *BTH*, set out a roadmap to implement the *BTH* recommendations, which included measures to respond to the needs of Stolen Generations Survivors, address intergenerational trauma, and create an environment for change, guided by the principles of *BTH*, namely, self-determination, non-discrimination, cultural renewal, a coherent policy base, and adequate funding (Healing Foundation, 2017, p. 27). Additionally, in 2021, the Healing Foundation released a four-point action plan calling for redress to Stolen Generations Survivors and their descendants; measures to meet the complex needs of Stolen Generations Survivors; provisions for healing intergenerational trauma and preventing new harm; and the implementation of a national accountability framework to monitor and report progress towards achieving better outcomes for Stolen Generations Survivors and their descendants. The report recognised the need for urgent, holistic responses that would be Survivor-centred and led, would adhere to the principle of self-determination, and would be trauma-aware, healing-informed, and evidenced-based. These reports indicate much change is needed, though it is not possible to elaborate on this here. As compensation was a key component of *BTH* and continues to be a concern of many affected by the forced child removal practice, the following section focuses on this measure.

Admittedly, compensation may not be a concern for everyone affected, and even when it is sought, it may prove to be woefully inadequate. A combination of individual and community-based healing strategies is needed (Healing Foundation, 2021, pp. 68–72) and even then, if they are not appropriately administered, they can become another source of injustice, as the experience in Canada demonstrates (see Chapter 7). Nevertheless, despite these shortcomings, *BTH* viewed compensation as a necessary response to the history and effects of the child removal practice, and after Rudd's apology it seems even more imperative. In terms of the transformative potential of an apology, an offer of compensation serves as a practical form of recognition that backs up the symbolic messages of an apology – to the recipients that what was done to them was wrong; and to the apologising nation that it now needs to pay for what it has done. Indeed, while successive Commonwealth governments continued to refuse to pay compensation to the Stolen Generations, the message of respect conveyed in Rudd's apology was further undermined (as was discussed in Chapter 4). As one descendent of a Stolen Generations Survivor stated more recently on the issue of compensation: 'When we think about how many elderly people have passed away since that apology [to the Stolen Generations] was given, I think it's a dodging of responsibility and it's extremely disrespectful' (Gooley, 2021).

Compensation

Of all the reparative measures *BTH* recommended, provision for 'monetary compensation' was the most detailed and included a broad range of heads of damages that could be claimed, which included (HREOC, 1997, p. 304):

1. Racial discrimination;
2. Arbitrary deprivation of liberty;
3. Pain and suffering;
4. Abuse, including physical, sexual and emotional abuse;
5. Disruption of family life;
6. Loss of cultural rights and fulfilment;
7. Loss of native title rights;
8. Labour exploitation;
9. Economic loss; and
10. Loss of opportunities.

Compensation would be funded by a joint National Fund ('Fund') established by COAG, which would be administered by a National Compensation Fund Board. Some of the benefits of this approach were its emphasis on ensuring Indigenous representation in the decision-making process, maximising claimants' access to the scheme by providing free legal advice and representation, ensuring that limitation periods and rules of evidence would not apply, and the process would have minimum formality and be culturally appropriate (including language) (HREOC, 1997, pp. 309–311).

In assessing compensation, *BTH* simplified the complexities of proving liability in civil litigation by recommending that claimants be paid minimum lump sums based on the fact of their forcible removal. These claims could be rebutted by the responsible government if there was proof that removal was in the child's best interests. Claimants, whether directly or indirectly harmed by the removal practice, could also seek additional compensation for specific harms and civil standards of proof would apply. To avoid double compensation, successful claims made under the Fund would preclude claims in court (HREOC, 1997, pp. 312–313).

In hindsight (and considering the obstacles Stolen Generations Survivors have subsequently experienced in court proceedings as discussed below), providing governments with a 'best interests' defence to the lump sum payments and setting the civil standard of proof for additional compensation could have defeated the creation of an accessible compensation scheme as *BTH* intended. In any event, Stolen Generations Survivors have never been provided with a national compensation package as envisaged by *BTH*. Attempts were made to enact Commonwealth legislation to set up a national scheme: the Stolen Generations Compensation Scheme Bill introduced in 2008 and the Stolen Generations Reparation Tribunal Bill, also introduced in 2008 and again in 2010. However, governments on both sides of politics have successfully resisted calls for a national compensation scheme.

More recently, in 2022, the former Morrison government established a AU$378.6 million Territories Stolen Generations Reparation Scheme ('the Territories Scheme') for the Commonwealth territories (the Northern Territory, the Australian Capital Territory, and Jervis Bay) as part of a AU$1 billion Commonwealth Implementation Plan for Closing the Gap. Eligible Survivors would be paid AU$75,000 in recognition for the harm caused; AU$7,000 for healing (e.g., for funeral expenses or to help return to country); free practical and emotional support; and each Survivor could receive a personal acknowledgement, if they wish (Healing Foundation, 2023).

Considering the stance of previous Commonwealth governments, this is a significant development, and especially so as the Morrison government was drawn from the Liberal–National Coalition Party, the same party as the Howard government that had steadfastly refused to apologise and offer compensation (see Chapter 3). The Morrison government's Territories Scheme has also gone further than Rudd's acceptance of responsibility in his apology in finally backing up this acknowledgement with redress. However, the Scheme does not extend to the acceptance of legal liability. Moreover, when setting up the scheme, the government did not expressly reject the logic (in federal decisions such as *Cubillo v. Commonwealth* (2001)) that the removal of children was in their best interests. When compared to the *BTH* recommendations, the Scheme also has notable shortcomings. It is not a national scheme, it does not provide holistic reparations as envisaged by *BTH*, nor does it provide compensation for the wide range of harms as identified by *BTH*. Moreover, anyone successful under the Territories Scheme is disallowed from making future claims for compensation for their removal in court.

Eligibility for the Scheme includes people who had been removed, and the descendants of those who have died, if the death was on or after the date the scheme was announced on 5 August 2021. This was found to be unsatisfactory by numerous Survivors and their families in the Northern Territory and they successfully negotiated a class action (valued AU$50.45 million) to recover compensation for all Survivors directly affected by removal and the descendants of any Survivors who have died prior to 5 August 2021 (Shine Lawyers, n.d.).

The Territories Scheme is one of several schemes that have been made available to Indigenous peoples across the Australian jurisdictions. As the discussion below demonstrates, while these schemes appear to avoid some of the pitfalls of litigation, they have created a patchwork approach to redress, which could be less than ideal, especially for Stolen Generations Survivors who may have shared experiences of harm but the response of governments across the country has lacked uniformity.

State and territory-based redress schemes

In establishing the Territories Scheme in 2022, the Commonwealth has now joined Tasmania (AU$5 million scheme under the *Stolen Generations of Aboriginal Children Act 2006* (Tas.)), South Australia (AU$11 million Stolen Generations Reparations Scheme, 2016–2018), New South Wales (AU$73 million Stolen Generations Reparations Scheme and Funeral Assistance Fund, 2017–2023), and Victoria (AU$155 million Stolen Generations Reparation Package, 2022–2027). Only Queensland and Western Australia have not committed to establishing schemes for Stolen Generations Survivors who had been removed within their borders.

At a symbolic level, the implementation of state and territory-based redress schemes has been more effective than the case law in conveying the message that the past practice of forcibly removing Indigenous children from their families was wrong. This contrasts starkly to Stolen Generations litigation, where of the four claims for common law compensation that have determined, only one has been successful (*Trevorrow v. South Australia* (2007)).

Behrendt, et al. (2019, p. 41), building on the analysis of Cunneen and Grix (2004, p. 4), have distilled the procedural and substantive legal issues that have posed obstacles to the success of Stolen Generations litigants in court, which may be summarised as follows:

1 Prohibitive financial cost;
2 Length of time involved before the outcome of litigation is finalised;
3 Emotional and psychological trauma experienced by claimants in the hostile environment of an adversarial court system;
4 Problems with establishing specific liability for harms that have been caused, in particular where documented evidence is accorded more authority than oral evidence, and governments were lax in keeping records and have lost and destroyed documents;
5 Problems Indigenous peoples have in overcoming statutory limitation periods, when these events occurred many decades ago;
6 Overcoming the judicial view that ‘standards of the time’ justified removal in the best interests of the child; and
7 Lack of constitutional protections.

Administratively assessed schemes could avoid these obstacles. The ones in Australia appear to indicate that governments have become more willing to accept that the removal of children was wrong and are no longer relying on the lack of legal rights and protections in Australian law to avoid responsibility for past injustices. Further, as these schemes relate to the history of forced child removals, they address the core issue (the removal of children), unlike in litigation where applicants are expected to establish liability according to specific legal duties (such as breaches of common law, statutory, and equitable duties). There are also the potential procedural advantages of these administratively assessed schemes in terms of providing Survivors with a cheaper, more cost- and time-effective, and less formal avenue of redress that can bypass the strict limitation periods and evidentiary rules in litigation. One example demonstrating these procedural benefits is the group action that was commenced in NSW in 2014 and settled out of court. The pitfalls of litigation were avoided as the claim was resolved with the cooperation of the NSW Crown Solicitors Office. This resulted in what has been described as a positive experience for Survivors as it was not as costly or time consuming as litigation, and Survivors were provided counselling to prevent re-traumatisation in giving evidence, and they were given the opportunity to retell their stories in ways that helped in the healing process (Aldrich, 2017).

However, the inconsistent approach to redress in Australia raises questions about how committed governments are to making amends to the Stolen Generations. For example, there are Australian jurisdictions (Queensland and Western Australia) that have not committed to establishing specific schemes for the Stolen Generations. Currently in these states, the courts are the only recourse available to Stolen Generations Survivors to make claims related to their removal, which as indicated above may merely expose claimants to more trauma and injustice. This is evident in the Western Australian case *Collard v. Western Australia* (2013) ('*Collard*'). In this case, the Collards, a Noongar family, pleaded solely on two grounds of breach of fiduciary duty: that the state had a fiduciary duty to the children not to fail to act in their best interests with respect to 'custody, maintenance and education', and in particular not to disregard 'the benefits of an upbringing within the family unit of their natural parents and siblings' (*Collard*, 2013, para. 1107); and the state had a duty to them as Aboriginal peoples in Western Australia as the result of colonisation, which created a relationship 'analogous to that of guardian and ward' (*Collard*, 2013, para. 1128). All these arguments failed mainly because it has never been decided that a fiduciary duty was owed to Indigenous peoples in Australia (*Collard*, 2013, para. 1130), nor has a fiduciary duty been found to protect non-commercial interests in Australian law (*Collard*, 2013, paras 1197–1198). The Court did consider whether, in the event a fiduciary duty was owed, it had been breached, and found that this would need to be determined according to whether the decisions to remove the children was in their best interests according to prevailing standards of the time (*Collard*, 2013, para. 1286). The Court found that these decisions were in the best interests of the children and that the impoverished conditions in which the Collard family was living, though possibly not legitimate grounds for the children's removal today, would not have been unreasonable at the time (*Collard*, 2013, paras 1338–1339).

Queensland and Western Australia may not have established Stolen Generations redress schemes but they, along with other jurisdictions, have established schemes for harms caused to children in institutional care (whether for sexual abuse or a combination of sexual, physical and emotional abuse, and neglect). These include the Abuse in Care Compensation Scheme (Tasmania, 2003–2013), the Redress Scheme (Queensland, 2007–2008), Redress WA (Western Australia, 2008–2009), the Ex Gratia Payment Scheme (South Australia, 2009–2019), and the National Redress Scheme (Commonwealth, 2018–2027). Stolen Generations Survivors have been eligible to apply to these schemes. However, while these schemes have been important in recognising the institutional abuse of children, and especially concerned with specific forms of abuse, such as sexual abuse (in the case of South Australia and the Commonwealth), they do not cover many of the other harms that may have been suffered. For instance, in not being Indigenous-specific, they have failed to provide for specific cultural harms, and in subsuming Indigenous peoples into mainstream non-Indigenous schemes, Indigenous Survivors can become marginalised. As a 2021 review of the National Redress Scheme found (among a range of things), Indigenous Survivors did not have equal access to the scheme, they were more likely to have their payments reduced than non-Indigenous applicants due to receiving other payments, Indigenous communities were more likely to be underserviced, particularly in regional and remote areas, and communication with Survivors and community members was often not culturally and trauma informed (Kruk, 2021, pp. 218–223). These concerns were compounded by delays in processing applications, and the inconsistencies and arbitrariness in how applications were processed and determined. The National Redress Scheme also has additional eligibility criteria for Survivors who are in gaol and/or have a criminal conviction of five years or more (National Redress Scheme, n.d.). Considering the disproportionate representation of Indigenous peoples in the criminal justice system, these requirements would disproportionately impact on Indigenous Survivors. These failures reveal how redress schemes can expose Indigenous peoples to further layers of discriminatory treatment and demonstrate how the exercise of state power in perpetrating past wrongs has not been held fully accountable.

But even in those jurisdictions that have set up redress schemes for the Stolen Generations, none of them provide a holistic response to the harms suffered consistent with international standards as recommended in *BTH*. Moreover, the approach to monetary redress has been compartmentalised, exemplified, for instance, by the establishment of separate stolen wages and

Stolen Generations schemes. Stolen wages schemes, which have been established in Queensland, NSW, and Western Australia, are relevant to Stolen Generations Survivors, as many were exploited for their labour as child apprentices and domestic servants (HREOC, 1997, p. 193). Notably, however, like the Stolen Generations schemes, not all jurisdictions have set up schemes for stolen wages. In this way, the connection between stolen children and stolen wages is lost through the creation of separate schemes, and so too is the understanding that the histories of the Stolen Generations and stolen wages are two of many interconnected injustices perpetrated under the auspices of the protection and assimilation regimes. The lack of reporting on these schemes, and indeed for most of the other schemes, also obscures their impacts on Survivors. The existence of multiple schemes within the same jurisdiction (e.g., in NSW where there has been a stolen wages scheme (the Aboriginal Trust Fund Repayment Scheme), the Stolen Generations Reparations Scheme and Funeral Assistance Fund, and the National Redress Scheme (for institutional child sexual assault)) means that Survivors may be required to retell their stories multiple times and be abreast of different application processes, which could result in re-traumatisation and compound disappointment, if unsuccessful. An important feature of the Stolen Generations Reparation Scheme and Funeral Assistance Fund and the National Redress Scheme is that Survivors may request an apology from government, but inconsistencies in the apologies received could result in one undermining the other (Aboriginal Affairs NSW, 2020, p. 39).

Moreover, with respect to the redress schemes that have been established, there are inconsistencies between them. This is exemplified by the different eligibility criteria set by the various Stolen Generations redress schemes. For example, some schemes (such as in NSW) have confined eligibility to those who were removed under Aboriginal protection legislation, to the exclusion of Survivors who were removed under more general child welfare legislation. This was subsequently tempered by the adoption of a 'contextual approach' that permitted claims of removal by the Child Welfare Department where there was evidence of '[Aborigines Welfare] Board involvement and/or an intention to "assimilate" the claimant' (Aboriginal Affairs NSW, 2020, p. 37). However, the scheme remained confined to the removal of Indigenous children under the policy of assimilation in NSW up to 2 June 1969 when the Aborigines Welfare Board ('the Board') was abolished. It excluded Survivors who were removed for child safety reasons up to this time (notwithstanding that any safety concerns may have been caused by the effects of colonisation, including past Indigenous child removals). This was rationalised as supported by *BTH*, presumably based on the understanding that removal for child welfare reasons was in the child's best interests. The scheme also excluded Survivors who were removed after the Board was abolished and prior to the enactment of the *Racial Discrimination Act 1975* (Cth) (notwithstanding that their removal may have been motivated by racial discrimination).

More broadly, this example highlights an issue with all the redress schemes whereby Survivor eligibility is limited to whether the wrongdoing (such as removal) occurred within the timeframe as set by the scheme itself. These schemes very much reinforce that past wrongdoing was exactly that – in the past – and do not account for continuing harms (such as more recent Indigenous child removals).

In addition to the problems that some direct Survivors have had meeting eligibility requirements, there are the issues facing their descendants, as only some Stolen Generations schemes have allowed descendant applications, and only in circumstances when the original Survivor has died (such as in Tasmania under the *Stolen Generations of Aboriginal Children Act 2006* (Tas.) and the Commonwealth's Territories Scheme). Even then, proving eligibility for descendants has been difficult due to lack of evidence and the process not easily accommodating Indigenous kinship structures (New South Wales, Parliament, Legislative Council, General Purpose Standing Committee No. 3, 2016, p. 94). These shortcomings further reflect a limited understanding of the history of the removal of Indigenous children by not accommodating the various rationales for removing children from their families and the intergenerational impacts of removal on Indigenous children and their families.

The payments offered by the schemes are also inconsistent across the board. For example, Stolen Generations Survivors were paid a lump sum of AU$20,000 (AU$10,000 added later) in South Australia, compared to being paid AU$75,000 in NSW and the Commonwealth, and AU$100,000 in Victoria. Some of these schemes have also included additional community-based restorative measures (in South Australia), support services for eligible Survivors (in Victoria and the Commonwealth), and forms of redress (such as a funeral fund and a government apology/personal acknowledgement in NSW, Victoria, and the Commonwealth), while others (notably in Tasmania) only offered lump sum payments. The disparity between the Stolen Generations schemes is even more striking when the amounts that can be achieved from litigation (e.g., in *Trevorrow v. South Australia* (2007) where the plaintiff was awarded $525,000 in damages) are also considered. Indeed, the South Australian Stolen Generations Reparation Scheme was established after the successful claim in *Trevorrow* and demonstrates how governments may use these schemes to reduce the cost of compensation on the state.

It may be that offering smaller amounts than what potentially could be awarded by court-ordered compensation is offset by requiring Survivors to meet lower thresholds of proof than is required in litigation. However, such a cost–benefit approach raises concerns about whether governments are more interested in reducing their costs instead of providing adequate redress. These concerns are heightened when it becomes apparent that the redress schemes have not necessarily overcome evidentiary burdens of litigation. This is exemplified when Survivors do not have the documentation (such as proof of Aboriginality) to substantiate their claims, as happened with the Stolen Generations scheme in Tasmania (Department of Premier and Cabinet, Tasmania, 2008, p. 13). The lack of supporting documentation is a problem that has arisen in litigation and is a particular concern for Stolen Generations Survivors when lost, destroyed, or poor recordkeeping by government results in their claims being rejected.

Apart from the amounts paid under the schemes being relatively low and varied, they also require different standards of proof to be met. The Stolen Generations schemes have provided lump sum payments to Survivors if certain eligibility criteria are met, while child institutional abuse schemes have offered additional payments based on severity of abuse (such as the Queensland Redress Scheme and Redress WA), which required claimants to provide evidence of harm and thus exposed claimants to more scrutiny (and possible re-traumatisation) (Royal Commission into Institutional Responses to Child Sexual Abuse, 2015, pp. 545–551).

Overall, the relatively low amounts paid by the redress schemes raise questions about whether the governments that have introduced them have accepted full responsibility for past wrongs. With respect to the Stolen Generations, the fact that Survivors in some schemes have been required to sign a deed of release (in South Australia and the Commonwealth), while others have not (in Tasmania, NSW, and Victoria), further undermines the integrity of such schemes, particularly as these schemes do not include admissions of liability. Notably, where jurisdictions have multiple schemes (such as the Commonwealth that has the National Redress Scheme for institutional child sexual abuse and the Territories Scheme for Stolen Generations Survivors), it is possible for Survivors to claim under both schemes because they cover different harms. However, if, for example, a Survivor has received a relevant prior payment from a scheme for sexual abuse (such as the South Australian Ex Gratia Payment Scheme), this may be deducted from the National Redress Scheme because both schemes relate to sexual abuse.

Evidently, this discussion has demonstrated that more is required to valorise Indigenous peoples' experiences of injustice through adequate measures of reparations. Monetary compensation is a reparative measure required by international standards. However, as noted above, some jurisdictions in Australia have made no attempt to establish redress schemes for the Stolen Generations. The jurisdictions that have may offer redress as a gesture of reconciliation, but the amounts offered appear token by comparison to the harms that have been suffered. It may be true that money cannot make up for what has been lost, and not everyone affected necessarily may want a monetary payment. Nevertheless, monetary payments serve as a form of recognition and are indicative of government commitment to acknowledge past wrongs. Ultimately, it is up to the recipients of the schemes to determine whether the payments are adequate or not. However, to date, there has not been a comprehensive review of redress in Australia to gauge Survivors' experiences. This contrasts with the reviews of the *Indian Residential Schools Settlement Agreement* in Canada discussed in Chapter 7. In Australia, it is apparent that Survivors' experiences of the schemes continue to be state-centric as governments continue to make the final decisions about what are necessary and appropriate measures. Accordingly, the exercise of state sovereignty continues to prevail unperturbed while Indigenous peoples' right to effective and adequate reparations remains unfulfilled. This issue is explored further with respect to the Closing the Gap policy.

Closing the gap

As was discussed in Chapter 4, the Closing the Gap policy was the key measure of redress offered in Rudd's apology to Indigenous peoples. This policy was implemented following the *National Indigenous Reform Agreement* (Council of Australian Governments ('COAG'), 2009), which was signed by the COAG in November 2008, and aimed (among other things) to 'close the gap' between Indigenous and non-Indigenous Australians with respect to six (and subsequently seven) targets related to health, employment, and education. However, as of 2020 only two of these targets (early childhood education and Year 12 attainment) were on track.

At the time of its implementation, the objective of the Closing the Gap policy was to achieve equality of outcomes for Indigenous Australians. Notably, it was recognised that closing the gap could only be achieved by working in partnership with Indigenous communities and by adopting a strengths-based approach which centralised the importance of Indigenous cultures and identities for spiritual, emotional, and physical wellbeing (Commonwealth of Australia, Department of the Prime Minister and Cabinet ('Commonwealth of Australia'), 2019, pp. 9–11). These were noble objectives, and the hope at the time was that there would be better coordination of activities at all levels of government and between organisations which would lead to better outcomes for Indigenous peoples, and a new way of working with Indigenous peoples would evolve. This was understood to be a flow-on effect of the Rudd apology (Commonwealth of Australia, 2019, p. 13) and reflects its potential to transform relations between Indigenous peoples and government as had been conveyed by some Indigenous peoples at the time of the apology (discussed in Chapter 3).

In a review in 2018 it was found that the Closing the Gap policy had been most successful where initiatives were community-led, and solutions were designed and implemented in partnership between communities and service providers. Unfortunately, it was found that this approach was not universally adopted and that a top-down approach was the most common experience of the policy (Commonwealth of Australia, 2019, p. 13). This outcome reflects problems that were intrinsic to the policy's framework.

First, and as foreshadowed in Chapter 4, the Closing the Gap policy as envisaged by Rudd may have sought to achieve a new partnership between Indigenous and non-Indigenous Australians, but Rudd only sought bipartisan support for this and other policies. This filtered through to the implementation of the policy by COAG, which failed to lay the foundation through appropriate consultation for a partnership approach to succeed, and this became a longstanding issue with the implementation of the policy (Commonwealth of Australia, 2019, p. 25).

Moreover, despite the aspirations to do things differently, the approach to closing to gap on closer examination revealed it was not a new approach to Indigenous policy, but a continuation of previous policies, such as the Howard government's policy of practical reconciliation, as noted in Chapter 4. As Pholi, Black and Richards (2009, p. 6) have explained, the approach to closing the gap continued to be based on a biomedical model aimed at achieving statistical equality between Indigenous and non-Indigenous people by focusing on what is measurable according to western scientific methods of data collection and management.

The effect of adopting a design model steeped in western scientific epistemology was to replicate many of the problems that past policies have posed for Indigenous peoples as exemplified by the following interrelated examples. First, the adoption of a therapeutic model depoliticised Indigenous peoples' collective experiences. A therapeutic model individualises Indigenous disadvantage and makes it an individual responsibility, which diverts attention from the structural and historical sources of disadvantage. Second, in focusing on improving socio-economic outcomes for individuals and not systemic inequalities created by lack of economic power, discrimination, and lack of control over outcomes, this approach failed to address the systemic causes of disadvantage in Indigenous communities and the need to address disadvantage more broadly within the political and legal system (Commonwealth of Australia, 2019, p. 24). As Pholi, Black and Richards identified, these structural issues (or gaps) were not construed as a problem and were therefore not measured for remediation (Pholi, Black and Richards, 2009, p. 6). Third, this approach effectively neutralised the structures of power that shape Indigenous socio-economic disadvantage to obscure how the identified inequalities between Indigenous and non-Indigenous peoples were themselves a result of violations of Indigenous peoples' rights. The focus was on the need to close socio-economic gaps, which continued to sideline the politico-legal gaps. Instead of focusing on the deficiencies of 'the system', the focus has been on Indigenous peoples as having deficiencies that need fixing. This is particularly troubling as they reinforce negative stereotypes of Indigenous peoples as 'sick, poor, under-educated, marginalised and oppressed' (Pholi, Black and Richards, 2009, p. 9, citing Paradies, 2006). These constructions reflect a deficit-based understanding of Indigeneity, which valorises mainstream standards and negates the existence and importance of Indigenous cultures and norms for Indigenous wellbeing. The fact that this occurred can be linked to government control over the available data relevant to Indigenous peoples. This leads to the next issue relating to the Closing the Gap targets. The data, as interpreted by government, resulted in targets that may measure success in mainstream Australian society, but made no allowance for the cultural differences that exist between (and among) Indigenous and non-Indigenous social norms (Altman and Fogarty, 2010). Thus, in practical terms, the Closing the Gap policy was assimilationist in orientation because it applied mainstream standards as the measure of wellbeing and erased the positive attributes of Indigenous cultures as the measure of wellbeing (Commonwealth of Australia, 2019, p. 23, citing Biddle and Markham, 2017; Pholi, Black and Richards, 2009). This ultimately defeated the culture-centred approach to closing the gap as was originally intended, which required a strengths-based, and not a deficit-based, approach to succeed in overcoming Indigenous disadvantage. This was somewhat inevitable as the policy was not explicitly underpinned by an Indigenous rights framework to support a culture-centred approach. In the absence of such a framework (especially the right of self-determination), the creation of a new partnership between Indigenous and non-Indigenous Australians was also thwarted.

However, even with respect to its stated aim of 'closing the gap' on socio-economic disadvantage, its focus on a relatively small set of targets was grossly inadequate in addressing the broad range of injustices experienced by Indigenous peoples. Moreover, while some Indigenous peoples may have welcomed the policy, its focus was on the delivery of services that should have been available to Indigenous peoples in any case (Durbach, 2008, p. 32, citing Dodson, 2000). Indeed, budget cuts to the policy over time by successive governments further undermined its construction as a measure of reparation and demonstrated that it did not have the status of a right that can be enforced against the government. Considering that it was Indigenous lives and life chances that the policy aimed to improve, the failure to deliver on its targets was (and is) arguably continuing the genocide – a 'slow death' – as it has been understood in Canada based on international legal developments (National Inquiry into Missing and Murdered Indigenous Women and Girls, 2019, pp. 8, 15).

More recently, the Closing the Gap policy was reset by the *National Agreement on Closing the Gap* ('*National Agreement*') (2020). This is the first agreement of its kind to be signed by COAG and Indigenous peak organisations (represented by the Lead Convenor of the Coalition of Peaks), having been negotiated through engagement with Indigenous peoples across Australia. The aim continues to be for government to work in partnership with Indigenous peoples on closing the gap. Accordingly, the *National Agreement* incorporates Priority Reforms to support changes to the way government works with Indigenous peoples that will:

1 Strengthen and establish formal partnerships and shared decision making;
2 Build the Aboriginal and Torres Strait Islander community-controlled sector;
3 Transform government organisations so they work better for Aboriginal and Torres Strait Islander people; and
4 Improve and share access to data and information to enable Aboriginal and Torres Strait Islander communities to make informed decisions (*National Agreement*, 2020, pp. 5–15).

These provisions appear aimed at building the institutional foundation that had previously been lacking to forge a new partnership on closing the gap. Within this partnership, Indigenous cultures would be prioritised and institutional racism within government organisations eliminated, and through strengthening the community-controlled sector there would, in accordance with the right of self-determination, be increased control over decision making and delivery of Indigenous services. Increasing Indigenous control over relevant data would also diminish how data is used by government to advance its policy agenda and instead would be used by Indigenous peoples to determine how the needs of their communities should be met. In terms of the discussion in the previous chapter, the *National Agreement* appears to align with what could be expected after an apology is made to Indigenous peoples in Australia according to the relational understanding. The *Agreement* embodies a 'New Approach' (*National Agreement*, 2020, p. 4) of listening and responding to the voices and aspirations of Indigenous peoples. Future decision making would be shared and by consensus, and 'where the voices of Aboriginal and Torres Strait Islander parties hold as much weight as the governments' (*National Agreement*, 2020, p. 6).

The other pillar of the *National Agreement* relates to Socio-Economic Reforms which aim to improve outcomes for Indigenous peoples. These are the Closing the Gap targets to be achieved by 2031 which, under the *Agreement* (when it was first released), were increased from seven to 16 and aim to improve life expectancy, increase child birthweight, increase early childhood education, improve early childhood development, increase Year 12 attainment, increase tertiary education for young adults, increase youth employment, increase adult employment, increase secure and affordable housing, reduce adult incarceration, reduce juvenile detention, reduce children in out-of-home care, eliminate violence and abuse against women and children, eliminate suicide, increase lands and waters covered by Indigenous peoples' legal rights and interests, and increase the number and strength of Indigenous languages spoken by Indigenous peoples. Since its release, the *Agreement* has added target 17 related to digital inclusion, measured by home access to the internet.

It is not possible to discuss each target in detail, but considering the focus of the Rudd apology on the Stolen Generations the following discussion examines the Closing the Gap target to reduce the number of Indigenous children removed from their families and placed in out-of-home care by 45% by 2031. This discussion is followed by an analysis of the *National Agreement*.

Closing the gap: Indigenous children in out-of-home care

It was well established at the time of Rudd's apology that Indigenous children were disproportionately represented in out-of-home care (Australian Institute of Health and Welfare, 2008). Responding to this issue should have been a priority, especially when Rudd declared in his apology that 'the injustices of the past must never, never happen again' (House of Representatives, Australia, 2008, p. 167). As has been claimed by Indigenous advocates Grandmothers Against Removals: 'Sorry means you don't do it again ...' (Thorburn and Syed, 2017, quoting Aunt Deb Swan from Grandmothers Against Removals). However, in their view, by not addressing contemporary Indigenous child removals, the apology implied that this practice had stopped. In turn, this reinforced the idea that the removal of children was in the past and all that was left to do was address the legacies of that history through the adoption of the Closing the Gap policy.

Rudd's silence on this issue contrasted with the pathway set out in the *BTH* report aimed to ensure the non-repetition of harm by addressing the issue of contemporary Indigenous child removals in line with international human rights standards related to principles of equality and non-discrimination (to address the structural inequalities experienced by Indigenous families related to housing, childcare, education, policing, and employment), the right of Indigenous peoples to self-determination (in leading decision making about Indigenous children), and the right of Indigenous children to their culture (to maintain connections with their families of origin) (HREOC, 1997, chap. 26). Encapsulating its reforms was a perceived need to introduce minimum national standards through legislation to overcome the dismal failure of the states and territories to protect these rights (HREOC, 1997, pp. 581–592).

BTH's recommendations were based on the presumption that it is in the child's best interest to remain with their Indigenous family, community, and culture and that their removal should be a measure of last resort (HREOC, 1997, p. 585, rec. 46a). This would require adequate early intervention measures for families and children to ensure rights to equality and non-discrimination (HREOC, 1997, p. 580, rec. 43a, 43b). If in the extreme case removal of a child was considered, Indigenous organisations were to be involved at every stage of the decision-making process (HREOC, 1997, p. 586, rec. 49) in line with the Indigenous right to self-determination. Furthermore, if a child was to be removed from their families, *BTH* recommended that the Indigenous Child Placement Principle ('the Placement Principle') apply according to the following order of preference to preserve the child's right to their culture:

1 Placement with a member of the child's family (as defined by local custom and practice) in the correct relationship to the child in accordance with Aboriginal or Torres Strait Islander law;
2 Placement with a member of the child's community in a relationship of responsibility for the child according to local custom and practice;
3 Placement with another member of the child's community; and
4 Placement with another Indigenous carer

(HREOC, 1997, p. 588, rec. 51b).

Children would only be placed with non-Indigenous carers as a last resort measure on condition that family reunion was a primary objective; the child continued to have contact with their Indigenous family, community, and culture; and the child lived in proximity to their Indigenous family and community (HREOC, 1997, p. 589, rec. 51d).

The states and territories have responded to *BTH* by incorporating versions of the Placement Principle in their own child welfare laws and to promote self-determination in decision making that affects Indigenous children and increase funding of services. However, national standards legislation as proposed by *BTH* has not been enacted, and the attempts made by the state and territories to uphold the Indigenous right of self-determination and the cultural rights of Indigenous children have not been sufficient to override institutional racism and stigmatisation within the child welfare system. The main issue remains – history is repeating itself as the rights of Indigenous peoples continue to be violated by the disproportionate removal of Indigenous children from their families.

In 2023, Indigenous children accounted for 42.8% of all children in out-of-home care even though they comprised only 5.98% of the total child population (SNAICC and Family Matters, 2023, p. 1). The statistics also indicate that in 2022 Indigenous children were 10.5 times more likely than non-Indigenous children to be in out-of-home care and between 2009 to 2022 the number of Indigenous children in out-of-home care more than doubled from 10,512 to 22,328 (Department of Families, Housing, Community Services and Indigenous Affairs and the National Framework Implementation Working Group, 2010, p. 7; SNAICC, 2023, p. 5). The fact that there has been an increase since the *National Agreement* was introduced in 2020 (there were 21,523 Indigenous children in out-of-home care on 30 June 2020 (SNAICC, Family Matters and University of Melbourne, 2021, p. 5)) shows the situation is worsening. This is further illuminated by the increase in the number of babies being removed from their mothers, which correlates with an increase in use of birth notifications with respect to mothers who had a child removed previously (Davis, 2019, p. 192). The data available indicates that Indigenous babies are at least twice as likely to have a pre-birth report than non-Indigenous babies (SNAICC, 2023, p. 21) and Indigenous babies under 12 months are 13.1 times more likely to be in out-of-home care (SNAICC and Family Matters, 2023, p. 1). These statistics combined raise concerns about government commitment to close the gap in out-of-home care.

National implementation of the Placement Principle was central to the *BTH* recommendations. This Principle continues to underpin the reform agendas of peak Indigenous child welfare advocacy groups and has been further developed to include five elements (prevention, partnership, placement, participation, and connection) (SNAICC, 2023, p. 64). However, with the rise of permanency planning in child welfare laws and administration, the best interests of the child has become associated with providing stability of care not in terms of Indigenous kinship care and attachment to culture (as embodied in the Placement Principle) but in terms of a narrow understanding of attachment theory which emphasises a singular attachment of a child to its carer (SNAICC, 2023, p. 30, citing SNAICC, 2016).

The emphasis on permanency planning is reflected in the statistics (in 2023, 80.9% of Indigenous children were on permanent care orders and 66.3% of all adoptions in the last ten years were of Indigenous children). At the same time, Indigenous children have increasingly been transferred to non-Indigenous care, evident in the number of children placed with Aboriginal and Torres Strait Islander carers having decreased from 53.6% in 2013 to 40.7% in 2022. All this is taking place within a context of inadequate and ineffective governmental responses to intergenerational trauma, homelessness, employment, education, and health to produce unacceptable levels of dislocation of children from their mothers and families. Instead of providing adequate early intervention supports and services to address these socio-economic factors, child welfare funding is channelled mostly to permanent interventions and not early interventions and reunification (84.1% spent on intervention services and out-of-home care and only 15.9% spent on support services) (SNAICC and Family Matters, 2023, pp. 1–2). This focus on permanency planning enables governments to shift some of their costs to private carers and to claim they are solving the crisis, as the number of children in permanent care may not be counted as being in out-of-home care. For Indigenous families, by contrast, the cycle of intergenerational trauma continues as children are removed at disproportionate rates (SNAICC, 2023, pp. 46–47). Moreover, and like what happened to previous Stolen Generations, Indigenous children are being targeted for removal, as demonstrated by the high investigation rates of Indigenous children when compared to non-Indigenous children, notwithstanding there are high rates of child mistreatment across all population groups in Australia (estimated at

62.2% in 2023 for people aged 16–65) (SNAICC, 2023, p. 24). Evidently, Indigenous children are no longer being removed under laws that specifically discriminate against Indigenous children and their families as they had been during the protection and assimilation eras. Instead, their removal is being authorised by general child welfare laws which, while appearing neutral, are administered by a system that continues to privilege middle-class non-Indigenous family values of permanent primary care giving while Indigenous child-rearing continues to be viewed through a culturally biased prism of deficiency. Thus, unaddressed social disadvantage and continuing over-surveillance of Indigenous families come together to create the conditions for the disproportionate removal of Indigenous children from their families.

There have been attempts to address the glaring deficiencies of Australia's child welfare systems. Nationally, the *Safe and Supported: Aboriginal and Torres Strait Islander First Action Plan 2023–26* ('*Action Plan*') (Australian Government, Department of Social Services, 2023a) followed the introduction of *Safe and Supported: the National Framework for Protecting Australia's Children 2021–2031* (Australian Government, Department of Social Services, 2023b). If properly resourced the *Action Plan* could (among other things) result in the transfer of authority in child protection to community and Indigenous organisations, investment in the community-controlled sector and workforce, data sovereignty, full implementation of the Placement Principle, and the establishment of nationals standards for Indigenous child welfare that would be overseen by state and territory Aboriginal and Torres Strait Islander Children's Commissioners, and would include establishing a National Commissioner (SNAICC, 2023, p. 7). Though welcome, these initiatives may not ultimately result in holistic change, as has been evidenced at the state level. In NSW, for example, there have been amendments to the *Children and Young Persons (Care and Protection) Act* (1998) ('*Children and Young Persons Act*') in response to the *Family Is Culture* report (Davis, 2019). Among them, caseworkers are now required to provide evidence to the Children's Court of all 'active efforts' taken to prevent children being removed from their families (New South Wales Government, Department of Communities and Justice, 2022; see also *Children and Young Persons Act*, 1998, ss 9A, 63, 79AA, 83, s 83A, and 266). However, not all recommendations in the *Family Is Culture* report have been implemented, and concerns have been raised that the government has merely tinkered around the edges (Aboriginal Legal Service NSW/ACT Ltd, 2022), evident in how provisions supporting the Placement Principle for Indigenous children must continue to compete with provisions aimed at permanency placement and adoption (cf., *Children and Young Persons Act*, 1998, ss 8 and 9 and ss 12A and 13). This is an issue not only for NSW but the entire nation as the focus continues to be on achieving permanency. Overall, the statistics reveal the need for a complete overhaul of child welfare legislation, policy, and practice because on current projections the number of Indigenous children separated from their families will not reach the Closing the Gap target of decreasing by 45% by 2031, but are projected to increase 39% by 2033 (SNAICC, 2023, p. 44).

The obstacles in the way of closing the gap in child welfare are representative of wider issues inherent in the Closing the Gap policy. On the face of it, the Priority Reforms in the new *National Agreement* could lead to the institutional changes required to close the gap on the Socio-Economic Reforms such as out-of-home care, among others. To paraphrase the Priority Reforms, these changes require the protection of Indigenous peoples' rights to self-determination and culture, the elimination of institutional racism, and an increase in government accountability through institutional reforms. Government provision of adequate and appropriate resources to implement these reforms would be vital to their success. Notably, however, as of July 2023 there was no data on progress in meeting the four Priority Reforms (Productivity Commission, 2023). Moreover, while the Commonwealth and state and territory governments have introduced Implementation Plans (as required under the *Agreement*) that are to varying degrees underpinned by the principles of self-determination and non-discrimination, the terms of these plans have been framed as policy and not law reform. This raises the question whether progress on meeting these Priority Reforms can be made while there are laws that condone discrimination against Indigenous peoples and there is an absence of laws upholding their rights.

The Socio-Economic Reforms also have their flaws. In covering a broader range of targets, they appear more attuned to Indigenous peoples' circumstances, especially by comparison to the former Closing the Gap targets. However, more recent research from the Healing Foundation (2021) has confirmed there is a 'gap within the gap' as Stolen Generations Survivors and their descendants are faring worse than Indigenous peoples not impacted by past child removal policies and laws. The Healing Foundation has set out an action plan to address this gap (as discussed above), but these recommendations have not been specifically incorporated in any of the Socio-Economic Reforms. The Healing Foundation's holistic approach also contrasts to the target-by-target approach to closing the gap in the *National Agreement*. Success of each target would require marked improvements in a range of other targets because of their interconnectedness, such as homelessness, child removal, and incarceration rates. However, there are instances where the set target is particularly underwhelming considering the gravity of the issue (such as reducing adult Indigenous incarceration rates only by 15% by 2031). Low targets like these bring the commitment of governments to make meaningful change in relation to this and the other targets into question. The current disproportionate incarceration rates are themselves a measure of socio-economic disadvantage in Indigenous communities – not to mention the institutional racism of the criminal justice system as demonstrated by notable instances of Indigenous deaths in custody (ANTaR, 2022).

Such relatively low targets could be rationalised as being realistic considering the challenges involved in closing the gaps; however, considering the urgency needed to address Indigenous socio-economic disadvantage, the low targets continue to normalise Indigenous peoples' disadvantaged status. Further, the absence of a comprehensive law reform agenda to change the laws that contribute to Indigenous socio-economic disadvantage (such as the disproportionate institutionalisation of Indigenous children in out-of-home care, and youth and adult incarceration) raises questions about whether the Socio-Economic targets can be achieved. As it is, there continues to be insufficient data to measure three of the 17 Closing the Gap targets (family violence, languages, digital inclusion); only four targets are on track (early childhood education, adult employment, youth incarceration, land rights and interests), seven targets are not on track (adult life expectancy, children's birthweight, attaining Year 12 or equivalent, attaining a tertiary qualification, youth employment/education/training, housing, sea rights and interests); and four are worsening (early childhood development, adult incarceration, out-of-home care, suicide) (Productivity Commission, 2023).[1]

Evidently, much more groundwork is needed if the terms of the *National Agreement* and its overarching promise of achieving a new way of working with Indigenous peoples are to be realised. The *Agreement* could support additional measures being implemented through its provisions for partnership actions, implementations plans, resourcing, and ensuring accountability through reporting on targets and reviews on progress. There are also provisions to change the *Agreement* to include new targets. Ultimately, however, the *Agreement* only has the status of a policy statement, and its focus is on delivery of services and programmes. It is not legally enforceable and therefore can be thwarted if not fully backed by government. Thus, while there is apparent commitment in the *Agreement* to the principle of Indigenous self-determination, eliminating institutional racism, and prioritising Indigenous cultures, in the absence of a robust legal framework protecting Indigenous rights (and an accessible mechanism for Indigenous peoples to enforce their rights and seek remedies for their violation), the aims of the *Agreement* may remain largely aspirational. Rudd in his apology may have declared that the Closing the Gap policy would be satisfying 'the unfulfilled spirit of the 1967 referendum' (House of Representatives, Australia, 2008, p. 170). At the time of the referendum, it was believed that giving the Commonwealth jurisdiction over Indigenous affairs would promote equal rights, end discrimination, and improve the standard of living of Indigenous peoples. Clearly, this has not happened. As a result of the 1967 referendum, the Commonwealth was given power over Indigenous peoples, enshrined in the 'race power' in s. 51(xxvi) of the *Commonwealth of Australia Constitution Act* (1900) ('*Constitution*'). However, this power has been found to not only support beneficial laws – it also has the potential to support discriminatory laws as well (*Kartinyeri v. Commonwealth* (1997)). Whether the *Agreement* can reset the path to closing the gap in the absence of a legal framework to support its aims remains to be seen when the success of closing the gap is contingent on political good will, which to date has been unreliable.

The *Uluru Statement from the Heart*

The discussion above has touched on only a few of the outstanding areas requiring resolution, but they speak to larger failures. Failure to deliver a just resolution of the wrongs inflicted on the Stolen Generations, and the continued pursuit of the Closing the Gap policy that has not advanced Indigenous rights but has enabled their continuing violation. Indeed, the continuing disproportionate removal of Indigenous children to out-of-home care exemplifies how the violation of Indigenous rights perpetuates the wrongs of the past and ultimately impedes the creation of a new partnership that was expected would emerge post-apology.

In the past, Indigenous peoples and their supporters have advocated a range of reforms encapsulating basic human rights and specific Indigenous rights in attempts to curb and overcome the structural violence of settler colonialism. These changes have been sought through different mechanisms, such as seeking constitutional recognition and representation in Parliament, establishing a treaty, recognising customary law, and enshrining a bill of rights (Behrendt, et al., 2019, chap. 14). Most recently, the Indigenous reform agenda has been framed by the *Uluru Statement from the Heart* ('*Uluru Statement*') (2017). This document is premised on the unceded sovereignty of Aboriginal and Torres Strait Islander Nations. As an expression of sovereignty, it is framed as an invitation to the Australian public 'to walk with us … for a better future'. This future requires addressing the negative impacts of colonisation evident in the over-representation of Indigenous peoples in prisons, out-of-home care, and juvenile detention – described as '*the torment of our powerless*'. The *Statement*'s proposed reforms are grounded on three pillars – 'Voice', 'Treaty', and 'Truth'. This would involve constitutionally enshrining a First Nations Voice in the *Constitution* and establishing a Makarrata Commission to oversee agreement making between First Nations and governments and a truth-telling process. The *Uluru Statement* reflects the aspirations of about 250 Indigenous delegates of the First Nations National Constitutional Convention, who had been drawn from 12 regional dialogues involving about 1,200 participants across Australia. The Convention was held in May 2017 near Uluru in central Australia as part of the movement to recognise Aboriginal and Torres Strait Islander peoples in the *Constitution*. By comparison to consultation processes in the past, consultation at the Convention was relatively extensive. Nevertheless, not all Indigenous communities were represented at Uluru, and not all Indigenous peoples supported the *Statement* (Wahlquist, 2017). This may indicate there were flaws in the consultation process, but more broadly, it demonstrates the flaws in the existing consultation processes in Australia that do not have a mechanism to oversee such consultations according to the Indigenous rights of self-determination and free, prior and informed consent as set out in the *United Nations Declaration of Indigenous Peoples* ('*UNDRIP*') (United Nations, 2007, arts, 3, 4, 19). Lack of proper consultation has also been an issue in Canada, exemplified by the process to implement *UNDRIP* there (discussed in Chapter 7).

The *Statement* has never succeeded in gaining bipartisan support from the two major political parties, but it does have the support of the Albanese Labor government despite the failed constitutional referendum on 14 October 2023 ('the Voice referendum'), which resulted in 39.94% 'yes' votes and 60.06% 'no' votes. A successful referendum would have, pursuant to the *Constitution Alteration (Aboriginal and Torres Strait Islander Voice) Act* (2023), inserted s. 129 in the *Constitution*, recognising Aboriginal and Torres Strait Islander peoples as the 'First Peoples of Australia', and providing for the establishment of an Aboriginal and Torres Strait Islander Voice ('the Voice) that 'may make representations to the Parliament and the Executive Government of the Commonwealth on matters relating to Aboriginal and Torres Strait Islander peoples', and giving the Parliament power 'to make laws with respect to matters relating to the ... Voice, including its composition, functions, powers and procedures'.[2]

A successful referendum could have functioned as a reparative measure by finally achieving constitutional recognition of Indigenous peoples and entrenching a mechanism for establishing an Indigenous representative body to advise parliaments and governments at the different jurisdictional levels. Constitutional recognition is a long-standing issue. Indigenous peoples were never consulted, nor did they participate in the Federation movement, which resulted in the enactment of the *Constitution* in 1900 and the establishment of the Commonwealth of Australia in 1901. At that time, their exclusion reflected the complete denial of Indigenous laws and governance systems, consistent with the discourses of terra nullius that constructed Indigenous peoples in racist terms as barbaric and uncivilised. The denial of their very existence is tellingly reflected by the fact there is no mention of Indigenous peoples in the preamble of the *Constitution*, while other provisions deprived them of basic citizenship rights to be counted in the national census (under s. 127) and vote in the elections of the Australian state parliaments (under s. 25). Section 127 was repealed by the 1967 referendum, though s. 25 remains.

Lack of proper Indigenous representation has also been a long-standing issue. In the past, Australian Governments (n.d.) have established Indigenous representative bodies,[3] such as the Aboriginal and Torres Strait Islander Commission ('ATSIC') (discussed in Chapter 3), which was created by legislation in 1989 and served, in part, as an advisory body to government. ATSIC was subsequently abolished by the Howard government in 2005, which exemplifies the vulnerability of Indigenous institutions to state power.

Entrenching the concept of the Voice in the *Constitution* would have made it harder to amend or repeal and potentially harder to erase and ignore the Voice once established. In terms of the themes of this book, if properly constituted, the Voice may have created official platforms for dialogue between Indigenous peoples and state actors. The aim, as stated in the *Uluru Statement*, was 'to empower our people and take a rightful place in our own country'.

The importance of the Voice to Indigenous peoples was demonstrated by the fact that a majority of voters in predominantly Indigenous electoral areas (mostly in remote communities) voted 'yes' in the referendum. Its ultimate failure was particularly traumatising for its Indigenous supporters. Several Indigenous representatives who supported the Voice responded to the abject rejection symbolised by the No result by declaring a week of silence. Their statement following the result highlight the main reasons why the referendum failed (*Open Letter: Statement for Our People and Country*, 2023). Foremost are the difficulties in changing the *Constitution*. A successful referendum in Australia requires Parliament to pass legislation setting out the proposed constitutional amendment. Once passed, the referendum requires a double majority, that is, a majority of voters across the country must support it as well as a majority of voters in a majority of states. The difficulty in achieving this level of support is exemplified by the fact that only 9 of 20 referendums have been successful. To achieve this level of support, bipartisan support was needed, and this was notably lacking with respect to the Voice referendum. The failed referendum illuminates the subordinate position of Indigenous peoples in Australia: Indigenous peoples may have the longest surviving cultures in the world, but after 235 years of colonisation they continue to be treated as undeserving of recognition in the nation's founding document and denied the possibility of having a say in their affairs.

Additional difficulties that faced a successful 'yes' vote were the conspiracy theories, and wilful and fearful ignorance among the broader public about the referendum that reflected racist, selfish, or indifferent attitudes, and normalised the increase of vilification of Indigenous peoples at this time. Exacerbating these sentiments was the conservative No campaign, which misrepresented and exaggerated the power the Voice would have had. These arguments were advanced not only by prominent non-Indigenous No campaigners, such as opposition Liberal Party leader Peter Dutton, but also prominent Indigenous No campaigners, such as Warlpiri/Celtic woman and Country Liberal senator Jacinta Nampijinpa Price, and Nyunggai man Warren Mundine.

Central to the conservative No campaign were arguments that the Voice would divide the country on race when the focus should continue to be on delivering practical outcomes for Indigenous peoples (Collard, 2022). Central to these concerns was that the Voice would undermine representative democracy by elevating the voices of Indigenous peoples above those of other Australians in the development of law and policy and result in Indigenous peoples having special rights and privileges that other Australians may not have.

The essence of these concerns was that the concept of the Voice violated the principle of equality, understood in Australia in a narrow sense as committed to equality of treatment and opportunity (discussed in Chapters 3 and 4). This approach accepts that special measures may be needed to overcome social disadvantage, but it does not extend to the provision of special rights to minority groups, as this would be divisive. Combined, these concerns effectively decontextualised the historical divisions in Australia created by the genocide and institutional racism inflicted on Indigenous peoples evident in the laws and policies that have singled Indigenous out for special (and adverse) treatment (such as past protection and assimilation policies and the more recent Northern Territory Emergency Response). The aim of the Voice was to temper this history by providing Indigenous peoples with a mechanism to help overcome the top-down approach to Indigenous affairs and institutionalise a more bottom-up approach consistent with the principle of self-determination.

The additional argument that the focus should be on practical outcomes related to the concern that the Voice would have added another layer of bureaucracy and obstruct tangible changes being made (Senate, Australia, 2023, p. 4 (Nampijinpa Price)). However, this concern appears to assume that current 'practical' approaches (such as the Closing the Gap policy) are working and ignores the evidence that when Indigenous peoples have a say in their own lives, outcomes improve. This was a key argument of the Yes campaign, which claimed that the Voice could lead to a cultural shift in the way that government approaches Indigenous affairs and have significant practical benefits for Indigenous peoples, especially in complementing closing the gap efforts. As Wiradjuri woman and Minister for Indigenous Australians Linda Burney claimed, the Voice was the 'best chance' to create 'a better future for Indigenous Australians after decades of failed government policies ... making sure voices in remote and regional communities are heard' (Visentin, 2022).

A constant criticism also expressed in the lead-up to the referendum was that the proposal lacked detail ('The lack of detail is killing the Voice', 2023). However, this ignored the information circulated by the government about the constitutional change and potential approaches to the establishment of the Voice (see, for example, Joint Select Committee on the Aboriginal and Torres Strait Islander Voice Referendum, 2023; Australian Government, 2023). More insidiously, this argument helped fuel public mistrust of the Voice proposal and the powers it would have had. While it was intended that a consultation process would follow the referendum, the Voice's powers would have ultimately been determined by Parliament through a legislative process. Indeed, the referendum would not have established the Voice. If it had succeeded, Parliament would have had to decide whether to enact legislation to create the Voice or not, and while the referendum would have given Parliament a mandate, there was no legal requirement for Parliament to establish the Voice. For example, s. 101 of the *Constitution* provides that 'there must be an inter-state commission, with such powers of adjudication and administration as the Parliament deems necessary', but no such body exists. Even if Parliament proceeded to establish the Voice, the legislation would not bind future parliaments and would be susceptible to political changes, as happened with ATSIC's abolition.

Concerns about the Voice also extended to how it would fit within the other constitutional structures of government (Parliament and the Executive) and whether its existence would result in High Court challenges. While the separation of powers precludes judicial interference in the exercise of the Commonwealth's parliamentary powers (and thereby would have precluded judicial interference in decisions made by Parliament with respect to the Voice's representations), concerns were raised about the exercise of the Commonwealth's Executive powers with respect the Voice's representations, and whether this could trigger judicial review of ministerial decision making. However, the wording of the proposed constitutional amendment was limited in scope in providing that the Voice 'may make' representations. It did not mandate that the Executive (or Parliament) must consider the Voice's representations. As Parliament would have determined the scope of the Voice's powers, it would have had the power to restrict judicial review of any consultations with the Voice. This may not have necessarily stopped High Court challenges. However, a literal interpretation of the proposed amendment indicates that the Voice's powers would have been limited to making representations. It may have been able to speak, but whether its representations would have been acted upon would have been more a policy than a legal question that the Parliament and the Executive would have decided. Indeed, the Voice's ability to speak would have depended on whether it had the resources to make effective representations, and its success would have depended on government willingness to support and fund its proposed reforms. Ultimately, accountability for these decisions (the scope of the Voice's powers, funding, etc.) would have been tested by the Australian public at election time. So understood, it becomes clearer that concerns about the Voice's functions and powers were misguided as the Voice would have been subject to the powers of Parliament and overseen by the voting public. Considering that Indigenous peoples' concerns are not usually given high priority at elections, this may not have provided a sufficient safeguard for the Voice's success.

Moreover, the idea that Parliament would decide the composition of the Voice was also met with the criticism that the Voice would be a 'Canberra Voice' and not representative of Indigenous peoples, especially in regional and remote regions (McIlroy and Coorey, 2023). Ensuring effective representation for Indigenous peoples has been a vexed issue. This was exemplified by ATSIC, which faced criticism with respect to its representative structure that resulted in local Indigenous communities experiencing detachment from the national board (Behrendt, et al., 2019, p. 236). Even more concerning have been the instances when Indigenous individuals were not representative at all because they had been handpicked by government.

For these reasons, establishing the Voice would have required extensive negotiations. These negotiations would have required faith in the Australian parliamentary system, an institution that historically has not consulted or represented the interests of Indigenous peoples very effectively and has largely functioned to subordinate the rights and interests of Indigenous peoples in favour of more dominant interests. It was these sorts of concerns that informed the progressive No position on the referendum.

It is important to acknowledge that not everyone was opposed the Voice because they perceived it would threaten non-Indigenous interests and state institutions. There were also concerns that the Voice would not have led to the change Indigenous peoples deserve. Former Greens senator, now Independent, Gunnai, Gunditjmara and Djab Wurring woman, Lidia Thorpe, was among those opposed to the Voice on grounds like these. She claimed the Voice proposal was another manifestation of racist colonial assimilation intent on undermining Indigenous sovereignty and eliminating Indigenous peoples. She was especially concerned that the Voice was not intended to be a decision-making body: it would have been an advisory body with non-binding powers. Instead of the Voice, Thorpe (and others like her) claimed that treaty should come first in conjunction with reparations consistent with the Royal Commission into Aboriginal Deaths in Custody and *BTH* (Senate, Australia, 2023, pp. 5–6).

These concerns were somewhat understandable. While it is true that Indigenous sovereignty is an inherent right that may only be ceded by Indigenous peoples, it remains the case that Indigenous claims to sovereignty have not been accepted in international or domestic laws. The Voice, as a non-binding advisory body, would not have addressed this issue, nor given Indigenous peoples' right to self-determination full expression. Rather, its non-binding status may have maintained Indigenous peoples' subordination to state laws and policies and rights violations may have continued. The Voice may have served to amplify Indigenous perspectives on matters that concern them, but because it would have been advisory only, decision-making power with respect to these matters would have continued to reside with Parliament and the Executive. As exemplified by the Howard government's abolition of ATSIC, Indigenous peoples' voices can be silenced completely if they contradict the official line (Thorne, 2004). Notably, while Thorpe rejected the Voice proposal, she has demonstrated commitment to Indigenous rights by introducing the United Nations Declaration on the Rights of Indigenous Peoples Bill (2022) aimed to incorporate *UNDRIP* in Australian law (cf., Australian Human Rights Commission, 2023). Aspects of this legislation are like the legislation adopted in Canada to incorporate *UNDRIP*, though not all Indigenous peoples in Canada support this process (see Chapter 7).

With respect to the treaty argument, it is also understandable that there are Indigenous peoples who see this as a pressing issue considering the longstanding failure in Australia to enter treaties with Indigenous peoples, but to criticise the Voice because it was not focused on treaty ignores how 'Treaty' is a pillar of the *Uluru Statement*. As sovereign peoples, the treaty issue should have been resolved when the Supreme Court of NSW considered the exercise of Indigenous jurisdiction in cases in the early 1800s (see Kercher, 1998). Presently, all states and territories (except Western Australia) are, to varying degrees, exploring official treaty processes with First Nations people, and some include truth telling (Queensland, Tasmania, the Northern Territory, Victoria) and voice (South Australia and Victoria). These jurisdictions are mostly under Labor and support the *Uluru Statement*. If the Liberals resume power in these jurisdictions, these processes could come under threat. Now that the Voice referendum has failed the message is not that Indigenous peoples deserve better (as the progressive No position claimed); rather, the No result has further entrenched the idea that any measures that appear to give Indigenous peoples 'special rights' are divisive and should be rejected.

Developments in Australia conform to a pattern of paying lip service to advancing Indigenous peoples' interests but falling short of protecting their rights. In the absence of rights protections, approaches in law and policy have tended to apply non-Indigenous norms and practices which often have not advanced the interests of Indigenous peoples at all. In this respect, after the referendum both sides of politics recommitted to closing the gap, but no commitment has been forthcoming to close the racism and ignorance gaps that contributed to the referendum's failure. Indigenous peoples continue to be cast as deficient while the democratic processes that created and sustain their unequal status remain unchallenged. Even so, the referendum exposed deep divisions in Australia and raised concerns about the fate of reconciliation that could not be ignored. The recommitment to closing the gap has sought to salvage the reconciliation movement in presenting the cause of overcoming Indigenous social disadvantage as an issue most Australians may agree on. In making this commitment, Australia may continue to portray its image as the land of the fair go. However, this image has, for many, never been the reality, and continues to wear thin as the gaps remain wide and in some cases are widening. Indeed, the genocide may only worsen if fairness continues to be equated with a notion of equality that results in attempts to achieve parity between Indigenous and non-Indigenous peoples in the absence of specific rights protections. Whether the Voice would have made any difference to closing the gap was uncertain as it would have only been authorised to provide non-binding advice. Nevertheless, a successful referendum would have powerfully affirmed Indigenous peoples as the 'First Peoples of Australia' in the *Constitution*. As 'Voice' is only one of the three pillars of the *Uluru Statement*, a successful referendum would have also provided the impetus for the establishment of the other two – 'Treaty' and 'Truth'. It could be that the support shown for the referendum by Indigenous and non-Indigenous peoples may be harnessed in future and result in the *Uluru Statement* being honoured by government to provide scope for rights and reparations for Indigenous peoples, and much-needed education for the broader population. But in the immediate aftermath of the referendum, it is uncertain whether

Australia will ever recognise Aboriginal and Torres Strait Islanders in the *Constitution*, as conservatives are at most only willing to support symbolic recognition while Indigenous peoples want (and are entitled to) more substantive changes. In the current status quo, the *Constitution* will continue to perpetuate a myth of settler colonialism that Indigenous peoples do not exist on their own lands (Allam, 2023). In terms of this book, it appears that at this time Australia has largely forgotten its apology to Indigenous peoples and its promise of establishing a new relationship with Indigenous peoples that should have led to the eventual demise of settler colonialism.

Conclusion

It is important to ensure Indigenous voices are heard and no longer patronised and silenced by state actors either by paternalistic claims to know what is best for Indigenous peoples or by discriminatory tactics that privilege non-Indigenous interests above the interests of Indigenous peoples. A rights framework could strengthen Indigenous voices being heard in law and policy. As discussed above, this was the approach advocated by *BTH* to address the injustices experienced by the Stolen Generations and which continue to be inflicted on Indigenous families in the contemporary child welfare system. Indeed, as governments in Australia are implementing measures (such as the *National Agreement*) that are at face value committed to listening to Indigenous voices and strengthening Indigenous control over their affairs, the absence of discussion to enshrine Indigenous rights, such as the right of self-determination, brings government commitment to such measures into serious question. A rights-based approach is explored further in the next chapter on Canada, but in terms of the Australian context, the failure to institutionalise rights protections demonstrates the politico-legal gaps that continue to exist between Indigenous peoples and government in the post-apology era. In the aftermath of the failed referendum the need for rights protections appears even more imperative, as it has become clear that if left to the majority in Australia, Indigenous peoples' interests will remain on the sidelines. However, this is where a conundrum arises: like the referendum, without majoritarian support, any attempt at rights implementation may likely face the same fate and be shut down as divisive.

Notes

1 Note that Target 15 covers land and sea rights and interests and the data suggests the former is on track, but the latter is not.
2 For a summary of the movement for constitutional recognition in Australia and discussion of the First Nations Voice to Parliament, see Mills, McNicol and Haughton (2023). In the meantime, South Australia has passed legislation to establish a First Nations Voice in that State (*First Nations Voice Act* (2023)).
3 For a coverage of Indigenous representative bodies in Australia see, Haughton (2023).

Reference list

Aboriginal Affairs NSW, 2020, *Stolen Generations reparations scheme interim report*, https://www.aboriginalaffairs.nsw.gov.au/healing-and-reparations/stolen-generations/2021-SGRS-Interim-Report-(Final)-%5Baccessible%5D.pdf

Aboriginal Legal Service NSW/ACT Ltd, 2022, *Family is culture bill has passed, but AbSec and ALS are calling for more*, 10 November, https://www.alsnswact.org.au/family-is-culture-bill-passed

Aboriginal and Torres Strait Islander Healing Foundation, 2017, *Bringing them home 20 years on: an action plan for healing*, https://healingfoundation.org.au/app/uploads/2017/05/Bringing-Them-Home-20-years-on-FINAL-SCREEN-1.pdf

Aboriginal and Torres Strait Islander Healing Foundation, 2021, *Make healing happen: it's time to act*, https://healingfoundation.org.au/app/uploads/2021/05/Make-Healing-Happen-Report-FINAL-May-2021.pdf

Aboriginal and Torres Strait Islander Healing Foundation, 2022, Stolen Generations collective healing initiatives: rounds 1–6: impacts and findings, https://healingfoundation.org.au//app/uploads/2022/12/Stolen_Generations_Collective_Healing_Rounds_1-6_Jun22_V5.pdf

Aldrich, H., 2017, 'The Stolen Generations group action: an alternative model to redress a traumatic past', *Precedent*, vol. *141*, https://classic.austlii.edu.au/au/journals/PrecedentAULA/2017/44.html

Allam, L., 2023, 'Rejecting the voice shows Australia is still in denial, its history of forgetting a festering wrong', *The Guardian*, 14 October, https://www.theguardian.com/australia-news/commentisfree/2023/oct/14/rejecting-the-voice-shows-australia-is-still-in-denial-its-history-of-forgetting-a-festering-wrong

Altman, J. and Fogarty, B., 2010, 'Indigenous Australians as "no gaps" subjects: education and development in remote Australia', in I. Snyder and J. Nieuwenhuysen (eds), *Closing the gap in education: improving outcomes in southern world societies*, Monash University Publishing, Victoria, pp. 109–128, https://hdl.handle.net/1885/9738

ANTaR, 2022, *Deaths in custody*, 27 October, https://antar.org.au/issues/justice/deaths-custody/

Australian Government, n.d., *Recognition through a Voice*, https://voice.gov.au/

Australian Government, 2023, *Voice principles*, https://webarchive.nla.gov.au/awa/20230929160619/https://voice.gov.au/about-voice/voice-principles

Australian Government, Department of Social Services, 2023a, *Safe and supported: Aboriginal and Torres Strait Islander First Action Plan 2023–26*, 31 January, https://www.dss.gov.au/families-and-children-programs-services-children-protecting-australias-children-safe-and-supported-the-national-framework-for-protecting-australias-children-2021-2031/safe-and-supported-aboriginal-and-torres-strait-islander-first-action-plan-2023-2026#:~:text=The%20Safe%20and%20Supported%3A%20Aboriginal,Torres%20Strait%20Islander%20Leadership%20Group

Australian Government, Department of Social Services, 2023b, *Safe and supported: the National Framework for Protecting Australia's Children 2021–2031*, 15 February, https://www.dss.gov.au/our-responsibilities/families-and-children/programs-services/protecting-australias-children

Australian Human Rights Commission, 2023, *A National Human Rights Act for Australia*, 7 March, https://humanrights.gov.au/human-rights-act-for-australia

Australian Institute of Health and Welfare, 2008, *Number of children in out-of-home care has increased significantly in five years*, 23 January, https://www.aihw.gov.au/news-media/media-releases/2008/jan/number-of-children-in-out-of-home-care-has-increas>

Behrendt, L., Cunneen, C., Libesman, T. and Watson, N., 2019, *Aboriginal and Torres Strait Islander legal relations*, 2nd edn, Oxford University Press, Australia.

Biddle, N. and Markham, F., 2017, 'Census data shows just how bad we've been at closing inequality gaps', *The Conversation*, 25 October, https://theconversation.com/census-data-shows-just-how-bad-weve-been-at-closing-inequality-gaps-86137

Children and Young Persons (Care and Protection) Act, 1998 (NSW).

Collard, S., 2022, 'NT Senator Jacinta Price urges govt to act on "practical" concerns as opposed to Voice', *NITV*, 8 June, https://www.sbs.com.au/nitv/the-point/article/nt-senator-jacinta-price-urges-govt-to-act-on-practical-concerns-as-opposed-to-voice/58bnllsa4

Collard v. Western Australia [No. 4] [2013] WASC 455.

Commonwealth of Australia Constitution Act, 1900, 63 & 64 Vict., c. 12, s. 9 (Imp.).

Commonwealth of Australia, Department of the Prime Minister and Cabinet, 2019, *Closing the Gap retrospective review*, https://www.niaa.gov.au/sites/default/files/publications/closing-gap-retrospective-review-accessible.pdf

Constitution Alteration (Aboriginal and Torres Strait Islander Voice), 2023 (Cth).

Council of Australian Governments, 2009, *National Indigenous Reform Agreement (Closing the Gap)*, https://www.voced.edu.au/content/ngv%3A49067

Cubillo v. Commonwealth, 2001, 174 ALR 97.

Cunneen, C. and Grix, J., 2004, *The limitations of litigation in Stolen Generations cases*, AIATSIS Research Discussion Paper Number 15, https://aiatsis.gov.au/sites/default/files/research_pub/cunneenc-grixj-dp15-limitations-litigation-stolen-generation-cases_0_2.pdf

Davis, M., 2019, *Family is culture: Independent Review of Aboriginal children and young people in OOHC*, https://www.familyisculture.nsw.gov.au/__data/assets/pdf_file/0011/726329/Family-Is-Culture-Review-Report.pdf

Department of Families, Housing, Community Services and Indigenous Affairs and the National Framework Implementation Working Group, 2010, *National standards for out of home care: consultation paper*, https://www.dss.gov.au/sites/default/files/documents/facs_37724_out_home_care.pdf

Department of Premier and Cabinet, Tasmania, 2008, *Report of the Stolen Generations Assessor: Stolen Generations of Aboriginal Children Act 2006*, https://nla.gov.au/nla.obj-1382145277/view

Durbach, A., 2008, '"The cost of a wounded society": reparations and the illusion of reconciliation', *Australian Indigenous Law Review*, vol. 12, no. 1, pp. 22–40.

Dodson, M., 2000, 'Mick Dodson at Corroboree 2000', *ABC Radio National*, 11 June, https://www.abc.net.au/radionational/archived/encounter/mick-dodson-at-corroboree-2000/3468418

First Nations Voice Act, 2023 (SA).

Gooley, C., 2021, 'Stolen Generations Survivors to sue the federal government for compensation', *The New Daily*, 28 April, https://thenewdaily.com.au/news/2021/04/28/stolen-generations-class-action/

Haughton, J., 2023, *Former Aboriginal and Torres Strait Islander Australian Government representative and advisory bodies: a quick guide*, Parliament of Australia, Department of Parliamentary Services, Research Paper Series, 2022–2023, 16 June, https://parlinfo.aph.gov.au/parlInfo/download/library/prspub/9221309/upload_binary/9221309.pdf

Healing Foundation, 2023, *Territories Stolen Generations Redress Scheme*, https://healingfoundation.org.au/territories-stolen-generations-redress-scheme/

House of Representatives, Australia, 2008, *Apology to Australia's Indigenous Peoples, Parliamentary Debates*, 13 February, https://parlinfo.aph.gov.au/parlInfo/genpdf/chamber/hansardr/2008-02-13/0003/hansard_frag.pdf;fileType=application/pdf

Human Rights and Equal Opportunity Commission, 1997, *Bringing them home: report of the National Inquiry into the Separation of Aboriginal and Torres Strait Islander Children from their Homes*, Sterling Press, Sydney.

Joint Select Committee on the Aboriginal and Torres Strait Islander Voice Referendum, 2023, *Advisory Report on the Constitution Alteration (Aboriginal and Torres Strait Islander Voice) 2023*, https://www.aph.gov.au/Parliamentary_Business/Committees/Joint/Former_Committees/Aboriginal_and_Torres_Strait_Islander_Voice_Referendum/VoiceReferendum/Report

Kartinyeri v. Commonwealth (1997) 195 CLR 337.

Kercher, B., 1998, 'R. v. Ballard, R. v. Murrell and R. v. Bonjon', *Australian Indigenous Law Reporter*, vol. 3, no. 3, pp. 410–425, https://www8.austlii.edu.au/cgi-bin/viewdoc/au/journals/AILR/1998/27.html

Kruk, R., 2021, *Final report: second year review of the National Redress Scheme*, https://www.nationalredress.gov.au/sites/default/files/documents/2021-06/d21-508932-final-report-second-year-review-national-redress-scheme.pdf

McIlroy, T. and Coorey, P., 2023, 'Dutton to oppose "Canberra Voice" in showdown with Albanese', *Financial Review*, 5 April, https://www.afr.com/politics/federal/dutton-to-oppose-canberra-voice-in-war-with-albanese-20230405-p5cy8g

Mills, J., McNicol, S. and Haughton, J., 2023, *Constitution Alteration (Aboriginal and Torres Strait Islander Voice) 2023*, Parliament of Australia, Department of Parliamentary Services, Bills Digest No. 80, 2022–2023, 19 May, https://parlinfo.aph.gov.au/parlInfo/download/legislation/billsdgs/9174583/upload_binary/9174583.pdf

National Agreement on Closing the Gap, 2020, https://www.closingthegap.gov.au/sites/default/files/files/national-agreement-ctg.pdf

National Inquiry into Missing and Murdered Indigenous Women and Girls, 2019, *A legal analysis of genocide: supplementary report*, https://www.mmiwg-ffada.ca/wp-content/uploads/2019/06/Supplementary-Report_Genocide.pdf

National Redress Scheme, n.d., *Serious criminal convictions – additional information form*, https://www.nationalredress.gov.au/sites/default/files/documents/2019-06/nrs004serious-criminal-convictions.pdf

New South Wales Government, Department of Community and Justice, 2022, *Family is culture bill passes the Upper House*, 21 October, https://dcj.nsw.gov.au/news-and-media/media-releases-archive/2022/family-is-culture-bill-passes-the-upper-house-.html

New South Wales, Parliament, Legislative Council, General Purpose Standing Committee No. 3, 2016, *Reparations for the Stolen Generations in New South Wales: unfinished business*, https://www.parliament.nsw.gov.au/lcdocs/inquiries/1645/Final%20report%20-%20Reparations%20for%20the%20Stolen%20Generations%20in%20NSW%20-%2023%20June%202016%20-%20with%20covers.pdf

Onus, F., 2023, *Healing Foundation: about us*, https://healingfoundation.org.au/about-us/

Open Letter: Statement for Our People and Country, 2023, 22 October, https://fpdn.org.au/open-letter-statement-for-our-people-and-country/

Paradies, Y., 2006, 'Beyond black and white: essentialism, hybridity and indigeniety', *Journal of Sociology*, vol. 42, no. 4, pp. 355–367.

Pholi, K., Black, D. and Richards, C., 2009, 'Is "close the gap" a useful approach to improving the health and wellbeing of Indigenous Australians?', *Australian Review of Public Affairs*, vol. 9, no. 2, pp. 1–14.

Productivity Commission, 2023, *Closing the Gap information repository: dashboard*, https://www.pc.gov.au/closing-the-gap-data/dashboard

Royal Commission into Institutional Responses to Child Sexual Abuse, 2015, *Redress and civil litigation report*, https://www.royalcommission.gov.au/system/files/2021-01/carc-final-report-redress-and-civil-litigation.pdf

Senate, Australia, 2023, *Hansard*, 19 June, https://parlinfo.aph.gov.au/parlInfo/download/chamber/hansards/26734/toc_pdf/Senate_2023_06_19.pdf;fileType=application%2Fpdf

Shine Lawyers, n.d., *Northern Territory Stolen Generations class action*, https://www.shine.com.au/service/class-actions/northern-territory-stolen-generations-class-action#:~:text=Proposed%20settlement%20of%20the%20class,is%20approved%20by%20the%20Court

SNAICC, 2016, *Achieving stability for Aboriginal and Torres Strait Islander children in out-of-home care: policy position statement*, https://www.snaicc.org.au/wp-content/uploads/2016/07/SNAICC-Achieving_stability-1.pdf

SNAICC (ed.), 2023, *The Family Matters report 2023*, https://www.snaicc.org.au/wp-content/uploads/2023/11/Family-Matters-Report-2023.pdf

SNAICC and Family Matters, 2023, *Family Matters: snapshot data*, https://www.snaicc.org.au/wp-content/uploads/2023/11/Family-Matters-Report-2023-data-snapshot.pdf

SNAICC, Family Matters and University of Melbourne, 2021, *The Family Matters report 2021*, https://www.familymatters.org.au/wp-content/uploads/2021/12/FamilyMattersReport2021.pdf

'The lack of detail is killing the Voice', 2023, *The Canberra Times*, 31 August, https://www.canberratimes.com.au/story/8329626/a-voice-needs-to-be-sold-with-clarity/

Thorburn, K. and Syed, J., 2017, '"Sorry means you don't do it again": Grandmothers Against Removals', *Honi Soit*, 26 January, https://honisoit.com/2017/01/sorry-means-you-dont-do-it-again-grandmothers-against-removals/

Thorne, A., 2004, 'ATSIC abolition creates opportunity to fight for something better!' *Freedom Socialist Party*, Winter/Spring, https://socialism.com/fsb-article/atsic-abolition-creates-opportunity-to-fight-for-something-better/

Trevorrow v. South Australia (No. 5) [2007] SASC 285.

Uluru Statement from the Heart, 2017, https://www.referendumcouncil.org.au/sites/default/files/2017-05/Uluru_Statement_From_The_Heart_0.PDF

United Nations, 2007, *United Nations Declaration on the Rights of Indigenous Peoples*, General Assembly Resolution 61/295.

United Nations Declaration on the Rights of Indigenous Peoples Bill 2022 (Cth).

van Boven, T., 1996, *The van Boven principles*, in Human Rights and Equal Opportunity Commission, 1997, *Bringing them home: report of the National Inquiry into the Separation of Aboriginal and Torres Strait Islander Children from their Homes*, Sterling Press, Sydney, pp. 649–650.

Visentin, L., 2022, 'Raised voices: the battle over Indigenous recognition turns ugly', *The Sydney Morning Herald*, 3 December, https://www.smh.com.au/politics/federal/raised-voices-the-battle-over-indigenous-recognition-turns-ugly-20221201-p5c2qg.html

Wahlquist, C., 2017, 'Uluru talks: delegates walk out due to sovereignty and treaty fears', *The Guardian*, 25 May, https://www.theguardian.com/australia-news/2017/may/25/uluru-talks-delegates-walk-out-due-to-sovereignty-and-treaty-fears#:~:text=The%20dissenting%20delegates%2C%20from%20New,the%20convention%20on%20Thursday%20afternoon

Chapter 7

Canada post-apology

Introduction

This chapter canvasses more recent developments in Canada post-apology. Like the previous chapter on Australia, this chapter recognises the importance of maintaining the apology's promise of 'never again' and the imperative for Indigenous peoples to guide the government in fulfilling this promise. By examining more recent developments through this relational understanding of apology making, this chapter assesses the approaches to providing redress to Residential School Survivors, fulfilling the Calls to Action of the Truth and Reconciliation Commission of Canada (TRC, 2015) with respect to ending the violence against Indigenous women and girls and implementing the *United Nations Declaration on the Rights of Indigenous Peoples* ('*UNDRIP*') (United Nations, 2007), and addressing the shortcomings of the child welfare system for Indigenous children and their families. These developments follow the *Indian Residential Settlement Agreement* ('*Settlement Agreement*') (2006), which was an important outcome for the Indigenous parties to the *Agreement* and was the only measure of redress Harper offered in his apology (House of Commons, Canada, 2008). Subsequently, the Trudeau government has committed to implement all the TRC's recommendations and has supported the findings of subsequent inquiries, most notably, the finding of genocide made by the National Inquiry into Murdered and Missing Indigenous Women and Girls. These developments reveal how Indigenous perspectives can change the national narrative and be the catalyst for further change. Despite this, poor implementation of the *Settlement Agreement*, and slow progress and often resistance to Indigenous claims has brought the government's commitment into question. This reveals how the government, by ostensibly implementing change, is maintaining the status quo as Indigenous peoples remain subordinate to state norms and thereby susceptible to further injustices. Indeed, while the government appears committed to changing law and policy to align with *UNDRIP*, its incremental approach and refusal to constitutionally enshrine these rights appears to undermine *UNDRIP* as the 'framework for reconciliation' (TRC, 2015,

DOI: 10.4324/9781003491019-7

p. 199). Currently, it would appear the government's efforts are proving inadequate in laying the foundation for the long-lasting changes needed to reset the nation-to-nation relationship in Canada.

Reparations and Residential School Survivors

As was noted in Chapter 3, the *Settlement Agreement* was implemented in Canada in 2007. This *Agreement* included C$1.9 billion for Common Experience Payments ('CEP') and C$960 million for an Independent Assessment Process ('IAP'). C$60 million was also allocated for a Truth and Reconciliation Commission ('TRC'), C$20 million for a Commemoration Fund, and another C$125 million to continue the Aboriginal Healing Foundation ('AHF'), which eventually closed in September 2014.

The *Settlement Agreement*, in combining compensation, truth-telling, commemorative, and rehabilitation measures for Residential School Survivors, appears more holistic than the state-by-state approach to redress for the Stolen Generations in Australia. Nevertheless, a different kind of patchwork to redress was created by the *Agreement*, for while there was scope to extend the *Agreement*, it ultimately was for Survivors who attended certain schools, and not all schools. In the intervening time, some of the Survivors excluded from the *Settlement Agreement* have been successful in securing other agreements. This has included the *Newfoundland and Labrador Residential Schools Class Action Settlement* (commenced in 2007 and 2008 and court-approved in 2016), which was between former Inuit students and the federal government; the *Federal Indian Day Schools (McLean) Settlement Agreement* (commenced in 2009 and court-approved in 2019), which was for students who had been forced to attend federally run day schools; and the *Indian Residential Schools Day Scholars (Gottfriedson) Settlement* (commenced in 2012 and court approved in 2021), which was for students who were forced to attend residential schools as day scholars. Funds for healing and commemoration have also been included in these agreements. In the case of the *Newfoundland and Labrador Settlement*, it was also followed by an apology by Prime Minister Trudeau in 2017 in response to criticisms of the Harper apology that did not acknowledge the students from these schools (discussed in Chapter 3). And in 2023, following the *Day Scholars Settlement*, the *Settlement Agreement in the Band Class Litigation* was established, whereby Canada will provide C$2.8 billion in funding for 325 Band class members to be placed in a not-for-profit trust to be used for language, culture, heritage, and healing projects (Government of Canada, 2023f).

Notwithstanding these are important milestones in the government's recognition of the individual and community harms caused by the school system in Canada, it is important to acknowledge that not all Survivors have been included in these agreements. This is evidenced by other class actions, such as the Île-à-la-Crosse Residential School Class Action for Métis Residential

School Survivors in Saskatchewan who had been excluded from the other residential school agreements (Waddle Phillips Professional Corporation, n.d.) and the Indian Boarding Homes Class Action for those who were housed in private boarding homes to attend public schools (Brackenbury, 2023). This latter class action follows the *Sixties Scoop Settlement Agreement* established in 2017 for Status First Nations and Inuit children who had been removed from their families and placed in non-Indigenous foster care or adoption.

Even with respect to the agreements that have been approved, not all Survivors have been eligible to apply. Thus, for instance, the *Newfoundland and Labrador Residential Schools Class Action Settlement* did not include day students or students who attended the schools prior to the province joining the Confederation in 1949 (Brake, 2018), while the *Sixties Scoop Settlement Agreement* did not include non-Status First Nations and Métis peoples. Overlapping claims were subsequently brought by these groups, but not without controversy (Provost, 2021). It also remains the case that these settlements are only with respect to federally run schools and continue to exclude students who attended provincial schools, nor are intergenerational Survivors eligible to make individual claims.

Furthermore, even for Survivors who have been eligible under these agreements they may not receive adequate redress and recognition. The section below examines the monetary, truth-telling, and healing measures of the *Settlement Agreement* to exemplify some (albeit not all) of the problems Survivors experienced. Drawing on reports documenting Survivor experiences of the *Agreement*, this discussion reveals the importance of Survivor-centred approaches to provide holistic, and culturally and trauma-informed, responses. In post-apology Canada, a Survivor-centred approach aligns with the relational understanding of apology making, but to the extent that the actual approach was state-centric, it proved harmful to Survivors.

The monetary payments

The CEP and IAP were the monetary measures of the *Settlement Agreement*. The CEP was an administrative process, in contrast to the IAP which was an adjudicated process. Survivors who were alive on 30 May 2005 and attended a school listed in the *Agreement* could apply.

The CEP (2007–2016) was paid as a lump sum to Survivors in recognition of loss of culture and language. It comprised of a C$10,000 payment and an additional C$3,000 for each year at the school. At the conclusion of the scheme, a total of approximately C$1.6 billion was paid to over 79,000 Survivors who on average received approximately C$20,000 each. Survivors could apply for the remaining CEP funds (maximum C$3,000) to be used for educational purposes either for themselves or for a family member. Survivors who were found ineligible for the CEP could appeal to the National

Administration Committee, and this decision could be further appealed in court. Despite this, almost 24,000 applicants were found ineligible (Government of Canada, 2019).

The IAP (2007–2019) was a separate process to settle outstanding legal claims for specific harms, including sexual and physical abuse while attending a residential school; other wrongful acts causing consequential psychological harm or a physical disability; and loss of opportunity, such as loss of income, due to abuse experienced at a residential school. The IAP had different processes for less and more complex cases and a process of review. In total more than C$3 billion was paid to more than 30,000 Survivors who on average were paid approximately C$111,000 each (including legal fees). More than 7,000 claims were not admitted, withdrawn, or dismissed (Government of Canada, 2019).

Notably in Canada, and unlike in Australia, reports specifically focused on Survivor experiences of the *Settlement Agreement* have been published by the AHF and the National Centre of Truth and Reconciliation ('NCTR') (Reimer et al., 2010; NCTR, 2020; cf., Government of Canada, 2017; Independent Assessment Process Oversight Committee 'IAP Committee', 2021, chap. 7).

With respect to the CEP and IAP, there were Survivors who reported positively about these processes in promoting healing and reconciliation (NCTR, 2020, pp. 8–9); in demonstrating government acknowledgement and recognition of harm; and in providing practical differences to their lives (NCTR, 2020, p. 10). However, there were also Survivors who reported negatively on these processes. Many of the criticisms of the processes related to the various ways they caused re-victimisation and re-traumatisation (through lack of, or lack of knowledge of, supports; having to repeatedly tell their stories; stories not being believed by officials; being denied compensation; and lack of acknowledgement as Survivors 'with a truth to be shared' (NCTR, 2020, pp. 28–31)). These processes were also criticised for reinforcing structural discrimination and inequalities (created by the complexity of the processes, their lack of impartiality, and dominance of western adversarial approaches, which compromised Indigenous practices and protocols) (NCTR, 2020, pp. 31–33). They were also difficult to access and poorly communicated to Survivors (NCTR, 2020, pp. 33–36). A striking example was how poor communication about the *Agreement* resulted in Survivors who had been incarcerated missing the deadlines to apply (NCTR, 2020, p. 22).

The attitudes of Survivors to the monetary payouts also revealed weaknesses. Survivor responses revealed that any positive outcomes achieved by the payments (e.g., contributing to their children's schooling) did not necessarily outweigh the negative effects (Reimer et al., 2010, pp. 44–46). The levels of payments were also criticised for being inadequate to make up for the trauma and harm suffered and improve Survivors' standards of living; they failed to take a holistic approach to harm (e.g., not enough scope was given to different forms of abuse in the IAP); and they imposed western standards on the value of work (e.g., by awarding more to men than women in the IAP) (NCTR, 2020, pp. 37–38). The methodology in assessing applications was also flawed (e.g., Survivors were found ineligible due to lost or poor recordkeeping in the CEP) (NCTR, 2020, p. 38). Indeed, there were notable instances when the government refused to release records, as occurred with respect to IAP proceedings brought by Survivors from St Anne's Residential School in Fort Albany, Ontario. Many claims were rejected as a result and Survivors were left with the hardship of challenging (unsuccessfully) the government's non-disclosure in the courts. Nevertheless, even when Survivors' claims were successful, there were instances where a lack of supports made it difficult for them to manage the payments, while racist attitudes resulted in their ability to manage the payments being questioned (NCTR, 2020, pp. 38–39).

Another significant issue with the CEP and IAP processes was a lack of professional and cultural competency in the staff involved, which resulted in re-traumatisation, but also jeopardised claims being fairly decided. This included lack of adequate legal representation (e.g., inadequate legal advice, unprofessional, negligent, and unethical behaviour, including overcharging of legal fees); and lack of adequate training and experience of the adjudicating officials, lawyers, therapists, and support workers (e.g., discrepancies in approaches between Indigenous and non-Indigenous adjudicators, exclusion of Indigenous therapists from the list of therapists, lack of training of support workers, which undermined their ability to support Survivors, and lack of supports for support workers, which resulted in vicarious trauma) (NCTR, 2020, pp. 40–42).

In the NCTR's *Lessons Learned* report Survivors provided insights on how the shortcomings of the CEP and IAP could be overcome by implementing more agreements to include Survivors excluded from the *Settlement Agreement*; extending the *Agreement* to intergenerational Survivors and including those Survivors who had died before the 30 May 2005 deadline; and initiating an independent legal review, which would include examining the CEP, reviewing the Law Societies' resolution of Survivor complaints about the mishandling of their compensation claims, and taking action against any legal practitioner found to have committed wrongdoing. Survivors also recommended improving information sharing about other settlements (such as the *Sixties Scoop Settlement Agreement*) (NCTR, 2020, p. 46–48).

In terms of future settlements, there were suggestions they should be treated more like 'Treaty-like agreements' to focus attention on reconciliation between First Nations and the Crown (NCTR, 2020, p. 58). Consistent with a Survivor-centred approach, this would require moving away from the dominant (western) model of conflict resolution and prioritising 'Indigenous law, cultural practices and protocols, and integrate Indigenous worldviews in design and implementation' (NCTR, 2020, p. 58). The need for processes to promote healing and prevent re-traumatisation and re-victimisation was also highlighted. This included reconsideration of the evidentiary standards (to accommodate the reality that records might be missing or incomplete) and changes to the way eligibility was determined (such as based on attendance and paying Survivors the same amount instead of payments based on harm suffered) (NCTR, 2020, pp. 46, 59). Ensuring that the professionals involved in any future settlements are culturally competent (and Indigenous professionals are included) was identified as crucial to prevent re-traumatisation and discrimination (NCTR, 2020, p. 60).

The fact that the needs of Survivors were not met by these processes exposed how each phase needed improvement. This included, among others, ensuring Survivors had access to information about the application processes through communication strategies that accommodated cultural, linguistic, and geographical differences; monitoring and evaluating the processes on an ongoing basis and making provisions for this in the actual settlement agreements; and providing adequate aftercare measures, the availability of which proved to be underutilised (NCTR, 2020, pp. 60–64; cf., IAP Committee, 2021, pp. 84–85).

Despite these recommendations, more recent Survivor experiences of other settlement agreements reveal that lessons of the *Settlement Agreement* still need to be learned. For example, the *Sixties Scoop Settlement Agreement* had an optional requirement to include a personal impact statement; however, there was a lack of support to help Survivors make a statement, which stifled Survivors making applications (Monkman, 2019). The *Lessons Learned* report also recommended that future settlements allow for progressive disclosure of harm to avoid re-traumatisation in the settlement process (NCTR, 2020, p. 59). This approach was not adopted in the *Day Schools Settlement Agreement*, which resulted in Survivors applying for lesser amounts (for verbal and physical harm that do not require proof) and not applying for higher amounts (for physical and sexual abuse that require a sworn declaration where no evidence exists) (Deer, 2022). These examples reveal that the processes are still not sufficiently trauma-informed and continue to lack cultural competency. Overall, more work is needed to overcome western approaches to redress and fully realise 'Indigenous sovereignty, ways of life and ceremonies' as recommended by the *Lessons Learned* report (NCTR, 2020, p. 60). They also reveal how these processes, in poorly responding to experiences of trauma, are posing obstacles to truth telling and healing. This was also evident during the work of the TRC, which further demonstrated the importance of Survivor-focused approaches to truth telling and healing.

Truth telling, healing, and reconciliation

A strength of the *Settlement Agreement*, as is evident in the *Lessons Learned* report, was that it created different forums for truth telling, and in some cases it was the first time Survivors had spoken out about their experiences (NCTR,

2020, p. 6). Through truth telling, healing and reconciliation became a real possibility, not only for Survivors as individuals, but also for their families and their broader relations with Canada (NCTR, 2020, pp. 7–8). Indeed, it was reported that any positive experiences of the CEP and IAP related not so much to the payment of money, but the opportunity for 'healing and resolution' these processes provided to Survivors (NCTR, 2020, p. 9). Community and commemoration events run by the TRC were also significant to healing in bringing groups of people together and enabling Survivors to forge friendships and establish collectives to continue their healing journeys beyond these events (NCTR, 2020, pp. 8–9). The commemoration events also had particular significance in providing opportunities to acknowledge former students, preserve knowledge of the residential schools, perform cultural activities, and pass knowledge to the next generations. This was significant not only for direct Survivors, but also for preserving the historical record in view of the number of Survivors who were ageing, dying, or had died, and promoting intergenerational healing and reconciliation for the children and descendants of Survivors (NCTR, 2020, pp. 9–10).

It is also apparent that Survivors had the most positive experiences when they were supported in culturally competent and trauma-informed ways, as did happen with the TRC and the IAP (NCTR, 2020, p. 16). However, where these supports were lacking or Survivors faced discriminatory and insensitive treatment (as happened with the CEP and IAP), this caused distress and re-traumatisation, and led to self-destructive behaviours in some cases (NCTR, 2020, p. 29).

Overall, however, Survivors reported being more appropriately supported in providing testimony to the TRC than the CEP or IAP (NCTR, 2020, p. 28). The *Lessons Learned* report identified the various ways that a culturally informed approach was adopted in the work of the TRC (NCTR, 2020, pp. 14–15). By comparison, for example, it reported how the hearings for the IAP were often reminiscent of the residential schools:

> Survivors were taken from their communities, brought to buildings that were like compounds, victimized by re-telling their stories in a culturally unsafe manner, and then returned to their communities without support, in a manner that was not trauma-informed.
>
> (NCTR, 2020, p. 32; cf., IAP Committee, 2021, p. 63)

Nevertheless, not all Survivors were completely satisfied with the TRC either, and believed, for example, it could have incorporated more cultural ceremony at its events, there could have been more Survivor involvement, and there could have been more media coverage of TRC events (NCTR, 2020, pp. 33, 35).

Any negative experiences of the *Agreement* undermined its potential for healing and reconciliation. This had flow-on consequences for its truth-telling potential. Most notably, it was found that experiences of re-traumatisation during the CEP and IAP discouraged Survivors from attending TRC events, and this is reflected by the fact that while there were about 38,000 IAP applications, there were only 7,800 TRC statements (NCTR, 2020, p. 30). Truth telling under the *Agreement* was also compromised by the reliance in the CEP and IAP processes on western legal norms that favour written records and not Survivor testimony. Missing or inaccurate records resulted in claims being rejected (NCTR, 2020, p. 38). This was devastating for Survivors, but it also had the potential effect of skewing the historical record based not on Survivor testimony, but on the number of applications that succeeded because of the available evidence.

Moreover, the capacity of the *Settlement Agreement* to engender truth telling was limited in scope to Residential School Survivors. While there have been settlements negotiated by other groups of Survivors, it has been found that truth telling and record collecting, which was a crucial part of the work of the TRC, have not been adequately provided for in these agreements (NCTR, 2020, p. 20). This raises the concern that more emphasis has been given 'to the process of settlement rather than to creation of a record of the collective truth telling' (NCTR, 2020, pp. 20–21). The effect is to close off the past rather than ensuring the past lives on through the creation of a historical record for future generations to remember what happened and better ensure the non-repetition of this history.

The TRC's mandate under the *Agreement* was to compile a history of the residential school system (*Schedule "N"*, n.d., p. 2). Yet, this work was hindered by instances where the Canadian government refused to release residential school records to the TRC, which forced the TRC to bring legal action to retrieve these records (NCTR, 2020, p. 33; *Fontaine v. Canada (Attorney General)*, 2013). Another dispute arose over the records used during the IAP and whether they should be preserved or destroyed. The *Agreement* may have given the TRC a mandate to create 'as complete an historical record of the IRS system and legacy', but it also provided that the IAP hearings and records would remain confidential (*Schedule "D"*, 2006, p. 15). The dispute was finally resolved by the Supreme Court of Canada in favour of preserving the confidentiality and privacy of the IAP hearings (*Canada (Attorney General) v. Fontaine*, 2017). Only some records of the proceedings would be preserved (the application forms, printed transcripts of claimants' testimony, voice recordings of claimants' testimony, and decisions on IAP claims), but after a 15-year retention period they would also be destroyed unless individual Survivors requested access for their own use, or consented to their release to the NCTR. A notice programme was subsequently implemented to inform Survivors about accessing these records or having them archived.

The Court's decision to maintain the confidentiality of the IAP proceedings was based on its understanding that the voluntariness of Survivors' participation in the IAP was dependent on its confidentiality. This conclusion was further supported by concerns that if the IAP records were released without consent, this could be traumatising for Survivors and their descendants and would undermine the healing and reconciliation that the *Settlement Agreement* sought to engender. Considering the severity of abuse in many cases, and especially the sensitivity surrounding student-on-student abuse cases, the Court's decision was understandable (*Canada (Attorney General) v. Fontaine*, 2017, para. 47). However, it was unclear to what extent Survivors were aware of the confidentiality provisions in the *Settlement Agreement*. According to the *Lessons Learned* report, there were differences in opinion among Survivors about what they thought would happen to these records, with some claiming they thought the records would be saved, and others claiming they thought they would be destroyed (NCTR, 2020, p. 45).

More recently, issues in relation to the retention of non-claim documents (i.e., the administrative records) of the IAP have arisen and whether statistical reports that provide details of how many and what types of the claims of abuse were made against specific schools should be released to the public. The Canadian government has so far been successful in opposing the release of these records. It has claimed this could inadvertently expose the identity of Survivors, which is contrary to the Supreme Court's decision in 2017, and compromise healing and reconciliation for Survivors. The NCTR, in contrast, has questioned the government's commitment to truth and reconciliation in contesting these records when there are measures that can be taken to protect the identities of Survivors (Barrera, 2020a). As has been claimed by Garnet Angeconeb, Pelican Lake Indian Residential School Survivor, the government's attempt to use the law to control the historical record 'looks like, smells like, feels like modern-day colonialism at its best' (Barrera, 2020b). In his view, as many records as possible should be preserved, as once all the Survivors are gone, only these records will remain to tell 'our history on the way Canada treated us'.

The above discussion reveals the tensions that can arise between truth telling and healing, and that to strike the right balance between them, future settlements would need to give Survivors more choice and control over their records, and not repeat what happened with the IAP when a notice programme was set up after many thousands of claims had been processed, including the applications of Survivors who had died and were not given a choice.

However, such measures may not be able to overcome the government's control over records. This is particularly poignant considering the dispute over records related to St Anne's Residential School. As noted above, to date, Survivors have been unsuccessful in gaining access to these records. Their struggles further illuminate the shortcomings of the legal system where decisions can be made without any Survivor involvement as happened in relation to a court review of some of these claims (Barrera, 2021). The ongoing struggles of Survivors for justice, exacerbated by the obstacles put in their way by

Canadian legal and political institutions, brings Canada's commitment to truth, healing, and reconciliation into question. However, at a deeper level, these problems were inevitable due to the way the *Settlement Agreement* was structured.

Under the *Agreement* the measures of reparations were compartmentalised, for instance, by the TRC, which was to facilitate truth telling; the CEP and IAP, which were to settle outstanding claims for compensation; and the AHF, which was to provide healing supports to Survivors. However, as seems apparent from the above discussion, appropriate supports were needed with respect to each measure. The need for healing was recognised in the work of the TRC and the IAP (IAP Committee, 2021, p. 25), though it was accommodated to varying degrees (NCTR, 2020). Furthermore, the AHF, which was the key healing measure under the *Agreement*, was disestablished in 2014. This left a huge gap in expertise to respond to the needs of Survivors in an effective manner (NCTR, 2020, p. 48), and clearly indicated that the *Settlement Agreement* underestimated the healing needs of Survivors as the other measures of the *Agreement* did not provide adequate healing measures either. Evidently, these issues demonstrated more trauma-informed supports were needed, and as the *Lessons Learned* report found, future settlements would need to provide more effective supports for Survivors and intergenerational Survivors alike (NCTR, 2020, p. 56). More recent agreements have incorporated measures that could be beneficial in this way; however, they are not as far-reaching as the recommendations in the *Lessons Learned* report. The section above has already identified how the CEP and IAP could have been improved and many of these recommendations would also help with healing. More broadly, the *Lessons Learned* report identified the need to address the intergenerational harms through community-based reforms across the socio-economic areas of education, employment, housing, and health (especially youth suicide and nutrition); law and justice areas of child welfare, social welfare, contact with the judicial system, and violence (especially related to missing and murdered Indigenous women and girls); and through culture and family supports (including cultural revival and strengthening families to meet their responsibilities) (NCTR, 2020, pp. 44–45). The need for self-sufficiency (using traditional and environmentally sustainable practices), a healthy environment (clean water, affordable housing, and other infrastructure), and sustainable resource management (in partnership between Indigenous communities, government, and corporations and according to sustainable practices and Indigenous knowledge) were also identified (NCTR, 2020, pp. 53–54). Re-establishing the AHF was also sought because of its past effectiveness in community healing, and other community healing initiatives were identified to respond to violence in communities (NCTR, 2020, p 48). Leadership for change was needed from Survivors, including intergenerational Survivors, but financial support was needed from government and the churches (NCTR, 2020, pp. 48–49).

The discussion above also illuminated how truth telling was compromised during the implementation of the *Agreement*, particularly exemplified by poor recordkeeping and government obstruction of records which hindered the success of claims, and the absence of a clear and transparent process for Survivors to determine the fate of their records, and in the case of children who had died, giving their families access (NCTR, 2020, p. 46). These issues illuminated the need for Survivors to have choice and control over their records, while also ensuring against re-traumatisation by preventing the misuse of their records by outsiders. Increased interest in the residential schools during the *Agreement* also confirmed the need to prevent unscrupulous practices of researchers as Survivors found some researchers violated their trust by using research data against them, while others thought researchers profited at the expense of their suffering. The need for ongoing research on the residential schools was identified, but it was emphasised that this needed to be community directed and controlled (NCTR, 2020, pp. 46, 57–58). The need for more apologies (notably by the Pope which was finally issued in 2022 ('I am deeply sorry', 2022) and commemoration events were also identified (NCTR, 2020, pp. 49–50). These included more events for Survivors to share stories with their descendants; compiling online photographic histories; a Memorial Day for Survivors who were also war veterans; creating national registries of the names of Survivors and erecting regional monuments in their honour; securing national recognition of the residential schools as a historic event; and introducing culturally appropriate commemoration events for children who died at the residential schools and protection of their graves (NCTR, 2020, pp. 50–51). The need for continuing education of the abuses (as well as of treaties and Indigenous rights) for the broader public and specifically for workers in social services was also highlighted, though some Survivors considered the need for cultural and language revitalisation as a higher priority, which would be community led, but financially supported by government and the churches (NCTR, 2020, pp. 50, 52–53). Finally, throughout the *Lesson Learned* report the importance of the TRC's Calls to Action was acknowledged; nevertheless, it ultimately concluded that information about these reforms and their implementation could be better relayed to Survivors (NCTR, 2020, pp. 49–50). The section below provides a general overview of these recommendations, while also recognising that Survivor concerns with respect to these and other matters raised in the *Lessons Learned* report have not been officially addressed.

The TRC Calls to Action

The discussion above demonstrated how Indigenous peoples continue to push the boundaries of the dominant structures of power to assert their claims. The *Settlement Agreement* represented the commitment of Indigenous peoples, the government, and the churches to truth, healing, and reconciliation. Survivors continue to draw on these principles to bring the government and the churches into account for the injustices they have suffered. It is also evident that the *Settlement Agreement* was far from adequate in providing redress. Survivors' perceptions of government actions, whether in trying to rectify these shortcomings or further obstructing them, broadly serves as a measure of the extent that government is committed to healing and reconciliation. Based on the above analysis it appears that on balance much more commitment to action is needed.

In its report, *Honouring the Truth, Reconciling for the Future* (TRC, 2015), the TRC formed the same conclusion and set out 94 Calls to Action needed to address the injustices facing Indigenous peoples. These were in addition to the 20 recommendations it made in its 2012 *Interim Report* (TRC, 2012).

In summary, the Calls to Action aim to address the injustices of the past and achieve reconciliation in the future. They can be broken down into these areas: children and youth; language and culture; health; justice in the legal system; history and commemoration; and reconciliation (Government of Canada, 2023b).

One initial observation is how the Calls to Action extended the reform agenda beyond the *Settlement Agreement* that Harper had confined himself to in his apology (discussed in Chapter 4). Yet, it was Harper's apology, as well as the other apologies made by political leaders at the time, and the church apologies that had been made previously to this, that justified the Calls to Action. According to the TRC, these apologies demanded action. They were the first step in fostering trust and reconciliation (TRC, 2015, p. 209). The next steps required institutionalising changes that would fulfil the promise of 'never again' which these apologies represented. This would require concrete actions that combined both material and symbolic measures. Importantly, the TRC recognised that to prevent the repetition of past injustices would require curbing the actions of government that had caused the atrocities of the residential schools. For the TRC, action required breaking the cycle of assimilation, addressing the legacies of the past, and creating the conditions for 'a mutually respectful relationship' (TRC, 2015, p. 210). Fundamentally, future action would require changing perceptions of what ostensibly is in the best interests of Indigenous peoples. As the residential schools clearly demonstrated, when government is in control of Indigenous peoples' lives, the outcomes are disastrous. The 'antidote', according to the TRC, was Indigenous rights protections, and most notably implementing the right of self-determination (TRC, 2015, p. 209). In this way, the TRC's recommendations aligned with the relational understanding of apology making in orienting reform according to Indigenous understandings and rights.

It is also evident from the wide-ranging areas covered by the Calls to Action that the TRC had a deeper understanding of the history of wrongdoing requiring remediation than Harper did in his apology. According to the TRC, the residential schools formed part of what it interchangeably referred to as a broader process of colonisation, assimilation, and cultural genocide (TRC, 2015, p. 133). Its response was to, in effect, decolonise the politico-legal order across all levels of government. Significantly, in this regard, the TRC's Call to Action 47 calls for the repudiation of 'concepts used to justify European sovereignty over Indigenous peoples and lands, such as the Doctrine of Discovery and *terra nullius*, and to reform those laws, government policies, and litigation strategies that continue to rely on such concepts' (TRC, 2015, p. 200). The TRC also called for reforms in line with Indigenous rights as reflected in treaty obligations owed to Indigenous peoples arising from the Royal Proclamation of 1763 and the Treaty of Niagara of 1764, and *UNDRIP*, which Canada had endorsed in 2010 (TRC, 2015, p. 137).

These reforms are encapsulated in Call to Action 45, which calls upon the government of Canada to jointly develop with Indigenous peoples a Royal Proclamation of Reconciliation ('the Proclamation') to be issued by the Crown. The Proclamation would include, but not be limited to, the following commitments:

1 Repudiate concepts used to justify European sovereignty over Indigenous lands and peoples such as the Doctrine of Discovery and terra nullius;
2 Adopt and implement the *United Nations Declaration on the Rights of Indigenous Peoples* as the framework for reconciliation;
3 Renew or establish Treaty relationships based on principles of mutual recognition, mutual respect, and shared responsibility for maintaining those relationships into the future; and
4 Reconcile Aboriginal and Crown constitutional and legal orders to ensure that Aboriginal peoples are full partners in Confederation, including the recognition and integration of Indigenous laws and legal traditions in negotiation and implementation processes involving Treaties, land claims, and other constructive agreements

(TRC, 2015, p. 199).

Call to Action 46 (TRC, 2015, p. 200) also calls on the parties to the *Settlement Agreement* to sign a Covenant of Reconciliation to advance reconciliation in Canadian society. Its aims largely mirrored the Proclamation, but also includes provisions for inclusion of those excluded from the *Settlement Agreement* to sign onto the Covenant of Reconciliation. Oversight of the progress made on reconciliation post-apology would be provided by a newly formed National Council for Reconciliation (Call to Action 53), which would also oversee progress on closing the gaps between Indigenous and non-Indigenous peoples (TRC, 2015, pp. 218, 329). In developing these recommendations, the TRC's overarching vision for Canada was to reset the nation-to-nation relationship 'that fully embraces Aboriginal peoples' right to self-determination within, and in partnership with, a viable Canadian sovereignty' (TRC, 2015, p. 184).

Notably, the Trudeau government committed to fulfilling all these recommendations, promising to do more than any previous Canadian government had done (and more than any Australian government as well). Nevertheless, these promises have not translated into meaningful change. Already, the discussion above revealed shortcomings in the government's handling of the *Settlement Agreement* spanning both Harper's and Trudeau's terms in office. In relation to the Calls to Action, progress on their implementation has been slow. According to the Indigenous Watchdog website, which monitors progress on the Calls to Action, as of 17 November 2023, 16% had not started; 49% were in progress; 21% had stalled; and 14% were completed (Indigenous Watchdog, 2023a). Notably, there has been no action to fulfil the Calls to Action that embody the spirit of reconciliation and decolonisation, such as developing the Proclamation and the Covenant of Reconciliation and repudiating the doctrines of discovery and terra nullius, while legislation to establish a National Council for Reconciliation to oversee the progress on reconciliation post-apology was only introduced in June 2022. Even with respect to the Calls to Action that have been implemented, or have progressed, further action is needed as is discussed below with respect to the Call to Actions related to murdered Indigenous women and girls and the implementation of *UNDRIP*.

Missing and murdered Indigenous women and girls

The TRC Call to Action 41 called for 'a public inquiry into the causes of, and remedies for, the disproportionate victimization of Aboriginal women and girls' (TRC, 2015, p. 181). In response, the National Inquiry into Missing and Murdered Indigenous Women and Girls ('National Inquiry') was established by the Trudeau government in 2016 and concluded in 2019 with the release of the Inquiry's report, *Reclaiming Power and Place* (National Inquiry, 2019c). The Métis Nation's Les Femmes Michif Otipemisiwak had its own inquiry and report (Les Femmes Michif Otipemisiwak – Women of the Métis Nation, 2019).

These inquiries were significant in finally providing an official forum for Indigenous women, girls, and 2SLGBTQQIA people and their families to recount their stories of violence and injustice. Their most significant finding was that genocide, as understood in the *Convention on the Prevention and Punishment of the Crime of Genocide* ('*Genocide Convention*') (United Nations, 1948), had been perpetrated against Indigenous peoples in Canada (National Inquiry, 2019a). This finding was stronger than the TRC's finding of cultural genocide perpetrated by the residential schools. Cultural genocide was deemed not to constitute genocide as it had been deliberately excluded from the *Genocide Convention* at the time of drafting at the behest of settler-colonised nations such as Canada (and Australia). More recently this attitude appears to have changed in Canada. In October 2022 the House of Commons unanimously passed a motion (albeit non-legally binding) to recognise Canada's residential schools as genocide according to the *Convention* (House of Commons, Canada, 2022, p. 8977). This motion followed Pope Francis' reference to the residential schools as genocide, and accords with the definition of genocide as understood by the National Inquiry. As the Inquiry stated, 'the debate around "cultural genocide" versus "real" genocide is misleading' (National Inquiry, 2019a, p. 7). According to its interpretation of more recent international legal developments, it concluded that 'the "specific intent to destroy" covers not only physical or biological destruction, but also, at a minimum, the destruction of a group as a social unit' (National Inquiry, 2019a, p. 23), and this included intent to destroy through 'a combination of violence, eradication of economic life, and incitement to assimilation' (National Inquiry, 2019a, p. 23, quoting Schabas, 2009, p. 271). These were some of the hallmarks of the violence perpetrated in the residential schools. Significantly, this understanding also encompasses genocide committed by lethal and non-lethal acts and thus accommodates gendered experiences of genocide through rape and sexual violence (National Inquiry, 2019a, p. 8).

In reaching its conclusions, the Inquiry extended the understanding of genocide beyond the dominant 'Holocaust prototype'. According to the Inquiry, the Holocaust model limits genocide to 'time-intensive, mass murder, which is calculated, coordinated within a nation-state, and well-planned by authoritarian leaders espousing ideological worldviews' (National Inquiry, 2019a, p. 9). While the Inquiry acknowledged that acts of genocide were perpetrated against Indigenous peoples in this way, the term 'colonial genocide' more accurately reflects Indigenous perspectives of the colonial violence that has, and continues to be, inflicted against them. According to the Inquiry:

> colonial genocide is ... a slow-moving process. ... [C]olonial destruction of Indigenous peoples has taken place insidiously and over centuries. The intent to destroy Indigenous peoples in Canada was implemented gradually and intermittently, using varied tactics against distinct Indigenous communities. These acts and omissions affected their rights to life and security, but also numerous economic, cultural and social rights. In addition to the lethal conduct, the non-lethal tactics used were no less destructive and fall within the scope of the crime of genocide. These policies fluctuated in time and space, and in different incarnations, are still ongoing.
>
> (National Inquiry, 2019a, pp. 9–10)

These actions, according to the Inquiry, constituted the crime of genocide in meeting the requisite *actus rea* and *mens rea* elements. According to the Inquiry, Canada's actions satisfied the *actus rea* of genocide as understood as a '"composite act", which is "a breach of an international obligation by a State through a series of actions or omissions defined in aggregate as wrongful"' (National Inquiry, 2019a, p. 10). The breach would last for as long as those acts or omissions continued and were not in conformity with the international prohibition on genocide. Additionally, the *mens rea* was satisfied by 'the existence of a genocidal policy or manifest pattern of conduct', which in the case of colonial genocide 'is slower, more insidious, structural, systemic, and often spans multiple administrations and political leadership' (National Inquiry, 2019a, p. 20). Moreover, the Inquiry found that despite the fact Canada was a liberal democracy and would itself be opposed to acts of genocide committed by nations that were authoritarian and did not adhere to democratic values, it could not escape the charge of genocide as this would ignore its '"genocidal foundations ... and fate"' of Indigenous peoples (National Inquiry, 2019a, p. 10, quoting Moses, 2008). This understanding implicates settler-colonised nations with similar histories (such as Australia and the United States).

Also of significance was the National Inquiry's conclusion that the genocide was ongoing. With respect to Indigenous women, girls, and 2SLGBTQQIA people the genocide continued through these four pathways:

1 Historical, multigenerational, and intergenerational trauma;
2 Social and economic marginalisation;
3 Maintaining the status quo and institutional lack of will; and
4 Ignoring the agency and expertise of Indigenous women, girls, and 2SLGBTQQIA people

(National Inquiry, 2019c, p. 111).

In response to its findings, the Inquiry set out 231 Calls for Justice (National Inquiry, 2019b). The Calls for Justice include 46 Inuit-specific, 29 Métis-specific (in addition to the Métis Inquiry's 62 Calls for Change or Miskotahâ), and 32 2SLGBTQQIA-specific Calls for Justice (National Inquiry, 2019b, pp. 202–218). The Inquiry also set out seven Principles for Change ('Principles') to guide the implementation of the Calls for Justice:

1 A focus on substantive equality and human and indigenous rights;
2 A decolonising approach;
3 Inclusion of families and Survivors;
4 Self-determined and Indigenous-led solutions and services;
5 Recognising distinctions;
6 Cultural safety; and
7 Trauma-informed approach

(National Inquiry, 2019b, pp. 169–173).

In setting out the Calls for Justice and accompanying Principles, the Inquiry expanded the normative framework for reform beyond the TRC's Calls for Action. Significantly, as the Inquiry noted, these Calls for Justice 'are legal imperatives – they are not optional' (National Inquiry, 2019b, p. 168) because they arise from a range of international and domestic human rights and Indigenous rights norms. To uphold these rights, Call for Justice 1.7 recommended the establishment of a National Indigenous and Human Rights Ombudsperson and a National Indigenous and Human Rights Tribunal, which would be independent of governments and would hear complaints from Indigenous individuals and communities in relation to Indigenous and human rights violations, and have the power to investigate government services provided to First Nations, Inuit, and Métis people and communities and determine their compliance with human and Indigenous rights laws (National Inquiry, 2019b, p. 178).

The Inquiry's findings are significant in demonstrating the power of truth telling to push the boundaries of official understandings of history and justify the introduction of additional measures of redress. The finding of genocide was particularly significant, as it was also officially accepted by Trudeau (with respect to Indigenous women, girls, and 2SLGBTQQIA people) against a history of denial of the genocide and continuing denial as became evident in the vehement backlash that was voiced in the media in response to this finding (Webster, 2019). The official acceptance of the finding of genocide is consistent with an underlying premise of this book that when Indigenous perspectives are placed at the centre of inquiry, dominant narratives can change. This change has thus far been eluded in Australia where claims of genocide have not been able to shake the narrative that settlement of Australia was peaceful and benevolent. Australia is also embarking on an inquiry into Murdered and Missing First Nations Women and Children, which is due to report on 30 June 2024 (Parliament of Australia, n.d.), but it is yet unknown whether this will reignite the genocide question. However, even with respect to Canada, the first step may have been taken to accept the genocide finding, but whether this translates into meaningful changes in Indigenous peoples' lives depends on government commitment to action. Trudeau's acceptance of the finding of genocide was important but it may become meaningless without concrete action to address the full effects of the genocide in law, policy, and practice. Unfortunately, to date, concrete changes have not become the reality.

In 2021, the *National Action Plan* (2021) and the *Federal Pathway*, which is the government's contribution to the *National Action Plan* (Government of Canada, 2021), were released. The Native Women's Association of Canada ('NWAC') released its own action plan at the same time (NWAC, 2021). The Inuit and Métis also released their own action plans in 2021 (Pauktuutit Inuit Women of Canada and Inuit Tapiriit Kanatami, 2021; Les Femmes Michif Otipemisiwak – Women of the Métis Nation, 2021) and the government released the *Federal 2SLGBTQI+ Action Plan* in 2022 (Government of Canada, 2023d). The *National Action Plan* is in response to Call for Justice 1.1 (National Inquiry, 2019b, p. 176), which is aimed to implement recommendations made by the National Inquiry and in other reports with respect to the violence against women, girls, and 2SLGBTQQIA people. However, these efforts have been heavily criticised for not setting out 'the comprehensive, system-wide, inter-governmental plan that is needed to end genocide' (Ontario Native Women's Association, 2021). Dissatisfaction with the government's progress was expressed by the Standing Senate Committee on Aboriginal Peoples (2022) and continues to be expressed by the NWAC (2023). These reports indicate that the government has done little to affect change. They also point to a wider overarching issue that there is a lack of coordination and accountability across governments in the implementation of the *National Action Plan*.

More recently, the government has reaffirmed its commitment to end systemic violence against Indigenous women, girls, and gender-diverse people in its *United Nations Declaration on the Rights of Indigenous Peoples Act Action Plan* ('*Action Plan*') (Department of Justice Canada, 2023). Nevertheless, the government's slow action brings its commitment to change into question and compromises the making of adequate and effective reparations to Indigenous peoples. This is not to discount how the Trudeau government's acceptance of the findings in the inquiries has served to vindicate Indigenous peoples' perspectives and rights. However, it remains the case that many of the government's promises are yet to be fulfilled and lead to meaningful change. And while Indigenous peoples wait for action, their rights continue to be violated.

Implementation of UNDRIP

As noted above, the TRC called for the government to implement *UNDRIP* as the framework for reconciliation in Canada (Call to Action 45). Furthermore, Calls to Action 43 and 44 call upon all levels of government to fully adopt and implement *UNDRIP* and for the federal government to develop a national plan, strategies, and other concrete measures to achieve the goals of *UNDRIP* (TRC, 2015, pp. 191).

Canada was originally opposed to *UNDRIP* when it was passed by the United Nations in 2007. It subsequently supported *UNDRIP* in 2010 and debate over whether UNDRIP should be implemented grew in momentum after the TRC's Calls to Action were released in 2015. In 2016, the Trudeau government agreed to implement *UNDRIP* in Canadian law, but it was not until 2021 (after a failed attempt in 2019 to enact Bill C-262 that was aimed to harmonise Canadian laws with *UNDRIP*) that the *United Nations Declaration on the Rights of Indigenous Peoples Act* (2021) ('Bill C-15') was enacted at the federal level for the purpose of implementing *UNDRIP* in Canadian law.

As some of the fundamental tenets of *UNDRIP* are the rights of self-determination and self-government; equality and non-discrimination; control over lands, territories, and resources; and freedom from assimilation and genocide, the prospect of aligning Canadian laws and policies with *UNDRIP* could, as some Indigenous supporters have contended, be 'the best chance' to 'break the colonial status quo' (Martisius, 2021). However, some Indigenous peoples are critical of Bill C-15's approach to *UNDRIP* (Watchmaker, 2021), while others have questioned whether the government is well-intended in implementing Bill C-15. This is especially so, considering Canada's past and present record of violating Indigenous peoples' rights, the obstacles faced by Indigenous peoples in proving rights violations, and the difficulties experienced by Indigenous peoples in enforcing measures of reparation, even when the government has accepted that violations have occurred. In view of these violations, and concerns (among others) over the lack of consultation at the drafting stage and prior to the enactment of Bill C-15, Indigenous groups have expressed serious reservations about Bill C-15 (Indigenous Watchdog, 2023e; Martisius, 2021).

Sections 6(1) and (4) of Bill C-15 requires the government to establish an action plan 'in consultation and cooperation with Indigenous peoples and with other federal ministers' to implement *UNDRIP* in Canadian law within two years and to table an annual report on progress made. A draft of the *Action Plan* was released in March 2023 and was finalised in June 2023 (Department of Justice Canada, 2023). Giving Indigenous peoples only two months for consultation and flaws with the consultation process itself were raised as serious concerns (Forester, 2023). The *Action Plan* has a five-year timeframe and sets out another 181 action items with respect to five areas: shared priorities, First Nations, Inuit, Métis, and Indigenous Modern Treaty Partner priorities. Some of the more promising aspects of the *Action Plan* are the recommendations to establish two Indigenous-led bodies: an Action Plan Advisory Committee (comprised of First Nations, Inuit, and Métis representatives to serve as counsel for *UNDRIP* implementation) and an independent Indigenous rights monitoring body (to provide oversight and accountability in implementing *UNDRIP*). However, doubts have been raised about whether these bodies, if established, will have effective powers and whether the *Action Plan* overall will lead to meaningful change (Leeson and Gallegos Dupuis, 2023). The *Action Plan* has been criticised (among other things) for being inadequate, as it 'echoes' government commitment to many earlier promises that to date have not been fulfilled; vague, as it lacks details about how the action items will be achieved, how they will be funded, and the timeframe for their completion; and insufficient, as it is only applies to federal laws and not provincial and territorial laws and therefore does not provide a coordinated approach to action items not under federal control (Leeson and Gallegos Dupuis, 2023). The *Action Plan* has also not resolved concerns expressed with respect to the draft *Action Plan* about the scope of the right of 'free, prior and informed consent' ('FPIC') as contained in *UNDRIP*, especially with respect to the approval of development projects on Indigenous lands and territories (United Nations, 2007, art 32). As recent history shows in relation to the Calls for Action and Calls for Justice, the Trudeau government has been slow to act, despite its promises to initiate change. Understandably, therefore, there is scepticism about whether the moves to implement *UNDRIP* signal true commitment to change, or whether the government is merely repackaging old colonialist approaches that subsume Indigenous peoples under the assumed sovereignty of the Crown in violation of their rights. The onus is on Indigenous peoples and their supporters to continue to hold government to account, but it may still take years before *UNDRIP* is fully implemented (and even then, implementation may be piecemeal and never completed).

Moreover, while the focus in this chapter has been largely on the developments at the national level, it is important to point out that almost all the provinces have not taken action to implement *UNDRIP* as required by the Calls to Action. The only province to enact legislation has been British Columbia in enacting the *Declaration on the Rights of Indigenous Peoples Act* (2019) ('*BC Act*') which, like Bill C-15, also aims to implement an action plan to align its laws with *UNDRIP*. In 2023, the Northwest Territories also introduced a bill to implement *UNDRIP* (though also not without criticism (Down, 2023)). This contrasts with six provinces (Ontario, Quebec, Alberta, Saskatchewan, Manitoba, and New Brunswick) whose premiers have been expressly opposed to *UNDRIP*. Of particular concern to these premiers has been whether incorporation of *UNDRIP*, especially its repeated references to the right to FPIC, as protected, for instance, by art. 32 with respect to proposed projects 'affecting Indigenous lands or territories and other resources', will give Indigenous peoples a veto power over development projects on their traditional lands and thereby undermine provincial authority over the land (Platt, 2020). These objections reflect the tenets of the doctrines of discovery and terra nullius and highlight the need to repudiate these doctrines as recommended in Calls to Action 45 and 46. However, to date, there have been no moves to repudiate these doctrines.

In the meantime, governments supportive of *UNDRIP* could speed up its implementation through agreement making, though this is a piecemeal approach. During the consultations that took place in relation to Bill C-15, there were Indigenous peoples who also expressed concerns about how FPIC as it relates to land and resource development will be implemented (Government of Canada, 2022). One suggestion was the creation of agreements between government and Indigenous governing bodies with respect to joint decision making. Notably, this idea was not adopted in Bill C-15, but it was adopted by British Columbia in the *BC Act*. British Columbia has since entered into its first agreement with the Tahltan Central Government (in 2022) with respect to the Eskay Creek Revitalisation Project (ahnationtalk, 2022). The *Declaration Act Consent Decision-Making Agreement* for Eskay Creek Project ('*Declaration Act Agreement*') is significant as it recognises the

Tahlton government's rights and title to their lands, their jurisdiction in land management over their lands, and ensures that development on their homelands will have Tahlton values at the centre. This approach in recognising the Tahlton government's inherent rights departs from past approaches to agreement making in historic and modern treaties, which often have extinguished these rights (National Inquiry, 2019c, pp. 134–135). Indeed, this *Agreement* could be interpreted as a positive step in advancing reconciliation in British Columbia as it was concluded consensually and in line with the Tahlton government's FPIC. However, this may be overstating the situation. Considering the long history of rights violations in British Columbia, whether an agreement would have been reached if there had been contention between the Indigenous parties and the government remains to be seen. This has been demonstrated by the conflicts over the construction of the Coastal Gaslink pipeline, the Trans Mountain pipeline, and the Site C dam.

In supporting these developments, the federal and provincial governments have violated the land rights of First Nations peoples (including the Wet'suwet'en Hereditory Chiefs (with respect to the Coastal Gaslink pipeline), the Squamish Nation, Tsleil-Waututh Nation, the Ts'elxwéyeqw Tribe, and Coldwater Indian Band (with respect to the Trans Mountain pipeline), and the Treaty 8 First Nations (with respect to the Site C dam). Moreover, the construction of these developments was authorised in contravention of the right in *UNDRIP* to FPIC, as consensus for the projects to proceed was never reached across the affected communities. These violations rightly bring government commitment to Indigenous rights into question. According to the United Nations, FPIC requires an independent process to be in place to determine which representative institutions can give consent on behalf of affected peoples or communities. It also requires the process to verify FPIC has been sought and for states to provide redress when it has not been sought (United Nations Human Rights Office of the High Commissioner, 2013). Most importantly, the focus of any process should be the outcome, which is to ensure that no decisions directly affecting Indigenous peoples' rights and interests are made without their informed consent (Committee on the Elimination of Racial Discrimination, 1997). All three developments have been criticised at the international level for not adhering to these principles (Pasternak, Spice and Feltes, 2021 p. 2). Indeed, these criticisms can be extended to other resource developments such as mineral claims which have revealed how easily British Columbian law has permitted mineral prospecting without consent or consultation with affected First Nations, as happened with respect to the Gitxaała and Ehattesaht First Nations (Fionda, 2023; see also *Gitxaała v. British Columbia (Chief Gold Commissioner)* (2023).

The courts have a chequered history in protecting Indigenous rights. The extensive litigation arising from approvals given to the Coastal Gaslink pipeline, the Trans Mountain pipeline, and the Site C dam provide just a few examples where the Indigenous peoples who are opposed to these developments have been thwarted in asserting their rights. By contrast, there are decisions such as *Yahey v. British Columbia* (2021), which was the first time a court has found that the cumulative effects of development within a First Nation's territory had infringed a treaty agreement.

The development of legal precedent in line with *UNDRIP* could contribute to ensure greater consistency in judicial approaches to Indigenous rights. Section 2(3) of Bill C-15 provides that: 'Nothing in this Act is to be construed as delaying the application of the Declaration in Canadian law'. This could be used to import Indigenous rights, such as FPIC, into the law. However, the courts have been reluctant to do this, as illustrated in *Thomas and Saik'uz First Nation v. Rio Tinto Alcan Inc* ('*Thomas*') (2022).

This decision reveals the differences between Indigenous rights in Canadian law and *UNDRIP*. In this case, the plaintiffs (the Saik'uz and Stellat'en First Nations) argued that the legislation to implement *UNDRIP* (enacted federally and in the province of British Columbia) could be interpreted as already requiring action to align Canadian law (specifically British Columbian law) with *UNDRIP*, and lead to changes to the common law approach to Aboriginal title (para. 210). Ultimately, the Court did not adopt this course as it found it was bound by existing Supreme Court precedent (*Thomas*, 2022, para. 212). Nevertheless, the Court did consider the rights to land protected by *UNDRIP* (arts 26–29) and opined that it would be 'unquestionable' that the plaintiffs' rights would be recognised according to these principles (*Thomas*, 2022, paras 207–208, 280). This conclusion can be contrasted with the Court's analysis of the existing common law recognition of Aboriginal title to land (as recognised by s. 35 of the *Constitution* (1982)), which it claimed imposes 'insurmountable obstacles ... in the path of Indigenous groups seeking to establish title even though they have occupied the land "since time immemorial" and notwithstanding purported affirmation of *UNDRIP* by both levels of government' (*Thomas*, 2022, para. 274).

Furthermore, while the Court found the plaintiffs had the Aboriginal right to fish, it did not find they had established their claim in nuisance for injunctive relief in relation to the adverse impact on their fishing rights caused by the construction of a dam within their traditional territories. The construction of the dam had been authorised by agreements and a licence from British Columbia issued to the defendant (now Rio Tinto) pursuant to provincial legislation. According to the plaintiffs, the authorisations for the dam were 'constitutionally inapplicable', partly because of the protection of their rights provided by s. 35 of the *Constitution*. In response, the Court claimed the plaintiffs were challenging the Crown's sovereignty to issue the authorisations for the construction of the dam (even though the plaintiffs had not made this claim) (*Thomas*, 2022, para. 199). Notably, the Court openly questioned the legitimacy of Crown sovereignty and title to land (and the doctrines of discovery and terra nullius upon which those constructs rely) (*Thomas*, 2022, paras 189–199), but found the 'harsh realities' were that the law and government of British Columbia (and presumably of Canada) had become 'firmly and intractably entrenched' in Canadian society and economy (*Thomas*, 2022, paras 201–202). In reaching this conclusion, the Court in effect reinforced how intractable it will be to change the status quo as the Court found it was bound to apply common law and statutory law, 'subject only to incremental changes not prohibited by precedent or legislative change' (*Thomas*, 2022, para. 204). Thus, according to the applicable law, the Court found that the plaintiffs could have succeeded in an action for private nuisance against the defendant, but because the defendant had complied with all government-imposed regulatory requirements, it was immune from liability on the defence of statutory authority (*Thomas*, 2022, para. 603).

Notably, s. 2(2) of Bill C-15 upholds the Indigenous rights recognised by s. 35 of the *Constitution* and does not abrogate or derogate from them. However, *Thomas* exemplifies how the exercise of state sovereignty can limit protection of these rights. This is important to bear in mind, considering art. 46(1) of *UNDRIP* also places limits on Indigenous rights in protecting (among other things) 'the territorial integrity or political unity of sovereign and independent States'.

Presently, if the reasoning in *Thomas* is accepted, the Supreme Court of Court is the final arbiter in determining the place of *UNDRIP* in the Canadian common law. Other decisions, such as *AltaLink Management Ltd v. Alberta (Utilities Commission)* (2021, paras 122–123) and *Laliberte v. Canada (Attorney General)* (2019, paras 55–56), have confirmed that *UNDRIP* could be used as an interpretative tool in the development of Canadian law, but it does not have constitutional status (*East Prairie Métis Settlement v. Alberta* (2021, para. 35)). This is consistent with the federal government's position that *UNDRIP* will not amend the *Constitution*; it will only inform how the *Constitution* will be interpreted (Government of Canada, 2023a). This raises questions about how the Supreme Court may in future interpret *UNDRIP* and its place within existing Canadian jurisprudence. It is well established in Canadian law that the Crown has a duty to consult and accommodate in relation to conduct that may adversely impact an Aboriginal rights or title. This duty was established by the Supreme Court of Canada in its decision in *Haida Nation v. British Columbia (Minister of Forests)* ('*Haida*') (2004). The Court found the duty flows from the honour of the Crown and the fiduciary duty it owes to Indigenous peoples as a consequence of the Royal Proclamation of 1763, and is embedded in the Aboriginal and treaty rights recognised in s. 35 of the *Constitution* that were formed prior to 1982 when the *Constitution* was enacted. Since *Haida*, the Supreme Court has maintained that the duty to consult does not give Indigenous peoples a veto power over infringement of their rights. This arguably provides lesser protection than is provided by FPIC in *UNDRIP*. FPIC does not expressly refer to a 'veto' power, but a plain understanding of giving 'consent' or not is saying 'yes' or 'no'. If this understanding is accepted by the Supreme Court, it could strengthen the common law duty to consult and accommodate in favour of Aboriginal rights and title. However, because *UNDRIP* does not (and will not) have constitutional force, it may be that the Court finds it is bound by its long-standing interpretation of the *Constitution*.

Moreover, with respect to legislation, the government has claimed that any amendments to existing laws or development of news laws in line with *UNDRIP* will proceed through the usual legislative process (Government of Canada, 2023a). However, until legislation is changed, *UNDRIP* may only be used as an interpretative tool. Presumably, if the text of the legislation conflicts with *UNDRIP*, the former will prevail considering it has legal status while *UNDRIP* does not.

There is also the issue of whether Indigenous peoples will be involved in the process of making any changes to legislation. In *Mikisew Cree First Nation v. Canada* (2018), a majority in the Supreme Court found that the common law duty to consult and accommodate did not extend to the legislative process. However, the more recent consultations between the Trudeau government and Indigenous peoples, such as in the development of the *Action Plan* to implement *UNDRIP*, while not changing existing constitutional arrangements (in fact, the government is resisting constitutional amendment to incorporate *UNDRIP*), indicate that consultation with Indigenous peoples may become standard practice. However, as previously noted, the government's level of engagement with Indigenous peoples has not been without criticism, and whether this will continue or will improve remains uncertain. Arguably, to uphold the right to FPIC would require change to the constitutional arrangements in Canada to give Indigenous peoples a platform on par with the other Canadian arms of government in recognition of their sovereignty and self-determination. However, this has not been proposed. It is also notable that the *Action Plan* is silent on how the government will implement art. 46 of *UNDRIP* and whether it will be used to limit the implementation of *UNDRIP*. Needless to say, the government's actions are already limited by its refusal to consider incorporating *UNDRIP* in the *Constitution*. In that respect, the government is maintaining Canada's sovereign status as art. 46 seemingly provides.

Indigenous child welfare

Child welfare is the final area canvassed in this chapter, which reveals a similar pattern in government approaches to Indigenous affairs discussed above. In Canada, like in Australia, Indigenous children continue to be removed from their families at disproportionate rates. In the 2016 census it was found that 7.7% of children aged under 14 were Indigenous, and 52.2% of Indigenous children aged under 14 were in foster care, which slightly increased in 2021 to 53.8% (Indigenous Watchdog, 2023a). The disproportionate representation of Indigenous children in care has also been linked to past Indigenous child removal laws and policies, such as the residential school system and the Sixties Scoop (TRC, 2015, p. 138). Responding to the child welfare crisis would contribute to overcoming the legacies of these past practices by breaking the cycle of child removals from their families. However, the government's response, similar to other contexts, has been to promise reform, only to then delay action, which has often been facilitated by government challenges to Indigenous claims for the just resolution of the issues facing Indigenous children and their families.

Both the TRC and the National Inquiry set out Calls to Action and Calls for Justice respectively in relation to child welfare, which the government accepted. With respect to the TRC, it identified key issues facing Indigenous children and their families: the discriminatory representation of children in care due to poverty and other social stresses caused by past policies and laws; the deaths and abuse of Indigenous children in foster care; the lack of Indigenous child and family services to cater especially for Métis and Inuit communities; and a lack of adequate funding for Indigenous child welfare services (TRC, 2015, pp. 138–142). The TRC recognised that to address the disproportionate number of Indigenous children in care required overcoming the consequences of past injustices and the challenges posed by the current welfare system that is plagued by a lack of regulatory consistency and funding for Indigenous child welfare services, research, and preventative measures. Central to these changes would be increasing Indigenous control over child welfare (TRC, 2015, p. 143).

The TRC also found these issues have been compounded by jurisdictional disputes over whether federal, provincial, or territorial governments have responsibility for child services (TRC, 2015, p. 142). In 2007, 'Jordan's Principle' was adopted by the House of Commons to resolve these jurisdictional issues. Jordan's Principle is named after five-year-old Jordan River Anderson, a child from the Norway House Cree Nation, who died in hospital as he had been unable to live in a home due to a jurisdictional dispute over funding for at-home care. In its original form, Jordan's Principle was to apply to on-reserve First Nations children to ensure that they have equitable access to services when they need them (Blackstock, 2012). Jordan's Principle requires the government department that is first contacted for a service to pay for it and any jurisdictional dispute over payment would be resolved later. However, as it had not been legislated, jurisdictional disputes over funding continued.

The TRC's vision for reform in relation to Indigenous child welfare was reflected in Calls to Action 1 to 5. In summary, they call on all levels of government (federal, provincial, territorial, and Aboriginal governments) to commit to reducing the number of Aboriginal children in care; improving data collection by introducing annual reports (by the federal government in collaboration with the provinces and territories) that detail the number of Aboriginal children in care compared to non-Aboriginal children, reasons for apprehension, total spending on preventative and care services, and the effectiveness of various interventions; fully implementing Jordan's Principle by all levels of government; enacting legislation at the federal level to establish national standards in child welfare in line with the Aboriginal right to self-government to ensure that the residential school legacy is taken into account in decision making, and that the placement of Aboriginal children into care is culturally appropriate; and developing appropriate parenting programmes for Aboriginal families by federal, provincial, territorial, and Aboriginal governments.

Concerns over Indigenous child welfare also featured strongly in the National Inquiry's report in which it made ten key findings (National Inquiry, 2019c, p. 355). These included that child welfare in Canada has been used as a 'tool in the genocide of Indigenous Peoples' (to oppress, displace, disrupt, and destroy); it has violated the Indigenous right of self-government in child welfare (because it is based on non-Indigenous laws, values, and worldviews); it is a form of violence (specifically, child apprehensions are a form of violence against mothers and children, and disrupt familial and cultural connections); it can be linked to violence (murdered and missing Indigenous women, girls, and 2SLGBTQQIA people); it can lead to more violence (abuse, exploitation, and human trafficking of children); and it violates other rights (for example, child removal is racially biased and discriminatory as poverty is often perceived as 'neglect', and birth alerts are also often used as the sole basis for apprehension of newborn children). The Inquiry also found that the state has infringed its duties (namely, its fiduciary duty) to children and youth in its care; the state funding model incentivises the apprehension of Indigenous children and youth (for example, in prioritising funding for foster homes over economic and support services to families); and that gaps in services and infrastructure in northern and remote communities can result in children being sent out to obtain services and care in other jurisdictions, which can result in jurisdictional neglect and culturally unsafe services and the denial of human rights and Indigenous rights of the children and their families.

Additionally, the National Inquiry included 15 Calls for Justice that specifically relate to child welfare (National Inquiry, 2019b, pp. 194–196). Encapsulating these recommendations is an Indigenous rights-based approach to ensure Indigenous control over child welfare and that 'the best interests' of children are met using distinction-based approaches. To ensure government compliance with Indigenous child rights, the Inquiry also called for a Child and Youth Advocate for Indigenous children in each jurisdiction. There were also calls to end discriminatory practices such as birth alerts and the apprehension of children based on poverty and culturally biased grounds, to ensure government compliance with Jordan's Principle with respect to all Indigenous children, and to end the discriminatory funding of services in line with the principle of substantive equity. Several of the Calls for Justice also relate to funding to provide the services and infrastructure required to keep children with their families, to ensure continuity of care in case of the death or disappearance of a caregiver, and that alternative family care is provided with equitable funding support. Other Calls for Justice relate to the recruitment of social workers and child welfare staff and ensuring they are culturally competent to respond to the needs of Indigenous children in care; introducing systems to detect and prevent Indigenous children being exploited and trafficked while in care; ensuring that child care agencies and all governments fully investigate the deaths of children in care; and reforming laws and services for Indigenous youth 'ageing out' of the system. Underpinning these Calls for Justice are distinction-based, culturally safe, and trauma-informed approaches.

The above account is only a summary of the discussion of child welfare in the TRC's report, which was further discussed in the Inquiry's report. However, it gives a sense of the range of the systemic issues in the Canadian child welfare system. Ultimately, it is whether action has been taken on these issues that matters. Some progress has been made in relation to all except one of the five Calls to Action on child welfare (Indigenous Watchdog, 2023a), but there has been little done to meet the Inquiry's Calls for Justice. The Native Women's Association Scorecard in 2021 noted that the *National Action Plan* to implement the Calls for Justice does not include plans to fulfil almost all the Calls for Justice on child welfare. Action has been commenced only partially with respect to Call to Justice 12.1 that calls for all governments to adopt an Indigenous rights approach in line with 'Indigenous self-determination and inherent jurisdiction over child welfare and support enhancements for child and family services' (NWAC, 2022, p. 21)

The following is a summary of what is being done, and still needs to be done, in relation to the five TRC Calls to Action:

1 Commit to reducing the number of Indigenous children in care. Budgets in 2020, 2021, and 2022 have allocated C$542 million over five years, C$1 billion over five years, and C$4.280 billion over five years respectively. The Canadian Association of Social Work Education Action Plan is being implemented and Provincial Social Work organisations have multiple initiatives under way. While the use of birth alerts has ended in most Canadian provinces, that has not stopped children being removed from their families at birth. There have also been no mechanisms or plans introduced at the governmental level to monitor and assess neglect investigations (Hwang, 2022; Indigenous Watchdog, 2023b).
2 Introduce child welfare reports that distinguish Indigenous and non-Indigenous children in care. Some announcements have been made such as in relation to Indigenous Services Canada launching national distinctions-based working groups with Indigenous (First Nations, Métis, and Inuit) and provincial and territorial partners co-developing data and reporting

strategies to increase data collection and reporting between jurisdictions and helping to better understand the number of Indigenous children and youth in care. However, there have been no progress reports on such initiatives (Indigenous Watchdog, 2021).

3 Fully implement Jordan's Principle. In December 2021, two Agreements-in-Principle were signed for a total settlement of C$40 billion. The first was for C$20 billion compensation to First Nations children and families for discrimination experienced in the First Nations Child and Family Services Program ('FNCFS') and the improper application of Jordan's Principle. In 2023, this was increased to C$23 billion after the Canadian Human Rights Tribunal ('CHRT') rejected the original agreement because it did not provide enough compensation to cover everyone affected. The second agreement is for C$19.807 billion to reform the FNCFS Program (Government of Canada, 2023c). These developments are highly significant considering that contestation over the scope of application of Jordan's Principle dates to 2007 when the first complaint of discrimination was made to the CHRT (Blackstock, 2016). The Harper government had been staunchly opposed to the claim and repeatedly refused to adhere to orders made by the CHRT in favour of the applicants. The Trudeau government also challenged findings of the CHRT. More recently, the government appears to have accepted its role to address these injustices inflicted by the Canadian child welfare system, but much more is needed. Off-reserve Status and non-Status Indians, Inuit, and Métis children removed from their families and placed in non-Indigenous care are yet to be similarly compensated and have begun their own class action for what has been termed the 'Millennium Scoop' ('Federal Court approves class action on behalf of off-reserve Indigenous children', 2022).

4 Enact legislation that establishes national standards for Indigenous children in line with the Indigenous right to self-determination. *An Act Respecting First Nations, Inuit and Métis Children, Youth and Families* (2019) ('Bill C-92') came into force in January 2020. The aim of the legislation is to change the way child services are delivered to Indigenous children and to move from the model where only federal, provincial, or territorial laws apply, to a model that affirms the inherent right of Indigenous peoples to exercise jurisdiction over child and family services. Notices of intention to exercise jurisdictional authority and requests to enter into coordination agreements to enforce Indigenous child welfare laws have been published by the government (Government of Canada, 2023e). The federal government has provided C$56 million to 115 Indigenous groups to undertake coordination discussions; the 2022 budget has allocated C$340.8 million over ten years to support Wabaseemoong Independent Nations' exercise of jurisdiction and C$87.3 million over three years to enable Indigenous communities to continue to work with the federal, provincial, and territory governments to support the

implementation of Indigenous child welfare laws. However, the Quebec government challenged the constitutionality of Bill C-92, and in 2019 the Quebec Court of Appeal held that all but two provisions (relating to Aboriginal self-government and regulation of child services) were constitutional. The province was asserting its exclusive jurisdiction in child welfare matters and thus the continued subordination of Indigenous child welfare to provincial law (Indigenous Watchdog, 2023c). Nevertheless, Bill C-92 has not avoided criticism from Indigenous peoples, which (among other things) relates to lack of recognition of Indigenous peoples' inherent jurisdiction over child welfare and lack of adequate up-front funding to facilitate the exercise of jurisdiction (Metallic, Friedland and Morales, 2019, pp. 7–9; Nation Talk, 2022).

5 Develop culturally appropriate parenting programmes for Aboriginal families. The budgets in 2016 and 2018 invested C$634.8 million and C$1.4 billion respectively in reducing the funding gap between Indigenous and non-Indigenous children. The budget in 2021 announced a C$1.147 billion and C$118.7 million ongoing starting in 2021–2022 to increase funding under the FNCFS Program to support families, including families not served by a delegated First Nations agency, to implement any orders of the CHRT, and support First Nations youth at the age of majority to successfully transition to independence for an additional two years (Indigenous Watchdog, 2023d).

Concluding comments

This book has argued that an apology to Indigenous peoples should advance their claims. This is supported by the relational understanding of apology making. However, as became clear, to realise this relational understanding, nation states need to be more attuned to the impacts of their laws and policies on Indigenous peoples and be prepared to make the necessary legal and structural changes to ensure that past injustices are not repeated in the future. It also became clear that adequate and effective reparations are required to make up for past injustices and that in the absence of appropriate reparations, the injustices suffered by Survivors, as exemplified by Stolen Generations and Residential School Survivors, may be compounded so that they suffer additional harm.

In exploring the Rudd and Harper apologies and the post-apology aftermath in Australia and Canada, differences in approaches to Indigenous peoples became evident. The Trudeau government appears to have been more receptive to change when compared to the former Harper government and any past or present government in Australia. The differences could be linked to different political outlooks. They may also be grounded in historical differences in settler–colonised relations in Australia and Canada, which is especially evident in their different histories with respect to treaties and rights protections. The effect of these historical differences appears to have placed Indigenous peoples in a stronger position vis-à-vis the state in Canada than in Australia. However, it is important not to confuse these differences as justification for the different treatment of Indigenous peoples in Australia and Canada. While the early treaties in Canada may be recognised as the foundation of the nation's legitimacy and provide a basis for placing Indigenous peoples on an equal footing with the state (TRC, 2015, p. 195), in Australia, the absence of treaties brings the legitimacy of the nation into question and has stunted Indigenous claims to be treated on an equal footing with the state.

Nevertheless, on closer examination, it is apparent that there is still much more to be done in both Australia and Canada to set them on the path towards a just resolution of past and present injustices. Notably, in the previous chapter on post-apology Australia, the importance of a rights-based approach became evident, while in this chapter, the difficulties associated with implementing a rights framework became clear. Ultimately, the difficulties can be traced back to the exercise of state sovereignty. As the Canadian example shows, when making reparations to Residential School Survivors, responding to the finding that genocide has been committed against Indigenous peoples, or setting the terms for Indigenous rights recognition within the Canadian politico-legal system, the state maintains the dominant position. However, it is important to recognise that the state is governed by state actors and that the difficulties to affect change have been created by them and are not intrinsic to the rights being sought to be upheld. This is clearly exemplified in Canada by the process of resolving the jurisdictional dispute over child welfare funding that vindicated the rights of First Nations children but which the Harper government, and subsequently the Trudeau government, challenged. At the present time, the governments in both Canada and Australia appear committed to change, but based on past failures their actions need to be constantly scrutinised. This is where the relational understanding of apology making serves to remind these governments to 'stay apologized' (Beales, 2008) by treating Indigenous peoples rights and interests as being of central importance.

Reference list

ahnationtalk, 2022, 'Tahltan Central Government, B.C. make history under Declaration Act', *Nation Talk*, 6 June, https://nationtalk.ca/story/tahltan-central-government-b-c-make-history-under-declaration-act

AltaLink Management Ltd v. Alberta (Utilities Commission), 2021 ABCA 342.

An Act Respecting First Nations, Inuit and Métis Children, youth and families, SC 2019, c. 24.

Barrera, J., 2020a, 'Ottawa's lack of co-operation over residential school claim records "tragic," says Murray Sinclair', *CBC News*, 2 June, https://www.cbc.ca/news/indigenous/murray-sinclair-iap-records-1.5593634

Barrera, J., 2020b, 'Ottawa's move to block statistical reports on residential schools "modern-day colonialism," says Survivor', *CBC News*, 27 May, https://www.cbc.ca/news/indigenous/iap-residential-school-records-holocaust-scholar-1.5586008

Barrera, J., 2021, '81 St. Anne's residential school compensation cases require "significant review," says court filing', *CBC News*, 2 September, https://www.cbc.ca/news/indigenous/st-annes-review-compensation-1.6161642

Beales, R., 2008, 'Federal government must "stay apologized" say Aboriginal leaders', *Brantford Expositer*, 15 December.

Blackstock, C., 2012, 'Jordan's Principle: Canada's broken promise to First Nations children?' *Paediatrics & Child Health*, vol. 17, no. 7, pp. 368–370, https://www.ncbi.nlm.nih.gov/pmc/articles/PMC3448536/

Blackstock, C., 2016, 'The complainant: the Canadian human rights case on First Nations child welfare', *McGill Law Journal*, vol. 62, no. 2, pp. 285–326, DOI:10.7202/1040049ar

Brackenbury, M., 2023, '"Indian boarding home" Survivors in the North eligible to receive thousands of dollars in compensation', *CBC News*, 9 January, https://www.cbc.ca/news/canada/north/indian-boarding-homes-nwt-1.6706364

Brake, J., 2018, 'Labrador Residential School Survivors left out of federal apology and settlement', *APTN News*, 19 March, https://www.aptnnews.ca/national-news/labrador-residential-school-survivors-left-federal-apology-settlement/

Canada (Attorney General) v. Fontaine, 2017 SCC 47.

Committee on the Elimination of Racial Discrimination, 1997, *General Recommendation No. 23: Indigenous peoples*, 18 August, https://www.uio.no/studier/emner/jus/jus/JUS5710/h13/undervisningsmateriale/general%2Brecommendation%2Bno23.pdf

Constitution Act, 1982, being Schedule B to the *Canada Act 1982* (UK), c. 11.

Declaration on the Rights of Indigenous Peoples Act, SBC 2019, c. 44.

Declaration on the Rights of Indigenous Peoples Act, SC 2021, c. 14.

Deer, K., 2022, 'Concerns raised by Survivors, advocates as Indian day school settlement deadline approaches', *CBC News*, 27 May, https://www.cbc.ca/news/indigenous/federal-day-school-settlement-deadline-1.6466640

Department of Justice Canada, 2023, *United Nations Declaration on the Rights of Indigenous Peoples Act Action Plan 2023–2028*, 21 November, https://www.justice.gc.ca/eng/declaration/ap-pa/index.html

Down, I., 2023, 'Dehcho First Nations' support of UNDRIP legislation "up in the air": grand chief', *CKLB Radio*, 28 April, https://cklbradio.com/2023/04/28/dehcho-first-nations-support-of-undrip-legislation-up-in-the-air-grand-chief/

East Prairie Métis Settlement v. Alberta, 2021 ABQB 762.

'Federal court approves class action on behalf of off-reserve Indigenous children', 2022, *CBC News*, 21 June, https://www.cbc.ca/news/canada/british-columbia/federal-court-certifies-millenium-scoop-lawsuit-1.6494816

Fionda, F., 2023, '"When is it going to stop?" Claims made on First Nations' territories even as they fight century-old mining laws', *The Narwhal*, 18 May, https://thenarwhal.ca/bc-supreme-court-gitxaala-ehattesaht/

Fontaine v. Canada (Attorney General), 2013 ONSC 684.

Forester, B., 2023, 'Assembly of First Nations wants federal UNDRIP plan overhauled, slams consultation process', *CBC News*, 6 April, https://www.cbc.ca/news/indigenous/afn-undrip-draft-plan-delay-1.6803777#:~:text=The%20resolution%20slams%20the%20consultation,of%20First%20Nations%20were%20excluded

Gitxaała v. British Columbia (Chief Gold Commissioner), 2023 BCSC 1680.
Government of Canada, 2017, *Lessons learned study of the Common Experience Payment process*, https://www.rcaanc-cirnac.gc.ca/eng/1468333119050/1537890150719
Government of Canada, 2019, *Statistics on the implementation of the Indian Residential Schools Settlement Agreement*, 19 February, https://www.rcaanc-cirnac.gc.ca/eng/1315320539682/1571590489978#sec1
Government of Canada, 2021, *Federal Pathway to address missing and murdered Indigenous women, girls and 2SLGBTQQIA+ people*, 3 June, https://www.rcaanc-cirnac.gc.ca/eng/1622233286270/1622233321912
Government of Canada, 2022, *Bill C-15: what we learned report*, 5 July, https://www.justice.gc.ca/eng/declaration/wwl-cna/c15/index.html
Government of Canada, 2023a, *About the Act*, 17 April, https://www.justice.gc.ca/eng/declaration/legislation.html
Government of Canada, 2023b, *Delivering on Truth and Reconciliation Commission Calls to Action*, 10 July, https://www.rcaanc-cirnac.gc.ca/eng/1524494530110/1557511412801
Government of Canada, 2023c, *Executive summary of Agreement-in-Principle on Long-Term Reform*, 13 September, https://www.sac-isc.gc.ca/eng/1644518166138/1644518227229
Government of Canada, 2023d, *Federal 2SLGBTQI+ Action Plan… Building our future, with pride*, 25 August, https://women-gender-equality.canada.ca/en/free-to-be-me/federal-2slgbtqi-plus-action-plan.html
Government of Canada, 2023e, *Notices and requests related to An Act respecting First Nations, Inuit and Métis children, youth and families*, 23 November, https://www.sac-isc.gc.ca/eng/1608565826510/1608565862367
Government of Canada, 2023f, *Settlement Agreement reached in Band class litigation*, 23 January, https://www.canada.ca/en/crown-indigenous-relations-northern-affairs/news/2023/01/settlement-agreement-reached-in-gottfriedson-band-class-litigation.html
Haida Nation v. British Columbia (Minister of Forests), [2004] 3 SCR 511.
House of Commons, Canada, 2008, *House of Commons Debates (Hansard)*, 39th Parl., 2nd Sess., vol. *142*, no. *110*, 11 June, https://www.ourcommons.ca/Content/House/392/Debates/110/HAN110-E.PDF
House of Commons, Canada, 2022, *House of Commons Debates (Hansard)*, 44th Parl., 1st Sess., vol. *151*, no. *119*, 27 October, https://www.ourcommons.ca/Content/House/441/Debates/119/HAN119-E.PDF
Hwang, P.K.S., 2022, 'Their newborns were taken at birth. Years later, these women still don't know why', *CBC News*, 30 September, https://www.cbc.ca/news/canada/ottawa/birth-alerts-indigenous-women-ottawa-stories-1.6591808#:~:text=Ontario%20ended%20the%20controversial%20practice,and%20illegal%2C%22%20said%20Yang
'"I am deeply sorry": full text of residential school apology from Pope Francis', 2022, *CBC News*, 25 July, https://www.cbc.ca/news/canada/edmonton/pope-francis-maskwacis-apology-full-text-1.6531341
Independent Assessment Process Oversight Committee, 2021, *Independent Assessment Process: final report*, https://www.iap-pei.ca/media/information/publication/pdf/FinalReport/IAP-FR-2021-03-11-eng.pdf
Indian Residential Schools Settlement Agreement, 2006, 8 May, https://residentialschoolsettlement.ca/IRS%20Settlement%20Agreement-%20ENGLISH.pdf

Indigenous Watchdog, 2021, *Call to Action # 2*, 22 December, https://www.indigenouswatchdog.org/cta/call-to-action-2/

Indigenous Watchdog, 2023a, *Calls to Action*, https://www.indigenouswatchdog.org/calls-to-action/

Indigenous Watchdog, 2023b, *Call to Action # 1*, 24 October, https://www.indigenouswatchdog.org/cta/call-to-action-1/

Indigenous Watchdog, 2023c, *Call to Action # 4*, 5 October, https://www.indigenouswatchdog.org/cta/call-to-action-4/

Indigenous Watchdog, 2023d, *Call to Action # 5*, 26 November, https://www.indigenouswatchdog.org/cta/call-to-action-5/

Indigenous Watchdog, 2023e, *United Nations Declaration on the Rights of Indigenous People (43–44)*, https://www.indigenouswatchdog.org/subcategory/united-nations-declaration-on-the-rights-of-indigenous-people/

Laliberte v. Canada (Attorney General), 2019 FC 766.

Les Femmes Michif Otipemisiwak – Women of the Métis Nation, 2019, *Métis perspectives of missing and murdered Indigenous women, girls and LGBTQ2S+ people*, https://metiswomen.org/wp-content/uploads/2021/06/LFMO-MMIWG-Report.pdf

Les Femmes Michif Otipemisiwak – Women of the Métis Nation, 2021, *Weaving Miskotaha: the Métis Nation's journey to ending missing and murdered women, girls and 2SLGBTQQIA+ people*, https://metiswomen.org/wp-content/uploads/2021/09/Weaving-Miskotaha-Report-July-2021.pdf

Leeson, N., and Gallegos Dupuis, M. 2023, 'Unravelling Canada's UN Indigenous action plan', *Law360 Canada*, LexisNexis, Canada, 2 August, https://www.law360.ca/articles/49015/unravelling-canada-s-un-indigenous-action-plan-nick-leeson-and-mariana-gallegos-dupuis

Martisius, V., 2021, 'Bill C-15 & implementing UNDRIP: what should this mean for the First Nations, Inuit and the Métis in relationship to Canada?', *British Columbia Civil Liberties Association*, 20 May, https://bccla.org/2021/05/bill-c-15-implementing-undrip-what-should-this-mean-for-the-first-nations-inuit-and-the-metis-in-relationship-to-canada/

Metallic, N.W., Friedland, H. and Morales, S., 2019, *The promise and pitfalls of C-92: An Act respecting First Nations, Inuit and Métis children, youth and families*, Yellowhead Institute, https://yellowheadinstitute.org/wp-content/uploads/2019/07/the-promise-and-pitfalls-of-c-92-report.pdf

Mikisew Cree First Nation v. Canada (Governor General in Council), [2018] 2 SCR 765.

Monkman, L., 2019, 'Sixties Scoop Survivors lament lack of support during compensation application process', *CBC News*, 30 August, https://www.cbc.ca/news/canada/manitoba/sixties-scoop-application-process-1.5265198

Moses, A.D., 2008, 'Toward a theory of critical genocide studies', *SciencesPo*, 18 April, https://www.sciencespo.fr/mass-violence-war-massacre-resistance/en/document/toward-theory-critical-genocide-studies.html

Nation Talk, 2022, 'Assembly of Manitoba Chiefs challenge Bill C-92 jurisdiction and provincial amendments to Child and Family Services Act', 26 May, https://www.indigenouswatchdog.org/current-problems/theme/government-and-institution-issues/child-welfare/#update-19088

National Action Plan, 2021, https://mmiwg2splus-nationalactionplan.ca/eng/1670511213459/1670511226843
National Centre for Truth and Reconciliation, 2020, *Lessons learned: Survivor perspectives*, https://nctr.ca/wp-content/uploads/2021/01/Lessons_learned_report_final_2020.pdf
National Inquiry into Missing and Murdered Indigenous Women and Girls, 2019a, *A legal analysis of genocide: supplementary report*, https://www.mmiwg-ffada.ca/wp-content/uploads/2019/06/Supplementary-Report_Genocide.pdf
National Inquiry into Missing and Murdered Indigenous Women and Girls, 2019b, *Calls for Justice*, https://www.mmiwg-ffada.ca/wp-content/uploads/2019/06/Calls_for_Justice.pdf
National Inquiry into Missing and Murdered Indigenous Women and Girls, 2019c, *Reclaiming power and place. The final report of the National Inquiry into Missing and Murdered Indigenous Women and Girls, volume 1a*, https://www.mmiwg-ffada.ca/wp-content/uploads/2019/06/Final_Report_Vol_1a-1.pdf
Native Women's Association of Canada, 2021, *NWAC Action Plan: our calls, our actions*, https://www.nwac.ca/assets-knowledge-centre/NWAC-action-plan-English.pdf
Native Women's Association of Canada, 2022, *Annual scorecard: an annual report outlining the federal government's progress on implementing the commitments made in their MMIWG2S National Action Plan*, https://nwac.ca/assets-knowledge-centre/FEDERAL_ANNUAL_SCORECARD_ACTIONPLAN_2022_2022-06-03-132116_mfnq.pdf
Native Women's Association of Canada, 2023, 'NWAC issues federal government a failing grade for continued inaction on its MMIWG2S+ National Action Plan', *Globe Newswire*, 1 June, https://www.globenewswire.com/news-release/2023/06/01/2680737/0/en/NWAC-Issues-Federal-Government-a-Failing-Grade-for-Continued-Inaction-on-its-MMIWG2S-National-Action-Plan.html
Ontario Native Women's Association, 2021, 'National Action Plan and Federal Pathway will not end genocide of Indigenous women and girls', *NationTalk*, 4 June, https://nationtalk.ca/story/national-action-plan-and-federal-pathway-will-not-end-genocide-of-indigenous-women-and-girls
Parliament of Australia, n.d., *Missing and murdered First Nations women and children*, https://www.aph.gov.au/Parliamentary_Business/Committees/Senate/Legal_and_Constitutional_Affairs/FirstNationswomenchildren
Pasternak, S., Spice, A. and Feltes, E., 2021, *The United Nations Committee on the Elimination of Racial Discrimination (CERD): a user guide for land defenders*, Yellowhead Institute, https://www.jstor.org/stable/resrep32684?seq=4
Pauktuutit Inuit Women of Canada and Inuit Tapiriit Kanatami, 2021, *National Inuit Action Plan on missing and murdered Inuit women, girls and 2SLGBTQQIA+ people*, https://pauktuutit.ca/wp-content/uploads/Pauktuutit_MMIWG_Action-Plan_English_PDF-Version.pdf
Platt, B., 2020, 'Six provinces object, but Liberals still move ahead with UN declaration on Indigenous rights', *National Post*, 3 December, https://nationalpost.com/news/politics/bill-to-enshrine-un-declaration-on-the-rights-of-indigenous-peoples-in-canadian-law

Provost, K., 2021, 'Sask. Man worried Métis and non-status Indian Sixties Scoop Survivors will have little say in class action' *CBC News*, 21 November, https://www.cbc.ca/news/canada/saskatoon/metis-non-status-indians-sixties-scoop-class-action-1.6255996

Reimer, G., Bombay, A., Ellsworth, L., Fryer, S., Logan, T., 2010, *The Indian Residential Schools Settlement Agreement's Common Experience Payment and healing: a qualitative study exploring impacts on recipients*, Aboriginal Healing Foundation, https://ehprnh2mwo3.exactdn.com/wp-content/uploads/2021/01/cep-2010-healing.pdf

Schabas, W.A., 2009, *Genocide in international law: the crime of crimes*, 2nd edn, Cambridge University Press, Cambridge.

Schedule "D": Independent Assessment Process (IAP) for continuing Indian residential school abuse claims, 2006, May, https://www.residentialschoolsettlement.ca/Schedule_D-IAP.PDF

Schedule "N": mandate for the Truth and Reconciliation Commission, n.d., https://www.residentialschoolsettlement.ca/schedule_n.pdf

Standing Senate Committee on Aboriginal Peoples, 2022, *Not enough: all words and no action on MMIWG: interim report of the Standing Senate Committee on Aboriginal peoples*, https://sencanada.ca/content/sen/committee/441/APPA/Reports/2022-06-22_APPA_SS-1_MMIWG_e_FINAL.pdf

Thomas and Saik'uz First Nation v. Rio Tinto Alcan Inc., 2022 BCSC 15.

Truth and Reconciliation Commission of Canada, 2012, *Truth and Reconciliation Commission of Canada: interim report*, https://www.bishop-accountability.org/reports/TRC_Canada/TRC_Canada_Interim_Report_2012_02_24_Original.pdf

Truth and Reconciliation Commission of Canada, 2015, *Honouring the truth, reconciling for the future: summary of the final report of the Truth and Reconciliation Commission of Canada*, https://ehprnh2mwo3.exactdn.com/wp-content/uploads/2021/01/Executive_Summary_English_Web.pdf

United Nations, 1948, *Convention on the Prevention and Punishment of the Crime of Genocide*, General Assembly Resolution 260 A (III).

United Nations, 2007, *United Nations Declaration on the Rights of Indigenous Peoples*, General Assembly Resolution 61/295.

United Nations Human Rights Office of the High Commissioner, 2013, *Free, prior and informed consent of Indigenous peoples*, https://www.ohchr.org/sites/default/files/Documents/Issues/IPeoples/FreePriorandInformedConsent.pdf

Waddle Phillips Professional Corporation, n.d., *Île-à-la-Crosse residential school classaction*,https://waddellphillips.ca/class-actions/ile-a-la-crosse-residential-school-class-action/

Watchmaker, Grand Chief O.V., 2021, *The Confederacy of Treaty No. 6 First Nations Chiefs reject flawed BILL C-15*, 1 April, https://e2e96e00-649d-436f-9a4b-ab1be9e78d97.filesusr.com/ugd/d347e6_a39e3656d90f45bc9e5d797b94e92726.pdf

Webster, D., 2019, 'Canada's non-conversation about genocide', *Active History*, 14 June, https://activehistory.ca/2019/06/canadas-non-conversation-about-genocide/

Yahey v. British Columbia, 2021 BCSC 1287.

Index

1967 referendum 70, 72, 184, 186

Aboriginal and Torres Strait Islander peoples, constitutional recognition of 21, 163, 185–192, 194–195
Aboriginal and Torres Strait Islander Commission (ATSIC) 70, 74, 186, 189, 190
Aboriginal and Torres Strait Islander Healing Foundation 76, 165–166, 183
Aboriginal Healing Foundation (AHF) 76–77, 120, 199, 201, 207
apology: and acceptance of responsibility 31, 45, 48, 49, 55; and power 8, 32–33, 36, 42, 52, 122; and respect 11, 36–37, 42, 47, 52; and sincerity 34–38, 40–44, 50, 53; and importance of context 10, 33–34, 43, 54; norm-setting function of 9, 48–50; role of victims and perpetrators 32, 35–37, 41–42, 45, 146; and reparations 4, 8–10, 40, 49, 53
apology making: as relational 2, 4–5, 7–8, 16–21; as speech act 1–2, 4, 7, 22, 32, 38; as transactional 9, 32, 35, 139; as transformative 9, 19, 49, 54; power dynamics of 32–33, 36, 41, 48; requirements of 38–39, 53–55
Apology to Australia's Indigenous Peoples *see* Rudd Apology
Apology to Former Students of Indian Residential Schools *see* Harper apology
apology, interpersonal: effectiveness of 38–41; functions of 34–37; role of victims and perpetrators 32–33, 35–37, 41, 146; *see also* forgiveness
apology, moral 31, 41, 46
apology, political: and the historical record 10, 17, 44–46; as reparative justice 45–48, 52; differences from interpersonal apology 6–7, 33, 43–45, 49, 52; effectiveness of 49–53; moral aspects of 9, 45–49, 55; power dynamics of 8, 17, 36, 47–48, 137–138, 145; and rights protection 47–48, 52; and role of head of state 4, 17, 50–51, 79, 150–151; significance to Indigenous peoples 43, 44, 45, 46–47; similarities to interpersonal apology 33, 41–43; and reparations 4, 8–9, 49, 51–53; *see also* forgiveness
assimilation policies (in Australia) 63–65, 118, 123, 172
assimilation policies (in Canada) 63, 66–67, 113, 123, 209

Basic Principles and Guidelines on the Right to a Remedy and Reparation for Victims of Gross Violations of Human Rights Law and Serious Violations of International Humanitarian Law 19, 46
Bill C-15 215–217, 219–220; *see also United Nations Declaration on the Rights of Indigenous Peoples* (*UNDRIP*); *United Nations*

Declaration on the Rights of Indigenous Peoples Act Action Plan
Brazeau, Patrick: response to Harper apology 2, 80
Bringing Them Home (*BTH*): and child welfare 179–180; and compensation 167–168; and race discrimination finding 69, 164, 167, 179; and genocide finding 64, 68–69, 164; Howard government rejection of 68, 70; recommendations of 67–69, 116, 144, 163–165; *see also* Aboriginal and Torres Strait Islander Healing Foundation; Stolen Generations

Calma, Tom: response to Rudd apology 4, 24n4, 80, 82–83, 86–87
Chartier, Clement: response to Harper apology 2, 80, 84
child welfare (in Australia) 65, 180–182, 192; and out-of-home care 5, 20–21, 123, 179
child welfare (in Canada) 221–225; and Jordan's Principle 6, 222, 223, 225
Closing the Gap policy: critique of 118–119, 125, 127, 175–177; and the 'fair go' 14, 82, 108, 117, 124, 136; in Rudd apology 14, 108, 115, 117; *see also National Agreement on Closing the Gap* (*National Agreement*)
collective apology *see* apology, political
commemoration 6, 199, 204, 208; Commemoration Fund 77, 199; *see also Settlement Agreement*; Truth and Reconciliation Commission of Canada (TRC)
Convention on the Prevention and Punishment of the Crime of Genocide 64, 69, 211–212; *see also* genocide
Corntassel, Jeff 156
Coulthard, Glen 18–19, 129
Council for Australian Reconciliation (CAR) 73–74

Declaration on the Rights of Indigenous Peoples Act, SC 2021 *see Bill C-15*
discrimination: and race 72, 157, 172, 184; and sex 94n6, 157; *see also* assimilation policies (in Australia); assimilation policies (in Canada); child welfare (in Australia); child welfare (in Canada); forced Indigenous child removal; *International Convention on the Elimination of All Forms of Racial Discrimination*
doctrines of discovery and terra nullius 12, 22, 46, 91, 210–211, 217, 219; *see also* terra nullius
Dodson, Patrick: and forgiveness 141, 148; response to Rudd apology 4, 24n4, 80, 83, 87–89

equality: formal 65, 74–75, 118, 126, 188; moral 36; of opportunity 70, 117, 188; of outcomes 136, 175; political 187

Fontaine, Phil: and Indigenous rights violations 91, 122–124, 179–180; response to Harper apology 2, 75, 78, 81, 85, 89–90; significance to Harper apology 153
forced Indigenous child removal: as genocide 13, 69, 90–91, 115; effects on Stolen Generations Survivors 69, 165–166, 183; *see also* assimilation policies (in Australia); residential school system
forgiveness: and gratitude 141–142, 152; and Harper apology 107, 149; and healing 50, 147–148; and Indigenous peoples 50, 139, 149, 152, 155; and political apology 41–42, 49–50, 53, 147, 149, 151; and power of victims 145–147; and Rudd apology 148, 151; and interpersonal apology 32, 35, 37, 39–40

Gathering Strength–Canada's Aboriginal Action Plan (Gathering Strength) 76–77; *see also* Aboriginal Healing Foundation (AHF); Royal Commission on Aboriginal Peoples (RCAP)
genocide: and Indigenous perspectives 76, 111–113, 142–143, 177; as cultural genocide 211–212; *see also* Harper apology; Rudd apology; assimilation policies (in Australia); assimilation policies (in Canada); forced Indigenous child removal; settler colonialism

genocide (in Australia) 177, 188, 191, 214; acceptance of 64, 69, 164; rejection of 14, 68, 75, 111; and Rudd apology 116, 127–128
genocide (in Canada) 14, 76; acceptance of 22, 198, 211–212; and Harper apology 90, 112–113, 120–121; *see also* National Inquiry into Missing and Murdered Indigenous Women and Girls
government accountability 21–22, 158, 182–183

Harper apology: and acceptance of responsibility 106–107; and acknowledgement of harm 104–105, 112–114; ceremonial aspects of 152–155; and genocide 113; and healing and reconciliation 108–109, 114, 120; history of 75–78; and *Settlement Agreement* 14–15, 109, 120–121, 126, 144; and settler colonialism 125, 128–129; *see also* Indigenous peoples, responses and role in Harper apology; politics of apology; residential school system; Truth and Reconciliation Commission of Canada (TRC)
Harper government 225, 227
Harper, S. 1, 78, 81
Healing *see* Aboriginal and Torres Strait Islander Healing Foundation, Aboriginal Healing Foundation (AHF), Calma, Tom; Harper apology, National Centre for Truth and Reconciliation (NCTR), *Lessons Learned* report
Healing Foundation *see* Aboriginal and Torres Strait Islander Healing Foundation
Howard government 68–69, 72–75, 110, 186, 190; and practical reconciliation 70, 118, 176; refusal to apologise 75, 82, 106, 168
Howard, J. 75; refusal to apologise 11, 81, 142

Indian Act (1876): attempts to repeal 3, 131n3; colonial patriarchy 94n6; compulsory enfranchisement 66–67, 114; Indian residential schools 67; *see also* Indigenous rights (in Canada)
Indian Residential Settlement Agreement see Settlement Agreement
Indigenous critical theory 18–19
Indigenous peoples: responses to Harper apology 42, 113–114, 143, 149, 154; responses to Rudd apology 42, 83, 89, 109–111, 116, 119, 140, 167, 179; role in apology making 5, 20, 54, 138–139, 155–156; role in Harper apology 79, 83, 107, 125–126, 152–155; role in Rudd apology 86–87, 125, 150–151; *see also* Calma, Tom; Chartier, Clement; Dodson, Patrick; Brazeau, Patrick; Fontaine, Phil; Jacobs, Beverley; Simon, Mary
Indigenous rights: and Rudd and Harper apologies 48, 119, 129–130; and self-determination 20, 143, 166, 178, 192, 225; and need for protection 12, 85–88, 121
Indigenous rights (in Australia): land rights 70–72; treaty 70–71, 73; *see also* child welfare (in Australia); Aboriginal and Torres Strait Islander peoples, constitutional recognition of
Indigenous rights (in Canada) 6, 22, 76, 157, 209–210; and free, prior and informed consent (FPIC) 216–218, 220–221; and the *Constitution* (1982) 219–221; and treaty 21–22, 114, 210, 227; *see also* child welfare (in Canada); *Bill C-15*; Truth and Reconciliation Commission of Canada (TRC); National Inquiry into Missing and Murdered Indigenous Women and Girls
Indigenous sovereignty: assertion of 22, 70, 92, 185, 191; denial of 126–130, 154–156, 190
International Convention on the Elimination of Racial Discrimination 69

Jacobs, Beverley: and Indigenous rights 85–86; response to Harper apology 2, 85, 92

laws, customary 71, 72, 74, 123, 156, 185

MoretonRobinson, A. 18

National Agreement on Closing the Gap (*National Agreement*) 177–178, 183–185
National Centre for Truth and Reconciliation (NCTR) 205–206; *Lessons Learned* report 202–206, 207–208
National Inquiry into Missing and Murdered Indigenous Women and Girls: Calls for Justice 213–214, 223–224; finding of genocide 6, 211–214; *National Action Plan* and *Federal Pathway* 214–215
Northern Territory Emergency Response 72, 74, 88, 157, 119, 188

Official apology *see* apology, political

politics of apology 11, 17, 32–33, 48, 78, 142; and Indigenous peoples 2, 16–18, 138, 144–145; *see also* Indigenous peoples, role in apology making
protection policy (in Australia) *see* assimilation policies (in Australia)
public apology *see* apology, political

reconciliation 145; and apology 8–9, 33, 35, 37, 42–44; Indigenous peoples' perspectives on 3, 80–81, 86–87, 143–144, 155; and Closing the Gap 136, 175, 178; in Australia 73–75; in Canada 209–210; *see also* Harper apology; Rudd apology; settler colonialism; Truth and Reconciliation Commission of Canada (TRC)
relational understanding of apology 17, 20–22, 139, 146; and 'never again 32, 139, 163, 198, 209; contrast to 'speech act 146, 150; relevance to Australia and Canada 154, 157–158, 163, 198, 226–227; *see also* apology making
reparations (in Australia): Commonwealth redress schemes 168–169, 171, 172, 174; state and territory-based redress schemes 169, 171–172; Stolen Generations compensation claims 166–168, 169–171; Stolen Generations redress schemes 168–170, 171–175; *see also* *Bringing Them Home* (*BTH*); Stolen Generations
reparations (in Canada) *see* *Gathering Strength–Canada's Aboriginal Action Plan* (*Gathering Strength*), National Centre for Truth and Reconciliation (NCTR), *Lessons Learned* report, National Inquiry into Missing and Murdered Indigenous Women and Girls, *Settlement Agreement*
residential school system: effects on Residential School Survivors 76, 221–222; Indigenous resistance to 83–84, 93, 128, 149, 152–153; kill the Indian in the child 67, 90, 105, 112; *see also* assimilation policies (in Canada); genocide (in Canada); National Centre for Truth and Reconciliation (NCTR), *Lessons Learned* report
Royal Commission into Aboriginal Deaths in Custody 72–73
Royal Commission on Aboriginal Peoples (RCAP) 76, 77, 113
Rudd apology: acceptance of responsibility 105–106; acknowledgement of harm 103–104, 111–112; and closing the gap 108, 117–119; and the 'fair go' 14, 108, 117–118, 124; history of 68–75; and refusal to accept genocide 110–111; and reconciliation 106–108, 151; and refusal to pay compensation 115–117; and settler colonialism 15–16, 119, 127–128; *see also* Indigenous peoples, responses and role in Rudd apology; politics of apology; Stolen Generations
Rudd government 14, 78, 116
Rudd, K. 111

self-determination: policy in Australia 70–72, 74; *see also* Indigenous rights
Settlement Agreement 6, 14–15, 136, 199, 207; and disputes over records 202, 206; and healing 203–204, 207; Indigenous critiques of 80, 84; and monetary payments 77, 199, 200–202; and other settlement agreements 199–200, 202–203, 205; *see also* Harper apology; National Centre for Truth and Reconciliation

(NCTR), *Lessons Learned* report; Truth and Reconciliation Commission of Canada (TRC)
settler colonialism: and the Rudd and Harper apologies 7–8, 13, 15–16, 19, 102, 127–130; as racist genocide 11–13, 90–92, 110–112; and decolonisation 5, 12, 19, 22, 139, 210–211; and *United Nations Declaration on the Rights of Indigenous People* 19; *see also* assimilation policies (in Australia); assimilation policies (in Canada); politics of apology
settler colonial theory 3, 62, 91
Simon, Mary: and forgiveness 141, 149–150; and Harper apology 2, 20, 81, 84, 86, 142
Smith, Linda Tuhiwai 5
speech act theory 8, 34–35, 37, 51, 122; *see also* apology making
state apology *see* apology, political
state sovereignty 16, 121–122, 138, 151, 175
Stolen Generations: and the 'history wars' 71, 81; legal treatment of 14, 68, 110–111, 168–171; needs of Survivors 164–167; *see also* assimilation policies (in Australia); forced Indigenous child removal; genocide (in Australia); reparations (in Australia)

terra nullius 71, 127, 186
treaty 114, 190–191, 217
Trudeau government 6, 198, 211, 215, 217, 221, 225
Trudeau, J. 21, 22, 24n3, 199, 214
Truth and Reconciliation Commission of Canada (TRC) 77, 198, 203–205; Calls to Action 21–22, 209–211, 215, 222–223, 224–225; and commemoration 204; and truth telling 204–205; and disputes over records 205–206; *see also* Harper apology; *Settlement Agreement*; National Centre for Truth and Reconciliation (NCTR); National Inquiry into Missing and Murdered Indigenous Women and Girls
truth: and power 17, 102, 119; power of 44, 55, 83, 89, 142, 214
truth telling (in Australia) *see Uluru Statement from the Heart*
truth telling (in Canada) *see* National Centre for Truth and Reconciliation (NCTR), *Lessons Learned* report, Truth and Reconciliation Commission of Canada (TRC)

Uluru Statement from the Heart see Aboriginal and Torres Strait Islander peoples, constitutional recognition of
United Nations Declaration on the Rights of Indigenous Peoples (UNDRIP) 5, 19, 157, 215–216; *see also* Indigenous rights (in Canada)
United Nations Declaration on the Rights of Indigenous Peoples Act Action Plan 215, 216–217, 221; *see also* Indigenous rights (in Canada)

Voice to Parliament *see* Aboriginal and Torres Strait Islander peoples, constitutional recognition of

Watson, Irene 156

FSC
www.fsc.org
MIX
Papier | Fördert
gute Waldnutzung
FSC® C083411

Kolibri 360 GmbH
Ferdinand-Jühlke-Straße 7
99095 Erfurt, Deutschland
produktsicherheit@kolibri360.de